EP Literature and Composition I Reader

Lessons 1-90

This book belongs to:

____

EP Literature and Composition I Reader Lessons 1-90

This book, made by Tina Rutherford with permission from Easy Peasy All-in-One Homeschool, is based on the Reading portion of the Literature and Composition I component of Easy Peasy's curriculum.
For EP's online curriculum visit allinonehighschool.com

This content was created in reference to the links used in the online Literature and Composition I course. The course page will contain any specific lesson source, as well as more practice in any concept that is difficult for the student to grasp. All written works contained in this book are either in the public domain or original to this author.

Cover design by Yuletide Media: www.yuletidemedia.com

Lovingly edited by Holly Dunn

ISBN: 9798501141100

First Edition: June, 2021

About this Book

This is an offline version of the reading selections for Lessons 1-90 of Easy Peasy All-in-One High School's Literature and Composition I course. We've modified and expanded upon the online activities and printable worksheets available at the Easy Peasy All-in-One High School website (allinonehighschool.com) so that you can work offline if desired. This book is ONLY the reading component of Literature and Composition I. It will not include any of the vocabulary, writing, or other language arts assignments and is not a complete English course on its own.

How to use this Book

This book is designed to be used in conjunction with the Literature and Composition I Language Arts and Vocabulary workbooks (for a full offline course) OR alongside the online Literature and Composition I course. As you proceed through this book, you will use the other Literature and Composition I workbooks or the online assignments to fill out the rest of the assignments.

This book follows the EP online Literature and Composition I course in sequential order, providing an offline version of the reading assignments. There will be slight differences from time to time, particularly where a reading assignment online was under copyright and a change needed to be made for the purposes of this book. But a student completing the assignments in this book along with the other Literature and Composition I workbooks or the other online assignments will complete one full high school English course.

Course Description: Reading Portion

This high school level course requires students to analyze a wide variety of literature. Students will be reading an autobiography, science fiction and allegorical novels, poetry, short stories, and plays. They will focus on poetic and literary devices such as metaphor and irony.

Course Reading List

Books: Historic autobiography of your choosing: *A Narrative of the Life of David Crockett*, Crockett; *Pilgrim's Progress*, Bunyan; *Twenty Thousand Leagues Under the Sea*, Verne

Plays: *Romeo and Juliet*, Shakespeare; *The Importance of Being Earnest*, Wilde

Short Stories: "The Gift of the Magi" and "The Ransom of Red Chief," O'Henry; "The Cask of Amontillado" (edited), Poe; "The Necklace," Maupassant; other excerpts

Poetry: Emily Dickinson and others

Table of Contents

Lessons 1-30

- For your first 30 lessons, you can choose which autobiography you'd like to read: Davy Crockett (included in this book) or an autobiography of your choosing. You'll need to budget your time to be sure you're done by lesson 31 when you'll have a new reading assignment. Davy Crockett is 17 chapters.
- **Note**: This autobiography contains the occasional use of the word "negro."

A Narrative of the Life of David Crockett
By Davy Crockett (1786-1836)

PREFACE

Fashion is a thing I care mighty little about, except when it happens to run just exactly according to my own notion; and I was mighty nigh sending out my book without any preface at all, until a notion struck me, that perhaps it was necessary to explain a little the reason why and wherefore I had written it.

Most of authors seek fame, but I seek for justice, — a holier impulse than ever entered into the ambitious struggles of the votaries of that *fickle, flirting* goddess.

A publication has been made to the world, which has done me much injustice; and the catchpenny errors which it contains, have been already too long sanctioned by my silence. I don't know the author of the book — and indeed I don't want to know him; for after he has taken such a liberty with my name, and made such an effort to hold me up to public ridicule, he cannot calculate on any thing but my displeasure. If he had been content to have written his opinions about me, however contemptuous they might have been, I should have had less reason to complain. But when he professes to give my narrative (as he often does) in my own language, and then puts into my mouth such language as would disgrace even an outlandish African, he must himself be sensible of the injustice he has done me, and the trick he has played off on the publick. I have met with hundreds, if not with thousands of people, who have formed their opinions of my appearance, habits, language, and every thing else from that deceptive work.

They have almost in every instance expressed the most profound astonishment at finding me in human shape, and with the *countenance*, *appearance*, and common *feelings* of a human being. It is to correct all these false notions, and to do justice to myself, that I have written.

It is certain that the writer of the book alluded to has gathered up many imperfect scraps of information concerning me, as in parts of his work there is some little semblance of truth. But I ask him, if this notice should ever reach his eye, how would he have liked it, if I had treated him so? — if I had put together such a bundle of ridiculous stuff, and headed it with his name, and sent it out upon the world without ever even condescending to ask his permission? To these questions, all upright men must give the same answer. It was wrong; and the desire to make money by it, is no apology for such injustice to a fellow man.

But I let him pass; as my wish is greatly more to vindicate myself, than to condemn him.

In the following pages I have endeavoured to give the reader a plain, honest, homespun account of my state in life, and some few of the difficulties which have attended me along its journey, down to this time. I am perfectly aware, that I have related many small and, as I fear, uninteresting circumstances; but if so, my apology is, that it was rendered necessary by a desire to link the different periods of my life together, as they have passed, from my childhood onward, and thereby to enable the reader to select such parts of it as he may relish most, if, indeed, there is any thing in it which may suit his palate.

I have also been operated on by another consideration. It is this: — I know, that obscure as I am, my name is making considerable deal of fuss in the world. I can't tell why it is, nor in what it is to end. Go where I will, everybody seems anxious to get a peep at me; and it would be hard to tell which would have the advantage, if I, and the "Government," and "Black Hawk," and a great eternal big caravan of *wild varments* were all to be showed at the same time in four different parts of any of the big cities in the nation. I am not so sure that I shouldn't get the most custom of any of the crew. There must therefore be something in me, or about me, that attracts attention, which is even mysterious to myself. I can't understand it, and I therefore put all the facts down, leaving the reader free to take his choice of them.

On the subject of my style, it is bad enough, in all conscience, to please critics, if that is what they are after. They are a sort of vermin, though, that I sha'n't even so much as stop to brush off. If they want to work on my book, just let them go ahead; and after they are done, they had better blot out all their criticisms, than to know what opinion I would express of *them*, and by what sort of a curious name I would call *them* if I was standing near them, and looking over their shoulders. They will, at most, have only their trouble for their pay. But I rather expect I shall have them on my side.

But I don't know of any thing in my book to be criticised on by honourable men. Is it on my spelling? — that's not my trade. Is it on my grammar? — I hadn't time to learn it, and make no pretensions to it. Is it on the order and arrangement of my book? — I never wrote one before, and never read very many; and, of course, know mighty little about that. Will it be on the authorship of the book? — this I claim, and I'll hang on to it, like a wax plaster. The whole book is my own, and every sentiment and sentence in it. I would not be such a fool, or knave either, as to deny that I have had it hastily run over by a friend or so, and that some little alterations have been made in the spelling and grammar; and I am not so sure that it is not the worse of even that, for I despise this way of spelling contrary to nature. And as for grammar, it's pretty much a thing of nothing at last, after all the fuss that's made about it. In some places, I wouldn't suffer either the spelling, or grammar, or any thing else to be touch'd; and therefore it will be found in my own way.

But if any body complains that I have had it looked over, I can only say to him, her, them — as the case may he — that while critics were learning grammar, and learning to spell, I, and "Doctor Jackson, L.L.D." were fighting in the wars; and if our books, and messages, and proclamations, and cabinet writings, and so forth, and so on, should need a little looking over, and a little correcting of the spelling and the grammar to make them fit for use, its just nobody's business. Big men have more important matters to attend to than crossing their *t*'s—, and dotting their *i*'s—, and such like small things. But the "Government's" name is to the proclamation, and my name's to the book; and if I didn't write the book, the "Government" didn't write the proclamation, which no man *dares to deny!*

But just read for yourself, and my ears for a, heel tap, if before you get through you don't say, with many a good-natured smile and hearty laugh, "This is truly the very thing itself — the exact image of its Author,

DAVID
CROCKETT."
Washington City,
February 1st, 1834.

CHAPTER I.

As the public seem to feel some interest in the history of an individual so humble as I am, and as that history can be so well known to no person living as to myself, I have, after so long a time, and under many pressing solicitations from my friends and acquaintances, at last determined to put my own hand to it, and lay before the world a narrative on which they may at least rely as being true. And seeking no ornament or colouring for a plain, simple tale of truth, I throw aside all hypocritical and fawning apologies, and, according to my own maxim, just "*go ahead.*" Where I am not known, I might, perhaps, gain some little credit by having thrown around this volume some of the flowers of learning; but where I am known, the vile cheatery would soon be detected, and like the foolish jackdaw, that with a *borrowed* tail attempted to play the peacock, I should be justly robbed of my pilfered ornaments, and sent forth to strut without a tail for the balance of my time. I shall commence my book with what little I have learned of the history of my father, as all *great men* rest many, if not most, of their hopes on their noble ancestry. Mine was poor, but I hope honest, and even that is as much as many a man can say. But to my subject.

My father's name was John Crockett, and he was of Irish descent. He was either born in Ireland or on a passage from that country to America across the Atlantic. He was by profession a farmer, and spent the early part of his life in the state of Pennsylvania. The name of my mother was Rebecca Hawkins. She was an American woman, born in the state of Maryland, between York and Baltimore. It is likely I may have heard where they were married, but if so, I have forgotten. It is, however, certain that they were, or else the public would never have been troubled with the history of David Crockett, their son.

I have an imperfect recollection of the part which I have understood my father took in the revolutionary war. I personally know nothing about it, for it happened to be a little before my day; but from himself, and many others who were well acquainted with its troubles and afflictions, I have learned that he was a soldier in the revolutionary war, and took part in that bloody struggle. He fought, according to my information, in the battle at Kings Mountain against the British and tories, and in some other engagements of which my remembrance is too imperfect to enable me to speak with any certainty. At some time, though I cannot say certainly when, my father, as I have understood, lived in Lincoln county, in the state of North Carolina. How long, I don't know. But when he removed from there, he settled in that district of country which is now embraced in the east division of Tennessee, though it was not then erected into a state.

He settled there under dangerous circumstances, both to himself and his family, as the country was full of Indians, who were at that time very troublesome. By the Creeks, my grandfather and grandmother Crockett were both, murdered, in their own house, and on the very spot of ground where Rogersville, in Hawkins county, now stands. At the same time, the Indians wounded Joseph Crockett, a brother to my father, by a ball, which broke his arm; and took James a prisoner, who was still a younger brother than Joseph, and who, from natural defects, was less able to make his escape, as he was both deaf and dumb. He remained with them for seventeen years and nine months, when he was discovered and recollected by my father and his eldest brother, William Crockett; and was purchased by them from an Indian trader, at a price which I do not now remember; but so it was, that he was delivered up to them, and they returned him to his relatives. He now lives in Cumberland county, in the state of Kentucky, though I have not seen him for many years.

My father and mother had six sons and three daughters. I was the fifth son. What a pity I hadn't been the seventh! For then I might have been, by *common consent*, called *doctor*, as a heap of people get to be great men. But, like many of them, I stood no chance to become great in any other way than by accident. As my father was very poor, and living as he did *far back in the back woods*, he had neither the means nor the opportunity to give me, or any of the rest of his children, any learning.

But before I get on the subject of my own troubles, and a great many very funny things that have happened to me, like all other historians and biographers, I should not only inform the public that I was born, myself, as well as other folks, but that this important event took place, according to the best information I have received on the subject, on the 17th of August, in the year 1786; whether by day or night, I believe I never heard, but if I did I, have forgotten. I suppose, however, it is not very material to my present purpose, nor to the world, as the more important fact is well attested, that I was born; and, indeed, it might be inferred, from my present size and appearance, that I was pretty *well born*, though I have never yet attached myself to that numerous and worthy society.

At that time my father lived at the mouth of Lime Stone, on the Nola-chucky river; and for the purpose not only of showing what sort of a man I now am, but also to show how soon I began to be a *sort of a little man*, I have endeavoured to take the *back track* of life, in order to fix on the first thing that I can remember. But even then, as now, so many things were happening, that as Major Jack Downing would say, they are all in "a pretty considerable of a snarl," and I find it "kinder hard" to fix on that thing, among them all, which really happened first. But I think it likely, I have hit on the outside line of my recollection; as one thing happened at which I was so badly scared, that it seems to me I could not have forgotten it, if it had happened a little time only after I was born. Therefore it furnishes me with no certain evidence of my age at the time; but I know one thing very well, and that is, that when it happened, I had no knowledge of the use of breeches, for I had never had any nor worn any.

But the circumstance was this: My four elder brothers, and a well-grown boy of about fifteen years old, by the name of Campbell, and myself, were all playing on the river's side; when all the rest of them got into my father's canoe, and put out to amuse themselves on the water, leaving me on the shore alone.

Just a little distance below them, there was a fall in the river, which went slap-right straight down. My brothers, though they were little fellows, had been used to paddling the canoe, and could have carried it safely anywhere about there; but this fellow Campbell wouldn't let them have the paddle, but, fool like, undertook to manage it himself. I reckon he had never seen a water craft before; and it went just any way but the way he wanted it. There he paddled, and paddled, and paddled — all the while going wrong, — until, in a short time, here they were all going, straight forward, stern foremost, right plump to the falls; and if they had only had a fair shake, they would have gone over as slick as a whistle. It was'ent this, though, that scared me; for I was so infernal mad that they had left me on the shore, that I had as soon have seen them all go over the falls a bit, as any other way. But their danger was seen by a man by the name of Kendall, but I'll be shot if it was Amos; for I believe I would know him yet if I was to see him. This man Kendall was working in a field on the bank, and knowing there was no time to lose, he started full tilt, and here he come like a cane brake afire; and as he ran, he threw off his coat, and then his jacket, and then his shirt, for I know when he got to the water he had nothing on but his breeches. But seeing him in such a hurry, and tearing off his clothes as he went, I had no doubt but that the devil or something else was after him — and close on him, too — as he was running within an inch of his life. This alarmed me, and I screamed out like a young painter. But Kendall didn't stop for this. He went ahead with all might, and as full bent on saving the boys, as Amos was on moving the deposites. When he came to the water he plunged in, and where it was too deep to wade he would swim, and where it was shallow enough he went bolting on; and by such exertion as I never saw at any other time in my life, he reached the canoe, when it was within twenty or thirty feet of the falls; and so great was the suck, and so swift the current, that poor Kendall had a hard time of it to stop them at last, as Amos will to stop the mouths of the people about his stockjobbing. But he hung on to the canoe, till he got it stop'd, and then draw'd it out of danger. When they got out, I found the boys were more scared than I had been, and the only thing that comforted me was, the belief that it was a punishment on them for leaving me on shore.

Shortly after this, my father removed, and settled in the same county, about ten miles above Greenville.

There another circumstance happened, which made a lasting impression on my memory, though I was but a small child. Joseph Hawkins, who was a brother to my mother, was in the woods hunting for deer. He was passing near a thicket of brush, in which one of our neighbours was gathering some grapes, as it was in the fall of the year, and the grape season. The body of the man was hid by the brush, and it was only as he would raise his hand to pull the bunches, that any part of him could be seen. It was a likely place for deer; and my uncle, having no suspicion that it was any human being, but supposing the raising of the hand to be the occasional twitch of a deer's ear, fired at the lump, and as the devil would have it, unfortunately shot the man through the body. I saw my father draw a silk handkerchief through the bullet hole, and entirely through his body; yet after a while he got well, as little as any one would have thought it. What become of him, or whether he is dead or alive, I don't know; but I reckon he did'ent fancy the business of gathering grapes in an out-of-the-way thicket soon again.

The next move my father made was to the mouth of Core creek, where he and a man by the name of Thomas Galbreath undertook to build a mill in partnership. They went on very well with their work until it was nigh done, when there came the second epistle to Noah's fresh [a flood], and away went their mill, shot, lock, and barrel. I remember the water rose so high, that it got up into the house we lived in, and my father moved us out of it, to keep us from being drowned. I was now about seven or eight years old, and have a pretty distinct recollection of every thing that was going on. From his bad luck in that business, and being ready to wash out from mill building, my father again removed, and this time settled in Jefferson county, now in the state of Tennessee; where he opened a tavern on the road from Abbingdon to Knoxville.

His tavern was on a small scale, as he was poor; and the principal accommodations which he kept, were for the waggoners who travelled the road. Here I remained with him until I was twelve years old; and about that time, you may guess, if you belong to Yankee land, or reckon, if like me you belong to the back-woods, that I began to make up my acquaintance with hard times, and a plenty of them.

An old Dutchman, by the name of Jacob Siler, who was moving from Knox county to Rockbridge, in the state of Virginia, in passing, made a stop at my father's house. He had a large stock of cattle, that he was carrying on with him; and I suppose made some proposition to my father to hire some one to assist him.

Being hard run every way, and having no thought, as I believe, that I was cut out for a Congressman or the like, young as I was, and as little as I knew about travelling, or being from home, he hired me to the old Dutchman, to go four hundred miles on foot, with a perfect stranger that I never had seen until the evening before. I set out with a heavy heart, it is true, but I went ahead, until we arrived at the place, which was three miles from what is called the Natural Bridge, and made a stop at the house of a Mr. Hartley, who was father-in-law to Mr. Siler, who had hired me. My Dutch master was very kind to me, and gave me five or six dollars, being pleased, as he said, with my services.

This, however, I think was a bait for me, as he persuaded me to stay with him, and not return any more to my father. I had been taught so many lessons of obedience by my father, that I at first supposed I was bound to obey this man, or at least I was afraid openly to disobey him; and I therefore staid with him, and tried to put on a look of perfect contentment until I got the family all to believe I was fully satisfied. I had been there about four or five weeks, when one day myself and two other boys were playing on the roadside, some distance from the house. There came along three waggoners. One belonged to an old man by the name of Dunn, and the others to two of his sons. They had each of them a good team, and were all bound for Knoxville. They had been in the habit of stopping at my father's as they passed the road, and I knew them. I made myself known to the old gentleman, and informed him of my situation; I expressed a wish to get back to my father and mother, if they could fix any plan for me to do so. They told me that they would stay that night at a tavern seven miles from there, and that if I could get to them before day the next morning, they would take me home; and if I was pursued, they would protect me. This was a Sunday evening; I went back to the good old Dutchman's house, and as good fortune would have it, he and the family were out on a visit. I gathered my clothes, and what little money I had, and put them all together under the head of my bed. I went to bed early that night, but sleep seemed to be a stranger to me. For though I was a wild boy, yet I dearly loved my father and mother, and their images appeared to be so deeply fixed in my mind, that I could not sleep for thinking of them. And then the fear that when I should attempt to go out, I should be discovered and called to a halt, filled me with anxiety; and between my childish love of home, on the one hand, and the fears of which I have spoken, on the other, I felt mighty queer.

But so it was, about three hours before day in the morning I got up to make my start. When I got out, I found it was snowing fast, and that the snow was then on the ground about eight inches deep. I had not even the advantage of moonlight, and the whole sky was hid by the falling snow, so that I had to guess at my way to the big road, which was about a half mile from the house. I however pushed ahead and soon got to it, and then pursued it, in the direction to the waggons.

I could not have pursued the road if I had not guided myself by the opening it made between the timber, as the snow was too deep to leave any part of it to be known by either seeing or feeling.

Before I overtook the waggons, the earth was covered about as deep as my knees; and my tracks filled so briskly after me, that by daylight, my Dutch master could have seen no trace which I left.

I got to the place about an hour before day. I found the waggoners already stirring, and engaged in feeding and preparing their horses for a start. Mr. Dunn took me in and treated me with great kindness. My heart was more deeply impressed by meeting with such a friend, and "at such a time," than by wading the snow-storm by night, or all the other sufferings which my mind had endured. I warmed myself by the fire, for I was very cold, and after an early breakfast, we set out on our journey. The thoughts of home now began to take the entire possession of my mind, and I almost numbered the sluggish turns of the wheels, and much more certainly the miles of our travel, which appeared to me to count mighty slow. I continued with my kind protectors, until we got to the house of a Mr. John Cole, on Roanoke, when my impatience became so great, that I determined to set out on foot and go ahead by myself, as I could travel twice as fast in that way as the waggons could.

Mr. Dunn seemed very sorry to part with me, and used many arguments to prevent me from leaving him. But home, poor as it was, again rushed on my memory, and it seemed ten times as dear to me as it ever had before. The reason was, that my parents were there, and all that I had been accustomed to in the hours of childhood and infancy was there; and there my anxious little heart panted also to be. We remained at Mr. Coles that night, and early in the morning I felt that I couldn't stay; so, taking leave of my friends the waggoners, I went forward on foot, until I was fortunately overtaken by a gentleman, who was returning from market, to which he had been with a drove of horses. He had a led horse, with a bridle and saddle on him, and he kindly offered to let me get on his horse and ride him. I did so, and was glad of the chance, for I was tired, and was, moreover, near the first crossing of Roanoke, which I would have been compelled to wade, cold as the water was, if I had not fortunately met this good man. I travelled with him in this way, without any thing turning up worth recording, until we got within fifteen miles of my father's house. There we parted, and he went on to Kentucky and I trudged on homeward, which place I reached that evening. The name of this kind gentleman I have entirely forgotten, and I am sorry for it; for it deserves a high place in my little book. A remembrance of his kindness to a little straggling boy, and a stranger to him, has however a resting place in my heart, and there it will remain as long as I live.

CHAPTER II.

Having gotten home, as I have just related, I remained with my father until the next fall, at which time he took it into his head to send me to a little country school, which was kept in the neighbourhood by a man whose name was Benjamin Kitchen; though I believe he was no way connected with the cabinet. I went four days, and had just began to learn my letters a little, when I had an unfortunate falling out with one of the scholars, — a boy much larger and older than myself I knew well enough that though the school-house might do for a still hunt, it wouldn't do for *a drive*, and so I concluded to wait until I could get him out, and then I was determined to give him salt and vinegar. I waited till in the evening, and when the larger scholars were spelling, I slip'd out, and going some distance along his road, I lay by the way-side in the bushes, waiting for him to come along. After a while he and his company came on sure enough, and I pitched out from the bushes and set on him like a wild cat. I scratched his face all to a flitter jig, and soon made him cry out for quarters in good earnest. The fight being over, I went on home, and the next morning was started again to school; but do you think I went? No, indeed. I was very clear of it; for I expected the master would lick me up, as bad as I had the boy. So, instead of going to the school-house, I laid out in the woods all day until in the evening the scholars were dismissed, and my brothers, who were also going to school, came along, returning home. I wanted to conceal this whole business from my father, and I therefore persuaded them not to tell on me, which they agreed to.

Things went on in this way for several days; I starting with them to school in the morning, and returning with them in the evening, but lying out in the woods all day. At last, however, the master wrote a note to my father, inquiring why I was not sent to school. When he read this note, he called me up, and I knew very well that I was in a devil of a hobble, for my father had been taking a few *horns*, and was in a good condition to make the fur fly. He called on me to know why I had not been at school? I told him I was afraid to go, and that the master would whip me; for I knew quite well if I was turned over to this old Kitchen, I should be cooked up to a cracklin, in little or no time. But I soon found that I was not to expect a much better fate at home; for my father told me, in a very angry manner, that he would whip me an eternal sight worse than the master, if I didn't start immediately to the school. I tried again to beg off; but nothing would do, but to go to the school. Finding me rather too slow about starting, he gathered about a two year old hickory, and broke after me. I put out with all my might, and soon we were both up to the top of our speed. We had a tolerable tough race for about a mile; but mind me, not on the school-house road, for I was trying to get as far the t'other way as possible. And I yet believe, if my father and the schoolmaster could both have levied on me about that time, I should never have been called on to sit in the councils of the nation, for I think they would have used me up. But fortunately for me, about this time, I saw just before me a hill, over which I made headway, like a young steamboat. As soon as I had passed over it, I turned to one side, and hid myself in the bushes. Here I waited until the old gentleman passed by, puffing and blowing, as tho' his steam was high enough to burst his boilers. I waited until he gave up the hunt, and passed back again: I then cut out, and went to the house of an acquaintance a few miles off, who was just about to start with a drove. His name was Jesse Cheek, and I hired myself to go with him, determining not to return home, as home and the school-house had both become too hot for me. I had an elder brother, who also hired to go with the same drove. We set out and went on through Abbingdon, and the county seat of Withe county, in the state of Virginia; and then through Lynchburgh, by Orange court-house, and Charlottesville, passing through what was called Chester Gap, on to a town called Front Royal, where my employer sold out his drove to a man by the name of Vanmetre; and I was started homeward again, in company with a brother of the first owner of the drove, with one horse between us; having left my brother to come on with the balance of the company.

I traveled on with my new comrade about three days' journey; but much to his discredit, as I then thought, and still think, he took care all the time to ride, but never to lie; at last I told him to go ahead, and I would come when I got ready. He gave me four dollars to bear my expenses upwards of four hundred miles, and then cut out and left me.

I purchased some provisions, and went on slowly, until at length I fell in with a waggoner, with whom I was disposed to scrape up a hasty acquaintance. I inquired where he lived, and where he was going, and all about his affairs. He informed me that he lived in Greenville, Tennessee, and was on his way to a place called Gerardstown, fifteen miles below Winchester. He also said, that after he should make his journey to that place, he would immediately return to Tennessee. His name was Adam Myers, and a jolly good fellow he seemed to be. On a little reflection, I determined to turn back and go with him, which I did; and we journeyed on slowly as waggons commonly do, but merrily enough. I often thought of home, and, indeed, wished bad enough to be there; but, when I thought of the school-house, and Kitchen, my master, and the race with my father, and the big hickory he carried, and of the fierceness of the storm of wrath that I had left him in, I was afraid to venture back; for I knew my father's nature so well, that I was certain his anger would hang on to him like a turkle does to a fisherman's toe, and that, if I went back in a hurry, he would give me the devil in three or four ways. But I and the waggoner had traveled two days, when we met my brother, who, I before stated, I had left behind when the drove was sold out. He persuaded me to go home, but I refused. He pressed me hard, and brought up a great many mighty strong arguments to induce me to turn back again. He pictured the pleasure of meeting my mother, and my sisters, who all loved me dearly, and told me what uneasiness they had already suffered about me. I could not help shedding tears, which I did not often do, and my affections all pointed back to those dearest friends, and as I thought, nearly the only ones I had in the world; but then the promised whipping — that was the thing. It came right slap down on every thought of home; and I finally determined that make or break, hit or miss, I would just hang on to my journey, and go ahead with the waggoner. My brother was much grieved at our parting, but he went his way, and so did I. We went on until at last we got to Gerardstown, where the waggoner tried to get a back load, but he could not without going to Alexandria. He engaged to go there, and I concluded that I would wait until he returned. I set in to work for a man by the name of John Gray, at twenty-five cents per day. My labour, however, was light, such as ploughing in some small grain, in which I succeeded in pleasing the old man very well. I continued working for him until the waggoner got back, and for a good long time afterwards, as he continued to run his team back and forward, hauling to and from Baltimore. In the next spring, from the proceeds of my daily labour, small as it was, I was able to get me some decent clothes, and concluded I would make a trip with the waggoner to Baltimore, and see what sort of a place that was, and what sort of folks lived there. I gave him the balance of what money I had for safe keeping, which, as well as I recollect, was about seven dollars. We got on well enough until we came near Ellicott's Mills. Our load consisted of flour, in barrels. Here I got into the waggon for the purpose of changing my clothing, not thinking that I was in any danger; but while I was in there we were met by some wheel-barrow men, who were working on the road, and the horses took a scare and away they went, like they had seen a ghost. They made a sudden wheel around, and broke the waggon tongue slap, short off, as a pipe-stem; and snap went both of the axletrees at the same time, and of all devlish flouncing about of flour barrels that ever was seen, I reckon this took the beat. Even *a rat* would have stood a bad chance in a *straight* race among them, and not much better in a crooked one; for he would have been in a good way to be ground up as fine as ginger by their rolling over him. But this proved to me, that if a fellow is born to be hung, he will never be drowned; and, further, that if he is born for a seat in Congress, even flour barrels can't make a mash of him. All these dangers I escaped unhurt, though, like most of the office-holders of these times, for a while I was afraid to say my soul was my own; for I didn't know how soon I should be knocked into a cocked hat, and get my walking papers for another country.

We put our load into another waggon, and hauled ours to a workman's shop in Baltimore, having delivered the flour, and there we intended to remain two or three days, which time was necessary to repair the runaway waggon. While I was there, I went, one day, down to the wharf, and was much delighted to see the big ships, and their sails all flying; for I had never seen any such things before, and, indeed, I didn't believe there were any such things in all nature. After a short time my curiosity induced me to step aboard of one, where I was met by the captain, who asked me if I didn't wish to take a voyage to London? I told him I did, for by this time I had become pretty well weaned from home, and I cared but little where I was, or where I went, or what become of me. He said he wanted just such a boy as I was, which I was glad to hear. I told him I would go and get my clothes, and go with him. He enquired about my parents, where they lived, and all about them. I let him know that they lived in Tennessee, many hundred miles off. We soon agreed about my intended voyage, and I went back to my friend, the waggoner, and informed him that I was going to London, and wanted my money and my clothes. He refused to let me have either, and swore that he would confine me, and take me back to Tennessee. I took it to heart very much, but he kept so close and constant a watch over me, that I found it impossible to escape from him, until he had started homeward, and made several days' journey on the road. He was, during this time, very ill to me, and threatened me with his waggon whip on several occasions. At length I resolved to leave him at all hazards; and so, before day, one morning, I got my clothes out of his waggon, and cut out, on foot, without a farthing of money to bear my expenses. For all other friends having failed, I determined then to throw myself on Providence, and see how that would use me. I had gone, however, only a few miles when I came up with another waggoner, and such was my situation, that I felt more than ever the necessity of endeavouring to find a friend. I therefore concluded I would seek for one in him. He was going westwardly, and very kindly enquired of me where I was travelling? My youthful resolution, which had brooked almost every thing else, rather gave way at this enquiry; for it brought the loneliness of my situation, and every thing else that was calculated to oppress me, directly to view. My first answer to his question was in a sprinkle of tears, for if the world had been given to me, I could not, at that moment, have helped crying. As soon as the storm of feeling was over, I told him how I had been treated by the waggoner but a little before, who kept what little money I had, and left me without a copper to buy even a morsel of food.

He became exceedingly angry, and swore that he would make the other waggoner give up my money, pronouncing him a scoundrel, and many other hard names. I told him I was afraid to see him, for he had threatened me with his waggon whip, and I believed he would injure me. But my new friend was a very large, stout-looking man, and as resolute as a tiger. He bid me not to be afraid, still swearing he would have my money, or whip it out of the wretch who had it.

We turned and went back about two miles, when we reached the place where he was. I went reluctantly; but I depended on my friend for protection. When we got there, I had but little to say; but approaching the waggoner, my friend said to him, "You rascal, you have treated this boy badly." To which he replied, it was my fault. He was then asked, if he did not get seven dollars of my money, which he confessed. It was then demanded of him; but he declared most solemnly, that he had not that amount in the world; that he had spent my money, and intended paying it back to me when we got to Tennessee. I then felt reconciled, and persuaded my friend to let him alone, and we returned to his waggon, geared up, and started. His name I shall never forget while my memory lasts; it was Henry Myers. He lived in Pennsylvania, and I found him what he professed to be, a faithful friend and a clever fellow.

We traveled together for several days, but at length I concluded to endeavour to make my way homeward; and for that purpose set out again on foot, and alone. But one thing I must not omit. The last night I staid with Mr. Myers, was at a place where several other waggoners also staid. He told them, before we parted, that I was a poor little straggling boy, and how I had been treated; and that I was without money, though I had a long journey before me, through a land of strangers, where it was not even a wilderness.

They were good enough to contribute a sort of money-purse, and presented me with three dollars. On this amount I travelled as far as Montgomery court-house, in the state of Virginia, where it gave out. I set in to work for a man by the name of James Caldwell, a month, for five dollars, which was about a shilling a day. When this time was out, I bound myself to a man by the name of Elijah Griffith, by trade a hatter, agreeing to work for him four years. I remained with him about eighteen months, when he found himself so involved in debt, that he broke up, and left the country. For this time I had received nothing, and was, of course, left without money, and with but very few clothes, and them very indifferent ones. I, however, set in again, and worked about as I could catch employment, until I got a little money, and some clothing; and once more cut out for home. When I reached New River, at the mouth of a small stream, called Little River, the white caps were flying so, that I couldn't not get any body to attempt to put me across. I argued the case as well as I could, but they told me there was great danger of being capsized, and drowned, if I attempted to cross. I told them if I could get a canoe I would venture, caps or no caps. They tried to persuade me out of it; but finding they could not, they agreed I might take a canoe, and so I did, and put off. I tied my clothes to the rope of the canoe, to have them safe, whatever might happen. But I found it a mighty ticklish business, I tell you. When I got out fairly on the river, I would have given the world, if it had belonged to me, to have been back on shore. But there was no time to lose now, so I just determined to do the best I could, and the devil take the hindmost. I turned the canoe across the waves, to do which, I had to turn it nearly up the river, as the wind came from that way; and I went about two miles before I could land. When I struck land, my canoe was about half full of water, and I was as wet as a drowned rat. But I was so much rejoiced, that I scarcely felt the cold, though my clothes were frozen on me; and in this situation, I had to go above three miles, before I could find any house, or fire to warm at. I, however, made out to get to one at last, and then I thought I would warm the inside a little, as well as the outside, that there might be no grumbling.

I passed on until I arrived in Sullivan county, in the state of Tennessee, and there I met with my brother, who had gone with me when I started from home with the cattle drove.

I staid with him a few weeks, and then went on to my father's, which place I reached late in the evening. Several waggons were there for the night, and considerable company about the house. I enquired if I could stay all night, for I did not intend to make myself known, until I saw whether any of the family would find me out. I was told that I could stay, and went in, but had mighty little to say to any body. I had been gone so long, and had grown so much, that the family did not at first know me. And another, and perhaps a stronger reason was, they had no thought or expectation of me, for they all long given me up for finally lost.

After a while, we were all called to supper. I went with the rest. We had sat down to the table and begun to eat, when my eldest sister recollected me: she sprung up, ran and seized me around the neck, and exclaimed, "Here is my lost brother." My feelings at this time it would be vain and foolish for me to attempt to describe. I had often thought I felt before, and I suppose I had, but sure I am, I never had felt as I then did. The joy of my sisters and my mother, and, indeed, of all the family, was such that it humbled me, and made me sorry that I hadn't submitted to a hundred whippings, sooner than cause so much affliction as they had suffered on my account. I found the family had never heard a word of me from the time my brother left me. I was now almost fifteen years old; and my increased age and size, together with the joy of my father, occasioned by my unexpected return, I was sure would secure me against my long dreaded whipping; and so they did. But it will be a source of astonishment to many, who reflect that I am now a member of the American Congress, — the most enlightened body of men in the world, — that at so advanced an age, the age of fifteen, I did not know the first letter in the book.

CHAPTER III.

I HAD remained for some short time at home with my father, when he informed me that he owed a man, whose name was Abraham Wilson, the sum of thirty-six dollars, and that if I would set in and work out the note, so as to lift it for him, he would discharge me from his service, and I might go free. I agreed to do this, and went immediately to the man who held my father's note, and contracted with him to work six months for it. I set in, and worked with all my might, not losing a single day in the six months. When my time was out, I got my father's note, and then declined working with the man any longer, though he wanted to hire me mighty bad. The reason was, it was a place where a heap of bad company met to drink and gamble, and I wanted to get away from them, for I know'd very well if I staid there, I should get a bad name, as nobody could be respectable that would live there. I therefore returned to my father, and gave him up his paper, which seemed to please him mightily, for though he was poor, he was an honest man, and always tried mighty hard to pay off his debts.

I next went to the house of an honest old Quaker, by the name of John Kennedy, who had removed from North Carolina, and proposed to hire myself to him, at two shillings a day. He agreed to take me a week on trial; at the end of which he appeared pleased with my work, and informed me that he held a note on my father for forty dollars, and that he would give me that note if I would work for him six months. I was certain enough that I should never get any part of the note; but then I remembered it was my father that owed it, and I concluded it was my duty as a child to help him along, and ease his lot as much as I could. I told the Quaker I would take him up at his offer, and immediately went to work. I never visited my father's house during the whole time of this engagement, though he lived only fifteen miles off. But when it was finished, and I had got the note, I borrowed one of my employer's horses, and, on a Sunday evening, went to pay my parents a visit. Some time after I got there, I pulled out the note and handed it to my father, who supposed Mr. Kennedy had sent it for collection. The old man looked mighty sorry, and said to me he had not the money to pay it, and didn't know what he should do. I then told him I had paid it for him, and it was then his own; that it was not presented for collection, but as a present from me. At this, he shed a heap of tears;

and as soon as he got a little over it, he said he was sorry he couldn't give me any thing, but he was not able, he was too poor.

The next day, I went back to my old friend, the Quaker, and set in to work for him for some clothes; for I had now worked a year without getting any money at all, and my clothes were nearly all worn out, and what few I had left were mighty indifferent. I worked in this way for about two months; and in that time a young woman from North Carolina, who was the Quaker's niece, came on a visit to his house. And now I am just getting on a part of my history that I know I never can forget. For though I have heard people talk about hard loving, yet I reckon no poor devil in this world was ever cursed with such hard love as mine has always been, when it came on me. I soon found myself head over heels in love with this girl, whose name the public could make no use of; and I thought that if all the hills about there were pure chink, and all belonged to me, I would give them if I could just talk to her as I wanted to; but I was afraid to begin, for when I would think of saying any thing to her, my heart would begin to flutter like a duck in a puddle; and if I tried to outdo it and speak, it would get right smack up in my throat, and choak me like a cold potatoe. It bore on my mind in this way, till at last I concluded I must die if I didn't broach the subject; and so I determined to begin and hang on a trying to speak, till my heart would get out of my throat one way or t'other. And so one day at it I went, and after several trials I could say a little. I told her how well I loved her; that she was the darling object of my soul and body; and I must have her, or else I should pine down to nothing, and just die away with the consumption.

I found my talk was not disagreeable to her; but she was an honest girl, and didn't want to deceive nobody. She told me she was engaged to her cousin, a son of the old Quaker. This news was worse to me than war, pestilence, or famine; but still I knowed I could not help myself. I saw quick enough my cake was dough, and I tried to cool off as fast as possible; but I had hardly safety pipes enough, as my love was so hot as mighty nigh to burst my boilers. But I didn't press my claims any more, seeing there was no chance to do any thing.

I began now to think, that all my misfortunes growed out of my want of learning. I had never been to school but four days, as the reader has already seen, and did not yet know a letter.

I thought I would try to go to school some; and as the Quaker had a married son, who was living about a mile and a half from him, and keeping a school, I proposed to him that I would go to school four days in the week, and work for him the other two, to pay my board and schooling. He agreed I might come on those terms; and so at it I went, learning and working back and forwards, until I had been with him nigh on to six months. In this time I learned to read a little in my primer, to write my own name, and to cypher some in the three first rules in figures. And this was all the schooling I ever had in my life, up to this day. I should have continued longer, if it hadn't been that I concluded I couldn't do any longer without a wife; and so I cut out to hunt me one.

I found a family of very pretty little girls that I had known when very young. They had lived in the same neighborhood with me, and I had thought very well of them. I made an offer to one of them whose name is nobody's business, no more than the Quaker girl's was, and I found she took it very well. I still continued paying my respects to her, until I got to love her as bad as I had the Quaker's niece; and I would have agreed to fight a whole regiment of wild cats if she would only have said she would have me. Several months passed in this way, during all of which time she continued very kind and friendly. At last, the son of the old Quaker and my first girl had concluded to bring their matter to a close, and my little queen and myself were called on to wait on them. We went on the day, and performed our duty as attendants. This made me worse than ever; and after it was over, I pressed my claim very hard on her, but she would still give me a sort of an evasive answer. However, I gave her mighty little peace, till she told me at last she would have me. I thought this was glorification enough, even without spectacles. I was then about eighteen years old. We fixed the time to be married; and I thought if that day come, I should be the happiest man in the created world, or in the moon, or any where else.

I had by this time got to be mighty fond of the rifle, and had bought a capital one. I most generally carried her with me whereever I went, and though I had got back to the old Quaker's to live, who was a very particular man, I would sometimes slip out and attend the shooting matches, where they shot for beef; I always tried, though, to keep it a secret from him. He had at the same time a bound boy living with him, who I had gotten into almost as great a notion of the girls as myself. He was about my own age, and was deeply smitten with the sister to my intended wife. I know'd it was in vain to try to get the leave of the old man for my young associate to go with me on any of my courting frolics; but I thought I could fix a plan to have him along, which would not injure the Quaker, as we had no notion that he should ever know it. We commonly slept up-stairs, and at the gable end of the house there was a window. So one Sunday, when the old man and his family were all gone to meeting, we went out and cut a long pole, and, taking it to the house, we set it up on end in the corner, reaching up the chimney as high as the window. After this we would go up-stairs to bed, and then putting on our Sunday clothes, would go out at the window, and climb down the pole, take a horse apiece, and ride about ten miles to where his sweetheart lived, and the girl I claimed as my wife. I was always mighty careful to be back before day, so as to escape being found out; and in this way I continued my attentions very closely until a few days before I was to be married, or at least thought I was, for I had no fear that any thing was about to go wrong.

Just now I heard of a shooting-match in the neighbourhood, right between where I lived and my girl's house; and I determined to kill two birds with one stone, — to go to the shooting match first, and then to see her. I therefore made the Quaker believe I was going to hunt for deer, as they were pretty plenty about in those parts; but, instead of hunting them, I went straight on to the shooting-match, where I joined in with a partner, and we put in several shots for the beef. I was mighty lucky, and when the match was over I had won the whole beef. This was on a Saturday, and my success had put me in the finest humour in the world. So I sold my part of the beef for five dollars in the real grit, for I believe that was before bank-notes was invented; at least, I had never heard of any. I now started on to ask for my wife; for, though the next Thursday was our wedding day, I had never said a word to her parents about it. I had always dreaded the under-taking so bad, that I had put the evil hour off as long as possible; and, indeed, I calculated they knowed me so well, they wouldn't raise any objection to having me for their son-in-law. I had a great deal better opinion of myself, I found, than other people had of me; but I moved on with a light heart, and my five dollars jingling in my pocket, thinking all the time there was but few greater men in the world than myself.

In this flow of good humour I went ahead, till I got within about two miles of the place, when I concluded I would stop awhile at the house of the girl's uncle; where I might enquire about the family, and so forth, and so on. I was indeed just about ready to consider her uncle, my uncle; and her affairs, my affairs. When I went in, tho' I found her sister there. I asked how all was at home? In a minute I found from her countenance something was wrong. She looked mortified, and didn't answer as quick as I thought she ought, being it was her *brother-in-law* talking to her. However, I asked her again. She then burst into tears, and told me her sister was going to deceive me; and that she was to be married to another man the next day. This was as sudden to me as a clap of thunder of a bright sunshiny day. It was the cap-stone of all the afflictions I had ever met with; and it seemed to me, that it was more than any human creature could endure. It struck me perfectly speechless for some time, and made me feel so weak, that I thought I should sink down. I however recovered from my shock after a little, and rose and started without any ceremony, or even bidding any body good-bye. The young woman followed me out to the gate, and entreated me to go on to her father's, and said she would go with me. She said the young man, who was going to marry her sister, had got his license, and had asked for her; but she assured me her father and mother both preferred me to him; and that she had no doubt but that, if I would go on, I could break off the match. But I found I could go no further. My heart was bruised, and my spirits were broken down; so I bid her farewell, and turned my lonesome and miserable steps back again homeward, concluding that I was only born for hardships, misery, and disappointment. I now began to think, that in making me, it was entirely forgotten to make my mate; that I was born odd, and should always remain so, and that nobody would have me.

But all these reflections did not satisfy my mind, for I had no peace day nor night for several weeks. My appetite failed me, and I grew daily worse and worse. They all thought I was sick; and so I was. And it was the worst kind of sickness, — a sickness of the heart, and all the tender parts, produced by disappointed love.

CHAPTER IV.

I CONTINUED in this down-spirited situation for a good long time, until one day I took my rifle and started a hunting. While out, I made a call at the house of a Dutch widow, who had a daughter that was well enough as to smartness, but she was as ugly as a stone fence. She was, however, quite talkative, and soon begun to laugh at me about my disappointment.

She seemed disposed, though, to comfort me as much as she could; and, for that purpose, told me to keep in good heart, that "there was as good fish in the sea as had ever been caught out of it." I doubted this very much; but whether or not, I was certain that she was not one of them, for she was so homely that it almost give me a pain in the eyes to look at her.

But I couldn't help thinking, that she had intended what she had said as a banter for me to court her ! ! ! — the last thing in creation I could have thought of doing. I felt little inclined to talk on the subject, it is true; but, to pass off the time, I told her I thought I was born odd, and that no fellow to me could be found. She protested against this, and said if I would come to their reaping, which was not far off, she would show me one of the prettiest little girls there I had ever seen. She added that the one who had deceived me was nothing to be compared with her. I didn't believe a word of all this, for I had thought that such a piece of flesh and blood as she was had never been manufactured, and never would again. I agreed with her, though, that the little varment had treated me so bad, that I ought to forget her, and yet I couldn't do it. I concluded the best way to accomplish it was to cut out again, and see if I could find any other that would answer me; and so I told the Dutch girl I would be at the reaping, and would bring as many as I could with me.

I employed my time pretty generally in giving information of it, as far as I could, until the day came; and I then offered to work for my old friend, the Quaker, two days, if he would let his bound boy go with me one to the reaping. He refused, and reproved me pretty considerable roughly for my proposition; and said, if he was in my place he wouldn't go; that there would be a great deal of bad company there; and that I had been so good a boy, he would be sorry for me to get a bad name. But I knowed my promise to the Dutch girl, and I was resolved to fulfil it; so I shouldered my rifle, and started by myself. When I got to the place, I found a large company of men and women, and among them an old Irish woman, who had a great deal to say. I soon found out from my Dutch girl, that this old lady was the mother of the little girl she had promised me, though I had not yet seen her. She was in an outhouse with some other youngsters, and had not yet made her appearance. Her mamma, however, was no way bashful. She came up to me, and began to praise my red cheeks, and said she had a sweetheart for me. I had no doubt she had been told what I come for, and all about it. In the evening I was introduced to her daughter, and I must confess, I was plaguy well pleased with her from the word go. She had a good countenance, and was very pretty, and I was full bent on making up an acquaintance with her.

It was not long before the dancing commenced, and I asked her to join me in a reel. She very readily consented to do so; and after we had finished our dance, I took a seat alongside of her, and entered into a talk. I found her very interesting; while I was setting by her, making as good a use of my time as I could, her mother came to us, and very jocularly called me her son-in-law. This rather confused me, but I looked on it as a joke of the old lady, and tried to turn it off as well as I could; but I took care to pay as much attention to her through the evening as I could. I went on the old saying, of salting the cow to catch the calf. I soon become so much pleased with this little girl, that I began to think the Dutch girl had told me the truth, when she said there was still good fish in the sea.

We continued our frolic till near day, when we joined in some plays, calculated to amuse youngsters. I had not often spent a more agreeable night. In the morning, however, we all had to part; and I found my mind had become much better reconciled than it had been for a long time. I went home to the Quaker's, and made a bargain to work with his son for a low-priced horse. He was the first one I had ever owned, and I was to work six months for him. I had been engaged very closely five or six weeks, when this little girl run in my mind so, that I concluded I must go and see her, and find out what sort of people they were at home. I mounted my horse and away I went to where she lived, and when I got there I found her father a very clever old man, and the old woman as talkative as ever. She wanted badly to find out all about me, and as I thought to see how I would do for her girl. I had not yet seen her about, and I began to feel some anxiety to know where she was.

In a short time, however, my impatience was relieved, as she arrived at home from a meeting to which she had been. There was a young man with her, who I soon found was disposed to set up claim to her, as he was so attentive to her that I could hardly get to slip in a word edgeways. I began to think I was barking up the wrong tree again; but I was determined to stand up to my rack, fodder or no fodder. And so, to know her mind a little on the subject, I began to talk about starting, as I knowed she would then show some sign, from which I could understand which way the wind blowed. It was then near night, and my distance was fifteen miles home. At this my little girl soon began to indicate to the other gentleman that his room would be the better part of his company. At length she left him, and came to me, and insisted mighty hard that I should not go that evening; and, indeed, from all her actions and the attempts she made to get rid of him, I saw that she preferred me all holler. But it wasn't long before I found trouble enough in another quarter. Her mother was deeply enlisted for my rival, and I had to fight against her influence as well as his. But the girl herself was the prize I was fighting for; and as she welcomed me, I was determined to lay siege to her, let what would happen. I commenced a close courtship, having cornered her from her old beau; while he set off, looking on, like a poor man at a country frolic, and all the time almost gritting his teeth with pure disappointment. But he didn't dare to attempt any thing more, for now I had gotten a start, and I looked at him every once in a while as fierce as a wild-cat. I staid with her until Monday morning, and then I put out for home.

It was about two weeks after this that I was sent for to engage in a wolf hunt, where a great number of men were to meet, with their dogs and guns, and where the best sort of sport was expected. I went as large as life, but I had to hunt in strange woods, and in a part of the country which was very thinly inhabited. While I was out it clouded up, and I began to get scared; and in a little while I was so much so, that I didn't know which way home was, nor any thing about it. I set out the way I thought it was, but it turned out with me, as it always does with a lost man, I was wrong, and took exactly the contrary direction from the right one. And for the information of young hunters, I will just say, in this place, that whenever a fellow gets bad lost, the way home is just the way he don't think it is. This rule will hit nine times out of ten. I went ahead, though, about six or seven miles, when I found night was coming on fast; but at this distressing time I saw a little woman streaking it along through the woods like all wrath, and so I cut on too, for I was determined I wouldn't lose sight of her that night any more. I run on till she saw me, and she stopped; for she was as glad to see me as I was to see her, as she was lost as well as me. When I came up to her, who should she be but my little girl, that I had been paying my respects to. She had been out hunting her father's horses, and had missed her way, and had no knowledge where she was, or how far it was to any house, or what way would take us there. She had been travelling all day, and was mighty tired; and I would have taken her up, and toated her, if it hadn't been that I wanted her just where I could see her all the time, for I thought she looked sweeter than sugar; and by this time I loved her almost well enough to eat her.

At last I came to a path, that I know'd must go somewhere, and so we followed it, till we came to a house, at about dark. Here we staid all night. I set up all night courting j and in the morning we parted. She went to her home, from which we were distant about seven miles, and I to mine, which was ten miles off.

I now turned in to work again; and it was about four weeks before I went back to see her. I continued to go occasionally, until I had worked long enough to pay for my horse, by putting in my gun with my work, to the man I had purchased from; and then I began to count whether I was to be deceived again or not. At our next meeting we set the day for our wedding; and I went to my father's, and made arrangements for an infair [Scottish: wedding reception], and returned to ask her parents for her. When I got there, the old lady appeared to be mighty wrathy; and when I broached the subject, she looked at me as savage as a meat axe. The old man appeared quite willing, and treated me very clever. But I hadn't been there long, before the old woman as good as ordered me out of her house. I thought I would put her in mind of old times, and see how that would go with her. I told her she had called me her son-in-law before I had attempted to call her my mother-in-law and I thought she ought to cool off. But her Irish was up too high to do any thing with her, and so I quit trying. All I cared for was, to have her daughter on my side, which I knowed was the case then; but how soon some other fellow might knock my nose out of joint again, I couldn't tell. I however felt rather insulted at the old lady, and I thought I wouldn't get married in her house. And so I told her girl, that I would come the next Thursday, and bring a horse, bridle, and saddle for her, and she must be ready to go. Her mother declared I shouldn't have her; but I know'd I should, if somebody else didn't get her before Thursday. I then started, bidding them good day, and went by the house of a justice of the peace, who lived on the way to my father's, and made a bargain with him to marry me.

When Thursday came, all necessary arrangements were made at my father's to receive my wife; and so I took my eldest brother and his wife, and another brother, and a single sister that I had, and two other young men with me, and cut out to her father's house to get her. We went on, until we got within two miles of the place, where we met a large company that had heard of the wedding, and were waiting. Some of that company went on with my brother and sister, and the young man I had picked out to wait on me. When they got there, they found the old lady as wrathy as ever. However the old man filled their bottle, and the young men returned in a hurry. I then went on with my company, and when I arrived I never pretended to dismount from my horse, but rode up to the door, and asked the girl if she was ready; and she said she was. I then told her to light on the horse I was leading; and she did so. Her father, though, had gone out to the gate, and when I started he commenced persuading me to stay and marry there; that he was entirely willing to the match, and that his wife, like most women, had entirely too much tongue; but that I oughtn't to mind her. I told him if she would ask me to stay and marry at her house, I would do so. With that he sent for her, and after they had talked for some time out by themselves, she came to me and looked at me mighty good, and asked my pardon for what she had said, and invited me stay. She said it was the first child she had ever had to marry; and she couldn't bear to see her go off in that way; that if I would light, she would do the best she could for us. I couldn't stand every thing, and so I agreed, and we got down, and went in. I sent off then for my parson, and got married in a short time; for I was afraid to wait long, for fear of another defeat. We had as good treatment as could be expected; and that night all went on well. The next day we cut out for my father's, where we met a large company of people, that had been waiting a day and a night for our arrival. We passed the time quite merrily, until the company broke up; and having gotten my wife, I thought I was completely made up, and needed nothing more in the whole world. But I soon found this was all a mistake — for now having a wife, I wanted every thing else; and, worse than all, I had nothing to give for it.

I remained a few days at my father's, and then went back to my new father-in-law's; where, to my surprise, I found my old Irish mother in the finest humour in the world.

She gave us two likely cows and calves, which, though it was a small marriage-portion, was still better than I had expected, and, indeed, it was about all I ever got. I rented a small farm and cabin, and went to work; but I had much trouble to find out a plan to get any thing to put in my house. At this time, my good old friend the Quaker came forward to my assistance, and gave me an order to a store for fifteen dollars' worth of such things as my little wife might choose. With this, we fixed up pretty grand, as we thought, and allowed to get on very well. My wife had a good wheel, and knowed exactly how to use it. She was also a good weaver, as most of the Irish are, whether men or women; and being very industrious with her wheel, she had, in little or no time, a fine web of cloth, ready to make up; and she was good at that too, and at almost any thing else that a woman could do.

We worked on for some years, renting ground, and paying high rent, until I found it wan't the thing it was cracked up to be; and that I couldn't make a fortune at it just at all. So I concluded to quit it, and cut out for some new country. In this time we had two sons, and I found I was better at increasing my family than my fortune. It was therefore the more necessary that I should hunt some better place to get along; and as I knowed I would have to move at some time, I thought it was better to do it before my family got too large, that I might have less to carry.

The Duck and Elk river country was just beginning to settle, and I determined to try that. I had now one old horse, and a couple of two year old colts. They were both broke to the halter, and my father-in-law proposed, that, if I went, he would go with me, and take one horse to help me move. So we all fixed up, and I packed my two colts with as many of my things as they could bear; and away we went across the mountains. We got on well enough, and arrived safely in Lincoln county, on the head of the Mulberry fork of Elk river. I found this a very rich country, and so new, that game, of different sorts, was very plenty. It was here that I began to distinguish myself as a hunter, and to lay the foundation for all my future greatness; but mighty little did I know of what sort it was going to be. Of deer and smaller game I killed abundance; but the bear had been much hunted in those parts before, and were not so plenty as I could have wished. I lived here in the years 1809 and '10, to the best of my recollection, and then I moved to Franklin county, and settled on Bean creek, where I remained till after the close of the last war.

CHAPTER V.

I WAS living ten miles below Winchester when the Creek war commenced; and as military men are making so much fuss in the world at this time, I must give an account of the part I took in the defence of the country. If it should make me president, why I can't help it; such things will sometimes happen; and my pluck is, never "to seek, nor decline office."

It is true, I had a little rather not; but yet, if the government can't get on without taking another president from Tennessee, to finish the work of "retrenchment and reform," why, then, I reckon I must go in for it. But I must begin about the war, and leave the other matter for the people to begin on.

The Creek Indians had commenced their open hostilities by a most bloody butchery at Fort Mines. There had been no war among us for so long, that but few, who were not too old to bear arms, knew any thing about the business. I, for one, had often thought about war, and had often heard it described; and I did verily believe in my own mind, that I couldn't fight in that way at all; but my after experience convinced me that this was all a notion. For when I heard of the mischief which was done at the fort, I instantly felt like going, and I had none of the dread of dying that I expected to feel. In a few days a general meeting of the militia was called for the purpose of raising volunteers; and when the day arrived for that meeting, my wife, who had heard me say I meant to go to the war, began to beg me not to turn out. She said she was a stranger in the parts where we lived, had no connexions living near her, and that she and our little children would be left in a lonesome and unhappy situation if I went away. It was mighty hard to go against such arguments as these; but my countrymen had been murdered, and I knew that the next thing would be, that the Indians would be scalping the women and children all about there, if we didn't put a stop to it. I reasoned the case with her as well as I could, and told her, that if every man would wait till his wife got willing for him to go to war, there would be no fighting done, until we would all be killed in our own houses; that I was as able to go as any man in the world; and that I believed it was a duty I owed to my country. Whether she was satisfied with this reasoning or not, she did not tell me; but seeing I was bent on it, all she did was to cry a little, and turn about to her work. The truth is, my dander was up, and nothing but war could bring it right again.

I went to Winchester, where the muster was to be, and a great many people had collected, for there was as much fuss among the people about the war as there is now about moving the deposites. When the men were paraded, a lawyer by the name of Jones addressed us, and closed by turning out himself, and enquiring, at the same time, who among us felt like we could fight Indians? This was the same Mr. Jones who afterwards served in Congress, from the state of Tennessee. He informed us he wished to raise a company, and that then the men should meet and elect their own officers. I believe I was about the second or third man that step'd out; but on marching up and down the regiment a few times, we found we had a large company. We volunteered for sixty days, as it was supposed our services would not be longer wanted. A day or two after this we met and elected Mr. Jones our captain, and also elected our other officers. We then received orders to start on the next Monday week; before which time, I had fixed as well as I could to go, and my wife had equip'd me as well as she was able for the camp. The time arrived; I took a parting farewell of my wife and my little boys, mounted my horse, and set sail, to join my company. Expecting to be gone only a short time, I took no more clothing with me than I supposed would be necessary, so that if I got into an Indian battle, I might not be pestered with any unnecessary plunder, to prevent my having a fair shake with them. We all met and went ahead, till we passed Huntsville, and camped at a large spring called Bealy's spring. Here we staid for several days, in which time the troops began to collect from all quarters. At last we mustered about thirteen hundred strong, all mounted volunteers, and all determined to fight, judging from myself, for I felt wolfish all over. I verily believe the whole army was of the real grit. Our captain didn't want any other sort; and to try them he several times told his men, that if any of them wanted to go back home, they might do so at any time, before they were regularly mustered into the service. But he had the honour to command all his men from first to last, as not one of them left him.

Gen'l. Jackson had not yet left Nashville with his old foot volunteers, that had gone with him to Natchez in 1812, the year before. While we remained at the spring, a Major Gibson came, and wanted some volunteers to go with him across the Tennessee river and into the Creek nation, to find out the movements of the Indians. He came to my captain, and asked for two of his best woodsmen, and such as were best with a rifle. The captain pointed me out to him, and said he would be security that I would go as far as the major would himself, or any other man. I willingly engaged to go with him, and asked him to let me choose my own mate to go with me, which he said I might do. I chose a young man by the name of George Russell, a son of old Major Russell, of Tennessee. I called him up, but Major Gibson said he thought he hadn't beard enough to please him, — he wanted men, and not boys. I must confess I was a little nettled at this; for I know'd George Russell, and I know'd there was no mistake in him; and I didn't think that courage ought to be measured by the beard, for fear a goat would have the preference over a man. I told the major he was on the wrong scent; that Russell could go as far as he could, and I must have him along. He saw I was a little wrathy, and said I had the best chance of knowing, and agreed that it should be as I wanted it. He told us to be ready early in the morning for a start; and so we were. We took our camp equipage, mounted our horses, and, thirteen in number, including the major, we cut out. We went on, and crossed the Tennessee river at a place called Ditto's Landing; and then traveled about seven miles further, and took up camp for the night. Here a man by the name of John Haynes overtook us. He had been an Indian trader in that part of the nation, and was well acquainted with it. He went with us as a pilot. The next morning, however, Major Gibson and myself concluded we should separate and take different directions to see what discoveries we could make; so he took seven of the men, and I five, making thirteen in all, including myself. He was to go by the house of a Cherokee Indian, named Dick Brown, and I was to go by Dick's father's; and getting all the information we could, we were to meet that evening where the roads came together, fifteen miles the other side of Brown's. At old Mr. Brown's I got a half blood Cherokee to agree to go with me, whose name was Jack Thompson. He was not then ready to start, but was to fix that evening, and overtake us at the fork road where I was to meet Major Gibson. I know'd it wouldn't be safe to camp right at the road; and so I told Jack, that when he got to the fork he must holler like an owl, and I would answer him in the same way; for I know'd it would be night before he got there. I and my men then started, and went on to the place of meeting, but Major Gibson was not there. We waited till almost dark, but still he didn't come. We then left the Indian trace a little distance, and turning into the head of a hollow, we struck up camp. It was about ten o'clock at night, when I heard my owl, and I answered him. Jack soon found us, and we determined to rest there during the night. We staid also next morning till after breakfast: but in vain, for the major didn't still come.

I told the men we had set out to hunt a fight, and I wouldn't go back in that way; that we must go ahead, and see what the red men were at. We started, and went to a Cherokee town about twenty miles off; and after a short stay there, we pushed on to the house of a man by the name of Radcliff. He was a white man, but had married a Creek woman, and lived just in the edge of the Creek nation. He had two sons, large likely fellows, and a great deal of potatoes and corn, and, indeed, almost every thing else to go on; so we fed our horses and got dinner with him, and seemed to be doing mighty well. But he was bad scared all the time. He told us there had been ten painted warriors at his house only an hour before, and if we were discovered there, they would kill us, and his family with us. I replied to him, that my business was to hunt for just such fellows as he had described, and I was determined not to gack until I had done it. Our dinner being over, we saddled up our horses, and made ready to start. But some of my small company I found were disposed to return. I told them, if we were to go back then, we should never hear the last of it; and I was determined to go ahead. I knowed some of them would go with me, and that the rest were afraid to go back by themselves; and so we pushed on to the camp of some of the friendly Creeks, which was distant about eight miles. The moon was about the full, and the night was clear; we therefore had the benefit of her light from night to morning, and I knew if we were placed in such danger as to make a retreat necessary, we could travel by night as well as in the day time.

We had not gone very far, when we met two negroes, well mounted on Indian ponies, and each with a good rifle. They had been taken from their owners by the Indians, and were running away from them, and trying to get back to their masters again. They were brothers, both very large and likely, and could talk Indian as well as English. One of them I sent on to Ditto's Landing, the other I took back with me. It was after dark when we got to the camp, where we found about forty men, women, and children.

They had bows and arrows, and I turned in to shooting with their boys by a pine light. In this way we amused ourselves very well for a while; but at last the negro, who had been talking to the Indians, came to me and told me they were very much alarmed, for the "red skins," as they called the war party of the Creeks, would come and find us there; and, if so, we should all be killed. I directed him to tell them that I would watch, and if one would come that night, I would carry the skin of his head home to make me a mockasin. When he made this communication, the Indians laughed aloud. At about ten o'clock at night we all concluded to try to sleep a little; but that our horses might be ready for use, as the treasurer said of the drafts on the United States' bank, on certain "contingences," we tied them up with our saddles on them, and every thing to our hand, if in the night our quarters should get uncomfortable. We lay down with our guns in our arms, and I had just gotten into a dose of sleep, when I heard the sharpest scream that ever escaped the throat of a human creature. It was more like a wrathy painter than any thing else. The negro understood it, and he sprang to me; for tho' I heard the noise well enough, yet I wasn't wide awake enough to get up. So the negro caught me, and said the red sticks was coming. I rose quicker then, and asked what was the matter? Our negro had gone and talked with the Indian who had just fetched the scream, as he come into camp, and learned from him, that the war party had been crossing the Coosa river all day at the Ten islands; and were going on to meet Jackson, and this Indian had come as a runner. This news very much alarmed the friendly Indians in camp, and they were all off in a few minutes. I felt bound to make this intelligence known as soon as possible to the army we had left at the landing; and so we all mounted our horses, and put out in a long lope to make our way back to that place. We were about sixty-five miles off. We went on to the same Cherokee town we had visited on our way out, having first called at Radcliff's, who was off with his family; and at the the town we found large fires burning, but not a single Indian was to be seen. They were all gone. These circumstances were calculated to lay our dander a little, as it appeared we must be in great danger; though we could easily have licked any force of not more than five to one. But we expected the whole nation would be on us, and against such fearful odds we were not so rampant for a fight.

We therefore staid only a short time in the light of the fires about the town, preferring the light of the moon and the shade of the woods. We pushed on till we got again to old Mr. Brown's, which was still about thirty miles from where we had left the main army. When we got there, the chickens were just at the first crowing for day. We fed our horses, got a morsel to eat ourselves, and again cut out. About ten o'clock in the morning we reached the camp, and I reported to Col. Coffee the news. He didn't seem to mind my report a bit, and this raised my dander higher than ever; but I knowed I had to be on my best behaviour, and so I kept it all to myself; though I was so mad that I was burning inside like a tar-kiln, and I wonder that the smoke hadn't been pouring out of me at all points.

Major Gibson hadn't yet returned, and we all began to think he was killed; and that night they put out a double guard. The next day the major got in, and brought a worse tale than I had, though he stated the same facts, so far as I went. This seemed to put our colonel all in a fidget; and it convinced me, clearly, of one of the hateful ways of the world. When I made my report, it wasn't believed, because I was no officer; I was no great man, but just a poor soldier. But when the same thing was reported by Major Gibson ! ! why, then, it was all as true as preaching, and the colonel believed it every word.

He, therefore, ordered breastworks to be thrown up, near a quarter of a mile long, and sent an express to Fayetteville, where General Jackson and his troops was, requesting them to push on like the very mischief, for fear we should all be cooked up to a cracklin before they could get there. Old Hickory-face made a forced march on getting the news; and on the next day, he and his men got into camp, with their feet all blistered from the effects of their swift journey. The volunteers, therefore, stood guard altogether, to let them rest.

CHAPTER VI. (*SENSITIVITY WARNING – war brutality and violence*)

About eight hundred of the volunteers, and of that number I was one, were now sent back, crossing the Tennessee river, and on through Huntsville, so as to cross the river again at another place, and to get on the Indians in another direction. After we passed Huntsville, we struck on the river at the Muscle Shoals, and at a place on them called Melton's Bluff. This river is here about two miles wide, and a rough bottom; so much so, indeed, in many places, as to be dangerous; and in fording it this time, we left several of the horses belonging to our men, with their feet fast in the crevices of the rocks. The men, whose horses were thus left, went ahead on foot. We pushed on till we got to what was called the Black Warrior's town, which stood near the very spot where Tuscaloosa now stands, which is the seat of government for the state of Alabama.

This Indian town was a large one; but when we arrived we found the Indians had all left it. There was a large field of corn standing out, and a pretty good supply in some cribs. There was also a fine quantity of dried leaves, which were very acceptable to us; and without delay we secured them as well as the corn, and then burned the town to ashes; after which we left the place.

In the field where we gathered the corn we saw plenty of fresh Indian tracks, and we had no doubt they had been scared off by our arrival.

We then went on to meet the main army at the fork road, where I was first to have met Major Gibson. We got that evening as far back as the encampment we had made the night before we reached the Black Warrior's town, which we had just destroyed. The next day we were entirely out of meat. I went to Col. Coffee, who was then in command of us, and asked his leave to hunt as we marched. He gave me leave, but told me to take mighty good care of myself. I turned aside to hunt, and had not gone far when I found a deer that had just been killed and skinned, and his flesh was still warm and smoking. From this I was sure that the Indian who had killed it had been gone only a very few minutes; and though I was never much in favour of one hunter stealing from another, yet meat was so scarce in camp, that I thought I must go in for it. So I just took up the deer on my horse before me, and carried it on till night. I could have sold it for almost any price I would have asked; but this wasn't my rule, neither in peace nor war. Whenever I had any thing, and saw a fellow being suffering, I was more anxious to relieve him than to benefit myself. And this is one of the true secrets of my being a poor man to this day. But it is my way; and while it has often left me with an empty purse, which is as near the devil as any thing else I have seen, yet it has never left my heart empty of consolations which money couldn't buy, — the consolations of having sometimes fed the hungry and covered the naked.

I gave all my deer away, except a small part I kept for myself, and just sufficient to make a good supper for my mess; for meat was getting to be a rarity to us all. We had to live mostly on parched corn. The next day we marched on, and at night took up camp near a large cane brake. While here, I told my mess I would again try for some meat; so I took my rifle and cut out, but hadn't gone far, when I discovered a large gang of hogs. I shot one of them down in his tracks, and the rest broke directly towards the camp. In a few minutes, the guns began to roar, as bad as if the whole army had been in an Indian battle; and the hogs to squeal as bad as the pig did, when the devil turned barber. I shouldered my hog, and went on to the camp; and when I got there I found they had killed a good many of the hogs, and a fine fat cow into the bargain, that had broke out of the cane brake. We did very well that night, and the next morning marched on to a Cherokee town, where our officers stop'd, and gave the inhabitants an order on Uncle Sam for their cow, and the hogs we had killed. The next day we met the main army, having had, as we thought, hard times, and a plenty of them, though we had yet seen hardly the beginning of trouble.

After our meeting we went on to Radcliff's, where I had been before while out as a spy; and when we got there, we found he had hid all his provisions. We also got into the secret, that he was the very rascal who had sent the runner to the Indian camp, with the news that the "red sticks" were crossing at the Ten Islands; and that his object was to scare me and my men away, and send us back with a false alarm.

To make some atonement for this, we took the old scroundrell's two big sons with us, and made them serve in the war.

We then marched to a place, which we called Camp Mills; and here it was that Captain Cannon was promoted to a colonel, and Colonel Coffee to a general. We then marched to the Ten Islands, on the Coosa river, where we established a fort; and our spy companies were sent out. They soon made prisoners of Bob Catala and his warriors, and, in a few days afterwards, we heard of some Indians in a town about eight miles off. So we mounted our horses, and put out for that town, under the direction of two friendly Creeks we had taken for pilots. We had also a Cherokee colonel, Dick Brown, and some of his men with us. When we got near the town we divided; one of our pilots going with each division. And so we passed on each side of the town, keeping near to it, until our lines met on the far side. We then closed up at both ends, so as to surround it completely; and then we sent Captain Hammond's company of rangers to bring on the affray. He had advanced near the town, when the Indians saw him, and they raised the yell, and came running at him like so many red devils. The main army was now formed in a hollow square around the town, and they pursued Hammond till they came in reach of us. We then gave them a fire, and they returned it, and then ran back into their town. We began to close on the town by making our files closer and closer, and the Indians soon saw they were our property. So most of them wanted us to take them prisoners; and their squaws and all would run and take hold of any of us they could, and give themselves up. I saw seven squaws have hold of one man, which made me think of the Scriptures. So I hollered out the Scriptures was fulfilling; that there was seven women holding to one man's coat tail. But I believe it was a hunting-shirt all the time. We took them all prisoners that came out to us in this way; but I saw some warriors run into a house, until I counted forty-six of them. We pursued them until we got near the house, when we saw a squaw sitting in the door, and she placed her feet against the bow she had in her hand, and then took an arrow, and, raising her feet, she drew with all her might, and let fly at us, and she killed a man, whose name, I believe, was Moore. He was a lieutenant, and his death so enraged us all, that she was fired on, and had at least twenty balls blown through her. This was the first man I ever saw killed with a bow and arrow. We now shot them like dogs; and then set the house on fire, and burned it up with the forty-six warriors in it. I recollect seeing a boy who was shot down near the house. His arm and thigh was broken, and he was so near the burning house that the grease was stewing out of him. In this situation he was still trying to crawl along; but not a murmur escaped him, though he was only about twelve years old. So sullen is the Indian, when his dander is up, that he had sooner die than make a noise, or ask for quarters.

The number that we took prisoners, being added to the number we killed, amounted to one hundred and eighty-six; though I don't remember the exact number of either. We had five of our men killed. We then returned to our camp, at which our fort was erected, and known by the name of Fort Strother. No provisions had yet reached us, and we had now been for several days on half rations. However we went back to our Indian town on the next day, when many of the carcasses of the Indians were still to be seen. They looked very awful, for the burning had not entirely consumed them, but given them a very terrible appearance, at least what remained of them. It was, somehow or other, found out that the house had a potatoe cellar under it, and an immediate examination was made, for we were all as hungry as wolves. We found a fine chance of potatoes in it, and hunger compelled us to eat them, though I had a little rather not, if I could have helped it, for the oil of the Indians we had burned up on the day before had run down on them, and they looked like they had been stewed with fat meat. We then again returned to the army, and remained there for several days almost starving, as all our beef was gone. We commenced eating the beef-hides, and continued to eat every scrap we could lay our hands on. At length an Indian came to our ground one night, and hollered, and said he wanted to see "Captain Jackson." He was conducted to the general's markee, into which he entered, and in a few minutes we received orders to prepare for marching.

In an hour we were all ready, and took up the line of march. We crossed the Coosa river, and went on in the direction to Fort Taladega. When we arrived near the place, we met eleven hundred painted warriors, the very choice of the Creek nation. They had encamped near the fort, and had informed the friendly Indians who were in it, that if they didn't come out, and fight with them against the whites, they would take their fort and all their ammunition and provision. The friendly party asked three days to consider of it, and agreed that if on the third day they didn't come out ready to fight with them, they might take their fort. Thus they put them off. They then immediately started their runner to General Jackson, and he and the army pushed over, as I have just before stated.

The camp of warriors had their spies out, and discovered us coming, some time before we got to the fort. They then went to the friendly Indians, and told them Captain Jackson was coming, and had a great many fine horses, and blankets, and guns, and every thing else; and if they would come out and help to whip him, and to take his plunder, it should all be divided with those in the fort. They promised that when Jackson came, they would then come out and help to whip him. It was about an hour by sun in the morning, when we got near the fort. We were piloted by friendly Indians, and divided as we had done on a former occasion, so as to go to the right and left of the fort, and, consequently, of the warriors who were camped near it. Our lines marched on, as before, till they met in front, and then closed in the rear, forming again into a hollow square. We then sent on old Major Russell, with his spy company, to bring on the battle; Capt. Evans' company went also. When they got near the fort, the top of it was lined with the friendly Indians, crying out as loud as they could roar, "How-dy-do, brother, how-dy-do?" They kept this up till Major Russel had passed by the fort, and was moving on towards the warriors. They were all painted as red as scarlet, and were just as naked as they were born. They had concealed themselves under the bank of a branch, that ran partly around the fort, in the manner of a half moon. Russel was going right into their circle, for he couldn't see them, while the Indians on the top of the fort were trying every plan to show him his danger. But he couldn't understand them. At last, two of them jumped from it, and ran, and took his horse by the bridle, and pointing to where they were, told him there were thousands of them lying under the bank. This brought them to a halt, and about this moment the Indians fired on them, and came rushing forth like a cloud of Egyptian locusts, and screaming like all the young devils had been turned loose, with the old devil of all at their head. Russel's company quit their horses, and took into the fort, and their horses ran up to our line, which was then in full view. The warriors then came yelling on, meeting us, and continued till they were within shot of us, when we fired and killed a considerable number of them. They then broke like a gang of steers, and ran across to our other line, where they were again fired on; and so we kept them running from one line to the other, constantly under a heavy fire, until we had killed upwards of four hundred of them. They fought with guns, and also with their bows and arrows; but at length they made their escape through a part of our line, which was made up of drafted militia, which broke ranks, and they passed. We lost fifteen of our men, as brave fellows as ever lived or died. We buried them all in one grave, and started back to our fort; but before we got there, two more of our men died of wounds they had received; making our total loss seventeen good fellows in that battle.

We now remained at the fort a few days, but no provision came yet, and we were all likely to perish. The weather also began to get very cold; and our clothes were nearly worn out, and horses getting very feeble and poor. Our officers proposed to Gen'l. Jackson to let us return home and get fresh horses, and fresh clothing, so as to be better prepared for another campaign; for our sixty days had long been out, and that was the time we entered for.

But the general took "the responsibility" on himself, and refused. We were, however, determined to go, as I am to put back the deposites, if I can. With this, the general issued his orders against it, as he has against the bank. But we began to fix for a start, as provisions were too scarce; just as Clay, and Webster, and myself are preparing to fix bank matters, on account of the scarcity of money. The general went and placed his cannon on a bridge we had to cross, and ordered out his regulars and drafted men to keep us from crossing; just as he has planted his Globe and K. C. to alarm the bank men, while his regulars and militia in Congress are to act as artillery men. But when the militia started to guard the bridge, they would holler back to us to bring their knapsacks along when we come, for they wanted to go as bad as we did; just as many a good fellow now wants his political knapsack brought along, that if, when we come to vote, he sees he has a fair shake to go, he may join in and help us to take back the deposites.

We got ready and moved on till we came near the bridge, where the general's men were all strung along on both sides, just like the office-holders are now, to keep us from getting along to the help of the country and the people. But we all had our flints ready picked, and our guns ready primed, that if we were fired on we might fight our way through, or all die together; just as we are now determined to save the country from ready ruin, or to sink down with it. When we came still nearer the bridge we heard the guards cocking their guns, and we did the same; just as we have had it in Congress, while the "government" regulars and the people's volunteers have all been setting their political triggers. But, after all, we marched boldly on, and not a gun was fired, nor a life lost; just as I hope it will be again, that we shall not be afraid of the general's Globe, nor his K. C, nor his regulars, nor their trigger snapping; but just march boldly over the executive bridge, and take the deposites back where the law placed them, and where they ought to be. When we had passed, no further attempt was made to stop us; but the general said, we were "the damned'st volunteers he had ever seen in his life; that we would volunteer and go out and fight, and then at our pleasure would *volunteer* and go home again, in spite of the devil." But we went on; and near Huntsville we met a reinforcement who were going on to join the army. It consisted of a regiment of volunteers, and was under the command of some one whose name I can't remember. They were sixty-day volunteers.

We got home pretty safely, and in a short time we had procured fresh horses and a supply of clothing better suited for the season; and then we returned to Fort Deposite, where our officers held a sort of a "national convention" on the subject of a message they had received from General Jackson, — demanding that on our return we should serve out six months. We had already served three months instead of two, which was the time we had volunteered for. On the next morning the officers reported to us the conclusions they had come to; and told us, if any of us felt bound to go on and serve out the six months, we could do so; but that they intended to go back home. I knowed if I went back home I couldn't rest, for I felt it my duty to be out; and when out was, somehow or other, always delighted to be in the very thickest of the danger. A few of us, therefore, determined to push on and join the army. The number I do not recollect, but it was very small.

When we got out there, I joined Major Russel's company of spies. Before we reached the place, General Jackson had started. We went on likewise, and overtook him at a place where we established a fort, called Fort Williams, and leaving men to guard it, we went ahead; intending to go to a place called the Horse-shoe bend of the Talapoosa river. When we came near that place, we began to find Indian sign plenty, and we struck up camp for the night. About two hours before day, we heard our guard firing, and we were all up in little or no time. We mended up our camp fires, and then fell back in the dark, expecting to see the Indians pouring in; and intending, when they should do so, to shoot them by the light of our own fires. But it happened that they did not rush in as we had expected, but commenced a fire on us as we were. We were encamped in a hollow square, and we not only returned the fire, but continued to shoot as well as we could in the dark, till day broke, when the Indians disappeared. The only guide we had in shooting was to notice the flash of their guns, and then shoot as directly at the place as we could guess.

In this scrape we had four men killed, and several wounded; but whether we killed any of the Indians or not we never could tell, for it is their custom always to carry off their dead, if they can possibly do so. We buried ours, and then made a large log heap over them, and set it on fire, so that the place of their deposite might not be known to the [Indians], who, we knew, would seek for them, that they might scalp them. We made some horse litters for our wounded, and took up a retreat. We moved on till we came to a large creek which we had to cross; and about half of our men had crossed, when the Indians commenced firing on our left wing, and they kept it up very warmly. We had left Major Russel and his brother at the camp we had moved from that morning, to see what discovery they could make as to the movements of the Indians; and about this time, while a warm fire was kept up on our left, as I have just stated, the major came up in our rear, and was closely pursued by a large number of Indians, who immediately commenced a fire on our artillery men. They hid themselves behind a large log, and could kill one of our men almost every shot, they being in open ground and exposed. The worst of all was, two of our colonels just at this trying moment left their men, and by a *forced march*, crossed the creek out of the reach of the fire. Their names, at this late day, would do the world no good, and my object is history alone, and not the slightest interference with character. An opportunity was now afforded for Governor Carroll to distinguish himself, and on this occasion he did so, by greater bravery than I ever saw any other man display. In truth, I believe, as firmly as I do that General Jackson is president, that if it hadn't been for Carroll, we should all have been genteely licked that time, for we were in a devil of a fix; part of our men on one side of the creek, and part on the other, and the Indians all the time pouring it on us, as hot as fresh mustard to a sore shin. I will not say exactly that the old general was whip'd; but I will say, that if we escaped it at all, it was like old Henry Snider going to heaven, "mita tam tite squeeze." I think he would confess himself, that he was nearer whip'd this time than he was at any other, for I know that all the world couldn't make him acknowledge that he was *pointedly* whip'd. I know I was mighty glad when it was over, and the [Indians] quit us, for I had begun to think there was one behind every tree in the woods.

We buried our dead, the number of whom I have also forgotten; and again made horse litters to carry our wounded, and so we put out, and returned to Fort Williams, from which place we had started. In the mean time, my horse had got crippled, and was unfit for service, and as another reinforcement had arrived, I thought they could get along without me for a short time; so I got a furlough and went home, for we had had hard times again on this hunt, and I began to feel as though I had done Indian fighting enough for one time. I remained at home until after the army had returned to the Horse-shoe bend, and fought the battle there. But not being with them at that time, of course no history of that fight can be expected of me.

CHAPTER VII.

Soon after this, an army was to be raised to go to Pensacola, and I determined to go again with them, for I wanted a small taste of British fighting, and I supposed they would be there.

Here again the entreaties of my wife were thrown in the way of my going, but all in vain; for I always had a way of just going ahead, at whatever I had a mind to. . One of my neighbours, hearing I had determined to go, came to me, and offered me a hundred dollars to go in his place as a substitute, as he had been drafted. I told him I was better raised than to hire myself out to be shot at; but that I would go, and he should go too, and in that way the government would have the services of us both. But we didn't call General Jackson "the government" in those days, though we used to go and fight under him in the war.

I fixed up, and joined old Major Russel again; but we couldn't start with the main army, but followed on, in a little time, after them. In a day or two, we had a hundred and thirty men in our company; and we went over and crossed the Muscle Shoals at the same place where I had crossed when first out, and where we burned the Black Warriors' town. We passed through the Choctaw and Chickesaw nations, on to Fort Stephens, and from thence to what is called the Cut-off, at the junction of the Tom-Bigby with the Alabama river. This place is near the old Fort Mimms, where the Indians committed the great butchery at the commencement of the war.

We were here about two days behind the main army, who had left their horses at the Cut-off, and taken it on foot; and they did this because there was no chance for forage between there and Pensacola. We did the same, leaving men enough to take care of our horses, and cut out on foot for that place. It was about eighty miles off; but in good heart we shouldered our guns, blankets, and provisions, and trudged merrily on. About twelve o'clock the second day, we reached the encampment of the main army, which was situated on a hill, overlooking the city of Pensacola. My commander. Major Russel, was a great favourite with Gen'l. Jackson, and our arrival was hailed with great applause, though we were a little after the feast; for they had taken the town and fort before we got there. That evening we went down into the town, and could see the British fleet lying in sight of the place. We got some liquor, and took a "horn" or so, and went back to the camp. We remained there that night, and in the morning we marched back towards the Cut-off. We pursued this direction till we reached old Fort Mimms, where we remained two or three days. It was here that Major Russel was promoted from his command, which was only that of a captain of spies, to the command of a major in the line. He had been known long before at home as old Major Russel, and so we all continued to call him in the army. A Major Childs, from East Tennessee, also commanded a battalion, and his and the one Russel was now appointed to command, composed a regiment, which, by agreement with General Jackson, was to quit his army and go to the south, to kill up the Indians on the Scamby river.

General Jackson and the main army set out the next morning for New Orleans, and a Colonel Blue took command of the regiment which I have before described. We remained, however, a few days after the general's departure, and then started also on our route.

As it gave rise to so much war and bloodshed, it may not be improper here to give a little description of Fort Mimms, and the manner in which the Indian war commenced. The fort was built right in the middle of a large old field, and in it the people had been forted so long and so quietly, that they didn't apprehend any danger at all, and had, therefore, become quite careless. A small negro boy, whose business it was to bring up the calves at milking time, had been out for that purpose, and on coming back, he said he saw a great many Indians. At this the inhabitants took the alarm, and closed their gates and placed out their guards, which they continued for a few days. But finding that no attack was made, they concluded the little negro had lied; and again threw their gates open, and set all their hands out to work their fields. The same boy was out again on the same errand, when, returning in great haste and alarm, he informed them that he had seen the Indians as thick as trees in the woods. He was not believed, but was tucked up to receive a flogging for the supposed lie; and was actually getting badly licked at the very moment when the Indians came in a troop, loaded with rails, with which they stop'd all the port-holes of the fort on one side except the bastion; and then they fell in to cutting down the picketing. Those inside the fort had only the bastion to shoot from, as all the other holes were spiked up; and they shot several of the Indians, while engaged in cutting. But as fast as one would fall, another would seize up the axe and chop away, until they succeeded in cutting down enough of the picketing to admit them to enter. They then began to rush through, and continued until they were all in. They immediately commenced scalping, without regard to age or sex; having forced the inhabitants up to one side of the fort, where they carried on the work of death as a butcher would in a slaughter pen.

The scene was particularly described to me by a young man who was in the fort when it happened, and subsequently went on with us to Pensacola. He said that he saw his father, and mother, his four sisters, and the same number of brothers, all butchered in the most shocking manner, and that he made his escape by running over the heads of the crowd, who were against the fort wall, to the top of the fort, and then jumping off, and taking to the woods. He was closely pursued by several Indians, until he came to a small byo, across which there was a log. He knew the log was hollow on the under side, so he slip'd under the log and hid himself. He said he heard the Indians walk over him several times back and forward. He remained, nevertheless, still till night, when he came out, and finished his escape. The name of this young man has entirely escaped my recollection, though his tale greatly excited my feelings. But to return to my subject. The regiment marched from where Gen'l. Jackson had left us to Fort Montgomery, which was distant from Fort Mimms about a mile and a half, and there we remained for some days.

Here we supplied ourselves pretty well with beef, by killing wild cattle which had formerly belonged to the people who perished in the fort, but had gone wild after their massacre.

When we marched from Fort Montgomery, we went some distance back towards Pensacola; then we turned to the left, and passed through a poor piny country, till we reached the Scamby river, near which we encamped. We had about one thousand men, and as a part of that number, one hundred and eighty-six Chickesaw and Choctaw Indians with us. That evening a boat landed from Pensacola, bringing many articles that were both good and necessary; such as sugar and coffee, and liquors of all kinds. The same evening, the Indians we had along proposed to cross the river, and the officers thinking it might be well for them to do so, consented; and Major Russell went with them, taking sixteen white men, of which number I was one. We camped on the opposite bank that night, and early in the morning we set out. We had not gone far before we came to a place where the whole country was covered with water, and looked like a sea. We didn't stop for this, tho', but just put in like so many spaniels, and waded on, sometimes up to our armpits, until we reached the pine hills, which made our distance through the water about a mile and a half. Here we struck up a fire to warm ourselves, for it was cold, and we were chilled through by being so long in the water. We again moved on, keeping our spies out; two to our left near the bank of the river, two straight before us, and two others on our right. We had gone in this way about six miles up the river, when our spies on the left came to us leaping the brush like so many old bucks, and informed us that they had discovered a camp of Creek Indians, and that we must kill them. Here we paused for a few minutes, and the prophets pow-wowed over their men awhile, and then got out their paint, and painted them, all according to their custom when going into battle. They then brought their paint to old Major Russell, and said to him, that as he was an officer, he must be painted too. He agreed, and they painted him just as they had done themselves. We let the Indians understand that we white men would first fire on the camp, and then fall back, so as to give the Indians a chance to rush in and scalp them. The Chickasaws marched on our left hand, and the Choctaws on our right, and we moved on till we got in hearing of the camp, where the Indians were employed in beating up what they called chainy briar root. On this they mostly subsisted. On a nearer approach we found they were on an island, and that we could get to them. While we were chatting about this matter, we heard some guns fired, and in a very short time after a keen whoop, which satisfied us, that where ever it was, there was war on a small scale. With that we all broke, like quarter horses, for the firing; and when we got there we found it was our two front spies, who related to us the following story: — As they were moving on, they had met with two Creeks who were out hunting their horses; as they approached each other, there was a large cluster of green bay bushes exactly between them, so that they were within a few feet of meeting before either was discovered. Our spies walked up to them, and speaking in the Shawnee tongue, informed them that General Jackson was at Pensacola, and they were making their escape, and wanted to know where they could get something to eat. The Creeks told them that nine miles up the Conaker, the river they were then on, there was a large camp of Creeks, and they had cattle and plenty to eat; and further, that their own camp was on an island about a mile off, and just below the mouth of the Conaker. They held their conversation and struck up a fire, and smoked together, and shook hands, and parted. One of the Creeks had a gun, the other had none; and as soon as they had parted, our Choctaws turned round and shot down the one that had the gun, and the other attempted to run off. They snapped several times at him, but the gun still missing fire, they took after him, and overtaking him, one of them struck him over the head with his gun, and followed up his blows till he killed him.

The gun was broken in the combat, and they then fired off the gun of the Creek they had killed, and raised the war-whoop. When we reached them, they had cut off the heads of both the Indians; and each of those Indians with us would walk up to one of the heads, and taking his war club would strike on it. This was done by every one of them; and when they had got done, I took one of their clubs, and walked up as they had done, and struck it on the head also. At this they all gathered round me, and patting me on the shoulder, would call me "Warrior — warrior."

They scalped the heads, and then we moved on a short distance to where we found a trace leading in towards the river. We took this trace and pursued it, till we came to where a Spaniard had been killed and scalped, together with a woman, who we supposed to be his wife, and also four children. I began to feel mighty ticklish along about this time, for I knowed if there was no danger then, there had been; and I felt exactly like there still was. We, however, went on till we struck the river, and then continued down it till we came opposite to the Indian camp, where we found they were still beating their roots.

It was now late in the evening, and they were in a thick cane brake. We had some few friendly Creeks with us, who said they could decoy them. So we all hid behind trees and logs, while the attempt was made. The Indians would not agree that we should fire, but pick'd out some of their best gunners, and placed them near the river. Our Creeks went down to the river's side, and hailed the camp in the Creek language. We heard an answer, and an Indian man started down towards the river, but didn't come in sight. He went back and again commenced beating his roots, and sent a squaw. She came down, and talked with our Creeks until dark came on. They told her they wanted her to bring them a canoe. To which she replied, that their canoe was on our side; that two of their men had gone out to hunt their horses and hadn't yet returned. They were the same two we had killed. The canoe was found, and forty of our picked Indian warriors were crossed over to take the camp. There was at last only one man in it, and he escaped; and they took two squaws, and ten children, but killed none of them, of course.

We had run nearly out of provisions, and Major Russell had determined to go up the Conaker to the camp we had heard of from the Indians we had killed. I was one that he selected to go down the river that night for provisions, with the canoe, to where we had left our regiment. I took with me a man by the name of John Guess, and one of the friendly Creeks, and cut out. It was very dark, and the river was so full that it overflowed the banks and the adjacent low bottoms. This rendered it very difficult to keep the channel, and particularly as the river was very crooked. At about ten o'clock at night we reached the camp, and were to return by morning to Major Russell, with provisions for his trip up the river; but on informing Colonel Blue of this arrangement, he vetoed it as quick as General Jackson did the bank bill; and said, if Major Russell didn't come back the next day, it would be bad times for him. I found we were not to go up the Conaker to the Indian camp, and a man of my company offered to go up in my place to inform Major Russell. I let him go; and they reached the major, as I was told, about sunrise in the morning, who immediately returned with those who were with him to the regiment, and joined us where we crossed the river, as hereafter stated.

The next morning we all fixed up, and marched down the Scamby to a place called Miller's Landing, where we swam our horses across, and sent on two companies down on the side of the bay opposite to Pensacola, where the Indians had fled when the main army first marched to that place. One was the company of Captain William Russell, a son of the old major, and the other was commanded by a Captain Trimble. They went on, and had a little skirmish with the Indians. They killed some, and took all the balance prisoners, though I don't remember the numbers. We again met those companies in a day or two, and sent the prisoners they had taken on to Fort Montgomery, in charge of some of our Indians.

I did hear, that after they left us, the Indians killed and scalped all the prisoners, and I never heard the report contradicted. I cannot positively say it was true, but I think it entirely probable, for it is very much like the Indian character.

CHAPTER VIII.

When we made a move from the point where we met the companies, we set out for Chatahachy, the place for which we had started when we left Fort Montgomery. At the start we had taken only twenty days' rations of flour, and eight days' rations of beef; and it was now thirty-four days before we reached that place. We were, therefore, in extreme suffering for want of something to eat, and exhausted with our exposure and the fatigues of our journey. I remember well, that I had not myself tasted bread but twice in nineteen days. I had bought a pretty good supply of coffee from the boat that had reached us from Pensacola, on the Scamby, and on that we chiefly subsisted. At length, one night our spies came in, and informed us they had found Holm's village on the Chatahachy river; and we made an immediate push for that place. We traveled all night, expecting to get something to eat when we got there. We arrived about sunrise, and near the place prepared for battle. We were all so furious, that even the certainty of a pretty hard fight could not have restrained us. We made a furious charge on the town, but to our great mortification and surprise, there wasn't a human being in it. The Indians had all run off and left it. We burned the town, however; but, melancholy to tell, we found no provision whatever. We then turned about, and went back to the camp we had left the night before, as nearly starved as any set of poor fellows ever were in the world.

We staid there only a little while, when we divided our regiment; and Major Childs, with his men, went back the way we had come for a considerable distance, and then turned to Baton-Rouge, where they joined General Jackson and the main army on their return from Orleans. Major Russell and his men struck for Fort Decatur, on the Talapoosa river. Some of our friendly Indians, who knew the country, went on ahead of us, as we had no trail except the one they made to follow. With them we sent some of our ablest horses and men, to get us some provisions, to prevent us from absolutely starving to death. As the army marched, I hunted every day, and would kill every hawk, bird, and squirrel that I could find. Others did the same; and it was a rule with us, that when we stop'd at night, the hunters would throw all they killed in a pile, and then we would make a general division among all the men. One evening I came in, having killed nothing that day. I had a very sick man in my mess, and I wanted something for him to eat, even if I starved myself. So I went to the fire of a Captain Cowen, who commanded my company after the promotion of Major Russell, and informed him that I was on the hunt of something for a sick man to eat. I knowed the captain was as bad off as the rest of us, but I found him broiling a turkey's gizzard. He said he had divided the turkey out among the sick, that Major Smiley had killed it, and that nothing else had been killed that day. I immediately went to Smiley's fire, where I found him broiling another gizzard. I told him, that it was the first turkey I had ever seen have two gizzards. But so it was, I got nothing for my sick man. And now seeing that every fellow must shift for himself, I determined that in the morning, I would come up missing; so I took my mess and cut out to go ahead of the army. We know'd that nothing more could happen to us if we went than if we staid, for it looked like it was to be starvation any way; we therefore determined to go on the old saying, root hog or die. We passed two camps, at which our men, that had gone on before us, had killed Indians. At one they had killed nine, and at the other three. About daylight we came to a small river, which I thought was the Scamby; but we continued on for three days, killing little or nothing to eat; till, at last, we all began to get nearly ready to give up the ghost, and lie down and die; for we had no prospect of provision, and we knew we couldn't go much further without it.

We came to a large prairie, that was about six miles across it, and in this I saw a trail which I knowed was made by bear, deer, and turkeys. We went on through it till we came to a large creek, and the low grounds were all set over with wild rye, looking as green as a wheat field. We here made a halt, unsaddled our horses, and turned them loose to graze.

One of my companions, a Mr. Vanzant, and myself, then went up the low grounds to hunt. We had gone some distance, finding nothing; when at last, I found a squirrel; which I shot, but he got into a hole in the tree. The game was small, but necessity is not very particular; so I thought I must have him, and I climbed that tree thirty feet high, without a limb, and pulled him out of his hole. I shouldn't relate such small matters, only to show what lengths a hungry man will go to, to get something to eat. I soon killed two other squirrels, and fired at a large hawk. At this a large gang of turkeys rose from the cane brake, and flew across the creek to where my friend was, who had just before crossed it. He soon fired on a large gobler, and I heard it fall. By this time my gun was loaded again, and I saw one sitting on my side of the creek, which had flew over when he fired; so I blazed away, and down I brought him. I gathered him up, and a fine turkey he was. I now began to think we had struck a breeze of luck, and almost forgot our past sufferings, in the prospect of once more having something to eat. I raised the shout, and my comrade came to me, and we went on to our camp with the game we had killed. While we were gone, two of our mess had been out, and each of them had found a bee tree. We turned into cooking some of our game, but we had neither salt nor bread. Just at this moment, on looking down the creek, we saw our men, who had gone on before us for provisions, coming to us. They came up, and measured out to each man a cupfull of flower. With this, we thickened our soup, when our turkey was cooked, and our friends took dinner with us, and then went on.

We now took our tomahawks, and went and cut our bee-trees, out of which we got a fine chance of honey; though we had been starving so long that we feared to eat much at a time, till, like the Irish by hanging, we got used to it again. We rested that night without moving our camp; and the next morning myself and Vanzant again turned out to hunt. We had not gone far, before I wounded a fine buck very badly; and while pursuing him, I was walking on a large tree that had fallen down, when from the top of it, a large bear broke out and ran off. I had no dogs, and I was sorry enough for it; for of all the hunting I ever did, I have always delighted most in bear hunting. Soon after this, I killed a large buck; and we had just gotten him to camp, when our poor starved army came up. They told us, that to lessen their sufferings as much as possible, Captain William Russell had had his horse led up to be shot for them to eat, just at the moment that they saw our men returning, who had carried on the flour.

We were now about fourteen miles from Fort Decatur, and we gave away all our meat, and honey, and went on with the rest of the army. When we got there, they could give us only one ration of meat, but not a mouthful of bread. I immediately got a canoe, and taking my gun, crossed over the river, and went to the Big Warrior's town. I had a large hat, and I offered an Indian a silver dollar for my hat full of corn. He told me that his corn was all "*shuestea*," which in English means, it was all gone. But he showed me where an Indian lived, who, he said, had corn. I went to him, and made the same offer. He could talk a little broken English, and said to me, "You got any powder? You got bullet?" I told him I had. He then said, "Me swap my corn, for powder and bullet." I took out about ten bullets, and showed him; and he proposed to give me a hat full of corn for them. I took him up, mighty quick. I then offered to give him ten charges of powder for another hat full of corn.

To this he agreed very willingly. So I took off my hunting-shirt, and tied up my corn; and though it had cost me very little of my powder and lead, yet I wouldn't have taken fifty silver dollars for it. I returned to the camp, and the next morning we started for the Hickory Ground, which was thirty miles off. It was here that General Jackson met the Indians, and made peace with the body of the nation. We got nothing to eat at this place, and we had yet to go forty-nine miles, over a rough and wilderness country, to Fort Williams. Parched corn, and but little even of that, was our daily subsistence. When we reached Fort Williams, we got one ration of pork and one of flour, which was our only hope until we could reach Fort Strother.

The horses were now giving out, and I remember to have seen thirteen good horses left in one day, the saddles and bridles being thrown away. It was thirty-nine miles to Fort Strother, and we had to pass directly by Fort Talladego, where we first had the big Indian battle with the eleven hundred painted warriors. We went through the old battle ground, and it looked like a great gourd patch; the sculls of the Indians who were killed still lay scattered all about, and many of their frames were still perfect, as the bones had not separated. But about five miles before we got to this battle ground, I struck a trail, which I followed until it led me to one of their towns. Here I swap'd some more of my powder and bullets for a little corn.

I pursued on, by myself, till some time after night, when I came up with the rest of the army. That night my company and myself did pretty well, as I divided out my corn among them. The next morning we met the East Tennessee troops, who were on their road to Mobile, and my youngest brother was with them. They had plenty of corn and provisions, and they gave me what I wanted for myself and my horse. I remained with them that night, though my company went across the Coosa river to the fort, where they also had the good fortune to find plenty of provisions. Next morning, I took leave of my brother and all my old neighbours, for there were a good many of them with him, and crossed over to my men at the fort. Here I had enough to go on, and after remaining a few days, cut out for home; Nothing more, worthy of the reader's attention, transpired till I was safely landed at home once more with my wife and children. I found them all well and doing well; and though I was only a rough sort of a backwoodsman, they seemed mighty glad to see me, however little the quality folks might suppose it. For I do reckon we love as hard in the backwood country, as any people in the whole creation.

But I had been home only a few days, when we received orders to start again, and go on to the Black Warrior and Cahawba rivers, to see if there was no Indians there. I know'd well enough there was none, and I wasn't willing to trust my craw any more where there was neither any fighting to do, nor any thing to go on; and so I agreed to give a young man, who wanted to go, the balance of my wages if he would serve out my time, which was about a month. He did so, and when they returned, sure enough they hadn't seen an Indian any more than if they had been all the time chopping wood in my clearing. This closed my career as a warrior, and I am glad of it, for I like life now a heap better than I did then; and I am glad all over that I lived to see these times, which I should not have done if I had kept fooling along in war, and got used up at it. When I say I am glad, I just mean I am glad I am alive, for there is a confounded heap of things I an't glad of at all. I an't glad, for example, that the "government" moved the deposites, and if my military glory should take such a turn as to make me president after the general's time, I'll move them back; yes, I, the "government," will "take the responsibility," and move them back again. If I don't, I wish I may be shot.

But I am glad that I am now through war matters, and I reckon the reader is too, for they have no fun in them at all; and less if he had had to pass through them first and then to write them afterwards. But for the dullness of their narrative, I must try to make amends by relating some of the curious things that happened to me in private life, and when forced to become a public man, as I shall have to be again, if ever I consent to take the presidential chair.

CHAPTER IX.

I CONTINUED at home now, working my farm for two years, as the war finally closed soon after I quit the service. The battle at New Orleans had already been fought, and treaties were made with the Indians which put a stop to their hostilities.

But in this time, I met with the hardest trial which ever falls to the lot of man. Death, that cruel leveller of all distinctions, — to whom the prayers and tears of husbands, and of even helpless infancy, are addressed in vain, — entered my humble cottage, and tore from my children an affectionate good mother, and from me a tender and loving wife.

It is a scene long gone by, and one which it would be supposed I had almost forgotten; yet when I turn my memory back on it, it seems as but the work of yesterday. It was the doing of the Almighty, whose ways are always right, though we sometimes think they fall heavily on us; and as painful as is even yet the remembrance of her sufferings, and the loss sustained by my little children and myself, yet I have no wish to lift up the voice of complaint. I was left with three children; the two oldest were sons, the youngest a daughter, and, at that time, a mere infant. It appeared to me, at that moment, that my situation was the worst in the world. I couldn't bear the thought of scattering my children, and so I got my youngest brother, who was also married, and his family to live with me. They took as good care of my children as they well could, but yet it wasn't all like the care of a mother. And though their company was to me in every respect like that of a brother and sister, yet it fell far short of being like that of a wife. So I came to the conclusion it wouldn't do, but that I must have another wife.

There lived in the neighbourhood, a widow lady whose husband had been killed in the war. She had two children, a son and daughter, and both quite small, like my own. I began to think, that as we were both in the same situation, it might be that we could do something for each other; and I therefore began to hint a little around the matter, as we were once and a while together. She was a good industrious woman, and owned a snug little farm, and lived quite comfortable. I soon began to pay my respects to her in real good earnest; but I was as sly about it as a fox when he is going to rob a hen-roost. I found that my company wasn't at all disagreeable to her; and I thought I could treat her children with so much friendship as to make her a good stepmother to mine, and in this I wan't mistaken, as we soon bargained, and got married, and then went ahead. In a great deal of peace we raised our first crop of children, and they are all married and doing well. But we had a second crop together; and I shall notice them as I go along, as my wife and myself both had a hand in them, and they therefore belong to the history of my second marriage.

The next fall after this marriage, three of my neighbours and myself determined to explore a new country. Their names were Robinson, Frazier, and Rich. We set out for the Creek country, crossing the Tennessee river; and after having made a day's travel, we stop'd at the house of one of my old acquaintances, who had settled there after the war. Resting here a day, Frazier turned out to hunt, being a great hunter; but he got badly bit by a very poisonous snake, and so we left him and went on. We passed through a large rich valley, called Jones's valley, where several other families had settled, and continued our course till we came near to the place where Tuscaloosa now stands. Here we camped, as there were no inhabitants, and hobbled out our horses for the night. About two hours before day, we heard the bells on our horses going back the way we had come, as they had started to leave us. As soon as it was daylight, I started in pursuit of them on foot, and carrying my rifle, which was a very heavy one. I went ahead the whole day, wading creeks and swamps, and climbing mountains; but I couldn't overtake our horses, though I could hear of them at every house they passed. I at last found I couldn't catch up with them, and so I gave up the hunt, and turned back to the last house I had passed, and staid there till morning. From the best calculation we could make, I had walked over fifty miles that day; and the next morning I was so sore, and fatigued, that I felt like I couldn't walk any more. But I was anxious to get back to where I had left my company, and so I started and went on, but mighty slowly, till after the middle of the day. I now began to feel mighty sick, and had a dreadful head-ache. My rifle was so heavy, and I felt so weak, that I lay down by the side of the trace, in a perfect wilderness too, to see if I wouldn't get better. In a short time some Indians came along. They had some ripe melons, and wanted me to eat some, but I was so sick I couldn't. They then signed to me, that I would die, and be buried; a thing I was confoundedly afraid of myself. But I asked them how near it was to any house? By their signs, again, they made me understand it was a mile and a half. I got up to go; but when I rose, I reeled about like a cow with the blind staggers, or a fellow who had taken too many "horns." One of the Indians proposed to go with me, and carry my gun. I gave him half a dollar, and accepted his offer. We got to the house, by which time I was pretty far gone, but was kindly received, and got on to a bed. The woman did all she could for me with her warm teas, but I still continued bad enough, with a high fever, and generally out of my senses. The next day two of my neighbours were passing the road, and heard of my situation, and came to where I was. They were going nearly the route I had intended to go, to look at the country; and so they took me first on one of their horses, and then on the other, till they got me back to where I had left my company. I expected I would get better, and be able to go on with them, but, instead of this, I got worse and worse; and when we got there, I wan't able to sit up at all. I thought now the jig was mighty nigh up with me, but I determined to keep a stiff upper lip. They carried me to a house, and each of my comrades bought him a horse, and they all set out together, leaving me behind. I knew but little that was going on for about two weeks; but the family treated me with every possible kindness in their power, and I shall always feel thankful to them. The man's name was Jesse Jones. At the end of two weeks I began to mend without the help of a doctor, or of any doctor's means. In this time, however, as they told me, I was speechless for five days, and they had no thought that I would ever speak again, — in Congress or any where else. And so the woman, who had a bottle of Batesman's draps ["medicine" probably consisting of opium and alcohol], thought if they killed me, I would only die any how, and so she would try it with me. She gave me the whole bottle, which throwed me into a sweat that continued on me all night; when at last I seemed to make up, and spoke, and asked her for a drink of water. This almost alarmed her, for she was looking every minute for me to die. She gave me the water, and, from that time, I began slowly to mend, and so kept on till I was able at last to walk about a little. I might easily have been mistaken for one of the Kitchen Cabinet, I looked so much like a ghost. I have been particular in giving a history of this sickness, not because I believe it will interest any body much now, nor, indeed, do I *certainly* know that it ever will. But if I should be forced to take the "white house," then it will be good history; and every one will look on it as important. And I can't, for my life, help laughing now, to think, that when all my folks get around me, wanting good fat offices, how so many of them will say, "What a good thing it was that that kind woman had the bottle of draps, that saved President Crockett's life, — the second greatest and best"! ! ! ! ! Good, says I, my noble fellow! You take the post office; or the navy; or the war office; or maybe the treasury. But if I give him the treasury, there's no devil if I don't make him agree first to fetch back them deposites. And if it's even the post-office, I'll make him promise to keep his money 'counts without any figuring, as that throws the whole concern heels over head in debt, in little or no time.

But when I got so I could travel a little, I got a waggoner who was passing along to hawl me to where he lived, which was about twenty miles from my house. I still mended as we went along, and when we got to his stopping place, I hired one of his horses, and went on home. I was so pale, and so much reduced, that my face looked like it had been half soled with brown paper.

When I got there, it was to the utter astonishment of my wife; for she supposed I was dead. My neighbours who had started with me had returned and took my horse home, which they had found with their's; and they reported that they had seen men who had helped to bury me; and who saw me draw my last breath. I know'd this was a whapper of a lie, as soon as I heard it. My wife had hired a man, and sent him out to see what had become of my money and other things; but I had missed the man as I went in, and he didn't return until some time after I got home, as he went all the way to where I lay sick, before he heard that I was still in the land of the living and a-kicking.

The place on which I lived was sickly, and I was determined to leave it. I therefore set out the next fall to look at the country which had been purchased of the Chickasaw tribe of Indians. I went on to a place called Shoal Creek, about eighty miles from where I lived, and here again I got sick. I took the ague and fever, which I supposed was brought on me by camping out. I remained here for some time, as I was unable to go farther; and in that time, I became so well pleased with the country about there, that I resolved to settle in it. It was just only a little distance in the purchase, and no order had been established there; but I thought I could get along without order as well as any body else. And so I moved and settled myself down on the head of Shoal Creek. We remained here some two or three years, without any law at all; and so many bad characters began to flock in upon us, that we found it necessary to set up a sort of temporary government of our own. I don't mean that we made any president, and called him the "government," but we met and made what we called a corporation; and I reckon we called it wrong, for it wa'n't a bank, and hadn't any deposites; and now they call the bank a corporation. But be this as it may, we lived in the back-woods, and didn't profess to know much, and no doubt used many wrong words. But we met, and appointed magistrates and constables to keep order. We didn't fix any laws for them, tho'; for we supposed they would know law enough, whoever they might be; and so we left it to themselves to fix the laws.

I was appointed one of the magistrates; and when a man owed a debt, and wouldn't pay it, I and my constable ordered our warrant, and then he would take the man, and bring him before me for trial. I would give judgment against him, and then an order of an execution would easily scare the debt out of him. If any one was charged with marking his neighbour's hogs, or with stealing any thing, which happened pretty often in those days, — I would have him taken, and if there was tolerable grounds for the charge, I would have him well whip'd and cleared. We kept this up till our Legislature added us to the white settlements in Giles county; and appointed magistrates by law, to organize matters in the parts where I lived. They appointed nearly every man a magistrate who had belonged to our corporation. I was then, of course, made a squire according to law; though now the honour rested more heavily on me than before. For, at first, whenever I told my constable, says I — "Catch that fellow, and bring him up for trial" — away he went, and the fellow must come, dead or alive; for we considered this a good warrant, though it was only in verbal writings. But after I was appointed by the assembly, they told me, my warrants must be in real writing, and signed; and that I must keep a book, and write my proceedings in it.

This was a hard business on me, for I could just barely write my own name; but to do this, and write the warrants too, was at least a huckleberry over my persimmon. I had a pretty well informed constable, however; and he aided me very much in this business. Indeed I had so much confidence in him, that I told him, when we should happen to be out anywhere, and see that a warrant was necessary, and would have a good effect, he need'nt take the trouble to come all the way to me to get one, but he could just fill out one; and then on the trial I could correct the whole business if he had committed any error. In this way I got on pretty well, till by care and attention I improved my handwriting in such manner as to be able to prepare my warrants, and keep my record book, without much difficulty. My judgments were never appealed from, and if they had been they would have stuck like wax, as I gave my decisions on the principles of common justice and honesty between man and man, and relied on natural born sense, and not on law, learning to guide me; for I had never read a page in a law book in all my life.

CHAPTER X.

About the time we were getting under good headway in our new government a Capt. Matthews came to me and told me he was a candidate for the office of colonel of a regiment, and that I must run for first major in the same regiment. I objected to this, telling him that I thought I had done my share of fighting, and that I wanted nothing to do with military appointments.

He still insisted, until at last I agreed, and of course had every reason to calculate on his support in my election. He was an early settler in that country, and made rather more corn than the rest of us; and knowing it would afford him a good opportunity to electioneer a little, he made a great corn husking, and a great frolic, and gave a general treat, asking every body over the whole country. Myself and my family were, of course, invited. When I got there, I found a very large collection of people, and some friend of mine soon informed me that the captain's son was going to offer against me for the office of major, which he had seemed so anxious for me to get. I cared nothing about the office, but it put my dander up high enough to see, that after he had pressed me so hard to offer, he was countenancing, if not encouraging, a secret plan to beat me. I took the old gentleman out, and asked him about it. He told me it was true his son was going to run as a candidate, and that he hated worse to run against me than any man in the county. I told him his son need give himself no uneasiness about that; that I shouldn't run against him for major, but against his daddy for colonel. He took me by the hand, and we went into the company. He then made a speech, and informed the people that I was his opponent. I mounted up for a speech too. I told the people the cause of my opposing him, remarking that as I had the whole family to run against any way, I was determined to levy on the head of the mess. When the time for the election came, his son was opposed by another man for major; and he and his daddy were both badly beaten. I just now began to take a rise, as in a little time I was asked to offer for the Legislature in the counties of Lawrence and Heckman.

I offered my name in the month of February, and started about the first of March with a drove of horses to the lower part of the state of North Carolina. This was in the year 1821, and I was gone upwards of three months. I returned, and set out electioneering, which was a bran-fire new business to me. It now became necessary that I should tell the people something about the government, and an eternal sight of other things that I knowed nothing more about than I did about Latin, and law, and such things as that. I have said before that in those days none of us called Gen'l. Jackson the government, nor did he seem in as fair a way to become so as I do now; but I knowed so little about it, that if any one had told me he was "the government," I should have believed it, for I had never read even a newspaper in my life, or any thing else, on the subject. But over all my difficulties, it seems to me I was born for luck, though it would be hard for any one to guess what sort. I will, however, explain that hereafter.

I went first into Heckman county, to see what I could do among the people as a candidate. Here they told me that they wanted to move their town nearer to the centre of the county, and I must come out in favour of it. There's no devil if I knowed what this meant, or how the town was to be moved; and so I kept dark, going on the identical same plan that I now find is called "*non-committal.*" About this time there was a great squirrel hunt on Duck river, which was among my people. They were to hunt two days: then to meet and count the scalps, and have a big barbecue, and what might be called a tip-top country frolic. The dinner, and a general treat, was all to be paid for by the party having taken the fewest scalps. I joined one side, taking the place of one of the hunters, and got a gun ready for the hunt. I killed a great many squirrels, and when we counted scalps, my party was victorious.

The company had every thing to eat and drink that could be furnished in so new a country, and much fun and good humour prevailed. But before the regular frolic commenced, I mean the dancing, I was called on to make a speech as a candidate; which was a business I was as ignorant of as an outlandish negro.

A public document I had never seen, nor did I know there were such things; and how to begin I couldn't tell. I made many apologies, and tried to get off, for I know'd I had a man to run against who could speak prime, and I know'd, too, that I wa'n't able to shuffle and cut with him. He was there, and knowing my ignorance as well as I did myself, he also urged me to make a speech. The truth is, he thought my being a candidate was a mere matter of sport; and didn't think, for a moment, that he was in any danger from an ignorant back-woods bear hunter. But I found I couldn't get off, and so I determined just to go ahead, and leave it to chance what I should say. I got up and told the people, I reckoned they know'd what I come for, but if not, I could tell them. I had come for their votes, and if they didn't watch mighty close, I'd get them too. But the worst of all was, that I couldn't tell them any thing about government. I tried to speak about something, and I cared very little what, until I choaked up as bad as if my mouth had been jam'd and cram'd chock full of dry mush. There the people stood, listening all the while, with their eyes, mouths and years all open, to catch every word I would speak.

At last I told them I was like a fellow I had heard of not long before. He was beating on the head of an empty barrel near the road-side, when a traveler, who was passing along, asked him what he was doing that for? The fellow replied, that there was some cider in that barrel a few days before, and he was trying to see if there was any then, but if there was he couldn't get at it. I told them that there had been a little bit of a speech in me a while ago, but I believed I couldn't get it out. They all roared out in a mighty laugh, and I told some other anecdotes, equally amusing to them, and believing I had them in a first-rate way, I quit and got down, thanking the people for their attention. But I took care to remark that I was as dry as a powder horn, and that I thought it was time for us all to wet our whistles a little; and so I put off to the liquor stand, and was followed by the greater part of the crowd.

I felt certain this was necessary, for I knowed my competitor could open government matters to them as easy as he pleased. He had, however, mighty few left to hear him, as I continued with the crowd, now and then taking a horn, and telling good humoured stories, till he was done speaking. I found I was good for the votes at the hunt, and when we broke up, I went on to the town of Vernon, which was the same they wanted me to move. Here they pressed me again on the subject, and I found I could get either party by agreeing with them. But I told them I didn't know whether it would be right or not, and so couldn't promise either way.

Their court commenced on the next Monday, as the barbacue was on a Saturday, and the candidates for governor and for Congress, as well as my competitor and myself, all attended.

The thought of having to make a speech made my knees feel mighty weak, and set my heart to fluttering almost as bad as my first love scrape with the Quaker's niece. But as good luck would have it, these big candidates spoke nearly all day, and when they quit, the people were worn out with fatigue, which afforded me a good apology for not discussing the government. But I listened mighty close to them, and was learning pretty fast about political matters. When they were all done, I got up and told some laughable story, and quit. I found I was safe in those parts, and so I went home, and didn't go back again till after the election was over. But to cut this matter short, I was elected, doubling my competitor, and nine votes over.

A short time after this, I was in Pulaski, where I met with Colonel Polk, now a member of Congress from Tennessee. He was at that time a member elected to the Legislature, as well as myself; and in a large company he said to me, "Well, colonel, I suppose we shall have a radical change of the judiciary at the next session of the Legislature." "Very likely, sir," says I, and I put out quicker, for I was afraid some one would ask me what the judiciary was; and if I knowed I wish I may be shot I don't indeed believe I had ever before heard that there was any such thing in all nature; but still I was not willing that the people there should know how ignorant I was about it.

When the time for meeting of the Legislature arrived, I went on, and before I had been there long, I could have told what the judiciary was, and what the government was too; and many other things that I had known nothing about before.

About this time I met with a very severe misfortune, which I may be pardoned for naming, as it made a great change in my circumstances, and kept me back very much in the world. I had built an extensive grist mill, and powder mill, all connected together, and also a large distillery. They had cost me upwards of three thousand dollars, more than I was worth in the world. The first news that I heard after I got to the Legislature, was, that my mills were — not blown up sky high, as you would guess, by my powder establishment, — but swept away all to smash by a large fresh, that came soon after I left home. I had, of course, to stop my distillery, as my grinding was broken up; and, indeed, I may say, that the misfortune just made a complete mash of me. I had some likely negroes, and a good stock of almost every thing about me, and, best of all, I had an honest wife. She didn't advise me, as is too fashionable, to smuggle up this, and that, and t'other, to go on at home; but she told me, says she, "Just pay up, as long as you have a bit's worth in the world; and then every body will be satisfied, and we will scuffle for more." This was just such talk as I wanted to hear, for a man's wife can hold him devlish uneasy, if she begins to scold, and fret, and perplex him, at a time when he has a full load for a rail-road car on his mind already.

And so, you see, I determined not to break full handed, but thought it better to keep a good conscience with an empty purse, than to get a bad opinion of myself, with a full one. I therefore gave up all I had, and took a bran-fire new start.

CHAPTER XI.

Having returned from the Legislature, I determined to make another move, and so I took my eldest son with me, and a young man by the name of Abram Henry, and cut out for the Obion. I selected a spot when I got there, where I determined to settle; and the nearest house to it was seven miles, the next nearest was fifteen, and so on to twenty. It was a complete wilderness, and full of Indians who were hunting. Game was plenty of almost every kind, which suited me exactly, as I was always fond of hunting. The house which was nearest me, and which, as I have already stated, was seven miles off, and on the different side of the Obion river, belonged to a man by the name of Owens; and I started to go there. I had taken one horse along, to pack our provision, and when I got to the water I hobbled him out to graze, until I got back; as there was no boat to cross the river in, and it was so high that it had overflowed all the bottoms and low country near it.

We now took water like so many beavers, notwithstanding it was mighty cold, and waded on. The water would sometimes be up to our necks, and at others not so deep; but I went, of course, before, and carried a pole, with which I would feel along before me, to see how deep it was, and to guard against falling into a slough, as there was many in our way. When I would come to one, I would take out my tomahawk and cut a small tree across it, and then go ahead again. Frequently my little son would have to swim, even where myself and the young man could wade; but we worked on till at last we got to the channel of the river, which made it about half a mile we had waded from where we took water. I saw a large tree that had fallen into the river from the other side, but it didn't reach across. One stood on the same bank where we were, that I thought I could fall, so as to reach the other; and so at it we went with my tomahawk, cutting away till we got it down; and, as good luck would have it, it fell right, and made us a way that we could pass.

When we got over this, it was still a sea of water as far as our eyes could reach. We took into it again, and went ahead, for about a mile, hardly ever seeing a single spot of land, and sometimes very deep. At last we come in sight of land, which was a very pleasing thing; and when we got out, we went but a little way, before we came in sight of the house, which was more pleasing than ever; for we were wet all over, and mighty cold. I felt mighty sorry when I would look at my little boy, and see him shaking like he had the worst sort of an ague, for there was no time for fever then. As we got near to the house, we saw Mr. Owens and several men that were with him, just starting away. They saw us, and stop'd, but looked much astonished until we got up to them, and I made myself known. The men who were with him were the owners of a boat which was the first that ever went that far up the Obion river; and some hands he had hired to carry it about a hundred miles still further up, by water, tho' it was only about thirty by land, as the river is very crooked.

They all turned back to the house with me, where I found Mrs. Owens, a fine, friendly old woman; and her kindness to my little boy did me ten times as much good as any thing she could have done for me, if she had tried her best. The old gentleman set out his bottle to us, and I concluded that if a horn wasn't good then, there was no use for its invention. So I swig'd off about a half pint, and the young man was by no means bashful in such a case; he took a strong pull at it too. I then gave my boy some, and in a little time we felt pretty well. We dried ourselves by the fire, and were asked to go on board of the boat that evening. I agreed to do so, but left my son with the old lady, and myself and my young man went to the boat with: Mr. Owens and the others. The boat was loaded with whiskey, flour, sugar, coffee, salt, castings, and other articles suitable for the country; and they were to receive five hundred dollars to land the load at M'Lemore's Bluff, beside the profit they could make on their load. This was merely to show that boats could get up to that point. We staid all night with them, and had a high night of it, as I took steam enough to drive out all the cold that was in me, and about three times as much more. In the morning we concluded to go on with the boat to where a great hurricane had crossed the river, and blowed all the timber down into it. When we got there, we found the river was falling fast, and concluded we couldn't get through the timber without more rise; so we drop'd down opposite Mr. Owens' again, where they determined to wait for more water.

The next day it rained rip-roriously, and the river rose pretty considerable, but not enough yet. And so I got the boatsmen all to go out with me to where I was going to settle, and we slap'd up a cabin in little or no time. I got from the boat four barrels of meal, and one of salt, and about ten gallons of whiskey.

To pay for these, I agreed to go with the boat up the river to their landing place. I got also a large middling of bacon, and killed a fine deer, and left them for my young man and my little boy, who were to stay at my cabin till I got back; which I expected would be in six or seven days. We cut out, and moved up to the harricane, where we stop'd for the night. In the morning I started about daylight, intending to kill a deer, as I had no thought they would get the boat through the timber that day. I had gone but a little way before I killed a fine buck, and started to go back to the boat; but on the way I came on the tracks of a large gang of elks, and so I took after them. I had followed them only a little distance when I saw them, and directly after I saw two large bucks. I shot one down, and the other wouldn't leave him; so I loaded my gun, and shot him down too. I hung them up, and went ahead again after my elks. I pursued on till after the middle of the day before I saw them again; but they took the hint before I got in shooting distance, and run off. I still pushed on till late in the evening, when I found I was about four miles from where I had left the boat, and as hungry as a wolf, for I hadn't eaten a bite that day.

I started down the edge of the river low grounds, giving out the pursuit of my elks, and hadn't gone hardly any distance at all, before I saw two more bucks, very large fellows too. I took a blizzard at one of them, and up he tumbled. The other ran off a few jumps and stop'd; and stood there till I loaded again, and fired at him. I knock'd his trotters from under him, and then I hung them both up. I pushed on again; and about sunset I saw three other bucks. I down'd with one of them, and the other two ran off. I hung this one up also, having now killed six that day. I then pushed on till I got to the harricane, and at the lower edge of it, about where I expected the boat was. Here I hollered as hard as I could roar, but could get no answer. I fired off my gun, and the men on the boat fired one too; but quite contrary/to my expectation, they had got through the timber, and were about two miles above me. It was now dark, and I had to crawl through the fallen timber the best way I could; and if the reader don't know it was bad enough, I am sure I do. For the vines and briers had grown all through it, and so thick, that a good fat coon couldn't much more than get along. I got through at last, and went on near to where I had killed my last deer, and once more fired off my gun, which was again answered from the boat, which was still a little above me. I moved on as fast as I could, but soon came to water, and not knowing how deep it was, I halted and hollered till they came to me with a skiff. I now got to the boat, without further difficulty; but the briers had worked on me at such a rate, that I felt like I wanted sewing up, all over. I took a pretty stiff horn, which soon made me feel much better; but I was so tired that I could hardly work my jaws to eat.

In the morning, myself and a young man started and brought in the first buck I had killed; and after breakfast we went and brought in the last one. The boat then started, but we again went and got the two I had killed just as I turned down the river in the evening; and we then pushed on and overtook the boat, leaving the other two hanging in the woods, as we had now as much as we wanted.

We got up the river very well, but quite slowly; and we landed, on the eleventh day, at the place the load was to be delivered at. They here gave me their skiff, and myself and a young man by the name of Flavins Harris, who had determined to go and live with me, cut out down the river for my cabin, which we reached safely enough.

We turned in and cleared a field, and planted our corn; but it was so late in the spring, we had no time to make rails, and therefore we put no fence around our field. There was no stock, however, nor any thing else to disturb our corn, except the wild *varments*, and the old serpent himself, with a fence to help him, couldn't keep them out. I made corn enough to do me, and during that spring I killed ten bears, and a great abundance of deer. But in all this time, we saw the face of no white person in that country, except Mr. Owens' family, and a very few passengers, who went out there, looking at the country. Indians, though, were still plenty enough. Having laid by my crap [solid material from melted fat, likely from his hunting spoils mentioned above], I went home, which was a distance of about a hundred and fifty miles; and when I got there, I was met by an order to attend a call-session of our Legislature. I attended it, and served out my time, and then returned, and took my family and what little plunder I had, and moved to where I had built my cabin, and made my crap.

I gathered my corn, and then set out for my Fall's hunt. This was in the last of October, 1822. I found bear very plenty, and, indeed, all sorts of game and wild varments, except buffalo. There was none of them. I hunted on till Christmass, having supplied my family very well all along with wild meat, at which time my powder gave out; and I had none either to fire Christmass guns, which is very common in that country, or to hunt with. I had a brother-in-law who had now moved out and settled about six miles west of me, on the opposite side of Rutherford's fork of the Obion river, and he had brought me a keg of powder, but I had never gotten it home. There had just been another of Noah's freshes, and the low grounds were flooded all over with water. I know'd the stream was at least a mile wide which I would have to cross, as the water was from hill to hill, and yet I determined to go on over in some way or other, so as to get my powder. I told this to my wife, and she immediately opposed it with all her might. I still insisted, telling her we had no powder for Christmass, and, worse than all, we were out of meat. She said, we had as well starve as for me to freeze to death or to get drowned, and one or the other was certain if I attempted to go.

But I didn't believe the half of this; and so I took my woolen wrappers, and a pair of mockasins, and put them on, and tied up some dry clothes and a pair of shoes and stockings, and started. But I didn't before know how much any body could suffer and not die. This, and some of my other experiments in water, learned me something about it, and I therefore relate them.

The snow was about four inches deep when I started; and when I got to the water, which was only about a quarter of a mile off, it look'd like an ocean. I put in, and waded on till I come to the channel, where I crossed that on a high log. I then took water again, having my gun and all my hunting tools along, and waded till I came to a deep slough, that was wider than the river itself. I had crossed it often on a log; but, behold, when I got there, no log was to be seen. I knowed of an island in the slough, and a sapling stood on it close to the side of that log, which was now entirely under water. I knowed further, that the water was about eight or ten feet deep under the log, and I judged it to be about three feet deep over it. After studying a little what I should do, I determined to cut a forked sapling, which stood near me, so as to lodge it against the one that stood on the island, in which I succeeded very well. I then cut me a pole, and crawled along on my sapling till I got to the one it was lodged against, which was about six feet above the water. I then felt about with my pole till I found the log, which was just about as deep under the water as I had judged. I then crawled back and got my gun, which I had left at the stump of the sapling I had cut, and again made my way to the place of lodgement, and then climb'd down the other sapling so as to get on the log. I then felt my way along with my feet, in the water, about waist deep, but it was a mighty ticklish business. However, I got over, and by this time I had very little feeling in my feet and legs, as I had been all the time in the water, except what time I was crossing the high log over the river, and climbing my lodged sapling.

I went but a short distance before I came to another slough, over which there was a log, but it was floating on the water. I thought I could walk it, and so I mounted on it; but when I had got about the middle of the deep water, somehow or somehow else, it turned over, and in I went up to my head. I waded out of this deep water, and went ahead till I came to the high-land, where I stop'd to pull of my wet clothes, and put on the others, which I had held up with my gun, above the water, when I fell in. I got them on, but my flesh had no feeling in it, I was so cold. I tied up the wet ones, and hung them up in a bush. I now thought I would run, so as to warm myself a little, but I couldn't raise a trot for some time; indeed, I couldn't step more than half the length of my foot. After a while I got better, and went on five miles to the house of my brother-in-law, having not even smelt fire from the time I started. I got there late in the evening, and he was much astonished at seeing me at such a time. I staid all night, and the next morning was most piercing cold, and so they persuaded me not to go home that day. I agreed, and turned out and killed him two deer; but the weather still got worse and colder, instead of better. I staid that night, and in the morning they still insisted I couldn't get home. I knowed the water would be frozen over, but not hard enough to bear me, and so I agreed to stay that day. I went out hunting again, and pursued a big *he-bear* all day, but didn't kill him. The next morning was bitter cold, but I knowed my family was without meat, and I determined to get home to them, or die a-trying.

I took my keg of powder, and all my hunting tools, and cut out. When I got to the water, it was a sheet of ice as far as I could see. I put on to it, but hadn't got far before it broke through with me; and so I took out my tomahawk, and broke my way along before me for a considerable distance. At last I got to where the ice would bear me for a short distance, and I mounted on it, and went ahead; but it soon broke in again, and I had to wade on till I came to my floating log. I found it so tight this time, that I know'd it couldn't give me another fall, as it was frozen in with the ice. I crossed over it without much difficulty, and worked along till I got to my lodged sapling, and my log under the water. The swiftness of the current prevented the water from freezing over it, and so I had to wade, just as I did when I crossed it before. When I got to my sapling, I left my gun and climbed out with my powder keg first, and then went back and got my gun. By this time I was nearly frozen to death, but I saw all along before me, where the ice had been fresh broke, and I thought it must be a bear straggling about in the water. I, therefore, fresh primed my gun, and, cold as I was, I was determined to make war on him, if we met. But I followed the trail till it led me home, and I then found it had been made by my young man that lived with me, who had been sent by my distressed wife to see, if he could, what had become of me, for they all believed that I was dead. When I got home I was'nt quite dead, but mighty nigh it; but I had my powder, and that was what I went for.

CHAPTER XII.

That night there fell a heavy rain, and it turned to a sleet. In the morning all hands turned out hunting. My young man, and a brother-in-law who had lately settled close by me, went down the river to hunt for turkeys; but I was for larger game. I told them, I had dreamed the night before of having a hard fight with a big black [man], and I knowed it was a sign that I was to have a battle with a bear; for in a bear country, I never know'd such a dream to fail. So I started to go up above the harricane, determined to have a bear. I had two pretty good dogs, and an old hound, all of which I took along. I had gone about six miles up the river, and it was then about four miles across to the main Obion; so I determined to strike across to that, as I had found nothing yet to kill. I got on to the river, and turned down it; but the sleet was still getting worse and worse. The bushes were all bent down, and locked together with ice, so that it was almost impossible to get along. In a little time my dogs started a large gang of old turkey goblers, and I killed two of them, of the biggest sort. I shouldered them up, and moved on, until I got through the harricane, when I was so tired that I laid my goblers down to rest, as they were confounded heavy, and I was mighty tired. While I was resting, my old hound went to a log, and smelt it awhile, and then raised his eyes toward the sky, and cried out. Away he went, and my other dogs with him, and I shouldered up my turkeys again, and followed on as hard as I could drive. They were soon out of sight, and in a very little time I heard them begin to bark. When I got to them, they were barking up a tree, but there was no game there. I concluded it had been a turkey, and that it had flew away.

When they saw me coming, away they went again; and, after a little time, began to bark as before. When I got near them, I found they were barking up the wrong tree again, as there was no game there. They served me in this way three or four times, until I was so infernal mad, that I determined, if I could get near enough, to shoot the old hound at least. With this intention I pushed on the harder, till I came to the edge of an open parara, and looking on before my dogs, I saw in and about the biggest bear that ever was seen in America. He looked, at the distance he was from me, like a large black bull. My dogs were afraid to attack him, and that was the reason they had stop'd so often, that I might overtake them. They were now almost up with him, and I took my goblers from my back and hung them up in a sapling, and broke like a quarter horse after my bear, for the sight of him had put new springs in me. I soon got near to them, but they were just getting into a roaring thicket, and so I couldn't run through it, but had to pick my way along, and had close work even at that.

In a little time I saw the bear climbing up a large black oak-tree, and I crawled on till I got within about eighty yards of him. He was setting with his breast to me; and so I put fresh priming in my gun, and fired at him. At this he raised one of his paws and snorted loudly. I loaded again as quick as I could, and fired as near the same place in his breast as possible. At the crack of my gun here he came tumbling down; and the moment he touched the ground, I heard one of my best dogs cry out. I took my tomahawk in one hand, and my big butcher-knife in the other, and run up within four or five paces of him, at which he let my dog go, and fixed his eyes on mc. I got back in all sorts of a hurry, for I know'd if he got hold of me, he would hug me altogether too close for comfort. I went to my gun and hastily loaded her again, and shot him the third time, which killed him good.

I now began to think about getting him home, but I didn't know how far it was. So I left him and started; and in order to find him again, I would blaze a sapling every little distance, which would show me the way back. I continued this till I got within about a mile of home, for there I know'd very well where I was, and that I could easily find the way back to my blazes. When I got home, I took my brother-in-law, and my young man, and four horses, and went back. We got there just before dark, and struck up a fire, and commenced butchering my bear. It was some time in the night before we finished it; and I can assert, on my honour, that I believe he would have weighed six hundred pounds. It was the second largest I ever saw. I killed one, a few years after, that weighed six hundred and seventeen pounds. I now felt fully compensated for my sufferings in going after my powder; and well satisfied that a dog might sometimes be doing a good business, even when he seemed to be *barking up the wrong tree*. We got our meat home, and I had the pleasure to know that we now had plenty, and that of the best; and I continued through the winter to supply my family abundantly with bear-meat and venison from the woods.

CHAPTER XIII.

I HAD on hand a great many skins, and so, in the month of February, I packed a horse with them, and taking my eldest son along with me, cut out for a little town called Jackson, situated about forty miles off. We got there well enough, and I sold my skins, and bought me some coffee, and sugar, powder, lead, and salt. I packed them all up in readiness for a start, which I intended to make early the next morning. Morning came, but I concluded, before I started, I would go and take a horn with some of my old fellow-soldiers that I had met with at Jackson.

I did so; and while we were engaged in this, I met with three candidates for the Legislature; a Doctor Butler, who was, by marriage, a nephew to General Jackson, a Major Lynn, and a Mr. McEver, all first-rate men. We all took a horn together, and some person present said to me, "Crockett, you must offer for the Legislature." I told him I lived at least forty miles from any white settlement, and had no thought of becoming a candidate at that time. So we all parted, and I and my little boy went on home.

It was about a week or two after this, that a man came to my house, and told me I was a candidate. I told him not so. But he took out a newspaper from his pocket, and show'd me where I was announced. I said to my wife that this was all a burlesque on me, but I was determined to make it cost the man who had put it there at least the value of the printing, and of the fun he wanted at my expense. So I hired a young man to work in my place on my farm, and turned out myself electioneering. I hadn't been out long, before I found the people began to talk very much about the bear hunter, the man from the cane; and the three gentlemen, who I have already named, soon found it necessary to enter into an agreement to have a sort of caucus at their March court, to determine which of them was the strongest, and the other two was to withdraw and support him. As the court came on, each one of them spread himself, to secure the nomination; but it fell on Dr. Butler, and the rest backed out. The doctor was a clever fellow, and I have often said he was the most talented man I ever run against for any office. His being related to Gen'l. Jackson also helped him on very much; but I was in for it, and I was determined to push ahead and go through, or stick. Their meeting was held in Madison county, which was the strongest in the representative district, which was composed of eleven counties, and they seemed bent on having the member from there.

At this time Col. Alexander was a candidate for Congress, and attending one of his public meetings one day, I walked to where he was treating the people, and he gave me an introduction to several of his acquaintances, and informed them that I was out electioneering. In a little time my competitor. Doctor Butler, came along; he passed by without noticing me, and I suppose, indeed, he did not recognise me. But I hailed him, as I was for all sorts of fun; and when he turned to me, I said to him, "Well, doctor, I suppose they have weighed you out to me; but I should like to know why they fixed your election for *March* instead *August*? This is," said I, "a branfire new way of doing business, if a caucus is to make a representative for the people!" He now discovered who I was, and cried out, "D — n it, Crockett, is that you?" — "Be sure it is," said I, "but I don't want it understood that I have come electioneering. I have just crept out of the cane, to see what discoveries I could make among the white folks." I told him that when I set out electioneering, I would go prepared to put every man on as good footing when I left him as I found him on. I would therefore have me a large buckskin hunting-shirt made, with a couple of pockets holding about a peck each; and that in one I would carry a great big twist of tobacco, and in the other my bottle of liquor; for I knowed when I met a man and offered him a dram, he would throw out his quid of tobacco to take one, and after he had taken his horn, I would out with my twist and give him another chaw. And in this way he would not be worse off than when I found him; and I would be sure to leave him in a first-rate good humour. He said I could beat him electioneering all hollow. I told him I would give him better evidence of that before August, notwithstanding he had many advantages over me, and particularly in the way of money; but I told him that I would go on the products of the country; that I had industrious children, and the best of coon dogs, and they would hunt every night till midnight to support my election; and when the coon fur wa'n't good, I would myself go a wolfing, and shoot down a wolf, and skin his head, and his scalp would be good to me for three dollars, in our state treasury money; and in this way I would get along on the big string. He stood like he was both amused and astonished, and the whole crowd was in a roar of laughter. From this place I returned home, leaving the people in a first-rate way; and I was sure I would do a good business among them. At any rate, I was determined to stand up to my lick-log, salt or no salt.

In a short time there came out two other candidates, a Mr. Shaw and a Mr. Brown. We all ran the race through; and when the election was over, it turned out that I beat them all by a majority of two hundred and forty-seven votes, and was again returned as a member of the Legislature from a new region of the country, without losing a session. This reminded me of the old saying — "A fool for luck, and a poor man for children."

I now served two years in that body from my new district, which was the years 1823 and '24. At the session of 1823, I had a small trial of my independence, and whether I would forsake principle for party, or for the purpose of following after big men.

The term of Col. John Williams had expired, who was a senator in Congress from the state of Tennessee. He was a candidate for another election, and was opposed by Pleasant M. Miller, Esq., who, it was believed, would not be able to beat the colonel. Some two or three others were spoken of, but it was at last concluded that the only man who could beat him was the present "government," General Jackson, So, a few days before the election was to come on, he was sent for to come and run for the senate. He was then in nomination for the presidency; but sure enough he came, and did run as the opponent of Colonel Williams, and beat him too, but not by my vote. The vote was, for Jackson, *thirty-five*; for Williams, *twenty-five*. I thought the colonel had honestly discharged his duty, and even the mighty name of Jackson couldn't make me vote against him.

But voting against the old chief was found a mighty up-hill business to all of them except myself. I never would, nor never did, acknowledge I had voted wrong; and I am more certain now that I was right than ever.

I told the people it was the best vote I ever gave; that I had supported the public interest, and cleared my conscience in giving it, instead of gratifying the private ambition of a man.

I let the people know as early as then, that I wouldn't take a collar around my neck with the letters engraved on it,

MY DOG. Andrew Jackson.

During these two sessions of the Legislature, nothing else turned up which I think it worth while to mention; and, indeed, I am fearful that I am too particular about many small matters; but if so, my apology is, that I want the world to understand my true history, and how I worked along to rise from a cane-brake to my present station in life.

Col. Alexander was the representative in Congress of the district I lived in, and his vote on the tariff law of 1824 gave a mighty heap of dissatisfaction to his people. They therefore began to talk pretty strong of running me for Congress against him. At last I was called on by a good many to be a candidate. I told the people that I couldn't stand that; it was a step above my knowledge, and I know'd nothing about Congress matters.

However, I was obliged to agree to run, and myself and two other gentlemen came out. But Providence was a little against two of us this hunt, for it was the year that cotton brought twenty-five dollars a hundred; and so Colonel Alexander would get up and tell the people, it was all the good effect of this tariff law; that it had raised the price of their cotton, and that it would raise the price of every thing else they made to sell. I might as well have sung *salms* over a dead horse, as to try to make the people believe otherwise; for they knowed their cotton had raised, sure enough, and if the colonel hadn't done it, they didn't know what had. So he rather made a mash of me this time, as he beat me exactly *two* votes, as they counted the polls, though I have always believed that many other things had been as fairly done as that same count.

He went on, and served out his term, and at the end of it cotton was down to six or eight dollars a hundred again; and I concluded I would try him once more, and see how it would go with cotton at the common price, and so I became a candidate.

CHAPTER XIV.

But the reader, I expect, would have no objection to know a little about my employment during the two years while my competitor was in Congress. In this space I had some pretty tuff times, and will relate some few things that happened to me. So here goes, as the boy said when he run by himself.

In the fall of 1825, I concluded I would build two large boats, and load them with pipe staves for market. So I went down to the lake, which was about twenty-five miles from where I lived, and hired some hands to assist me, and went to work; some at boat building, and others to getting staves. I worked on with my hands till the bears got fat, and then I turned out to hunting, to lay in a supply of meat. I soon killed and salted down as many as were necessary for my family; but about this time one of my old neighbours, who had settled down on the lake about twenty-five miles from me, came to my house and told me he wanted me to go down and kill some bears about in his parts. He said they were extremely fat, and very plenty. I know'd that when they were fat, they were easily taken, for a fat bear can't run fast or long. But I asked a bear no favours, no way, further than civility, for I now had eight large dogs, and as fierce as painters; so that a bear stood no chance at all to get away from them. So I went home with him, and then went on down towards the Mississippi, and commenced hunting.

We were out two weeks, and in that time killed fifteen bears. Having now supplied my friend with plenty of meat, I engaged occasionally again with my hands in our boat building, and getting staves. But I at length couldn't stand it any longer without another hunt. So I concluded to take my little son, and cross over the lake, and take a hunt there. We got over, and that evening turned out and killed three bears, in little or no time. The next morning we drove up four forks, and made a sort of scaffold, on which we salted up our meat, so as to have it out of the reach of the wolves, for as soon as we would leave our camp, they would take possession. We had just eat our breakfast, when a company of hunters came to our camp, who had fourteen dogs, but all so poor, that when they would bark they would almost have to lean up against a tree and take a rest. I told them their dogs couldn't run in smell of a bear, and they had better stay at my camp, and feed them on the bones I had cut out of my meat. I left them there, and cut out; but I hadn't gone far, when my dogs took a first-rate start after a very large fat old *he-bear*, which run right plump towards my camp. I pursued on, but my other hunters had heard my dogs coming, and met them, and killed the bear before I got up with him. I gave him to them, and cut out again for a creek called Big Clover, which wa'n't very far off. Just as I got there, and was entering a cane brake, my dogs all broke and went ahead, and, in a little time, they raised a fuss in the cane, and seemed to be going every way. I listened a while, and found my dogs was in two companies, and that both was in a snorting fight. I sent my little son to one, and I broke for t'other. I got to mine first, and found my dogs had a two-year-old bear down, a-wooling away on him; so I just took out my big butcher, and went up and slap'd it into him, and killed him without shooting. There was five of the dogs in my company. In a short time, I heard my little son fire at his bear; when I went to him he had killed it too. He had two dogs in his team. Just at this moment we heard my other dog barking a short distance off, and all the rest immediately broke to him. We pushed on too, and when we got there, we found he had still a larger bear than either of them we had killed, treed by himself. We killed that one also, which made three we had killed in less than half an hour. We turned in and butchered them, and then started to hunt for water, and a good place to camp. But we had no sooner started, than our dogs took a start after another one, and away they went like a thunder-gust, and was out of hearing in a minute. We followed the way they had gone for some time, but at length we gave up the hope of finding them, and turned back. As we were going back, I came to where a poor fellow was grubbing, and he looked like the very picture of hard times. I asked him what he was doing away there in the woods by himself? He said he was grubbing for a man who intended to settle there; and the reason why he did it was, that he had no meat for his family, and he was working for a little.

I was mighty sorry for the poor fellow, for it was not only a hard, but a very slow way to get meat for a hungry family; so I told him if he would go with me, I would give him more meat than he could get by grubbing in a month. I intended to supply him with meat, and also to get him to assist my little boy in packing in and salting up my bears. He had never seen a bear killed in his life. I told him I had six killed then, and my dogs were hard after another. He went off to his little cabin, which was a short distance in the brush, and his wife was very anxious he should go with me. So we started and went to where I had left my three bears, and made a camp. We then gathered my meat and salted, and scaffled it, as I had done the other. Night now came on, but no word from my dogs yet. I afterwards found they had treed the bear about five miles off, near to a man's house, and had barked at it the whole enduring night. Poor fellows ! many a time they looked for me, and wondered why I didn't come, for they knowed there was no mistake in me, and I know'd they were as good as ever fluttered. In the morning, as soon as it was light enough to see, the man took his gun and went to them, and shot the bear, and killed it. My dogs, however, wouldn't have any thing to say to this stranger; so they left him, and came early in the morning back to me.

We got our breakfast, and cut out again; and we killed four large and very fat bears that day. We hunted out the week, and in that time we killed seventeen, all of them first-rate. When we closed our hunt, I gave the man over a thousand weight of fine fat bear-meat, which pleased him mightily, and made him feel as rich as a Jew. I saw him the next fall, and he told me he had plenty of meat to do him the whole year from his week's hunt. My son and me now went home. This was the week between Christmass and New-year that we made this hunt. When I got home, one of my neighbours was out of meat, and wanted me to go back, and let him go with me, to take another hunt. I couldn't refuse; but I told him I was afraid the bear had taken to house by that time, for after they get very fat in the fall and early part of the winter, they go into their holes, in large hollow trees, or into hollow logs, or their cane-houses, or the harricanes; and lie there till spring, like frozen snakes. And one thing about this will seem mighty strange to many people. From about the first of January to about the last of April, these varments lie in their holes altogether. In all that time they have no food to eat; and yet when they come out, they are not an ounce lighter than when they went to house. I don't know the cause of this, and still I know it is a fact; and I leave it for others who have more learning than myself to account for it. They have not a particle of food with them, but they just lie and suck the bottom of their paw all the time. I have killed many of them in their trees, which enables me to speak positively on this subject. However, my neighbour, whose name was McDaniel, and my little son and me, went on down to the lake to my second camp, where I had killed my seventeen bears the week before, and turned out to hunting. But we hunted hard all day without getting a single start. We had carried but little provisions with us, and the next morning was entirely out of meat. I sent my son about three miles off, to the house of an old friend, to get some. The old gentleman was much pleased to hear I was hunting in those parts, for the year before the bears had killed a great many of his hogs. He was that day killing his bacon hogs, and so he gave my son some meat, and sent word to me that I must come in to his house that evening, that he would have plenty of feed for my dogs, and some accommodations for ourselves; but before my son got back, we had gone out hunting, and in a large cane brake my dogs found a big bear in a cane-house, which he had fixed for his winter-quarters, as they sometimes do.

When my lead dog found him, and raised the yell, all the rest broke to him, but none of them entered his house until we got up. I encouraged my dogs, and they knowed me so well, that I could have made them seize the old serpent himself, with all his horns and heads, and cloven foot and ugliness into the bargain, if he would only have come to light, so that they could have seen him. They bulged in, and in an instant the bear followed them out, and I told my friend to shoot him, as he was mighty wrathy to kill a bear. He did so, and killed him prime. We carried him to our camp, by which time my son had returned; and after we got our dinners we packed up, and cut for the house of my old friend, whose name was Davidson.

We got there, and staid with him that night; and the next morning, having salted up our meat, we left it with him, and started to take a hunt between the Obion lake and the Red-foot lake; as there had been a dreadful harricane, which passed between them, and I was sure there must be a heap of bears in the fallen timber. We had gone about five miles without seeing any sign at all; but at length we got on some high cany ridges, and, as we rode along, I saw a hole in a large black oak, and on examining more closely, I discovered that a bear had clomb the tree. I could see his tracks going up, but none coming down, and so I was sure he was in there. A person who is acquainted with bear-hunting, can tell easy enough when the varment is in the hollow; for as they go up they don't slip a bit, but as they come down they make long scratches with their nails.

My friend was a little ahead of me, but I called him back, and told him there was a bear in that tree, and I must have him out. So we lit from our horses, and I found a small tree which I thought I could fall so as to lodge against my bear tree, and we fell to work chopping it with our tomahawks. I intended, when we lodged the tree against the other, to let my little son go up, and look into the hole, for he could climb like a squirrel. We had chop'd on a little time and stop'd to rest, when I heard my dogs barking mighty severe at some distance from us, and I told my friend I knowed they had a bear; for it is the nature of a dog, when he finds you are hunting bears, to hunt for nothing else; he becomes fond of the meat, and considers other game as "not worth a notice," as old Johnson said of the devil.

We concluded to leave our tree a bit, and went to my dogs, and when we got there, sure enough they had an eternal great big fat bear up a tree, just ready for shooting. My friend again petitioned me for liberty to shoot this one also. I had a little rather not, as the bear was so big, but I couldn't refuse; and so he blazed away, and down came the old fellow like some great log had fell. I now missed one of my dogs, the same that I before spoke of as having treed the bear by himself sometime before, when I had started the three in the cane break. I told my friend that my missing dog had a bear somewhere, just as sure as fate; so I left them to butcher the one we had just killed, and I went up on a piece of high ground to listen for my dog. I heard him barking with all his might some distance off, and I pushed ahead for him. My other dogs hearing him broke to him, and when I got there, sure enough again he had another bear ready treed; if he hadn't, I wish I may be shot. I fired on him, and brought him down; and then went back, and help'd finish butchering the one at which I had left my friend. We then packed both to our tree where we had left my boy. By this time, the little fellow had cut the tree down that we intended to lodge, but it fell the wrong way; he had then feather'd in on the big tree, to cut that, and had found that it was nothing but a shell on the outside, and all doted in the middle, as too many of our big men are in these days, having only an outside appearance. My friend and my son cut away on it, and I went off about a hundred yards with my dogs to keep them from running under the tree when it should fall. On looking back at the hole, I saw the bear's head out of it, looking down at them as they were cutting. I hollered to them to look up, and they did so; and McDaniel catched up his gun, but by this time the bear was out, and coming down the tree. He fired at it, and as soon as it touch'd ground the dogs were all round it, and they had a roll-and-tumble fight to the foot of the hill, where they stop'd him. I ran up, and putting my gun against the bear, fired and killed him. We now had three, and so we made our scaffold and salted them up.

CHAPTER XV.

In the morning I left my son at the camp, and we started on towards the harricane; and when we had went about a mile, we started a very large bear, but we got along mighty slow on account of the cracks in the earth occasioned by the earthquakes. We, however, made out to keep in hearing of the dogs for about three miles, and then we come to the harricane. Here we had to quit our horses, as old Nick himself couldn't have got through it without sneaking it along in the form that he put on, to make a fool of our old grandmother Eve. By this time several of my dogs had got tired and come back; but we went ahead on foot for some little time in the harricane, when we met a bear coming straight to us, and not more than twenty or thirty yards off. I started my tired dogs after him, and McDaniel pursued them, and I went on to where my other dogs were. I had seen the track of the bear they were after, and

I knowed he was a screamer. I followed on to about the middle of the harricane; but my dogs pursued him so close, that they made him climb an old stump about twenty feet high. I got in shooting distance of him and fired, but I was all over in such a flutter from fatigue and running, that I couldn't hold steady; but, however, I broke his shoulder, and he fell. I run up and loaded my gun as quick as possible, and shot him again and killed him. When I went to take out my knife to butcher him, I found I had lost it in coming through the harricane. The vines and briers was so thick that I would sometimes have to get down and crawl like a varment to get through at all; and a vine had, as I supposed, caught in the handle and pulled it out. While I was standing and studying what to do, my friend came to me. He had followed my trail throughthe harricane, and had found my knife, which was mighty good news to me; as a hunter hates the worst in the world to lose a good dog, or any part of his hunting-tools. I now left McDaniel to butcher the bear, and I went after our horses, and brought them as near as the nature of case would allow. I then took our bags, and went back to where he was; and when we had skin'd the bear, we fleeced off the fat and carried it to our horses at several loads. We then packed it up on our horses, and had a heavy pack of it on each one. We now started and went on till about sunset, when I concluded we must be near our camp; so I hollered and my son answered me, and we moved on in the direction to the camp. We had gone but a little way when I heard my dogs make a warm start again; and I jumped down from my horse and gave him up to my friend, and told him I would follow them. He went on to the camp, and I went ahead after my dogs with all my might for a considerable distance, till at last night came on. The woods were very rough and hilly, and all covered over with cane.

I now was compel'd to move on more slowly; and was frequently falling over logs, and into the cracks made by the earthquakes, so that I was very much afraid I would break my gun. However I went on about three miles, when I came to a good big creek, which I waded. It was very cold, and the creek was about knee-deep; but I felt no great inconvenience from it just then, as I was all over wet with sweat from running, and I felt hot enough. After I got over this creek and out of the cane, which was very thick on all our creeks, I listened for my dogs. I found they had either treed or brought the bear to a stop, as they continued barking in the same place. I pushed on as near in the direction to the noise as I could, till I found the hill was too steep for me to climb, and so I backed and went down the creek some distance till I came to a hollow, and then took up that, till I come to a place where I could climb up the hill. It was mighty dark, and was difficult to see my way or any thing else. When I got up the hill, I found I had passed the dogs; and so I turned and went to them. I found, when I got here, they had treed the bear in a large forked poplar, and it was setting in the fork.

I could see the lump, but not plain enough to shoot with any certainty, as there was no moonlight; and so I set in to hunting for some dry brush to make me a light; but I could find none, though I could find that the ground was torn mightily to pieces by the cracks.

At last I thought I could shoot by guess, and kill him; so I pointed as near the lump as I could, and fired away. But the bear didn't come he only clomb up higher, and got out on a limb, which helped me to see him better. I now loaded up again and fired, but this time he didn't move at all. I commenced loading for a third fire, but the first thing I knowed, the bear was down among my dogs, and they were fighting all around me.

I had my big butcher in my belt, and I had a pair of dressed buckskin breeches on. So I took out my knife, and stood, determined, if he should get hold of me, to defend myself in the best way I could. I stood there for some time, and could now and then see a white dog I had, but the rest of them, and the bear, which were dark coloured, I couldn't see at all, it was so miserable dark. They still fought around me, and sometimes within three feet of me; but, at last, the bear got down into one of the cracks, that the earthquakes had made in the ground, about four feet deep, and I could tell the biting end of him by the hollering of my dogs. So I took my gun and pushed the muzzle of it about, till I thought I had it against the main part of his body, and fired; but it happened to be only the fleshy part of his foreleg. With this, he jumped out of the crack, and he and the dogs had another hard fight around me, as before. At last, however, they forced him back into the crack again, as he was when I had shot.

I had laid down my gun in the dark, and I now began to hunt for it; and, while hunting, I got hold of a pole, and I concluded I would punch him awhile with that. I did so, and when I would punch him, the dogs would jump in on him, when he would bite them badly, and they would jump out again. I concluded, as he would take punching so patiently, it might be that he would lie still enough for me to get down in the crack, and feel slowly along till I could find the right place to give him a dig with my butcher. So I got down, and my dogs got in before him and kept his head towards them, till I got along easily up to him; and placing my hand on his rump, felt for his shoulder, just behind which I intended to stick him. I made a lounge with my long knife, and fortunately stuck him right through the heart; at which he just sank down, and I crawled out in a hurry. In a little time my dogs all come out too, and seemed satisfied, which was the way they always had of telling me that they had finished him.

I suffered very much that night with cold, as my leather breeches, and every thing else I had on, was wet and frozen. But I managed to get my bear out of this crack after several hard trials, and so I butchered him, and laid down to try to sleep. But my fire was very bad, and I couldn't find any thing that would burn well to make it any better; and I concluded I should freeze, if I didn't warm myself in some way by exercise. So I got up, and hollered a while, and then I would just jump up and down with all my might, and throw myself into all sorts of motions. But all this wouldn't do; for my blood was now getting cold, and the chills coming all over me, I was so tired, too, that I could hardly walk; but I thought I would do the best I could to save my life, and then, if I died, nobody would be to blame. So I went to a tree about two feet through, and not a limb on it for thirty feet, and I would climb up it to the limbs, and then lock my arms together around it, and slide down to the bottom again. This would make the insides of my legs and arms feel mighty warm and good. I continued this till daylight in the morning, and how often I clomb up my tree and slid down I don't know, but I reckon at least a hundred times.

In the morning I got my bear hung up so as to be safe, and then set out to hunt for my camp. I found it after a while, and McDaniel and my son were very much rejoiced to see me get back, for they were about to give me up for lost. We got our breakfasts, and then secured our meat by building a high scaffold, and covering it over. We had no fear of its spoiling, for the weather was so cold that it couldn't.

We now started after my other bear, which had caused me so much trouble and suffering; and before we got him, we got a start after another, and took him also. We went on to the creek I had crossed the night before and camped, and then went to where my bear was, that I had killed in the crack. When we examined the place, McDaniel said he wouldn't have gone into it, as I did, for all the bears in the woods.

We took the meat down to our camp and salted it, and also the last one we had killed; intending, in the morning, to make a hunt in the harricane again.

We prepared for resting that night, and I can assure the reader I was in need of it. We had laid down by our fire, and about ten o'clock there came a most terrible earthquake, which shook the earth so, that we were rocked about like we had been in a cradle. We were very much alarmed; for though we were accustomed to feel earthquakes, we were now right in the region which had been torn to pieces by them in 1812, and we thought it might take a notion and swallow us up, like the big fish did Jonah.

In the morning we packed up and moved to the harricane, where we made another camp, and turned out that evening and killed a very large bear, which made eight we had now killed in this hunt.

The next morning we entered the harricane again, and in little or no time my dogs were in full cry. We pursued them, and soon came to a thick cane-brake, in which they had stop'd their bear. We got up close to him, as the cane was so thick that we couldn't see more than a few feet. Here I made my friend hold the cane a little open with his gun till I shot the bear, which was a mighty large one. I killed him dead in his tracks. We got him out and butchered him, and in a little time started another and killed him, which now made ten we had killed; and we know'd we couldn't pack any more home, as we had only five horses along; therefore we returned to the camp and salted up all our meat, to be ready for a start homeward next morning.

The morning came, and we packed our horses with the meat, and had as much as they could possibly carry, and sure enough cut out for home. It was about thirty miles, and we reached home the second day. I had now accommodated my neighbour with meat enough to do him, and had killed in all, up to that time, fifty-eight bears, during the fall and winter.

As soon as the time come for them to quit their houses and come out again in the spring, I took a notion to hunt a little more, and in about one month I killed forty-seven more, which made one hundred and five bears I had killed in less than one year from that time.

CHAPTER XVI.

Having now closed my hunting for that winter, I returned to my hands, who were engaged about my boats and staves, and made ready for a trip down the river. I had two boats and about thirty thousand staves, and so I loaded with them, and set out for New Orleans. I got out of the Obion river, in which I had loaded my boats, very well; but when I got into the Mississippi, I found all my hands were bad scared, and in fact I believe I was scared a little the worst of any; for I had never been down the river, and I soon discovered that my pilot was as ignorant of the business as myself. I hadn't gone far before I determined to lash the two boats together; we did so, but it made them so heavy and obstinate, that it was next akin to impossible to do any thing at all with them, or to guide them right in the river.

That evening we fell in company with some Ohio boats; and about night we tried to land, but we could not. The Ohio men hollered to us to go on and run all night. We took their advice, though we had a good deal rather not; but we couldn't do any other way. In a short distance we got into what is called the "*Devil's Elbow*;" and if any place in the wide creation has its own proper name, I thought it was this. Here we had about the hardest work that I ever was engaged in, in my life, to keep out of danger; and even then we were in it all the while. We twice attempted to land at Wood-yards, which we could see, but couldn't reach.

The people would run out with lights, and try to instruct us how to get to shore; but all in vain. Our boats were so heavy that we couldn't take them much any way, except the way they wanted to go, and just the way the current would carry them. At last we quit trying to land, and concluded just to go ahead as well as we could, for we found we couldn't do any better. Some time in the night I was down in the cabin of one of the boats, sitting by the fire, thinking on what a hobble we had got into; and how much better bear-hunting was on hard land, than floating along on the water, when a fellow had to go ahead whether he was exactly willing or not.

The hatchway into the cabin came slap down, right through the top of the boat; and it was the only way out except a small hole in the side, which we had used for putting our arms through to dip up water before we lashed the boats together.

We were now floating sideways, and the boat I was in was the hindmost as we went. All at once I heard the hands begin to run over the top of the boat in great confusion, and pull with all their might; and the first thing I know'd after this we went broadside full tilt against the head of an island where a large raft of drift timber had lodged. The nature of such a place would be, as every body knows, to suck the boats down, and turn them right under this raft; and the uppermost boat would, of course, be suck'd down and go under first. As soon as we struck, I bulged for my hatchway, as the boat was turning under sure enough. But when I got to it, the water was pouring thro' in a current as large as the hole would let it, and as strong as the weight of the river could force it. I found I couldn't get out here, for the boat was now turned down in such a way, that it was steeper than a house-top. I now thought of the hole in the side, and made my way in a hurry for that. With difficulty I got to it, and when I got there, I found it was too small for me to get out by my own dower, and I began to think that I was in a worse box than ever. But I put my arms through and hollered as loud as I could roar, as the boat I was in hadn't yet quite filled with water up to my head, and the hands who were next to the raft, seeing my arms out, and hearing me holler, seized them, and began to pull. I told them I was sinking, and to pull my arms off, or force me through, for now I know'd well enough it was neck or nothing, come out or sink.

By a violent effort they jerked me through; but I was in a pretty pickle when I got through. I had been sitting without any clothing over my shirt: this was torn off, and I was literally skin'd like a rabbit. I was, however, well pleased to get out in any way, even without shirt or hide; as before I could straighten myself on the boat next to the raft, the one they pull'd me out of went entirely under, and I have never seen it any more to this day. We all escaped on to the raft, where we were compelled to sit all night, about a mile from land on either side. Four of my company were bareheaded, and three barefooted; and of that number I was one. I reckon I looked like a pretty cracklin ever to get to Congress ! ! !

We had now lost all our loading; and every particle of our clothing, except what little we had on; but over all this, while I was setting there, in the night, floating about on the drift, I felt happier and better off than I ever had in my life before, for I had just made such a marvellous escape, that I had forgot almost every thing else in that; and so I felt prime.

In the morning about sunrise, we saw a boat coming down, and we hailed her. They sent a large skiff, and took us all on board, and carried us down as far as Memphis. Here I met with a friend, that I never can forget as long as I am able to go ahead at any thing; it was a Major Winchester, a merchant of that place: he let us all have hats, and shoes, and some little money to go upon, and so we all parted.

A young man and myself concluded to go on down to Natchez, to see if we could hear any thing of our boats; for we supposed they would float out from the raft, and keep on down the river. We got on a boat at Memphis, that was going down, and so cut out. Our largest boat, we were informed, had been seen about fifty miles below where we stove, and an attempt had been made to land her, but without success, as she was as hardheaded as ever.

This was the last of my boats, and of my boating; for it went so badly with me, along at the first, that I hadn't much mind to try it any more. I now returned home again, and as the next August was the Congressional election, I began to turn my attention a little to that matter, as it was beginning to be talked of a good deal among the people.

CHAPTER XVII.

I HAVE, heretofore, informed the reader that I had determined to run this race to see what effect *the price of cotton* could have again on it. I now had Col. Alexander to run against once more, and also General William Arnold.

I had difficulties enough to fight against this time, as every one will suppose; for I had no money, and a very bad prospect, so far as I know'd, of getting any to help me along. I had, however, a good friend, who sent for me to come and see him. I went, and he was good enough to offer me some money to help me out. I borrowed as much as I thought I needed at the start, and went ahead. My friend also had a good deal of business about over the district at the different courts; and if he now and then slip'd in a good word for me, it is nobody's business. We frequently met at different places, and, as he thought I needed, he would occasionally hand me a little more cash; so I was able to buy a little of "the *creature*," to put my friends in a good humour, as well as the other gentlemen, for they all treat in that country; not to get elected, of course — for that would be against the law; but just, as I before said, to make themselves and their friends feel their keeping a little.

Nobody ever did know how I got money to get along on, till after the election was over, and I had beat my competitors twenty-seven hundred and forty-eight votes. Even the price of cotton couldn't save my friend Aleck this time. My rich friend, who had been so good to me in the way of money, now sent for me, and loaned me a hundred dollars, and told me to go ahead; that that amount would bear my expenses to Congress, and I must then shift for myself. I came on to Washington, and draw'd two hundred and fifty dollars, and purchased with it a check on the bank at Nashville, and enclosed it to my friend; and I may say, in truth, I sent this money with a mighty good will, for I reckon nobody in this world loves a friend better than me, or remembers a kindness longer.

I have now given the close of the election, but I have skip'd entirely over the canvass, of which I will say a very few things in this place; as I know very well how to tell the truth, but not much about placing them in book order, so as to please critics.

Col. Alexander was a very clever fellow, and principal surveyor at that time; so much for one of the men I had to run against. My other competitor was a major-general in the militia, and an attorney-general at the law, and quite a smart, clever man also; and so it will be seen I had war work as well as law trick, to stand up under. Taking both together, they make a pretty considerable of a load for any one man to carry. But for war claims, I consider myself behind no man except "the government," and mighty little, if any, behind him; but this the people will have to determine hereafter, as I reckon it won't do to quit the work of "reform and retrenchment" yet for a spell.

But my two competitors seemed some little afraid of the influence of each other, but not to think me in their way at all. They, therefore, were generally working against each other, while I was going ahead for myself, and mixing among the people in the best way I could. I was as cunning as a little red fox, and wouldn't risk my tail in a "committal" trap.

I found the sign was good, almost everywhere I went. On one occasion, while we were in the eastern counties of the district, it happened that we all had to make a speech, and it fell on me to make the first one. I did so after my manner, and it turned pretty much on the old saying, "A short horse is soon curried," as I spoke not very long. Colonel Alexander followed me, and then General Arnold come on.

The general took much pains to reply to Alexander, but didn't so much as let on that there was any such candidate as myself at all. He had been speaking for a considerable time, when a large flock of guinea-fowls came very near to where he was, and set up the most unmerciful chattering that ever was heard, for they are a noisy little brute any way. They so confused the general, that he made a stop, and requested that they might be driven away. I let him finish his speech, and then walking up to him, said aloud, "Well, colonel, you are the first man I ever saw that understood the language of fowls." I told him that he had not had the politeness to name me in his speech, and that when my little friends, the guinea-fowls, had come up and began to holler "Crockett, Crockett, Crockett," he had been ungenerous enough to stop, and drive *them* all away. This raised a universal shout among the people for me, and the general seemed mighty bad plagued. But he got more plagued than this at the polls in August, as I have stated before.

This election was in 1827, and I can say, on my conscience, that I was, without disguise, the friend and supporter of General Jackson, upon his principles as he laid them down, and as "*I understood them*," before his election as president. During my two first sessions in Congress, Mr. Adams was president, and I worked along with what was called the Jackson party pretty well. I was re-elected to Congress, in 1829, by an overwhelming majority; and soon after the commencement of this second term, I saw, or thought I did, that it was expected of me that I was to bow to the name of Andrew Jackson, and follow him in all his motions, and mindings, and turnings, even at the expense of my conscience and judgment. Such a thing was new to me, and a total stranger to my principles. I know'd well enough, though, that if I didn't "hurra" for his name, the hue and cry was to be raised against me, and I was to be sacrificed, if possible. His famous, or rather I should say his in-*famous*, Indian bill was brought forward, and I opposed it from the purest motives in the world. Several of my colleagues got around me, and told me how well they loved me, and that I was ruining myself. They said this was a favourite measure of the president, and I ought to go for it. I told them I believed it was a wicked, unjust measure, and that I should go against it, let the cost to myself be what it might; that I was willing to go with General Jackson in every thing that I believed was honest and right; but, further than this, I wouldn't go for him, or any other man in the whole creation; that I would sooner be honestly and politically d — nd, than hypocritically immortalized. I had been elected by a majority of three thousand five hundred and eighty-five votes, and I believed they were honest men, and wouldn't want me to vote for any unjust notion, to please Jackson or any one else; at any rate, I was of age, and was determined to trust them. I voted against this Indian bill, and my conscience yet tells me that I gave a good honest vote, and one that I believe will not make me ashamed in the day of judgment. I served out my term, and though many amusing things happened, I am not disposed to swell my narrative by inserting them.

When it closed, and I returned home, I found the storm had raised against me sure enough; and it was echoed from side to side, and from end to end of my district, that I had turned against Jackson. This was considered the unpardonable sin. I was hunted down like a wild varment, and in this hunt every little newspaper in the district, and every little pin-hook lawyer was engaged. Indeed, they were ready to print any and every thing that the ingenuity of man could invent against me. Each editor was furnished with the journals of Congress from head-quarters; and hunted out every vote I had missed in four sessions, whether from sickness or not, no matter, and each one was charged against me at eight dollars. In all I had missed about *seventy* votes, which they made amount to five hundred and sixty dollars; and they contended I had swindled the government out of this sum, as I had received my pay, as other members do. I was now again a candidate in 1830, while all the attempts were making against me; and every one of these little papers kept up a constant war on me, fighting with every scurrilous report they could catch.

Over all I should have been elected, if it hadn't been, that but a few weeks before the election, the little four-pence-ha'penny limbs of the law fell on a plan to defeat me, which had the desired effect. They agreed to spread out over the district, and make appointments for me to speak, almost every-where, to clear up the Jackson question. They would give me no notice of these appointments, and the people would meet in great crowds to hear what excuse Crockett had to make for quitting Jackson.

But instead of Crockett's being there, this small-fry of lawyers would be there, with their saddle-bags full of the little newspapers and their journals of Congress; and would get up and speak, and read their scurrilous attacks on me, and would then tell the people that I was afraid to attend; and in this way would turn many against me. All this intrigue was kept a profound secret from me, till it was too late to counteract it; and when the election came, I had a majority in seventeen counties, putting all their votes together, but the eighteenth beat me; and so I was left out of Congress during those two years. The people of my district were induced, by these tricks, to take a stay on me for that time; but they have since found out that they were imposed on, and on re-considering my case, have reversed that decision; which, as the Dutchman said, "is as fair a ding as eber was."

When I last declared myself a candidate, I knew that the district would be divided by the Legislature before the election would come on; and I moreover knew, that from the geographical situation of the country, the county of Madison, which was very strong, and which was the county that had given the majority that had beat me in the former race, should be left off from my district.

But when the Legislature met, as I have been informed, and I have no doubt of the fact, Mr. Fitzgerald, my competitor, went up, and informed his friends in that body, that if Madison county was left off, he wouldn't run; for "that Crockett could beat Jackson himself in those parts, in any way they could fix it."

The liberal Legislature you know, of course, gave him that county; and it is too clear to admit of dispute, that it was done to make a mash of me. In order to make my district in this way, they had to form the southern district of a string of counties around three sides of mine, or very nearly so. Had my old district been properly divided, it would have made two nice ones, in convenient nice form. But as it is, they are certainly the most unreasonably laid off of any in the state, or perhaps in the nation, or even in the te-total creation.

However, when the election came on, the people of the district, and of Madison county among the rest, seemed disposed to prove to Mr. Fitzgerald and the Jackson Legislature, that they were not to be transferred like hogs, and horses, and cattle in the market; and they determined that I shouldn't be broke down, though I had to carry Jackson, and the enemies of the bank, and the legislative works all at once. I had Mr. Fitzgerald, it is true, for my open competitor, but he was helped along by all his little lawyers again, headed by old Black Hawk, as he is sometimes called, (alias) Adam Huntsman, with all his talents for writing "*Chronicles*," and such like foolish stuff.

But one good thing was, and I must record it, the papers in the district were now beginning to say "fair play a little," and they would publish on both sides of the question. The contest was a warm one, and the battle well-fought; but I gained the day, and the Jackson horse was left a little behind. When the polls were compared, it turned out I had beat Fitz just two hundred and two votes, having made a mash of all their intrigues. After all this, the reader will perceive that I am now here in Congress, this 28th day of January, in the year of our Lord one thousand eight hundred and thirty-four; and that, what is more agreeable to my feelings as a freeman, I am at liberty to vote as my conscience and judgment dictates to be right, without the yoke of any party on me, or the driver at my heels, with his whip in hand, commanding me to ge-wo-haw, just at his pleasure. Look at my arms, you will find no party hand-cuff on them ! Look at my neck, you will not find there any collar, with the engraving

MY DOG.

Andrew Jackson.

But you will find me standing up to my rack, as the people's faithful representative, and the public's most obedient, very humble servant,

DAVID CROCKETT.

THE END.

- Note: Davy Crockett served in Congress until 1835. He left Tennessee to explore Texas in November, 1835. He died at the Battle of the Alamo on March 6, 1836 at age 49.

Lesson 31

- Read "The Gift of the Magi" by O. Henry (1905).

The Gift Of The Magi

One dollar and eighty-seven cents. That was all. And sixty cents of it was in pennies. Pennies saved one and two at a time by bulldozing the grocer and the vegetable man and the butcher until one's cheeks burned with the silent imputation of parsimony that such close dealing implied. Three times Della counted it. One dollar and eighty- seven cents. And the next day would be Christmas.

There was clearly nothing to do but flop down on the shabby little couch and howl. So Della did it. Which instigates the moral reflection that life is made up of sobs, sniffles, and smiles, with sniffles predominating.

While the mistress of the home is gradually subsiding from the first stage to the second, take a look at the home. A furnished flat at $8 per week. It did not exactly beggar description, but it certainly had that word on the lookout for the mendicancy squad.

In the vestibule below was a letter-box into which no letter would go, and an electric button from which no mortal finger could coax a ring. Also appertaining thereunto was a card bearing the name "Mr. James Dillingham Young."

The "Dillingham" had been flung to the breeze during a former period of prosperity when its possessor was being paid $30 per week. Now, when the income was shrunk to $20, though, they were thinking seriously of contracting to a modest and unassuming D. But whenever Mr. James Dillingham Young came home and reached his flat above he was called "Jim" and greatly hugged by Mrs. James Dillingham Young, already introduced to you as Della. Which is all very good.

Della finished her cry and attended to her cheeks with the powder rag. She stood by the window and looked out dully at a gray cat walking a gray fence in a gray backyard. Tomorrow would be Christmas Day, and she had only $1.87 with which to buy Jim a present. She had been saving every penny she could for months, with this result. Twenty dollars a week doesn't go far. Expenses had been greater than she had calculated. They always are. Only $1.87 to buy a present for Jim. Her Jim.

Many a happy hour she had spent planning for something nice for him. Something fine and rare and sterling–something just a little bit near to being worthy of the honor of being owned by Jim.

There was a pier-glass between the windows of the room. Perhaps you have seen a pierglass in an $8 flat. A very thin and very agile person may, by observing his reflection in a rapid sequence of longitudinal strips, obtain a fairly accurate conception of his looks. Della, being slender, had mastered the art.

Suddenly she whirled from the window and stood before the glass. Her eyes were shining brilliantly, but her face had lost its color within twenty seconds. Rapidly she pulled down her hair and let it fall to its full length.

Now, there were two possessions of the James Dillingham Youngs in which they both took a mighty pride. One was Jim's gold watch that had been his father's and his grandfather's. The other was Della's hair. Had the queen of Sheba lived in the flat across the airshaft, Della would have let her hair hang out the window some day to dry just to depreciate Her Majesty's jewels and gifts. Had King Solomon been the janitor, with all his treasures piled up in the basement, Jim would have pulled out his watch every time he passed, just to see him pluck at his beard from envy.

So now Della's beautiful hair fell about her rippling and shining like a cascade of brown waters. It reached below her knee and made itself almost a garment for her. And then she did it up again nervously and quickly. Once she faltered for a minute and stood still while a tear or two splashed on the worn red carpet.

On went her old brown jacket; on went her old brown hat. With a whirl of skirts and with the brilliant sparkle still in her eyes, she fluttered out the door and down the stairs to the street.

Where she stopped the sign read: "Mne. Sofronie. Hair Goods of All Kinds." One flight up Della ran, and collected herself, panting. Madame, large, too white, chilly, hardly looked the "Sofronie."

"Will you buy my hair?" asked Della.

"I buy hair," said Madame. "Take yer hat off and let's have a sight at the looks of it."

Down rippled the brown cascade.

"Twenty dollars," said Madame, lifting the mass with a practised hand.

"Give it to me quick," said Della.

Oh, and the next two hours tripped by on rosy wings. Forget the hashed metaphor. She was ransacking the stores for Jim's present.

She found it at last. It surely had been made for Jim and no one else. There was no other like it in any of the stores, and she had turned all of them inside out. It was a platinum fob chain simple and chaste in design, properly proclaiming its value by substance alone and not by meretricious ornamentation–as all good things should do. It was even worthy of The Watch. As soon as she saw it she knew that it must be Jim's. It was like him. Quietness and value–the description applied to both. Twenty-one dollars they took from her for it, and she hurried home with the 87 cents. With that chain on his watch Jim might be properly anxious about the time in any company. Grand as the watch was, he sometimes looked at it on the sly on account of the old leather strap that he used in place of a chain.

When Della reached home her intoxication gave way a little to prudence and reason. She got out her curling irons and lighted the gas and went to work repairing the ravages made by generosity added to love. Which is always a tremendous task, dear friends–a mammoth task.

Within forty minutes her head was covered with tiny, close-lying curls that made her look wonderfully like a truant schoolboy. She looked at her reflection in the mirror long, carefully, and critically.

"If Jim doesn't kill me," she said to herself, "before he takes a second look at me, he'll say I look like a Coney Island chorus girl. But what could I do–oh! what could I do with a dollar and eighty- seven cents?"

At 7 o'clock the coffee was made and the frying-pan was on the back of the stove hot and ready to cook the chops.

Jim was never late. Della doubled the fob chain in her hand and sat on the corner of the table near the door that he always entered. Then she heard his step on the stair away down on the first flight, and she turned white for just a moment. She had a habit for saying little silent prayer about the simplest everyday things, and now she whispered: "Please God, make him think I am still pretty."

The door opened and Jim stepped in and closed it. He looked thin and very serious. Poor fellow, he was only twenty-two–and to be burdened with a family! He needed a new overcoat and he was without gloves.

Jim stopped inside the door, as immovable as a setter at the scent of quail. His eyes were fixed upon Della, and there was an expression in them that she could not read, and it terrified her. It was not anger, nor surprise, nor disapproval, nor horror, nor any of the sentiments that she had been prepared for. He simply stared at her fixedly with that peculiar expression on his face.

Della wriggled off the table and went for him.

"Jim, darling," she cried, "don't look at me that way. I had my hair cut off and sold because I couldn't have lived through Christmas without giving you a present. It'll grow out again–you won't mind, will you? I just had to do it. My hair grows awfully fast. Say `Merry Christmas!' Jim, and let's be happy. You don't know what a nice–what a beautiful, nice gift I've got for you."

"You've cut off your hair?" asked Jim, laboriously, as if he had not arrived at that patent fact yet even after the hardest mental labor.

"Cut it off and sold it," said Della. "Don't you like me just as well, anyhow? I'm me without my hair, ain't I?"

Jim looked about the room curiously.

"You say your hair is gone?" he said, with an air almost of idiocy.

"You needn't look for it," said Della. "It's sold, I tell you–sold and gone, too. It's Christmas Eve, boy. Be good to me, for it went for you. Maybe the hairs of my head were numbered," she went on with sudden serious sweetness, "but nobody could ever count my love for you. Shall I put the chops on, Jim?"

Out of his trance Jim seemed quickly to wake. He enfolded his Della. For ten seconds let us regard with discreet scrutiny some inconsequential object in the other direction. Eight dollars a week or a million a year–what is the difference? A mathematician or a wit would give you the wrong answer. The magi brought valuable gifts, but that was not among them. This dark assertion will be illuminated later on.

Jim drew a package from his overcoat pocket and threw it upon the table.

"Don't make any mistake, Dell," he said, "about me. I don't think there's anything in the way of a haircut or a shave or a shampoo that could make me like my girl any less. But if you'll unwrap that package you may see why you had me going a while at first."

White fingers and nimble tore at the string and paper. And then an ecstatic scream of joy; and then, alas! a quick feminine change to hysterical tears and wails, necessitating the immediate employment of all the comforting powers of the lord of the flat.

For there lay The Combs–the set of combs, side and back, that Della had worshipped long in a Broadway window. Beautiful combs, pure tortoise shell, with jewelled rims–just the shade to wear in the beautiful vanished hair. They were expensive combs, she knew, and her heart had simply craved and yearned over them without the least hope of possession. And now, they were hers, but the tresses that should have adorned the coveted adornments were gone.

But she hugged them to her bosom, and at length she was able to look up with dim eyes and a smile and say: "My hair grows so fast, Jim!"

And them Della leaped up like a little singed cat and cried, "Oh, oh!"

Jim had not yet seen his beautiful present. She held it out to him eagerly upon her open palm. The dull precious metal seemed to flash with a reflection of her bright and ardent spirit.

"Isn't it a dandy, Jim? I hunted all over town to find it. You'll have to look at the time a hundred times a day now. Give me your watch. I want to see how it looks on it."

Instead of obeying, Jim tumbled down on the couch and put his hands under the back of his head and smiled.

"Dell," said he, "let's put our Christmas presents away and keep 'em a while. They're too nice to use just at present. I sold the watch to get the money to buy your combs. And now suppose you put the chops on."

The magi, as you know, were wise men–wonderfully wise men–who brought gifts to the Babe in the manger. They invented the art of giving Christmas presents. Being wise, their gifts were no doubt wise ones, possibly bearing the privilege of exchange in case of duplication. And here I have lamely related to you the uneventful chronicle of two foolish children in a flat who most unwisely sacrificed for each other the greatest treasures of their house. But in a last word to the wise of these days let it be said that of all who give gifts these two were the wisest. Of all who give and receive gifts, such as they are wisest. Everywhere they are wisest. They are the magi.

Lesson 32

- Read this bio of O. Henry, the author of the story you read in the previous lesson.

O. Henry was born William Sidney Porter on September 11, 1862. He was born in Greensboro, North Carolina. His mother died when he was only three, and his father was a medical doctor. He was raised by his aunt and grandmother.

In 1896, Porter was accused of embezzlement and he fled the country to Honduras. He came back to the US when he learned his wife was dying, and there he surrendered to police. He was convicted and sent to jail in 1898.

In order to support his daughter while in prison, he began writing short stories. Not wanting his readers to know he was a prisoner, he used the pen name Olivier Henry, shortening it to O. Henry after only one story.

O. Henry was released from prison 2 years early for good behavior, and he moved to New York, New York. He wrote a story a week for various publications, all in all writing nearly 600 stories about life in America. But he struggled with alcoholism, eventually dying of cirrhosis of the liver in 1910 at age 47.

- Read this guide to the story.

Plot Summary

On Christmas Eve, Della had scraped together all she could, but only had $1.87 with which to buy her husband James a Christmas gift.

She and her husband only had two prized possessions: her beautiful, long hair, and his gold pocket watch given to him by his father. Della went down the street to Madame Sofronie's shop and sold her hair for $20. She found and bought a platinum chain for her husband's gold watch.

When Jim got home, he walked in and stared at his wife. Worried that he didn't like the way she looked with short hair, Della explained that she couldn't bear not to get him a Christmas gift. He hugged her and tossed a package onto the table. Della opened the present and immediately understood his stares. Her husband had bought a set of expensive combs she had been wishing for. Della reassured her husband that her hair would grow back quickly.

When Della gave her present to Jim, the reader is told what they've already suspected: he had sold his pocket watch to buy the combs. But like the magi of old, the two had given each other the perfect gifts. By sacrificing for each other, their presents were worth more than just a chain and some combs.

Setting
The story is set in New York City (Coney Island, a famous amusement park in Brooklyn, is mentioned in the story). A simple apartment and a hair shop down the street fill out the setting.

Characters
Della Young: A woman with beautiful, long hair which she cuts and sells to buy a Christmas gift for her husband.

James Dillingham Young: Della's husband who sells his gold watch to buy a gift for Della.

Madame Sofronie: Shop owner who buys Della's hair.

Type of Work and Year of Publication
"The Gift of the Magi" is a short story, written by O. Henry. It was published in a New York City newspaper in 1905.

The Three Magi
The Magi were the three wise men from the east who traveled to Bethlehem, following a bright star, to present gifts to the infant Jesus, famously bringing gifts of gold, frankincense, and myrrh (see Matthew 2:11).

The Number Three
There are lots of "3s" in the story. Here are just some examples. Can you find others?

- The story has three characters.
- In the first paragraph, Della counts her money three times.
- In the second paragraph, we find the sentence: "Life is made up of sobs, sniffles, and smiles.
- Della as speaks with "sudden serious sweetness" (this is a great example of **alliteration**).
- There are three valuable things in the story: Jim's watch, Della's hair, and Jim and Della's love.

Theme: Love
The theme of the story is the love Della and Jim show in their sacrificial gifts for one another.

Climax
The climax occurs when the gifts are opened.

Lesson 34 (no reading for Lesson 33)

- Read this bio of Edgar Allan Poe (1809-1849).

Edgar Allan Poe was born in Boston, Massachusetts on January 19, 1809. Both of his parents died before his third birthday, so he was raised as a foster child. His foster parents sent him to good schools, but when he ran up gambling debts less than a year into his college education, his foster father refused to pay the debts and Poe was forced to leave his university.

Poe went on to enlist in the army, beginning to write short stories and poems as time traveled on. In 1835, he became the editor of a magazine and then went on to edit several literary journals. These were the years where he most strongly established himself as a short story writer and poet. He married his thirteen year old cousin, but when she died in 1847, the depression and alcoholism he had been struggling with became even worse. On October 3, 1849, he was found partially conscious. He died four days later. His official cause of death was "acute congestion of the brain," but later study found that he might have had rabies.

Poe's mark on American literature can't be overlooked. He is considered one of the founders of both horror and detective fiction. He paved the way for the modern short story. And he was one of the first American writers to become a major player on the world stage of literature.

- Read the short story, "The Cask of Amontillado" **Warning:** This is edited. You don't want to read the gross ending. He kills his friend. He builds him a tomb out of bricks (masonry).

The Cask of Amontillado
Edgar Allan Poe

THE thousand injuries of Fortunato I had borne as I best could, but when he ventured upon insult, I vowed revenge. You, who so well know the nature of my soul, will not suppose, however, that I gave utterance to a threat. At length I would be avenged; this was a point definitively settled -- but the very definitiveness with which it was resolved precluded the idea of risk. I must not only punish, but punish with impunity. A wrong is unredressed when retribution overtakes its redresser. It is equally unredressed when the avenger fails to make himself felt as such to him who has done the wrong.

It must be understood that neither by word nor deed had I given Fortunato cause to doubt my good will. I continued as was my wont, to smile in his face, and he did not perceive that my smile now was at the thought of his immolation.

He had a weak point -- this Fortunato -- although in other regards he was a man to be respected and even feared. He prided himself on his connoisseurship in wine. Few Italians have the true virtuoso spirit. For the most part their enthusiasm is adopted to suit the time and opportunity to practise imposture upon the British and

Austrian millionaires. In painting and gemmary, Fortunato, like his countrymen , was a quack, but in the matter of old wines he was sincere. In this respect I did not differ from him materially; I was skilful in the Italian vintages myself, and bought largely whenever I could.

It was about dusk, one evening during the supreme madness of the carnival season, that I encountered my friend. He accosted me with excessive warmth, for he had been drinking much. The man wore motley. He had on a tight-fitting parti-striped dress and his head was surmounted by the conical cap and bells. I was so pleased to see him, that I thought I should never have done wringing his hand.

I said to him – "My dear Fortunato, you are luckily met. How remarkably well you are looking to-day! But I have received a pipe of what passes for Amontillado, and I have my doubts."

"How?" said he, "Amontillado? A pipe? Impossible? And in the middle of the carnival?"

"I have my doubts," I replied; "and I was silly enough to pay the full Amontillado price without consulting you in the matter. You were not to be found, and I was fearful of losing a bargain."

"Amontillado!"

"I have my doubts."

"Amontillado!"

"And I must satisfy them."

"Amontillado!"

"As you are engaged, I am on my way to Luchesi. If any one has a critical turn, it is he. He will tell me"–

"Luchesi cannot tell Amontillado from Sherry."

"And yet some fools will have it that his taste is a match for your own."

"Come let us go."

"Whither?"

"To your vaults."

"My friend, no; I will not impose upon your good nature. I perceive you have an engagement. Luchesi"—

"I have no engagement; come."

"My friend, no. It is not the engagement, but the severe cold with which I perceive you are afflicted. The vaults are insufferably damp. They are encrusted with nitre."

"Let us go, nevertheless. The cold is merely nothing. Amontillado! You have been imposed upon; and as for Luchesi, he cannot distinguish Sherry from Amontillado."

Thus speaking, Fortunato possessed himself of my arm. Putting on a mask of black silk and drawing a roquelaire closely about my person, I suffered him to hurry me to my palazzo.

There were no attendants at home; they had absconded to make merry in honour of the time. I had told them that I should not return until the morning and had given them explicit orders not to stir from the house. These orders were sufficient, I well knew, to insure their immediate disappearance, one and all, as soon as my back was turned.

I took from their sconces two flambeaux, and giving one to Fortunato bowed him through several suites of rooms to the archway that led into the vaults. I passed down a long and winding staircase, requesting him to be cautious as he followed. We came at length to the foot of the descent, and stood together on the damp ground of the catacombs of the Montresors.

The gait of my friend was unsteady, and the bells upon his cap jingled as he strode.

"The pipe," said he.

"It is farther on," said I; "but observe the white webwork which gleams from these cavern walls."

He turned towards me and looked into my eyes with two filmy orbs that distilled the rheum of intoxication.

"Nitre?" he asked, at length.

"Nitre," I replied. "How long have you had that cough!"

"Ugh! ugh! ugh! -- ugh! ugh! ugh! -- ugh! ugh! ugh! -- ugh! ugh! ugh! -- ugh! ugh! ugh!"

My poor friend found it impossible to reply for many minutes.

"It is nothing," he said, at last.

"Come," I said, with decision, "we will go back; your health is precious. You are rich, respected, admired, beloved; you are happy as once I was. You are a man to be missed. For me it is no matter. We will go back; you will be ill and I cannot be responsible. Besides, there is Luchesi"—

"Enough," he said; "the cough is a mere nothing; it will not kill me. I shall not die of a cough."

"True -- true," I replied; "and, indeed, I had no intention of alarming you unnecessarily -- but you should use all proper caution. A draught of this Medoc will defend us from the damps."

Here I knocked off the neck of a bottle which I drew from a long row of its fellows that lay upon the mould.

"Drink," I said, presenting him the wine.

He raised it to his lips with a leer. He paused and nodded to me familiarly, while his bells jingled.

“I drink,” he said, “to the buried that repose around us.”

“And I to your long life.”

He again took my arm and we proceeded.

“These vaults," he said, “are extensive.”

“The Montresors,” I replied, “were a great numerous family.”

“I forget your arms.”

“A huge human foot d’or, in a field azure; the foot crushes a serpent rampant whose fangs are imbedded in the heel.”

“And the motto?”

“Nemo me impune lacessit.”

“Good!” he said.

The wine sparkled in his eyes and the bells jingled. My own fancy grew warm with the Medoc. We had passed through walls of piled bones, with casks and puncheons intermingling, into the inmost recesses of the catacombs. I paused again, and this time I made bold to seize Fortunato by an arm above the elbow.

“The nitre!” I said: “see it increases. It hangs like moss upon the vaults. We are below the river’s bed. The drops of moisture trickle among the bones. Come, we will go back ere it is too late. Your cough”—

“It is nothing” he said; “let us go on. But first, another draught of the Medoc.”

I broke and reached him a flagon of De Grave. He emptied it at a breath. His eyes flashed with a fierce light. He laughed and threw the bottle upwards with a gesticulation I did not understand.

I looked at him in surprise. He repeated the movement -- a grotesque one.

"You do not comprehend?" he said.

"Not I," I replied.

"Then you are not of the brotherhood."

"How?"

"You are not of the masons."

"Yes, yes," I said "yes! yes."

"You? Impossible! A mason?"

"A mason," I replied.

"A sign," he said.

"It is this," I answered, producing a trowel from beneath the folds of my roquelaire.

"You jest," he exclaimed, recoiling a few paces. "But let us proceed to the Amontillado."

"Be it so," I said, replacing the tool beneath the cloak, and again offering him my arm. He leaned upon it heavily. We continued our route in search of the Amontillado. We passed through a range of low arches, descended, passed on, and descending again, arrived at a deep crypt, in which the foulness of the air caused our flambeaux rather to glow than flame.

- NOTE: Poe is very famous, but very dark. I don't recommend any further reading of his works, but you should know who he is and the type of literature he wrote. Do you think his childhood influenced his writing?

Lesson 35

- Read this guide to the story.

Setting
It is near dusk during carnival season in Europe. The cheerful atmosphere of the carnival activities is contrasted drastically when the setting shifts to the dark, descending vaults under Montressor's home.

Characters
The two main characters in the story are Montressor, the narrator of the story who wants revenge upon his friend Fortunato for insulting him. Fortunato has a fancy taste for wine and is drunk throughout the story. Montressor uses his drunkenness and his taste for wine to his own advantage.

Point of View
The story is written from the perspective of Montressor. In true Poe style, the reader is asked to enter into the mind of a disturbing individual, thus increasing the shock and horror once the murder takes place.

Style
There are many examples of irony throughout the story. A few include: the name of the character "Fortunato" who meets an *un*fortunate end; the fact that Fortunato is dressed in a jester costume for carnival season and is then made a fool; Montresor toasting Fortunato's long life; Fortunato saying, "I will not die of a cough."

Theme
There are many dark themes in the story. Alongside the obvious theme of revenge, there are also themes of selfishness, deceit, hatred, pride, and more.

Lesson 36

- You're going to be reading Guy de Maupassant's short story "The Necklace" (or "La parure" in its original language). It was first published in a Paris newspaper in February of 1884. The story is Maupassant's most widely read story, partly because of its "whip-crack" or "O. Henry" ending. (O. Henry wrote the story from a few lessons ago, "The Gift of the Magi.") This type of ending is one where a plot twist completely changes the story right at the end. Most of Maupassant's other works don't include this device. Though it's unknown where he got the idea for "The Necklace," his mentor and friend, Gustave Flaubert, wrote a novel called *Madame Bovary* which has some similarities. Both Madame Bovary and Maupassant's character Mathidle Loisel try to escape their social situation.
- What are some things wrong with her attitude as shown in the 5th paragraph?
- **Note**: you might want to read the questions in your Language Arts workbook or on the site before you start to read the story so you can answer them as you read. They are a graded assignment.

The Necklace
Guy de Maupassant (1850-1893)

She was one of those pretty and charming girls, born by a blunder of destiny in a family of employees. She had no dowry, no expectations, no means of being known, understood, loved, married by a man rich and distinguished; and she let them make a match for her with a little clerk in the Department of Education.

She was simple because she could not be adorned; but she was as unhappy as though kept out of her own class; for women have no caste and no descent, their beauty, their grace, and their charm serving them instead of birth and fortune. Their native keenness, their instinctive elegance, their flexibility of mind, and their only hierarchy; and these make the daughters of the people the equals of the most lofty dames.

She suffered intensely, feeling herself born for every delicacy and every luxury. She suffered from the poverty of her dwelling, from the worn walls, the abraded chairs, the ugliness of the stuffs. All these things, which another woman of her caste would not even have noticed, tortured her and made her indignant. The sight of the little girl from Brittany who did her humble housework awoke in her desolated regrets and distracted dreams. She let her mind dwell on the quiet vestibules, hung with Oriental tapestries, lighted by tall lamps of bronze, and on the two tall footmen in knee breeches who dozed in the large armchairs, made drowsy by the heat of the furnace. She let her mind dwell on the large parlors, decked with old silk, with their delicate furniture, supporting precious bric-a-brac, and on the coquettish little rooms, perfumed, prepared for the five o'clock chat with the most intimate friends, men well known and sought after, whose attentions all women envied and desired.

When she sat down to dine, before a tablecloth three days old, in front of her husband, who lifted the cover of the tureen, declaring with an air of satisfaction, "Ah, the good *pot-au-feu.* I don't know anything better than that," she was thinking of delicate repasts, with glittering silver, with tapestries peopling the walls with ancient figures and with strange birds in a fairy-like forest; she was thinking of exquisite dishes, served in marvelous platters, of compliment whispered and heard with a sphinx-like smile, while she was eating the rosy flesh of a trout or the wings of a quail.

She had no dresses, no jewelry, nothing. And she loved nothing else; she felt herself made for that only. She would so much have liked to please, to be envied, to be seductive and sought after.

She had a rich friend, comrade of her convent days, whom she did not want to go and see any more, so much did she suffer as she came away. And she wept all day long, from chagrin, from regret, from despair, and from distress.

***

But one evening her husband came in with a proud air, holding in his hand a large envelope.

"There," said he, "there's something for you."

She quickly tore the paper and took out of it a printed card which bore these words:—

"The Minister of Education and Mme. Georges Rampouneau beg M. and Mme. Loisel to do them the honor to pass the evening with them at the palace of the Ministry, on Monday, January 18."

Instead of being delighted, as her husband had hoped, she threw the invitation on the table with annoyance, murmuring—

"What do you want me to do with that?"

"But, my dear, I thought you would be pleased. You never go out, and here's a chance, a fine one. I had the hardest work to get it. Everybody is after them; they are greatly sought for and not many are given to the clerks. You will see there all the official world."

She looked at him with an irritated eye and she declared with impatience:—

"What do you want me to put on my back to go there?"

He had not thought of that; he hesitated:—

"But the dress in which you go to the theater. That looks very well to me—"

He shut up, astonished and distracted at seeing that his wife was weeping. Two big tears were descending slowly from the corners of the eyes to the corners of the mouth. He stuttered:—

"What's the matter? What's the matter?"

But by a violent effort she had conquered her trouble, and she replied in a calm voice as she wiped her damp cheeks:—

"Nothing. Only I have no clothes, and in consequence I cannot go to this party. Give your card to some colleague whose wife has a better outfit than I."

He was disconsolate. He began again:—

"See here, Mathilde, how much would this cost, a proper dress, which would do on other occasions; something very simple?"

She reflected a few seconds, going over her calculations, and thinking also of the sum which she might ask without meeting an immediate refusal and a frightened exclamation from the frugal clerk.

At last, she answered hesitatingly:—

"I don't know exactly, but it seems to me that with four hundred francs I might do it."

He grew a little pale, for he was reserving just that sum to buy a gun and treat himself to a little shooting, the next summer, on the plain of Nanterre, with some friends who used to shoot larks there on Sundays.

But he said:—

"All right. I will give you four hundred francs. But take care to have a pretty dress."

***

The day of the party drew near, and Mme. Loisel seemed sad, restless, anxious. Yet her dress was ready. One evening her husband said to her:—

"What's the matter? Come now, You've been quite queer these last three days."

And she answered:—

"It annoys me not to have a jewel, not a single stone, to put on. I shall look like distress. I would almost rather not go to this party."

He answered:—

"You will wear some natural flowers. They are very stylish this time of the year. For ten francs you will have two or three magnificent roses."

But she was not convinced.

"No; there's nothing more humiliating than to look poor among of a lot of rich women."

But her husband cried:—

"What a goose you are! Go find your friend, Mme. Forester, and ask her to lend you some jewelry. You know her well enough to do that."

She gave a cry of joy:—

"That's true. I had not thought of it."

The next day she went to her friend's and told her about her distress.

Mme. Forester went to her mirrored wardrobe, took out a large casket, brought it, opened it, and said to Mme. Loisel:—

"Choose, my dear."

She saw at first bracelets, then a necklace of pearls, then a Venetian cross of gold set with precious stones of an admirable workmanship. She tried on the ornaments before the glass, hesitated, and could not decide to take them off and to give them up. She kept on asking:—

"You haven't anything else/"

"Yes, yes. Look. I do not know what will happen to please you."

All at once she discovered, in a box of black satin, a superb necklace of diamonds, and her heart began to beat with boundless desire. Her hands trembled in taking it up. She fastened it round her throat, on her high dress, and remained in ecstasy before herself.

Then, she asked, hesitating, full of anxiety:—

"Can you lend me this, only this?"

"Yes, yes, certainly."

She sprang to her friend's neck, kissed her with ardor, and then escaped with her treasure.

***

The day of the party arrived. Mme. Loisel was a success. She was the prettiest of them all, elegant, gracious, smiling, and mad with joy. All the men were looking at her, inquiring her name, asking to be introduced. All the attaches of the Cabinet wanted to dance with her. The Minister took notice of her.

She danced with delight, with passion, intoxicated with pleasure, thinking of nothing, in the triumph of her beauty, in the glory of her success, in a sort of cloud of happiness made up of all these tributes, of all the admirations, of all these awakened desires, of this victory so complete and so sweet to a woman's heart.

She went away about four in the morning. Since midnight—her husband has been dozing in a little anteroom with three other men whose wives were having a good time.

He threw over her shoulders the wraps he had brought to go home in, modest garments of every-day life, the poverty of which was out of keeping with the elegance of the ball dress. She felt this, and wanted to fly so as not to be noticed by the other women, who were wrapping themselves up in rich furs.

Loisel kept her back—

"Wait a minute; you will catch cold outside; I'll call a cab."

But she did not listen to him, and went downstairs rapidly. When they were in the street, they could not find a carriage, and they set out in search of one, hailing the drivers whom they saw passing in the distance.

They went down toward the Seine, disgusted, shivering. Finally, they found on the Quai one of those old night-hawk cabs which one sees in Paris only after night has fallen, as though they are ashamed of their misery in the daytime.

It brought them to their door, rue des Martyrs; and they went up their own stairs sadly. For her it was finished. And he was thinking that he would have to be at the Ministry at ten o'clock.

She took off the wraps with which she had covered her shoulders, before the mirror, so as to see herself once more in her glory. But suddenly she gave a cry. She no longer had the necklace around her throat!

Her husband, half undressed already, asked—

"What is the matter with you?"

She turned to him, terror-stricken:—

"I—I—I have not Mme. Forester's diamond necklace!"

He jumped up, frightened—

"What? How? It is not possible!"

And they searched in the folds of the dress, in the folds of the wrap, in the pockets, everywhere. They did not find it.

He asked:—

"Are you sure you still had it when you left the ball?"

"Yes, I touched it in the vestibule of the Ministry."

"But if you had lost it in the street, we should have heard it fall. It must be in the cab."

"Yes. That is probable. Did you take the number?"

"No. And you—you did not even look at it?"

"No."

They gazed at each other, crushed. At last Loisel dressed himself again.

"I'm going," he said, "back the whole distance we came on foot, to see if I cannot find it."

And he went out. She stayed there, in her ball dress, without strength to go to bed, overwhelmed, on a chair, without a fire, without a thought.

Her husband came back about seven o'clock. He had found nothing.

Then he went to police headquarters, to the newspapers to offer a reward, to the cab company; he did everything, in fact, that a trace of hope could urge him to.

She waited all day, in the same dazed state in face of this horrible disaster.

Loisel came back in the evening, with his face worn and white; he had discovered nothing.

"You must write to your friend," he said, "that you have broken the clasp of her necklace and that you are having it repaired. That will give us time to turn around."

She wrote as he dictated.

***

At the end of a week they had lost all hope. And Loisel, aged by five years, declared:—

"We must see how we can replace those jewels."

The next day they took the case which had held them to the jeweler whose name was in the cover. He consulted his books.

"It was not I, madam, who sold this necklace. I only supplied the case."

Then they went from jeweler to jeweler, looking for a necklace like the other, consulting their memory,—sick both of them with grief and anxiety.

In a shop in the Palais Royal, they found a diamond necklace that seemed to them absolutely like the one they were seeking. It was priced forty thousand francs. They could have it for thirty-six.

They begged the jeweler not to sell it for three days. And they made a bargain that he should take it back for thirty-four thousand, if the first was found before the end of February.

Loisel possessed eighteen thousand francs which his father had left him. He had to borrow the remainder.

He borrowed, asking a thousand francs from one, five hundred from another, five here, three louis there. He gave promissory notes, made ruinous agreements, dealt with usurers, with all kinds of lenders. He compromised the end of his life, risked his signature without even knowing whether it could be honored; and, frightened by all the anguish of the future, by the black misery which was about to settle down on him, by the perspective of all sorts of physical deprivations and of all sorts of moral tortures, he went to buy the new diamond necklace, laying down on the jeweler's counter thirty-six thousand francs.

When Mme. Loisel took back the necklace to Mme. Forester, the latter said, with an irritated air:—

"You ought to have brought it back sooner, for I might have needed it."

She did not open the case, which her friend had been fearing. If she had noticed the substitution, what would she have thought? What would she have said? Might she not have been taken for a thief?

***

Mme. Loisel learned the horrible life of the needy. She made the best of it, moreover, frankly, heroically. The frightful debt must be paid. She would pay it. They dismissed the servant; they changed their rooms; they took an attic under the roof.

She learned the rough work of the household, the odious labors of the kitchen. She washed the dishes, wearing out her pink nails on the greasy pots and the bottoms of the pans. She washed the dirty linen, the shirts and the towels, which she dried on a rope; she carried down the garbage to the street every morning, and she carried up the water, pausing for breath on every floor. And, dressed like a woman of the people, she went to the fruiterer, the grocer, the butcher, a basket on her arm, bargaining, insulted, fighting for her wretched money, sou by sou.

Every month they had to pay notes, to renew others to gain time.

The husband worked in the evening keeping up the books of a shopkeeper, and at night often he did copying at five sous the page.

And this life lasted ten years.

At the end of ten years they had paid everything back, everything, with the rates of usury and all the accumulation of heaped-up interest.

Mme. Loisel seemed aged now. She had become the robust woman, hard and rough, of a poor household. Badly combed, with her skirts awry and her hands red, her voice was loud, and she washed the floor with splashing water.

But sometimes, when her husband was at the office, she sat down by the window and she thought of that evening long ago, of that ball, where she had been so beautiful and so admired.

What would have happened if she had not lost that necklace? Who knows? Who knows? How singular life is, how changeable! What a little thing it takes to save you or to lose you.

Then, one Sunday, as she was taking a turn in the Champs Elysées, as a recreation after the labors of the week, she perceived suddenly a woman walking with a child. It was Mme. Forester, still young, still beautiful, still seductive.

Mme. Loisel felt moved. Should she speak to her? Yes, certainly. And now that she had paid up, she would tell her all. Why not?

She drew near.

"Good morning, Jeanne."

The other did not recognize her, astonished to be hailed thus familiarly by this woman of the people. She hesitated—

"But—madam—I don't know—are you not making a mistake?"

"No, I am Mathilde Loisel."

Her friend gave a cry—

"Oh!—My poor Mathilde, how you are changed."

"Yes, I have had hard days since I saw you, and many troubles,—and that because of you."

"Of me?—How so?"

"You remember that diamond necklace that you lent me to go to the ball at the Ministry?"

"Yes. And then?"

"Well, I lost it."

"How can that be?—since you brought it back to me?"

"I brought you back another just like it. And now for ten years we have been paying for it. You will understand that it was not easy for us, who had nothing. At last, it is done, and I am mighty glad."

Mme. Forester had guessed.

"You say that you bought a diamond necklace to replace mine?"

"Yes. You did not notice it, even, did you? They were exactly alike?"

And she smiled with proud and naïve joy.

Mme. Forester, much moved, took her by both hands:—

"Oh my poor Mathilde. But mine were false. At most they were worth five hundred francs!"

Lesson 38 (no reading for Lesson 37)

- Read "The Ransom of Red Chief" by O. Henry.

IT LOOKED like a good thing: but wait till I tell you. We were down South, in Alabama -- Bill Driscoll and myself -- when this kidnapping idea struck us. It was, as Bill afterward expressed it, "during a moment of temporary mental apparition"; but we didn't find that out till later.

There was a town down there, as flat as a flannel-cake, and called Summit, of course. It contained inhabitants of as undeleterious and self-satisfied a class of peasantry as ever clustered around a Maypole.

Bill and me had a joint capital of about six hundred dollars, and we needed just two thousand dollars more to pull off a fraudulent town-lot scheme in Western Illinois with. We talked it over on the front steps of the hotel. Philoprogenitiveness, says we, is strong in semi-rural communities; therefore and for other reasons, a kidnapping project ought to do better there than in the radius of newspapers that send reporters out in plain clothes to stir up talk about such things. We knew that Summit couldn't get after us with anything stronger than constables and maybe some lackadaisical bloodhounds and a diatribe or two in the Weekly Farmers' Budget. So, it looked good.

We selected for our victim the only child of a prominent citizen named Ebenezer Dorset. The father was respectable and tight, a mortgage fancier and a stern, upright collection-plate passer and forecloser. The kid was a boy of ten, with bas-relief freckles, and hair the colour of the cover of the magazine you buy at the news-stand when you want to catch a train. Bill and me figured that Ebenezer would melt down for a ransom of two thousand dollars to a cent. But wait till I tell you.

About two miles from Summit was a little mountain, covered with a dense cedar brake. On the rear elevation of this mountain was a cave. There we stored provisions. One evening after sundown, we drove in a buggy past old Dorset's house. The kid was in the street, throwing rocks at a kitten on the opposite fence. "Hey, little boy!" says Bill, "would you like to have a bag of candy and a nice ride?" The boy catches Bill neatly in the eye with a piece of brick.

"That will cost the old man an extra five hundred dollars," says Bill, climbing over the wheel.

That boy put up a fight like a welter-weight cinnamon bear; but, at last, we got him down in the bottom of the buggy and drove away. We took him up to the cave and I hitched the horse in the cedar brake. After dark I drove the buggy to the little village, three miles away, where we had hired it, and walked back to the mountain. Bill was pasting court-plaster over the scratches and bruises on his features. There was a burning behind the big rock at the entrance of the cave, and the boy was watching a pot of boiling coffee, with two buzzard tailfeathers stuck in his red hair. He points a stick at me when I come up, and says:

"Ha! cursed paleface, do you dare to enter the camp of Red Chief, the terror of the plains?"

"He's all right now," says Bill, rolling up his trousers and examining some bruises on his shins. "We're playing Indian. We're making Buffalo Bill's show look like magic-lantern views of Palestine in the town hall. I'm Old Hank, the Trapper, Red Chief's captive, and I'm to be scalped at daybreak. By Geronimo! that kid can kick hard."

Yes, sir, that boy seemed to be having the time of his life. The fun of camping out in a cave had made him forget that he was a captive, himself. He immediately christened me Snake-eye, the Spy, and announced that, when his braves returned from the warpath, I was to be broiled at the stake at the rising of the sun.

Then we had supper; and he filled his mouth full of bacon and bread and gravy, and began to talk. He made a during-dinner speech something like this:

"I like this fine. I never camped out before; but I had a pet 'possum once, and I was nine last birthday. I hate to go to school. Rats ate up sixteen of Jimmy Talbot's aunt's speckled hen's eggs. Are there any real Indians in these woods? I want some more gravy. Does the trees moving make the wind blow? We had five puppies. What makes your nose so red, Hank? My father has lots of money. Are the stars hot? I whipped Ed Walker twice, Saturday. I don't like girls. You dassent catch toads unless with a string. Do oxen make any noise? Why are oranges round? Have you got beds to sleep on in this cave? Amos Murray has got Six toes. A parrot can talk, but a monkey or a fish can't. How many does it take to make twelve?"

Every few minutes he would remember that he was a pesky redskin, and pick up his stick rifle and tiptoe to the mouth of the cave to rubber for the scouts of the hated paleface. Now and then he would let out a war-whoop that made Old Hank the Trapper shiver. That boy had Bill terrorized from the start.

"Red Chief," says I to the kid, "would you like to go home?"

"Aw, what for?" says he. "I don't have any fun at home. I hate to go to school. I like to camp out. You won't take me back home again, Snake-eye, will you?"

"Not right away," says I. "We'll stay here in the cave a while."

"All right!" says he. "That'll be fine. I never had such fun in all my life."

We went to bed about eleven o'clock. We spread down some wide blankets and quilts and put Red Chief between us. We weren't afraid he'd run away. He kept us awake for three hours, jumping up and reaching for his rifle and screeching: "Hist! pard," in mine and Bill's ears, as the fancied crackle of a twig or the rustle of a leaf revealed to his young imagination the stealthy approach of the outlaw band. At last, I fell into a troubled sleep, and dreamed that I had been kidnapped and chained to a tree by a ferocious pirate with red hair.

Just at daybreak, I was awakened by a series of awful screams from Bill. They weren't yells, or howls, or shouts, or whoops, or yalps, such as you'd expect from a manly set of vocal organs -- they were simply indecent, terrifying, humiliating screams, such as women emit when they see ghosts or caterpillars. It's an awful thing to hear a strong, desperate, fat man scream incontinently in a cave at daybreak. I jumped up to see what the matter was. Red Chief was sitting on Bill's chest, with one hand twined in Bill's hair. In the other he had the sharp case-knife we used for slicing bacon; and he was industriously and realistically trying to take Bill's scalp, according to the sentence that had been pronounced upon him the evening before.

I got the knife away from the kid and made him lie down again. But, from that moment, Bill's spirit was broken. He laid down on his side of the bed, but he never closed an eye again in sleep as long as that boy was with us. I dozed off for a while, but along toward sun-up I remembered that Red Chief had said I was to be burned at the stake at the rising of the sun. I wasn't nervous or afraid; but I sat up and lit my pipe and leaned against a rock.

"What you getting up so soon for, Sam?" asked Bill.

"Me?" says I. "Oh, I got a kind of a pain in my shoulder. I thought sitting up would rest it."

"You're a liar!" says Bill. "You're afraid. You was to be burned at sunrise, and you was afraid he'd do it. And he would, too, if he could find a match. Ain't it awful, Sam? Do you think anybody will pay out money to get a little imp like that back home?"

"Sure," said I. "A rowdy kid like that is just the kind that parents dote on. Now, you and the Chief get up and cook breakfast, while I go up on the top of this mountain and reconnoitre."

I went up on the peak of the little mountain and ran my eye over the contiguous vicinity. Over toward Summit I expected to see the sturdy yeomanry of the village armed with scythes and pitchforks beating the countryside for the dastardly kidnappers. But what I saw was a peaceful landscape dotted with one man ploughing with a dun mule. Nobody was dragging the creek; no couriers dashed hither and yon, bringing tidings of no news to the distracted parents. There was a sylvan attitude of somnolent sleepiness pervading that section of the external outward surface of Alabama that lay exposed to my view. "Perhaps," says I to myself, "it has not yet been discovered that the wolves have home away the tender lambkin from the fold. Heaven help the wolves!" says I, and I went down the mountain to breakfast.

When I got to the cave I found Bill backed up against the side of it, breathing hard, and the boy threatening to smash him with a rock half as big as a cocoanut.

"He put a red-hot boiled potato down my back," explained Bill, "and the mashed it with his foot; and I boxed his ears. Have you got a gun about you, Sam?"

I took the rock away from the boy and kind of patched up the argument. "I'll fix you," says the kid to Bill. "No man ever yet struck the Red Chief but what he got paid for it. You better beware!"

After breakfast the kid takes a piece of leather with strings wrapped around it out of his pocket and goes outside the cave unwinding it.

"What's he up to now?" says Bill, anxiously. "You don't think he'll run away, do you, Sam?"

"No fear of it," says I. "He don't seem to be much of a home body. But we've got to fix up some plan about the ransom. There don't seem to be much excitement around Summit on account of his disappearance; but maybe they haven't realized yet that he's gone. His folks may think he's spending the night with Aunt Jane or one of the neighbours. Anyhow, he'll be missed to-day. To-night we must get a message to his father demanding the two thousand dollars for his return."

Just then we heard a kind of war-whoop, such as David might have emitted when he knocked out the champion Goliath. It was a sling that Red Chief had pulled out of his pocket, and he was whirling it around his head.

I dodged, and heard a heavy thud and a kind of a sigh from Bill, like a horse gives out when you take his saddle off. A rock the size of an egg had caught Bill just behind his left ear. He loosened himself all over and fell in the fire across the frying pan of hot water for washing the dishes. I dragged him out and poured cold water on his head for half an hour.

By and by, Bill sits up and feels behind his ear and says: "Sam, do you know who my favourite Biblical character is?"

"Take it easy," says I. "You'll come to your senses presently."

"King Herod," says he. "You won't go away and leave me here alone, will you, Sam?"

I went out and caught that boy and shook him until his freckles rattled.

"If you don't behave," says I, "I'll take you straight home. Now, are you going to be good, or not?"

"I was only funning," says he sullenly. "I didn't mean to hurt Old Hank. But what did he hit me for? I'll behave, Snake-eye, if you won't send me home, and if you'll let me play the Black Scout to-day."

"I don't know the game," says I. "That's for you and Mr. Bill to decide. He's your playmate for the day. I'm going away for a while, on business. Now, you come in and make friends with him and say you are sorry for hurting him, or home you go, at once."

I made him and Bill shake hands, and then I took Bill aside and told him I was going to Poplar Cove, a little village three miles from the cave, and find out what I could about how the kidnapping had been regarded in Summit. Also, I thought it best to send a peremptory letter to old man Dorset that day, demanding the ransom and dictating how it should be paid.

"You know, Sam," says Bill, "I've stood by you without batting an eye in earthquakes, fire and flood -- in poker games, dynamite outrages, police raids, train robberies and cyclones. I never lost my nerve yet till we kidnapped that two-legged skyrocket of a kid. He's got me going. You won't leave me long with him, will you, Sam?"

"I'll be back some time this afternoon," says I. "You must keep the boy amused and quiet till I return. And now we'll write the letter to old Dorset."

Bill and I got paper and pencil and worked on the letter while Red Chief, with a blanket wrapped around him, strutted up and down, guarding the mouth of the cave. Bill begged me tearfully to make the ransom fifteen hundred dollars instead of two thousand. "I ain't attempting," says he, "to decry the celebrated moral aspect of parental affection, but we're dealing with humans, and it ain't human for anybody to give up two thousand dollars for that forty-pound chunk of freckled wildcat. I'm willing to take a chance at fifteen hundred dollars. You can charge the difference up to me."

So, to relieve Bill, I acceded, and we collaborated a letter that ran this way:

Ebenezer Dorset, Esq.:

We have your boy concealed in a place far from Summit. It is useless for you or the most skilful detectives to attempt to find him. Absolutely, the only terms on which you can have him restored to you are these: We demand fifteen hundred dollars in large bills for his return; the money to be left at midnight to-night at the same spot and in the same box as your reply -- as hereinafter described. If you agree to these terms, send your answer in writing by a solitary messenger to-night at half-past eight o'clock. After crossing Owl Creek, on the road to Poplar Cove, there are three large trees about a hundred yards apart, close to the fence of the wheat field on the right-hand side. At the bottom of the fence-post, opposite the third tree, will be found a small pasteboard box. The messenger will place the answer in this box and return immediately to Summit.

If you attempt any treachery or fail to comply with our demand as stated, you will never see your boy again.

If you pay the money as demanded, he will be returned to you safe and well within three hours. These terms are final, and if you do not accede to them no further communication will be attempted.

TWO DESPERATE MEN.

I addressed this letter to Dorset, and put it in my pocket. As I was about to start, the kid comes up to me and says:

"Aw, Snake-eye, you said I could play the Black Scout while you was gone."

"Play it, of course," says I. "Mr. Bill will play with you. What kind of a game is it?"

"I'm the Black Scout," says Red Chief, "and I have to ride to the stockade to warn the settlers that the Indians are coming. I'm tired of playing Indian myself. I want to be the Black Scout."

"All right," says I. "It sounds harmless to me. I guess Mr. Bill will help you foil the pesky [Indians]."

"What am I to do?" asks Bill, looking at the kid suspiciously.

"You are the hoss," says Black Scout. "Get down on your hands and knees. How can I ride to the stockade without a hoss?"

"You'd better keep him interested," said I, "till we get the scheme going. Loosen up."

Bill gets down on his all fours, and a look comes in his eye like a rabbit's when you catch it in a trap.

"How far is it to the stockade, kid?" he asks, in a husky manner of voice.

"Ninety miles," says the Black Scout. "And you have to hump yourself to get there on time. Whoa, now!"

The Black Scout jumps on Bill's back and digs his heels in his side.

"For Heaven's sake," says Bill, "hurry back, Sam, as soon as you can. I wish we hadn't made the ransom more than a thousand. Say, you quit kicking me or I'll get up and warm you good."

I walked over to Poplar Cove and sat around the post-office and store, talking with the chawbacons that came in to trade. One whiskerando says that he hears Summit is all upset on account of Elder Ebenezer Dorset's boy having been lost or stolen. That was all I wanted to know. I bought some smoking tobacco, referred casually to the price of black-eyed peas, posted my letter surreptitiously and came away. The postmaster said the mail-carrier would come by in an hour to take the mail on to Summit.

When I got back to the cave Bill and the boy were not to be found. I explored the vicinity of the cave, and risked a yodel or two, but there was no response.

So I lighted my pipe and sat down on a mossy bank to await developments.

In about half an hour I heard the bushes rustle, and Bill wabbled out into the little glade in front of the cave. Behind him was the kid, stepping softly like a scout, with a broad grin on his face. Bill stopped, took off his hat and wiped his face with a red handkerchief. The kid stopped about eight feet behind him.

"Sam," says Bill, "I suppose you'll think I'm a renegade, but I couldn't help it. I'm a grown person with masculine proclivities and habits of self-defense, but there is a time when all systems of egotism and predominance fail. The boy is gone. I have sent him home. All is off. There was martyrs in old times," goes on Bill, "that suffered death rather than give up the particular graft they enjoyed. None of 'em ever was subjugated to such supernatural tortures as I have been. I tried to be faithful to our articles of depredation; but there came a limit."

"What's the trouble, Bill?" I asks him.

"I was rode," says Bill, "the ninety miles to the stockade, not barring an inch. Then, when the settlers was rescued, I was given oats. Sand ain't a palatable substitute. And then, for an hour I had to try to explain to him why there was nothin' in holes, how a road can run both ways and what makes the grass green. I tell you, Sam, a human can only stand so much. I takes him by the neck of his clothes and drags him down the mountain. On the way he kicks my legs black-and-blue from the knees down; and I've got to have two or three bites on my thumb and hand cauterized.

"But he's gone" -- continues Bill – "gone home. I showed him the road to Summit and kicked him about eight feet nearer there at one kick. I'm sorry we lose the ransom; but it was either that or Bill Driscoll to the madhouse."

Bill is puffing and blowing, but there is a look of ineffable peace and growing content on his rose-pink features.

"Bill," says I, "there isn't any heart disease in your family, is there?"

"No," says Bill, "nothing chronic except malaria and accidents. Why?"

"Then you might turn around," says I, "and have a took behind you."

Bill turns and sees the boy, and loses his complexion and sits down plump on the round and begins to pluck aimlessly at grass and little sticks. For an hour I was afraid for his mind. And then I told him that my scheme was to put the whole job through immediately and that we would get the ransom and be off with it by midnight if old Dorset fell in with our proposition. So Bill braced up enough to give the kid a weak sort of a smile and a promise to play the Russian in a Japanese war with him as soon as he felt a little better.

I had a scheme for collecting that ransom without danger of being caught by counterplots that ought to commend itself to professional kidnappers. The tree under which the answer was to be left -- and the money later on -- was close to the road fence with big, bare fields on all sides. If a gang of constables should be watching for any one to come for the note they could see him a long way off crossing the fields or in the road. But no, sirree! At half-past eight I was up in that tree as well hidden as a tree toad, waiting for the messenger to arrive.

Exactly on time, a half-grown boy rides up the road on a bicycle, locates the pasteboard box at the foot of the fence-post, slips a folded piece of paper into it and pedals away again back toward Summit.

I waited an hour and then concluded the thing was square. I slid down the tree, got the note, slipped along the fence till I struck the woods, and was back at the cave in another half an hour. I opened the note, got near the lantern and read it to Bill. It was written with a pen in a crabbed hand, and the sum and substance of it was this:

Two Desperate Men.

Gentlemen: I received your letter to-day by post, in regard to the ransom you ask for the return of my son. I think you are a little high in your demands, and I hereby make you a counter-proposition, which I am inclined to believe you will accept. You bring Johnny home and pay me two hundred and fifty dollars in cash, and I agree to take him off your hands. You had better come at night, for the neighbours believe he is lost, and I couldn't be responsible for what they would do to anybody they saw bringing him back.

Very respectfully,

EBENEZER DORSET.

"Great pirates of Penzance!" says I; "of all the impudent – "

But I glanced at Bill, and hesitated. He had the most appealing look in his eyes I ever saw on the face of a dumb or a talking brute.

"Sam," says he, "what's two hundred and fifty dollars, after all? We've got the money. One more night of this kid will send me to a bed in Bedlam. Besides being a thorough gentleman, I think Mr. Dorset is a spendthrift for making us such a liberal offer. You ain't going to let the chance go, are you?"

"Tell you the truth, Bill," says I, "this little he ewe lamb has somewhat got on my nerves too. We'll take him home, pay the ransom and make our get-away."

We took him home that night. We got him to go by telling him that his father had bought a silver-mounted rifle and a pair of moccasins for him, and we were going to hunt bears the next day.

It was just twelve o'clock when we knocked at Ebenezer's front door. Just at the moment when I should have been abstracting the fifteen hundred dollars from the box under the tree, according to the original proposition, Bill was counting out two hundred and fifty dollars into Dorset's hand.

When the kid found out we were going to leave him at home he started up a howl like a calliope and fastened himself as tight as a leech to Bill's leg. His father peeled him away gradually, like a porous plaster.

"How long can you hold him?" asks Bill.

"I'm not as strong as I used to be," says old Dorset, "but I think I can promise you ten minutes."

"Enough," says Bill. "In ten minutes I shall cross the Central, Southern and Middle Western States, and be legging it trippingly for the Canadian border."

And, as dark as it was, and as fat as Bill was, and as good a runner as I am, he was a good mile and a half out of Summit before I could catch up with him.

Lesson 40 (no reading for Lesson 39)

- Review "The Gift of the Magi" by rereading the story guide in Lesson 32.

Lesson 41

- Read about the themes of "The Necklace."

Are people victims of fate or victims of their own choices and the desires they pursue? What do you think in the case of Mathilde? The author, Maupassant, starts the story by insinuating "a blunder of destiny" is responsible:

> "She was one of those pretty and charming girls, born by a blunder of destiny in a family of employees" (first paragraph).

Mathilde borrows a necklace from her friend, loses the necklace, then replaces it with an expensive lookalike of authentic diamonds. She works ten years to pay for it, only to find out that the original was a fake. These parts of the story seem to suggest that Mathilde is just a victim of fate.

The story also tells us, however, that Mathilde deeply desired to be thought of as a wealthy, well-to-do woman:

> "She suffered intensely, feeling herself born for every delicacy and every luxury" (third paragraph).

Her views of success included dresses and jewelry. How people perceived her from the outside was very important to her. These parts of the story point to it being Mathilde's own desires, and not fate, that caused her ten years of grief. It's ultimately up to the reader to decide if Mathilde is ruled by fate or desire. What do you think?

What are some other themes of the story? We should never judge a person by their outward appearance. Who they are – their character, personality, spiritual self – is more important than what they possess. Mathilde learned this lesson in the most difficult way possible. Also, "looks can be deceiving!" Mathilde saw the people at the party as "authentic" simply because they were of the social status she so desired to be. She assumed the necklace was expensive and authentic as soon as she saw it. The necklace turned out to be fake. And based on the way the people at the party judge Mathilde by her appearance, the story seems to imply that they were as fake as the necklace.

Lesson 42

- Reread the story guide for "The Cask of Amontillado" in Lesson 35.

Lesson 44 (no reading for Lesson 43)

- Read this biography of William Shakespeare.

Who Was William Shakespeare?

William Shakespeare was an English poet, playwright, and actor. He's considered the greatest dramatist of all time. He was a part of the Renaissance era. Not much is known about his personal life.

Scholars recognize Shakespeare's birthday as April 23, 1564, based on a baptism record from April 26, 1564. Stratford-upon-Avon, located about 100 miles northwest of London, was his home. He was the third child of six children.

He married Anne Hathaway on November 28, 1582 in Worcester. He was 18 and she was 26. They had three children, including a set of twins. One of the twins died at 11 years old.

There are gaps in the accounts of Shakespeare's life. But in the 1590s, there are records of Shakespeare being a managing partner in an acting company in London, the Lord Chamberlain's Men, as well as evidence he earned a living as an actor and a playwright.

By 1597, 15 of Shakespeare's 37 plays had been written and published. He purchased the second-largest house in Stratford, so he was obviously doing well for himself. By 1599, Shakespeare and his business partners had built their own theater, the Globe Theater.

Most of Shakespeare's plays were written using a cadenced pattern of lines of unrhymed, blank verse. However, each of his plays also contain parts that deviate from this and use various forms of poetry or simple prose.

The order in which he wrote them can be unclear, but between 1590 and 1613, Shakespeare wrote 37 plays consisting primarily of histories (*Henry VI, Richard II, Henry V, Julius Caesar*), tragedies (*Romeo and Juliet, Hamlet, Othello, King Lear, Macbeth*), comedies (*A Midsummer Night's Dream, Merchant of Venice, Much Ado about Nothing, Twelfth Night*), and tragicomedies (*Cymbeline, The Winter's Tale, The Tempest* – these are darker than his comedies, but end with reconciliation or forgiveness as opposed to the tragedies he wrote).

Popular belief is that Shakespeare died on his 52nd birthday, April 23, 1616, though some think this is a myth. However, church records show he was interred at Trinity Church on April 25, 1616. His exact cause of death is unknown, though many believe he was briefly ill before dying.

Over the centuries, many groups have arisen that question the origin of Shakespeare's plays. Critics mention well-known playwrights such as Christopher Marlowe, Francis Bacon, and Edward de Vere as the true authors of the plays. This likely comes from the sparse details of Shakespeare's life, and the lack of proof of his education coupled with the cerebral and poetic nature of his plays.

But most Shakespearean scholars do believe Shakespeare wrote all his own plays. They mention other playwrights of the time who also had sparse histories and came from modest backgrounds. They also point out an education including Latin and the classics would provide a good foundation for writing. They also show records that exist acknowledging him as the author of some of his plays, and showing he was a recognized member of certain theater companies that performed his plays.

The Romantic and Victorian periods were when Shakespeare's works reached the peak of their popularity. In the 20th century, a fresh focus on the arts allowed his works to be rediscovered and treasured once more. Today, they are still performed, read, and studied. Shakespeare's characters are relatable in emotion and conflict, which makes them appeal to wide audiences across varied cultures and contexts.

- Read about these drama terms.

Soliloquy: A soliloquy is when a character reveals their thoughts to the audience onstage and alone. There are some famous soliloquys in *Romeo and Juliet*. Perhaps the most famous is from the balcony scene in Act 2, Scene 2: "But soft, what light through yonder window breaks? It is the East, and Juliet is the sun."

Aside: An aside is a stage direction used to allow characters to address the audience without the other characters noticing. It's written into the play like this: [Aside]. An example of is found in Act 2, Scene 2 where Juliet is talking and Romeo says, as if thinking aloud: "*[Aside]* Shall I hear more, or shall I speak at this?"

Simile: Simile is making a comparison using like or as. An example is in Act 5, Scene 3: "This sight of death is as a bell That warns my old age to a sepulcher"

Personification: Personification involves giving non-human items human feelings or characteristics. You can see an example in Act 1, Scene 1: "Alas that love, so gentle in his view, Should be so tyrannous and rough in proof!"

Metaphor: A metaphor makes a comparison between two seemingly unrelated things (without using like or as). Act 1, Scene 5 has an example in this line: "My lips, two blushing pilgrims, ready stand To smooth that rough touch with a tender kiss."

Dramatic Irony: In dramatic irony, the audience knows something that the characters do not. The Prologue has a couple of lines of dramatic irony, such as this one: "pair of star-cross'd lovers take their life…"

Oxymoron: An oxymoron is made up of contradictory terms such as "jumbo shrimp," "awfully good," or "act naturally." There are several in this line from Act 1, Scene 1 "Feather of lead, bright smoke, cold fire, sick health, Still-waking sleep that is not what it is!"

Lesson 45

- Read this summary of *Romeo and Juliet* by Jennifer Appel.

Romeo and Juliet – romance or tragedy? You decide after reading this story fueled by revenge, attraction, secrecy and rivalry.

This play takes place in Verona, Italy, in a time when families are feuding and whom one is related to is of the upmost importance for whom one can befriend or marry.

The story opens with a street fight between the servants of the dueling families – the Montagues and Capulets. The Prince stops everything and sets up a new rule that any further fights that threaten the peace are punishable by death.

Count Paris wants to marry Juliet, but Juliet's father asks him to wait a couple of years and invites him to a ball that he has planned. Her mother and nurse try to convince Juliet to court the Count.

Meanwhile, when Romeo attends a banquet put on by his family's rival, the Capulets, while trying to see the woman he loves – spoiler alert, it's not Juliet – he instead finds himself drawn to the very young Juliet. Not knowing that she herself is a Capulet and therefore the sworn enemy of his family, the Montagues, he kisses her and falls head over heels with her in one night. They determine to marry the next day with the help of Juliet's nurse.

Before they can make it to the wedding, another street fight breaks out. In the midst of Romeo trying to stop the fight, Juliet's cousin, Tybalt, is killed. Romeo is banished for the killing.

Aided by the friar, Juliet fakes her own death in order to be free to marry Romeo. A note is sent to Romeo to let him in on the scheme, but he doesn't receive the note in time. Instead, he sees what he believes to be her lifeless body in the tomb and drinks poison to die. She wakes up and finds him dead next to her and losing all hope for life, she stabs herself. The family discovers the twisted fates of the young lovers and calls off the long-standing family feud. The pair were able to accomplish in their deaths the one thing that had never been possible before – peace between their families.

- Here is a list of the characters in the play. You might want to mark this page and refer to it as you read to help keep track of who is whom.

Characters

Romeo: Of the Montague family; incredibly impulsive.

Juliet: Of the Capulet family; fakes death to avoid marriage, but causes problems for those who think her death was real.

Montague: Romeo's father, head of a powerful family in Verona; in a feud with the Capulets.

Capulet: Juliet's father, head of another powerful family in Verona; in a feud with the Montagues.

Benvolio: Nephew of Montague and Romeo's best friend. He brings Romeo to the Capulet feast to help him meet other women and move on from Rosaline.

Tybalt: A Capulet who hates the Montagues. Very hot-tempered.

Prince Escalus: Prince of Verona. He wants peace between the Capulets and Montagues because their feud is causing disorder in Verona.

Paris: Friend of Prince Escalus. Betrothed (engaged) to Juliet.

Mercutio: Friend of Romeo and Prince Escalus. He likes to fight and challenges Tybalt to a duel for insulting Romeo.

Nurse: Has taken care of Juliet since she was a baby and tries to help her get together with Romeo.

Friar Lawrence: Friend of Romeo. He agrees to marry Romeo and Juliet in hopes that their marriage will bring the Capulets and Montagues together.

Montague's wife: Romeo's mother who is emotionally affected by the feud.

Capulet's wife: Juliet's mother; very protective of her family.

Minor Characters

Sampson: Capulet family servant.

Gregory: Capulet family servant.

Anthony: Capulet family servant who helps set up the feast.

Potpan: Capulet family servant who helps set up the feast.

Peter: Servant to Juliet's nurse; responsible for finding the people on the guest list for the feast.

Abram: Montague family servant.

Balthasar: Montague family servant.

Apothecary: Sells Romeo illegal poison because he needs the money.

Friar John: Tasked to deliver Friar Laurence's message to Romeo that says that Juliet is not really dead.

Lesson 46

- Read the Prologue and Act 1, Scene 1 of *Romeo and Juliet*. You'll notice stage directions in brackets and italics, as well as line numbers on the right side every 5 lines.
- **Note** – If you struggle to read this play, there's a site linked in the online course that offers a translation of what's happening in the different scenes. There is also a link to watch the play.

Romeo and Juliet
Prologue

Chorus. Two households, both alike in dignity,
In fair Verona, where we lay our scene,
From ancient grudge break to new mutiny,

Where civil blood makes civil hands unclean.
From forth the fatal loins of these two foes
A pair of star-cross'd lovers take their life;
Whose misadventured piteous overthrows
Do with their death bury their parents' strife.
The fearful passage of their death-mark'd love,
And the continuance of their parents' rage,
Which, but their children's end, nought could remove,
Is now the two hours' traffic of our stage;
The which if you with patient ears attend,
What here shall miss, our toil shall strive to mend.

Act 1, Scene 1
Verona. A Public Place.

[Enter SAMPSON and GREGORY, of the house of Capulet, armed with swords and bucklers]

Sampson. Gregory, o' my word, we'll not carry coals.

Gregory. No, for then we should be colliers.

Sampson. I mean, an we be in choler, we'll draw.

Gregory. Ay, while you live, draw your neck out o' the collar.

Sampson. I strike quickly, being moved.

Gregory. But thou art not quickly moved to strike.

Sampson. A dog of the house of Montague moves me.

Gregory. To move is to stir; and to be valiant is to stand:
therefore, if thou art moved, thou runn'st away.

Sampson. A dog of that house shall move me to stand: I will take the wall of any man or maid of Montague's.

Gregory. That shows thee a weak slave; for the weakest goes to the wall.

Sampson. True; and therefore women, being the weaker vessels, are ever thrust to the wall: therefore I will push Montague's men from the wall, and thrust his maids to the wall.

Gregory. The quarrel is between our masters and us their men.

Sampson. 'Tis all one, I will show myself a tyrant: when I have fought with the men, I will be cruel with the maids, and cut off their heads.

Gregory. The heads of the maids?

Sampson. Ay, the heads of the maids, or their maidenheads; take it in what sense thou wilt.

Gregory. They must take it in sense that feel it.

Sampson. Me they shall feel while I am able to stand: and 'tis known I am a pretty piece of flesh.

Gregory. 'Tis well thou art not fish; if thou hadst, thou hadst been poor John. Draw thy tool! here comes two of the house of the Montagues.

Sampson. My naked weapon is out: quarrel, I will back thee.

Gregory. How! turn thy back and run?

Sampson. Fear me not.

Gregory. No, marry; I fear thee!

Sampson. Let us take the law of our sides; let them begin.

Gregory. I will frown as I pass by, and let them take it as they list.

Sampson. Nay, as they dare. I will bite my thumb at them; which is a disgrace to them, if they bear it.

[Enter ABRAHAM and BALTHASAR]

Abraham. Do you bite your thumb at us, sir?

Sampson. I do bite my thumb, sir.

Abraham. Do you bite your thumb at us, sir?

Sampson. *[Aside to GREGORY]* Is the law of our side, if I say ay?

Gregory. No.

Sampson. No, sir, I do not bite my thumb at you, sir, but I bite my thumb, sir.

Gregory. Do you quarrel, sir?

Abraham. Quarrel sir! no, sir.

Sampson. If you do, sir, I am for you: I serve as good a man as you.

Abraham. No better.

Sampson. Well, sir.

Gregory. Say 'better:' here comes one of my master's kinsmen.

Sampson. Yes, better, sir.

Abraham. You lie.

Sampson. Draw, if you be men. Gregory, remember thy swashing blow.

[They fight]

[Enter BENVOLIO]

Benvolio. Part, fools!
Put up your swords; you know not what you do.

[Beats down their swords]

[Enter TYBALT]

Tybalt. What, art thou drawn among these heartless hinds?
Turn thee, Benvolio, look upon thy death.

Benvolio. I do but keep the peace: put up thy sword,
Or manage it to part these men with me.

Tybalt. What, drawn, and talk of peace! I hate the word,
As I hate hell, all Montagues, and thee:
Have at thee, coward!
[They fight]
[Enter, several of both houses, who join the fray;
then enter Citizens, with clubs]

First Citizen. Clubs, bills, and partisans! strike! beat them down!
Down with the Capulets! down with the Montagues!

[Enter CAPULET in his gown, and LADY CAPULET]

Capulet. What noise is this? Give me my long sword, ho!

Lady Capulet. A crutch, a crutch! why call you for a sword?

Capulet. My sword, I say! Old Montague is come,
And flourishes his blade in spite of me.

[Enter MONTAGUE and LADY MONTAGUE]

Montague. Thou villain Capulet,—Hold me not, let me go.

Lady Montague. Thou shalt not stir a foot to seek a foe.

[Enter PRINCE, with Attendants]

Prince Escalus. Rebellious subjects, enemies to peace,
Profaners of this neighbour-stained steel,—
Will they not hear? What, ho! you men, you beasts,
That quench the fire of your pernicious rage
With purple fountains issuing from your veins,
On pain of torture, from those bloody hands
Throw your mistemper'd weapons to the ground,
And hear the sentence of your moved prince.
Three civil brawls, bred of an airy word,
By thee, old Capulet, and Montague,
Have thrice disturb'd the quiet of our streets,
And made Verona's ancient citizens
Cast by their grave beseeming ornaments,
To wield old partisans, in hands as old,
Canker'd with peace, to part your canker'd hate:
If ever you disturb our streets again,
Your lives shall pay the forfeit of the peace.
For this time, all the rest depart away:
You Capulet; shall go along with me:
And, Montague, come you this afternoon,
To know our further pleasure in this case,
To old Free-town, our common judgment-place.
Once more, on pain of death, all men depart.

[Exeunt all but MONTAGUE, LADY MONTAGUE, and BENVOLIO]

Montague. Who set this ancient quarrel new abroach?
Speak, nephew, were you by when it began?

Benvolio. Here were the servants of your adversary,
And yours, close fighting ere I did approach:
I drew to part them: in the instant came
The fiery Tybalt, with his sword prepared,
Which, as he breathed defiance to my ears,
He swung about his head and cut the winds,
Who nothing hurt withal hiss'd him in scorn:
While we were interchanging thrusts and blows,
Came more and more and fought on part and part,
Till the prince came, who parted either part.

Lady Montague. O, where is Romeo? saw you him to-day?
Right glad I am he was not at this fray.

Benvolio. Madam, an hour before the worshipp'd sun
Peer'd forth the golden window of the east,
A troubled mind drave me to walk abroad;
Where, underneath the grove of sycamore
That westward rooteth from the city's side,
So early walking did I see your son:
Towards him I made, but he was ware of me
And stole into the covert of the wood:
I, measuring his affections by my own,
That most are busied when they're most alone,
Pursued my humour not pursuing his,
And gladly shunn'd who gladly fled from me.

Montague. Many a morning hath he there been seen,
With tears augmenting the fresh morning dew.
Adding to clouds more clouds with his deep sighs;
But all so soon as the all-cheering sun
Should in the furthest east begin to draw

The shady curtains from Aurora's bed,
Away from the light steals home my heavy son,
And private in his chamber pens himself,
Shuts up his windows, locks far daylight out
And makes himself an artificial night:
Black and portentous must this humour prove,
Unless good counsel may the cause remove.

Benvolio. My noble uncle, do you know the cause?

Montague. I neither know it nor can learn of him.

Benvolio. Have you importuned him by any means?

Montague. Both by myself and many other friends:
But he, his own affections' counsellor,
Is to himself—I will not say how true—
But to himself so secret and so close,
So far from sounding and discovery,
As is the bud bit with an envious worm,
Ere he can spread his sweet leaves to the air,
Or dedicate his beauty to the sun.
Could we but learn from whence his sorrows grow.
We would as willingly give cure as know.

[Enter ROMEO]

Benvolio. See, where he comes: so please you, step aside;
I'll know his grievance, or be much denied.

Montague. I would thou wert so happy by thy stay,
To hear true shrift. Come, madam, let's away.

[Exeunt MONTAGUE and LADY MONTAGUE]

Benvolio. Good-morrow, cousin.

Romeo. Is the day so young?

Benvolio. But new struck nine.

Romeo. Ay me! sad hours seem long.
Was that my father that went hence so fast?

Benvolio. It was. What sadness lengthens Romeo's hours?

Romeo. Not having that, which, having, makes them short.

Benvolio. In love?

Romeo. Out—

Benvolio. Of love?

Romeo. Out of her favour, where I am in love.

Benvolio. Alas, that love, so gentle in his view,
Should be so tyrannous and rough in proof!

Romeo. Alas, that love, whose view is muffled still,
Should, without eyes, see pathways to his will!
Where shall we dine? O me! What fray was here?
Yet tell me not, for I have heard it all.
Here's much to do with hate, but more with love.
Why, then, O brawling love! O loving hate!
O any thing, of nothing first create!
O heavy lightness! serious vanity!
Mis-shapen chaos of well-seeming forms!
Feather of lead, bright smoke, cold fire,
sick health!
Still-waking sleep, that is not what it is!
This love feel I, that feel no love in this.
Dost thou not laugh?

Benvolio. No, coz, I rather weep.

Romeo. Good heart, at what?

Benvolio. At thy good heart's oppression.

Romeo. Why, such is love's transgression.
Griefs of mine own lie heavy in my breast,
Which thou wilt propagate, to have it prest
With more of thine: this love that thou hast shown
Doth add more grief to too much of mine own.
Love is a smoke raised with the fume of sighs;
Being purged, a fire sparkling in lovers' eyes;
Being vex'd a sea nourish'd with lovers' tears:
What is it else? a madness most discreet,
A choking gall and a preserving sweet.
Farewell, my coz.

Benvolio. Soft! I will go along;
An if you leave me so, you do me wrong.

Romeo. Tut, I have lost myself; I am not here;
This is not Romeo, he's some other where.

Benvolio. Tell me in sadness, who is that you love.

Romeo. What, shall I groan and tell thee?

Benvolio. Groan! why, no.
But sadly tell me who.

Romeo. Bid a sick man in sadness make his will:
Ah, word ill urged to one that is so ill!
In sadness, cousin, I do love a woman.

Benvolio. I aim'd so near, when I supposed you loved.

Romeo. A right good mark-man! And she's fair I love.

Benvolio. A right fair mark, fair coz, is soonest hit.

Romeo. Well, in that hit you miss: she'll not be hit
With Cupid's arrow; she hath Dian's wit;
And, in strong proof of chastity well arm'd,
From love's weak childish bow she lives unharm'd.
She will not stay the siege of loving terms,
Nor bide the encounter of assailing eyes,
Nor ope her lap to saint-seducing gold:
O, she is rich in beauty, only poor,
That when she dies with beauty dies her store.

Benvolio. Then she hath sworn that she will still live chaste?

Romeo. She hath, and in that sparing makes huge waste,
For beauty starved with her severity
Cuts beauty off from all posterity.
She is too fair, too wise, wisely too fair,
To merit bliss by making me despair:
She hath forsworn to love, and in that vow
Do I live dead that live to tell it now.

Benvolio. Be ruled by me, forget to think of her.

Romeo. O, teach me how I should forget to think.

Benvolio. By giving liberty unto thine eyes;
Examine other beauties.

Romeo. 'Tis the way
To call hers exquisite, in question more:
These happy masks that kiss fair ladies' brows
Being black put us in mind they hide the fair;
He that is strucken blind cannot forget
The precious treasure of his eyesight lost:

Show me a mistress that is passing fair,
What doth her beauty serve, but as a note
Where I may read who pass'd that passing fair?
Farewell: thou canst not teach me to forget.

Benvolio. I'll pay that doctrine, or else die in debt.

[Exeunt]

Lesson 47

- Read Act 1, Scenes 2 and 3 of *Romeo and Juliet*.

Act 1, Scene 2
A Street

[Enter CAPULET, PARIS, and Servant]

Capulet. But Montague is bound as well as I,
In penalty alike; and 'tis not hard, I think,
For men so old as we to keep the peace.

Paris. Of honourable reckoning are you both;
And pity 'tis you lived at odds so long.
But now, my lord, what say you to my suit?

Capulet. But saying o'er what I have said before:
My child is yet a stranger in the world;
She hath not seen the change of fourteen years,
Let two more summers wither in their pride,
Ere we may think her ripe to be a bride.

Paris. Younger than she are happy mothers made.

Capulet. And too soon marr'd are those so early made.
The earth hath swallow'd all my hopes but she,
She is the hopeful lady of my earth:
But woo her, gentle Paris, get her heart,
My will to her consent is but a part;
An she agree, within her scope of choice
Lies my consent and fair according voice.
This night I hold an old accustom'd feast,
Whereto I have invited many a guest,
Such as I love; and you, among the store,
One more, most welcome, makes my number more.
At my poor house look to behold this night
Earth-treading stars that make dark heaven light:
Such comfort as do lusty young men feel
When well-apparell'd April on the heel
Of limping winter treads, even such delight
Among fresh female buds shall you this night
Inherit at my house; hear all, all see,
And like her most whose merit most shall be:
Which on more view, of many mine being one
May stand in number, though in reckoning none,
Come, go with me.
[To Servant, giving a paper]
Go, sirrah, trudge about
Through fair Verona; find those persons out
Whose names are written there, and to them say,
My house and welcome on their pleasure stay.

[Exeunt CAPULET and PARIS]

Servant. Find them out whose names are written here! It is written, that the shoemaker should meddle with his yard, and the tailor with his last, the fisher with his pencil, and the painter with his nets; but I am sent to find those persons whose names are here writ, and can never find what names the writing person hath here writ. I must to the learned.—In good time.

[Enter BENVOLIO and ROMEO]

Benvolio. Tut, man, one fire burns out another's burning,
One pain is lessen'd by another's anguish;
Turn giddy, and be holp by backward turning;
One desperate grief cures with another's languish:
Take thou some new infection to thy eye,
And the rank poison of the old will die.

Romeo. Your plaintain-leaf is excellent for that.

Benvolio. For what, I pray thee?

Romeo. For your broken shin.

Benvolio. Why, Romeo, art thou mad?

Romeo. Not mad, but bound more than a mad-man is;
Shut up in prison, kept without my food,
Whipp'd and tormented and—God-den, good fellow.

Servant. God gi' god-den. I pray, sir, can you read?

Romeo. Ay, mine own fortune in my misery.

Servant. Perhaps you have learned it without book: but, I pray, can you read any thing you see?

Romeo. Ay, if I know the letters and the language.

Servant. Ye say honestly: rest you merry!

Romeo. Stay, fellow; I can read.
[Reads]
'Signior Martino and his wife and daughters;
County Anselme and his beauteous sisters; the lady widow of Vitravio; Signior Placentio and his lovely

nieces; Mercutio and his brother Valentine; mine uncle Capulet, his wife and daughters; my fair niece Rosaline; Livia; Signior Valentio and his cousin Tybalt, Lucio and the lively Helena.' A fair assembly: whither should they come?

Servant. Up.

Romeo. Whither?

Servant. To supper; to our house.

Romeo. Whose house?

Servant. My master's.

Romeo. Indeed, I should have ask'd you that before.

Servant. Now I'll tell you without asking: my master is the great rich Capulet; and if you be not of the house of Montagues, I pray, come and crush a cup of wine. Rest you merry!

[Exit]

Benvolio. At this same ancient feast of Capulet's
Sups the fair Rosaline whom thou so lovest,
With all the admired beauties of Verona:
Go thither; and, with unattainted eye,
Compare her face with some that I shall show,
And I will make thee think thy swan a crow.

Romeo. When the devout religion of mine eye
Maintains such falsehood, then turn tears to fires;
And these, who often drown'd could never die,
Transparent heretics, be burnt for liars!

One fairer than my love! the all-seeing sun
Ne'er saw her match since first the world begun.

Benvolio. Tut, you saw her fair, none else being by,
Herself poised with herself in either eye:
But in that crystal scales let there be weigh'd
Your lady's love against some other maid
That I will show you shining at this feast,
And she shall scant show well that now shows best.

Romeo. I'll go along, no such sight to be shown,
But to rejoice in splendor of mine own.

[Exeunt]

Act 1, Scene 3
A Room in Capulet's House

[Enter LADY CAPULET and Nurse]

Lady Capulet. Nurse, where's my daughter? call her forth to me.

Nurse. Now, by my maidenhead, at twelve year old,
I bade her come. What, lamb! what, ladybird!
God forbid! Where's this girl? What, Juliet!

[Enter JULIET]

Juliet. How now! who calls?

Nurse. Your mother.

Juliet. Madam, I am here.
What is your will?

Lady Capulet. This is the matter:—Nurse, give leave awhile,
We must talk in secret:—nurse, come back again;
I have remember'd me, thou's hear our counsel.
Thou know'st my daughter's of a pretty age.

Nurse. Faith, I can tell her age unto an hour.

Lady Capulet. She's not fourteen.

Nurse. I'll lay fourteen of my teeth,—
And yet, to my teeth be it spoken, I have but four—
She is not fourteen. How long is it now
To Lammas-tide?

Lady Capulet. A fortnight and odd days.

Nurse. Even or odd, of all days in the year,
Come Lammas-eve at night shall she be fourteen.
Susan and she—God rest all Christian souls!—
Were of an age: well, Susan is with God;
She was too good for me: but, as I said,
On Lammas-eve at night shall she be fourteen;
That shall she, marry; I remember it well.
'Tis since the earthquake now eleven years;
And she was wean'd,—I never shall forget it,—
Of all the days of the year, upon that day:
For I had then laid wormwood to my dug,
Sitting in the sun under the dove-house wall;
My lord and you were then at Mantua:—
Nay, I do bear a brain:—but, as I said,
When it did taste the wormwood on the nipple
Of my dug and felt it bitter, pretty fool,
To see it tetchy and fall out with the dug!
Shake quoth the dove-house: 'twas no need, I trow,
To bid me trudge:
And since that time it is eleven years;
For then she could stand alone; nay, by the rood,

She could have run and waddled all about;
For even the day before, she broke her brow:
And then my husband—God be with his soul!
A' was a merry man—took up the child:
'Yea,' quoth he, 'dost thou fall upon thy face?
Thou wilt fall backward when thou hast more wit;
Wilt thou not, Jule?' and, by my holidame,
The pretty wretch left crying and said 'Ay.'
To see, now, how a jest shall come about!
I warrant, an I should live a thousand years,
I never should forget it: 'Wilt thou not, Jule?' quoth he;
And, pretty fool, it stinted and said 'Ay.'

Lady Capulet. Enough of this; I pray thee, hold thy peace.

Nurse. Yes, madam: yet I cannot choose but laugh,
To think it should leave crying and say 'Ay.'
And yet, I warrant, it had upon its brow
A bump as big as a young cockerel's stone;
A parlous knock; and it cried bitterly:
'Yea,' quoth my husband, 'fall'st upon thy face?
Thou wilt fall backward when thou comest to age;
Wilt thou not, Jule?' it stinted and said 'Ay.'

Juliet. And stint thou too, I pray thee, nurse, say I.

Nurse. Peace, I have done. God mark thee to his grace!
Thou wast the prettiest babe that e'er I nursed:
An I might live to see thee married once,
I have my wish.

Lady Capulet. Marry, that 'marry' is the very theme
I came to talk of. Tell me, daughter Juliet,
How stands your disposition to be married?

Juliet. It is an honour that I dream not of.

Nurse. An honour! were not I thine only nurse,
I would say thou hadst suck'd wisdom from thy teat.

Lady Capulet. Well, think of marriage now; younger than you,
Here in Verona, ladies of esteem,
Are made already mothers: by my count,
I was your mother much upon these years
That you are now a maid. Thus then in brief:
The valiant Paris seeks you for his love.

Nurse. A man, young lady! lady, such a man
As all the world—why, he's a man of wax.

Lady Capulet. Verona's summer hath not such a flower.

Nurse. Nay, he's a flower; in faith, a very flower.

Lady Capulet. What say you? can you love the gentleman?
This night you shall behold him at our feast;
Read o'er the volume of young Paris' face,
And find delight writ there with beauty's pen;
Examine every married lineament,
And see how one another lends content
And what obscured in this fair volume lies
Find written in the margent of his eyes.
This precious book of love, this unbound lover,
To beautify him, only lacks a cover:
The fish lives in the sea, and 'tis much pride
For fair without the fair within to hide:
That book in many's eyes doth share the glory,
That in gold clasps locks in the golden story;
So shall you share all that he doth possess,
By having him, making yourself no less.

Nurse. No less! nay, bigger; women grow by men.

Lady Capulet. Speak briefly, can you like of Paris' love?

Juliet. I'll look to like, if looking liking move:
But no more deep will I endart mine eye
Than your consent gives strength to make it fly.

[Enter a Servant]

Servant. Madam, the guests are come, supper served up, you called, my young lady asked for, the nurse cursed in the pantry, and every thing in extremity. I must hence to wait; I beseech you, follow straight.

Lady Capulet. We follow thee.
[Exit Servant]
Juliet, the county stays.

Nurse. Go, girl, seek happy nights to happy days.

[Exeunt]

Lesson 48

- Read Act 1, Scenes 4 and 5 of *Romeo and Juliet.*

Act 1, Scene 4
A Street

[Enter ROMEO, MERCUTIO, BENVOLIO, with five or six [p]Maskers, Torch-bearers, and others]

Romeo. What, shall this speech be spoke for our excuse?
Or shall we on without a apology?

Benvolio. The date is out of such prolixity:
We'll have no Cupid hoodwink'd with a scarf,
Bearing a Tartar's painted bow of lath,
Scaring the ladies like a crow-keeper;
Nor no without-book prologue, faintly spoke
After the prompter, for our entrance:
But let them measure us by what they will;
We'll measure them a measure, and be gone.

Romeo. Give me a torch: I am not for this ambling;
Being but heavy, I will bear the light.

Mercutio. Nay, gentle Romeo, we must have you dance.

Romeo. Not I, believe me: you have dancing shoes
With nimble soles: I have a soul of lead
So stakes me to the ground I cannot move.

Mercutio. You are a lover; borrow Cupid's wings,
And soar with them above a common bound.

Romeo. I am too sore enpierced with his shaft
To soar with his light feathers, and so bound,
I cannot bound a pitch above dull woe:
Under love's heavy burden do I sink.

Mercutio. And, to sink in it, should you burden love;
Too great oppression for a tender thing.

Romeo. Is love a tender thing? it is too rough,
Too rude, too boisterous, and it pricks like thorn.

Mercutio. If love be rough with you, be rough with love;
Prick love for pricking, and you beat love down.
Give me a case to put my visage in:
A visor for a visor! what care I

What curious eye doth quote deformities?
Here are the beetle brows shall blush for me.

Benvolio. Come, knock and enter; and no sooner in,
But every man betake him to his legs.

Romeo. A torch for me: let wantons light of heart
Tickle the senseless rushes with their heels,
For I am proverb'd with a grandsire phrase;
I'll be a candle-holder, and look on.
The game was ne'er so fair, and I am done.

Mercutio. Tut, dun's the mouse, the constable's own word:
If thou art dun, we'll draw thee from the mire
Of this sir-reverence love, wherein thou stick'st
Up to the ears. Come, we burn daylight, ho!

Romeo. Nay, that's not so.

Mercutio. I mean, sir, in delay
We waste our lights in vain, like lamps by day.
Take our good meaning, for our judgment sits
Five times in that ere once in our five wits.

Romeo. And we mean well in going to this mask;
But 'tis no wit to go.

Mercutio. Why, may one ask?

Romeo. I dream'd a dream to-night.

Mercutio. And so did I.

Romeo. Well, what was yours?

Mercutio. That dreamers often lie.

Romeo. In bed asleep, while they do dream things true.

Mercutio. O, then, I see Queen Mab hath been with you.
She is the fairies' midwife, and she comes
In shape no bigger than an agate-stone
On the fore-finger of an alderman,
Drawn with a team of little atomies
Athwart men's noses as they lie asleep;
Her wagon-spokes made of long spiders' legs,
The cover of the wings of grasshoppers,
The traces of the smallest spider's web,
The collars of the moonshine's watery beams,
Her whip of cricket's bone, the lash of film,
Her wagoner a small grey-coated gnat,
Not so big as a round little worm
Prick'd from the lazy finger of a maid;
Her chariot is an empty hazel-nut
Made by the joiner squirrel or old grub,
Time out o' mind the fairies' coachmakers.
And in this state she gallops night by night
Through lovers' brains, and then they dream of love;
O'er courtiers' knees, that dream on court'sies straight,
O'er lawyers' fingers, who straight dream on fees,
O'er ladies' lips, who straight on kisses dream,
Which oft the angry Mab with blisters plagues,
Because their breaths with sweetmeats tainted are:
Sometime she gallops o'er a courtier's nose,
And then dreams he of smelling out a suit;
And sometime comes she with a tithe-pig's tail
Tickling a parson's nose as a' lies asleep,
Then dreams, he of another benefice:
Sometime she driveth o'er a soldier's neck,
And then dreams he of cutting foreign throats,
Of breaches, ambuscadoes, Spanish blades,
Of healths five-fathom deep; and then anon
Drums in his ear, at which he starts and wakes,
And being thus frighted swears a prayer or two

And sleeps again. This is that very Mab
That plats the manes of horses in the night,
And bakes the elflocks in foul sluttish hairs,
Which once untangled, much misfortune bodes:
This is the hag, when maids lie on their backs,
That presses them and learns them first to bear,
Making them women of good carriage:
This is she—

Romeo. Peace, peace, Mercutio, peace!
Thou talk'st of nothing.

Mercutio. True, I talk of dreams,
Which are the children of an idle brain,
Begot of nothing but vain fantasy,
Which is as thin of substance as the air
And more inconstant than the wind, who wooes
Even now the frozen bosom of the north,
And, being anger'd, puffs away from thence,
Turning his face to the dew-dropping south.

Benvolio. This wind, you talk of, blows us from ourselves;
Supper is done, and we shall come too late.

Romeo. I fear, too early: for my mind misgives
Some consequence yet hanging in the stars
Shall bitterly begin his fearful date
With this night's revels and expire the term
Of a despised life closed in my breast
By some vile forfeit of untimely death.
But He, that hath the steerage of my course,
Direct my sail! On, lusty gentlemen.

Benvolio. Strike, drum.

[Exeunt]

Act 1, Scene 5
A hall in Capulet's house

[Musicians waiting. Enter Servingmen with napkins]

First Servant. Where's Potpan, that he helps not to take away? He shift a trencher? he scrape a trencher!

Second Servant. When good manners shall lie all in one or two men's hands and they unwashed too, 'tis a foul thing.

First Servant. Away with the joint-stools, remove the court-cupboard, look to the plate. Good thou, save me a piece of marchpane; and, as thou lovest me, let the porter let in Susan Grindstone and Nell. Antony, and Potpan!

Second Servant. Ay, boy, ready.

First Servant. You are looked for and called for, asked for and sought for, in the great chamber.

Second Servant. We cannot be here and there too. Cheerly, boys; be brisk awhile, and the longer liver take all.

[Enter CAPULET, with JULIET and others of his house, meeting the Guests and Maskers]

Capulet. Welcome, gentlemen! ladies that have their toes
Unplagued with corns will have a bout with you.
Ah ha, my mistresses! which of you all
Will now deny to dance? she that makes dainty,
She, I'll swear, hath corns; am I come near ye now?
Welcome, gentlemen! I have seen the day
That I have worn a visor and could tell
A whispering tale in a fair lady's ear,

Such as would please: 'tis gone, 'tis gone, 'tis gone:
You are welcome, gentlemen! come, musicians, play.
A hall, a hall! give room! and foot it, girls.
[Music plays, and they dance]
More light, you knaves; and turn the tables up,
And quench the fire, the room is grown too hot.
Ah, sirrah, this unlook'd-for sport comes well.
Nay, sit, nay, sit, good cousin Capulet;
For you and I are past our dancing days:
How long is't now since last yourself and I
Were in a mask?

Second Capulet. By'r lady, thirty years.

Capulet. What, man! 'tis not so much, 'tis not so much:
'Tis since the nuptials of Lucentio,
Come pentecost as quickly as it will,
Some five and twenty years; and then we mask'd.

Second Capulet. 'Tis more, 'tis more, his son is elder, sir;
His son is thirty.

Capulet. Will you tell me that?
His son was but a ward two years ago.

Romeo. *[To a Servingman]* What lady is that, which doth enrich the hand
Of yonder knight?

Servant. I know not, sir.

Romeo. O, she doth teach the torches to burn bright!
It seems she hangs upon the cheek of night
Like a rich jewel in an Ethiope's ear;
Beauty too rich for use, for earth too dear!
So shows a snowy dove trooping with crows,
As yonder lady o'er her fellows shows.

The measure done, I'll watch her place of stand,
And, touching hers, make blessed my rude hand.
Did my heart love till now? forswear it, sight!
For I ne'er saw true beauty till this night.

Tybalt. This, by his voice, should be a Montague.
Fetch me my rapier, boy. What dares the slave
Come hither, cover'd with an antic face,
To fleer and scorn at our solemnity?
Now, by the stock and honour of my kin,
To strike him dead, I hold it not a sin.

Capulet. Why, how now, kinsman! wherefore storm you so?

Tybalt. Uncle, this is a Montague, our foe,
A villain that is hither come in spite,
To scorn at our solemnity this night.

Capulet. Young Romeo is it?

Tybalt. 'Tis he, that villain Romeo.

Capulet. Content thee, gentle coz, let him alone;
He bears him like a portly gentleman;
And, to say truth, Verona brags of him
To be a virtuous and well-govern'd youth:
I would not for the wealth of all the town
Here in my house do him disparagement:
Therefore be patient, take no note of him:
It is my will, the which if thou respect,
Show a fair presence and put off these frowns,
And ill-beseeming semblance for a feast.

Tybalt. It fits, when such a villain is a guest:
I'll not endure him.

Capulet. He shall be endured:
What, goodman boy! I say, he shall: go to;
Am I the master here, or you? go to.
You'll not endure him! God shall mend my soul!
You'll make a mutiny among my guests!
You will set cock-a-hoop! you'll be the man!

Tybalt. Why, uncle, 'tis a shame.

Capulet. Go to, go to;
You are a saucy boy: is't so, indeed?
This trick may chance to scathe you, I know what:
You must contrary me! marry, 'tis time.
Well said, my hearts! You are a princox; go:
Be quiet, or—More light, more light! For shame!
I'll make you quiet. What, cheerly, my hearts!

Tybalt. Patience perforce with wilful choler meeting
Makes my flesh tremble in their different greeting.
I will withdraw: but this intrusion shall
Now seeming sweet convert to bitter gall.

[Exit]

Romeo. *[To JULIET]* If I profane with my unworthiest hand
This holy shrine, the gentle sin is this:
My lips, two blushing pilgrims, ready stand
To smooth that rough touch with a tender kiss.

Juliet. Good pilgrim, you do wrong your hand too much,
Which mannerly devotion shows in this;
For saints have hands that pilgrims' hands do touch,
And palm to palm is holy palmers' kiss.

Romeo. Have not saints lips, and holy palmers too?

Juliet. Ay, pilgrim, lips that they must use in prayer.

Romeo. O, then, dear saint, let lips do what hands do;
They pray, grant thou, lest faith turn to despair.

Juliet. Saints do not move, though grant for prayers' sake.

Romeo. Then move not, while my prayer's effect I take.
Thus from my lips, by yours, my sin is purged.

Juliet. Then have my lips the sin that they have took.

Romeo. Sin from thy lips? O trespass sweetly urged!
Give me my sin again.

Juliet. You kiss by the book.

Nurse. Madam, your mother craves a word with you.

Romeo. What is her mother?

Nurse. Marry, bachelor,
Her mother is the lady of the house,
And a good lady, and a wise and virtuous
I nursed her daughter, that you talk'd withal;
I tell you, he that can lay hold of her
Shall have the chinks.

Romeo. Is she a Capulet?
O dear account! my life is my foe's debt.

Benvolio. Away, begone; the sport is at the best.

Romeo. Ay, so I fear; the more is my unrest.

Capulet. Nay, gentlemen, prepare not to be gone;
We have a trifling foolish banquet towards.
Is it e'en so? why, then, I thank you all
I thank you, honest gentlemen; good night.

More torches here! Come on then, let's to bed.
Ah, sirrah, by my fay, it waxes late:
I'll to my rest.

[Exeunt all but JULIET and Nurse]

Juliet. Come hither, nurse. What is yond gentleman?

Nurse. The son and heir of old Tiberio.

Juliet. What's he that now is going out of door?

Nurse. Marry, that, I think, be young Petrucio.

Juliet. What's he that follows there, that would not dance?

Nurse. I know not.

Juliet. Go ask his name: if he be married.
My grave is like to be my wedding bed.

Nurse. His name is Romeo, and a Montague;
The only son of your great enemy.

Juliet. My only love sprung from my only hate!
Too early seen unknown, and known too late!
Prodigious birth of love it is to me,
That I must love a loathed enemy.

Nurse. What's this? what's this?

Juliet. A rhyme I learn'd even now
Of one I danced withal.

[One calls within 'Juliet.']

Nurse. Anon, anon!
Come, let's away; the strangers all are gone.

[Exeunt]

Lesson 49

- Read the Prologue and Act 2, Scenes 1 through 3 of *Romeo and Juliet.*

Prologue

[Enter Chorus]

Chorus. Now old desire doth in his death-bed lie,
And young affection gapes to be his heir;
That fair for which love groan'd for and would die,
With tender Juliet match'd, is now not fair.
Now Romeo is beloved and loves again,
Alike betwitched by the charm of looks,
But to his foe supposed he must complain,
And she steal love's sweet bait from fearful hooks:
Being held a foe, he may not have access
To breathe such vows as lovers use to swear;
And she as much in love, her means much less
To meet her new-beloved any where:
But passion lends them power, time means, to meet
Tempering extremities with extreme sweet.

[Exit]

Act 2, Scene 1
A lane by the wall of Capulet's orchard

[Enter ROMEO]

Romeo. Can I go forward when my heart is here?
Turn back, dull earth, and find thy centre out.

[He climbs the wall, and leaps down within it]

[Enter BENVOLIO and MERCUTIO]

Benvolio. Romeo! my cousin Romeo!

Mercutio. He is wise;
And, on my lie, hath stol'n him home to bed.

Benvolio. He ran this way, and leap'd this orchard wall:
Call, good Mercutio.

Mercutio. Nay, I'll conjure too.
Romeo! humours! madman! passion! lover!
Appear thou in the likeness of a sigh:
Speak but one rhyme, and I am satisfied;
Cry but 'Ay me!' pronounce but 'love' and 'dove;'
Speak to my gossip Venus one fair word,
One nick-name for her purblind son and heir,
Young Adam Cupid, he that shot so trim,
When King Cophetua loved the beggar-maid!
He heareth not, he stirreth not, he moveth not;
The ape is dead, and I must conjure him.
I conjure thee by Rosaline's bright eyes,
By her high forehead and her scarlet lip,
By her fine foot, straight leg and quivering thigh
And the demesnes that there adjacent lie,
That in thy likeness thou appear to us!

Benvolio. And if he hear thee, thou wilt anger him.

Mercutio. This cannot anger him: 'twould anger him
To raise a spirit in his mistress' circle
Of some strange nature, letting it there stand
Till she had laid it and conjured it down;
That were some spite: my invocation
Is fair and honest, and in his mistress' name
I conjure only but to raise up him.

Benvolio. Come, he hath hid himself among these trees,
To be consorted with the humorous night:
Blind is his love and best befits the dark.

Mercutio. If love be blind, love cannot hit the mark.
Now will he sit under a medlar tree,
And wish his mistress were that kind of fruit
As maids call medlars, when they laugh alone.
Romeo, that she were, O, that she were
An open et cetera, thou a poperin pear!
Romeo, good night: I'll to my truckle-bed;
This field-bed is too cold for me to sleep:
Come, shall we go?

Benvolio. Go, then; for 'tis in vain
To seek him here that means not to be found.

[Exeunt]

Act 2, Scene 2
Capulet's orchard

[Enter ROMEO]

Romeo. He jests at scars that never felt a wound.
[JULIET appears above at a window]
But, soft! what light through yonder window breaks?

It is the east, and Juliet is the sun.
Arise, fair sun, and kill the envious moon,
Who is already sick and pale with grief,
That thou her maid art far more fair than she:
Be not her maid, since she is envious;
Her vestal livery is but sick and green
And none but fools do wear it; cast it off.
It is my lady, O, it is my love!
O, that she knew she were!
She speaks yet she says nothing: what of that?
Her eye discourses; I will answer it.
I am too bold, 'tis not to me she speaks:
Two of the fairest stars in all the heaven,
Having some business, do entreat her eyes
To twinkle in their spheres till they return.
What if her eyes were there, they in her head?
The brightness of her cheek would shame those stars,
As daylight doth a lamp; her eyes in heaven
Would through the airy region stream so bright
That birds would sing and think it were not night.
See, how she leans her cheek upon her hand!
O, that I were a glove upon that hand,
That I might touch that cheek!

Juliet. Ay me!

Romeo. She speaks:
O, speak again, bright angel! for thou art
As glorious to this night, being o'er my head
As is a winged messenger of heaven
Unto the white-upturned wondering eyes
Of mortals that fall back to gaze on him
When he bestrides the lazy-pacing clouds
And sails upon the bosom of the air.

Juliet. O Romeo, Romeo! wherefore art thou Romeo?
Deny thy father and refuse thy name;

Or, if thou wilt not, be but sworn my love,
And I'll no longer be a Capulet.

Romeo. *[Aside]* Shall I hear more, or shall I speak at this?

Juliet. 'Tis but thy name that is my enemy;
Thou art thyself, though not a Montague.
What's Montague? it is nor hand, nor foot,
Nor arm, nor face, nor any other part
Belonging to a man. O, be some other name!
What's in a name? that which we call a rose
By any other name would smell as sweet;
So Romeo would, were he not Romeo call'd,
Retain that dear perfection which he owes
Without that title. Romeo, doff thy name,
And for that name which is no part of thee
Take all myself.

Romeo. I take thee at thy word:
Call me but love, and I'll be new baptized;
Henceforth I never will be Romeo.

Juliet. What man art thou that thus bescreen'd in night
So stumblest on my counsel?

Romeo. By a name
I know not how to tell thee who I am:
My name, dear saint, is hateful to myself,
Because it is an enemy to thee;
Had I it written, I would tear the word.

Juliet. My ears have not yet drunk a hundred words
Of that tongue's utterance, yet I know the sound:
Art thou not Romeo and a Montague?

Romeo. Neither, fair saint, if either thee dislike.

Juliet. How camest thou hither, tell me, and wherefore?
The orchard walls are high and hard to climb,
And the place death, considering who thou art,
If any of my kinsmen find thee here.

Romeo. With love's light wings did I o'er-perch these walls;
For stony limits cannot hold love out,
And what love can do that dares love attempt;
Therefore thy kinsmen are no let to me.

Juliet. If they do see thee, they will murder thee.

Romeo. Alack, there lies more peril in thine eye
Than twenty of their swords: look thou but sweet,
And I am proof against their enmity.

Juliet. I would not for the world they saw thee here.

Romeo. I have night's cloak to hide me from their sight;
And but thou love me, let them find me here:
My life were better ended by their hate,
Than death prorogued, wanting of thy love.

Juliet. By whose direction found'st thou out this place?

Romeo. By love, who first did prompt me to inquire;
He lent me counsel and I lent him eyes.
I am no pilot; yet, wert thou as far
As that vast shore wash'd with the farthest sea,
I would adventure for such merchandise.

Juliet. Thou know'st the mask of night is on my face,
Else would a maiden blush bepaint my cheek
For that which thou hast heard me speak to-night
Fain would I dwell on form, fain, fain deny
What I have spoke: but farewell compliment!
Dost thou love me? I know thou wilt say 'Ay,'

And I will take thy word: yet if thou swear'st,
Thou mayst prove false; at lovers' perjuries
Then say, Jove laughs. O gentle Romeo,
If thou dost love, pronounce it faithfully:
Or if thou think'st I am too quickly won,
I'll frown and be perverse an say thee nay,
So thou wilt woo; but else, not for the world.
In truth, fair Montague, I am too fond,
And therefore thou mayst think my 'havior light:
But trust me, gentleman, I'll prove more true
Than those that have more cunning to be strange.
I should have been more strange, I must confess,
But that thou overheard'st, ere I was ware,
My true love's passion: therefore pardon me,
And not impute this yielding to light love,
Which the dark night hath so discovered.

Romeo. Lady, by yonder blessed moon I swear
That tips with silver all these fruit-tree tops—

Juliet. O, swear not by the moon, the inconstant moon,
That monthly changes in her circled orb,
Lest that thy love prove likewise variable.

Romeo. What shall I swear by?

Juliet. Do not swear at all;
Or, if thou wilt, swear by thy gracious self,
Which is the god of my idolatry,
And I'll believe thee.

Romeo. If my heart's dear love—

Juliet. Well, do not swear: although I joy in thee,
I have no joy of this contract to-night:
It is too rash, too unadvised, too sudden;
Too like the lightning, which doth cease to be

Ere one can say 'It lightens.' Sweet, good night!
This bud of love, by summer's ripening breath,
May prove a beauteous flower when next we meet.
Good night, good night! as sweet repose and rest
Come to thy heart as that within my breast!

Romeo. O, wilt thou leave me so unsatisfied?

Juliet. What satisfaction canst thou have to-night?

Romeo. The exchange of thy love's faithful vow for mine.

Juliet. I gave thee mine before thou didst request it:
And yet I would it were to give again.

Romeo. Wouldst thou withdraw it? for what purpose, love?

Juliet. But to be frank, and give it thee again.
And yet I wish but for the thing I have:
My bounty is as boundless as the sea,
My love as deep; the more I give to thee,
The more I have, for both are infinite.
[Nurse calls within]
I hear some noise within; dear love, adieu!
Anon, good nurse! Sweet Montague, be true.
Stay but a little, I will come again.

[Exit, above]

Romeo. O blessed, blessed night! I am afeard.
Being in night, all this is but a dream,
Too flattering-sweet to be substantial.

[Re-enter JULIET, above]

Juliet. Three words, dear Romeo, and good night indeed.
If that thy bent of love be honourable,

Thy purpose marriage, send me word to-morrow,
By one that I'll procure to come to thee,
Where and what time thou wilt perform the rite;
And all my fortunes at thy foot I'll lay
And follow thee my lord throughout the world.

Nurse. *[Within]* Madam!

Juliet. I come, anon.—But if thou mean'st not well,
I do beseech thee—

Nurse. *[Within]* Madam!

Juliet. By and by, I come:—
To cease thy suit, and leave me to my grief:
To-morrow will I send.

Romeo. So thrive my soul—

Juliet. A thousand times good night!

[Exit, above]

Romeo. A thousand times the worse, to want thy light.
Love goes toward love, as schoolboys from
their books,
But love from love, toward school with heavy looks.

[Retiring]

[Re-enter JULIET, above]

Juliet. Hist! Romeo, hist! O, for a falconer's voice,
To lure this tassel-gentle back again!
Bondage is hoarse, and may not speak aloud;
Else would I tear the cave where Echo lies,

And make her airy tongue more hoarse than mine,
With repetition of my Romeo's name.

Romeo. It is my soul that calls upon my name:
How silver-sweet sound lovers' tongues by night,
Like softest music to attending ears!

Juliet. Romeo!

Romeo. My dear?

Juliet. At what o'clock to-morrow
Shall I send to thee?

Romeo. At the hour of nine.

Juliet. I will not fail: 'tis twenty years till then.
I have forgot why I did call thee back.

Romeo. Let me stand here till thou remember it.

Juliet. I shall forget, to have thee still stand there,
Remembering how I love thy company.

Romeo. And I'll still stay, to have thee still forget,
Forgetting any other home but this.

Juliet. 'Tis almost morning; I would have thee gone:
And yet no further than a wanton's bird;
Who lets it hop a little from her hand,
Like a poor prisoner in his twisted gyves,
And with a silk thread plucks it back again,
So loving-jealous of his liberty.

Romeo. I would I were thy bird.

Juliet. Sweet, so would I:
Yet I should kill thee with much cherishing.
Good night, good night! parting is such
sweet sorrow,
That I shall say good night till it be morrow.

[Exit above]

Romeo. Sleep dwell upon thine eyes, peace in thy breast!
Would I were sleep and peace, so sweet to rest!
Hence will I to my ghostly father's cell,
His help to crave, and my dear hap to tell.

[Exit]

Act 2, Scene 3
Friar Laurence's cell

[Enter FRIAR LAURENCE, with a basket]

Friar Laurence. The grey-eyed morn smiles on the frowning night,
Chequering the eastern clouds with streaks of light,
And flecked darkness like a drunkard reels
From forth day's path and Titan's fiery wheels:
Now, ere the sun advance his burning eye,
The day to cheer and night's dank dew to dry,
I must up-fill this osier cage of ours
With baleful weeds and precious-juiced flowers.
The earth that's nature's mother is her tomb;
What is her burying grave that is her womb,
And from her womb children of divers kind
We sucking on her natural bosom find,
Many for many virtues excellent,
None but for some and yet all different.
O, mickle is the powerful grace that lies
In herbs, plants, stones, and their true qualities:
For nought so vile that on the earth doth live

But to the earth some special good doth give,
Nor aught so good but strain'd from that fair use
Revolts from true birth, stumbling on abuse:
Virtue itself turns vice, being misapplied;
And vice sometimes by action dignified.
Within the infant rind of this small flower
Poison hath residence and medicine power:
For this, being smelt, with that part cheers each part;
Being tasted, slays all senses with the heart.
Two such opposed kings encamp them still
In man as well as herbs, grace and rude will;
And where the worser is predominant,
Full soon the canker death eats up that plant.

[Enter ROMEO]

Romeo. Good morrow, father.

Friar Laurence. Benedicite!
What early tongue so sweet saluteth me?
Young son, it argues a distemper'd head
So soon to bid good morrow to thy bed:
Care keeps his watch in every old man's eye,
And where care lodges, sleep will never lie;
But where unbruised youth with unstuff'd brain
Doth couch his limbs, there golden sleep doth reign:
Therefore thy earliness doth me assure
Thou art up-roused by some distemperature;
Or if not so, then here I hit it right,
Our Romeo hath not been in bed to-night.

Romeo. That last is true; the sweeter rest was mine.

Friar Laurence. God pardon sin! wast thou with Rosaline?

Romeo. With Rosaline, my ghostly father? no;
I have forgot that name, and that name's woe.

Friar Laurence. That's my good son: but where hast thou been, then?

Romeo. I'll tell thee, ere thou ask it me again.
I have been feasting with mine enemy,
Where on a sudden one hath wounded me,
That's by me wounded: both our remedies
Within thy help and holy physic lies:
I bear no hatred, blessed man, for, lo,
My intercession likewise steads my foe.

Friar Laurence. Be plain, good son, and homely in thy drift;
Riddling confession finds but riddling shrift.

Romeo. Then plainly know my heart's dear love is set
On the fair daughter of rich Capulet:
As mine on hers, so hers is set on mine;
And all combined, save what thou must combine
By holy marriage: when and where and how
We met, we woo'd and made exchange of vow,
I'll tell thee as we pass; but this I pray,
That thou consent to marry us to-day.

Friar Laurence. Holy Saint Francis, what a change is here!
Is Rosaline, whom thou didst love so dear,
So soon forsaken? young men's love then lies
Not truly in their hearts, but in their eyes.
Jesu Maria, what a deal of brine
Hath wash'd thy sallow cheeks for Rosaline!
How much salt water thrown away in waste,
To season love, that of it doth not taste!
The sun not yet thy sighs from heaven clears,
Thy old groans ring yet in my ancient ears;
Lo, here upon thy cheek the stain doth sit
Of an old tear that is not wash'd off yet:
If e'er thou wast thyself and these woes thine,
Thou and these woes were all for Rosaline:

And art thou changed? pronounce this sentence then,
Women may fall, when there's no strength in men.

Romeo. Thou chid'st me oft for loving Rosaline.

Friar Laurence. For doting, not for loving, pupil mine.

Romeo. And bad'st me bury love.

Friar Laurence. Not in a grave,
To lay one in, another out to have.

Romeo. I pray thee, chide not; she whom I love now
Doth grace for grace and love for love allow;
The other did not so.

Friar Laurence. O, she knew well
Thy love did read by rote and could not spell.
But come, young waverer, come, go with me,
In one respect I'll thy assistant be;
For this alliance may so happy prove,
To turn your households' rancour to pure love.

Romeo. O, let us hence; I stand on sudden haste.

Friar Laurence. Wisely and slow; they stumble that run fast.

[Exeunt]

Lesson 50

- Read Act 2, Scenes 4-6 of *Romeo and Juliet.*

Act 2, Scene 4
A street

[Enter BENVOLIO and MERCUTIO]

Mercutio. Where the devil should this Romeo be?
Came he not home to-night?

Benvolio. Not to his father's; I spoke with his man.

Mercutio. Ah, that same pale hard-hearted wench, that Rosaline.
Torments him so, that he will sure run mad.

Benvolio. Tybalt, the kinsman of old Capulet,
Hath sent a letter to his father's house.

Mercutio. A challenge, on my life.

Benvolio. Romeo will answer it.

Mercutio. Any man that can write may answer a letter.

Benvolio. Nay, he will answer the letter's master, how he dares, being dared.

Mercutio. Alas poor Romeo! he is already dead; stabbed with a white wench's black eye; shot through the ear with a love-song; the very pin of his heart cleft with the blind bow-boy's butt-shaft: and is he a man to encounter Tybalt?

Benvolio. Why, what is Tybalt?

Mercutio. More than prince of cats, I can tell you. O, he is the courageous captain of compliments. He fights as you sing prick-song, keeps time, distance, and proportion; rests me his minim rest, one, two, and the third in your bosom: the very butcher of a silk button, a duellist, a duellist; a gentleman of the very first house, of the first and second cause: ah, the immortal passado! the punto reverso! the hai!

Benvolio. The what?

Mercutio. The pox of such antic, lisping, affecting fantasticoes; these new tuners of accents! 'By Jesu, a very good blade! a very tall man! a very good whore!' Why, is not this a lamentable thing, grandsire, that we should be thus afflicted with these strange flies, these fashion-mongers, these perdona-mi's, who stand so much on the new form, that they cannot at ease on the old bench? O, their bones, their bones!

[Enter ROMEO]

Benvolio. Here comes Romeo, here comes Romeo.

Mercutio. Without his roe, like a dried herring: flesh, flesh, how art thou fishified! Now is he for the numbers that Petrarch flowed in: Laura to his lady was but a kitchen-wench; marry, she had a better love to be-rhyme her; Dido a dowdy; Cleopatra a gipsy; Helen and Hero hildings and harlots; Thisbe a grey eye or so, but not to the purpose. Signior Romeo, bon jour! there's a French salutation to your French slop. You gave us the counterfeit fairly last night.

Romeo. Good morrow to you both. What counterfeit did I give you?

Mercutio. The slip, sir, the slip; can you not conceive?

Romeo. Pardon, good Mercutio, my business was great; and in such a case as mine a man may strain courtesy.

Mercutio. That's as much as to say, such a case as yours constrains a man to bow in the hams.

Romeo. Meaning, to court'sy.

Mercutio. Thou hast most kindly hit it.

Romeo. A most courteous exposition.

Mercutio. Nay, I am the very pink of courtesy.

Romeo. Pink for flower.

Mercutio. Right.

Romeo. Why, then is my pump well flowered.

Mercutio. Well said: follow me this jest now till thou hast worn out thy pump, that when the single sole of it is worn, the jest may remain after the wearing sole singular.

Romeo. O single-soled jest, solely singular for the singleness.

Mercutio. Come between us, good Benvolio; my wits faint.

Romeo. Switch and spurs, switch and spurs; or I'll cry a match.

Mercutio. Nay, if thy wits run the wild-goose chase, I have done, for thou hast more of the wild-goose in one of thy wits than, I am sure, I have in my whole five: was I with you there for the goose?

Romeo. Thou wast never with me for any thing when thou wast not there for the goose.

Mercutio. I will bite thee by the ear for that jest.

Romeo. Nay, good goose, bite not.

Mercutio. Thy wit is a very bitter sweeting; it is a most sharp sauce.

Romeo. And is it not well served in to a sweet goose?

Mercutio. O here's a wit of cheveril, that stretches from an inch narrow to an ell broad!

Romeo. I stretch it out for that word 'broad;' which added to the goose, proves thee far and wide a broad goose.

Mercutio. Why, is not this better now than groaning for love? now art thou sociable, now art thou Romeo; now art thou what thou art, by art as well as by nature: for this drivelling love is like a great natural, that runs lolling up and down to hide his bauble in a hole.

Benvolio. Stop there, stop there.

Mercutio. Thou desirest me to stop in my tale against the hair.

Benvolio. Thou wouldst else have made thy tale large.

Mercutio. O, thou art deceived; I would have made it short: for I was come to the whole depth of my tale; and meant, indeed, to occupy the argument no longer.

Romeo. Here's goodly gear!

[Enter Nurse and PETER]

Mercutio. A sail, a sail!

Benvolio. Two, two; a shirt and a smock.

Nurse. Peter!

Peter. Anon!

Nurse. My fan, Peter.

Mercutio. Good Peter, to hide her face; for her fan's the fairer face.

Nurse. God ye good morrow, gentlemen.

Mercutio. God ye good den, fair gentlewoman.

Nurse. Is it good den?

Mercutio. 'Tis no less, I tell you, for the bawdy hand of the dial is now upon the prick of noon.

Nurse. Out upon you! what a man are you!

Romeo. One, gentlewoman, that God hath made for himself to mar.

Nurse. By my troth, it is well said; 'for himself to mar,' quoth a'? Gentlemen, can any of you tell me where I may find the young Romeo?

Romeo. I can tell you; but young Romeo will be older when you have found him than he was when you sought him: I am the youngest of that name, for fault of a worse.

Nurse. You say well.

Mercutio. Yea, is the worst well? very well took, i' faith; wisely, wisely.

Nurse. if you be he, sir, I desire some confidence with you.

Benvolio. She will indite him to some supper.

Mercutio. A bawd, a bawd, a bawd! so ho!

Romeo. What hast thou found?

Mercutio. No hare, sir; unless a hare, sir, in a lenten pie, that is something stale and hoar ere it be spent.
[Sings]
An old hare hoar,
And an old hare hoar,
Is very good meat in lent
But a hare that is hoar
Is too much for a score,
When it hoars ere it be spent.

Romeo, will you come to your father's? we'll to dinner, thither.

Romeo. I will follow you.

Mercutio. Farewell, ancient lady; farewell,
[Singing]
'lady, lady, lady.'

[Exeunt MERCUTIO and BENVOLIO]

Nurse. Marry, farewell! I pray you, sir, what saucy merchant was this, that was so full of his ropery?

Romeo. A gentleman, nurse, that loves to hear himself talk, and will speak more in a minute than he will stand to in a month.

Nurse. An a' speak any thing against me, I'll take him down, an a' were lustier than he is, and twenty such Jacks; and if I cannot, I'll find those that shall. Scurvy knave! I am none of his flirt-gills; I am none of his skains-mates. And thou must stand by too, and suffer every knave to use me at his pleasure?

Peter. I saw no man use you a pleasure; if I had, my weapon should quickly have been out, I warrant you: I dare draw as soon as another man, if I see occasion in a good quarrel, and the law on my side.

Nurse. Now, afore God, I am so vexed, that every part about me quivers. Scurvy knave! Pray you, sir, a word: and as I told you, my young lady bade me inquire you out; what she bade me say, I will keep to myself: but first let me tell ye, if ye should lead her into a fool's paradise, as they say, it were a very gross kind of behavior, as they say: for the gentlewoman is young; and, therefore, if you should deal double with her, truly it were an ill thing to be offered to any gentlewoman, and very weak dealing.

Romeo. Nurse, commend me to thy lady and mistress. I protest unto thee—

Nurse. Good heart, and, i' faith, I will tell her as much: Lord, Lord, she will be a joyful woman.

Romeo. What wilt thou tell her, nurse? thou dost not mark me.

Nurse. I will tell her, sir, that you do protest; which, as I take it, is a gentlemanlike offer.

Romeo. Bid her devise
Some means to come to shrift this afternoon;
And there she shall at Friar Laurence' cell
Be shrived and married. Here is for thy pains.

Nurse. No truly sir; not a penny.

Romeo. Go to; I say you shall.

Nurse. This afternoon, sir? well, she shall be there.

Romeo. And stay, good nurse, behind the abbey wall:
Within this hour my man shall be with thee
And bring thee cords made like a tackled stair;
Which to the high top-gallant of my joy
Must be my convoy in the secret night.
Farewell; be trusty, and I'll quit thy pains:
Farewell; commend me to thy mistress.

Nurse. Now God in heaven bless thee! Hark you, sir.

Romeo. What say'st thou, my dear nurse?

Nurse. Is your man secret? Did you ne'er hear say,
Two may keep counsel, putting one away?

Romeo. I warrant thee, my man's as true as steel.

Nurse. Well, sir; my mistress is the sweetest lady—Lord, Lord! when 'twas a little prating thing:—O, there is a nobleman in town, one Paris, that would fain lay knife aboard; but she, good soul, had as lief see a toad, a very toad, as see him. I anger her sometimes and tell her that Paris is the properer man; but, I'll warrant you, when I say so, she looks as pale as any clout in the versal world. Doth not rosemary and Romeo begin both with a letter?

Romeo. Ay, nurse; what of that? both with an R.

Nurse. Ah. mocker! that's the dog's name; R is for the—No; I know it begins with some other letter:—and she hath the prettiest sententious of it, of you and rosemary, that it would do you good to hear it.

Romeo. Commend me to thy lady.

Nurse. Ay, a thousand times.
[Exit Romeo]
Peter!

Peter. Anon!

Nurse. Peter, take my fan, and go before and apace.

[Exeunt]

Act 2, Scene 5
Capulet's Orchard

[Enter JULIET]

Juliet. The clock struck nine when I did send the nurse;
In half an hour she promised to return.
Perchance she cannot meet him: that's not so.
O, she is lame! love's heralds should be thoughts,
Which ten times faster glide than the sun's beams,
Driving back shadows over louring hills:
Therefore do nimble-pinion'd doves draw love,
And therefore hath the wind-swift Cupid wings.
Now is the sun upon the highmost hill
Of this day's journey, and from nine till twelve
Is three long hours, yet she is not come.
Had she affections and warm youthful blood,

She would be as swift in motion as a ball;
My words would bandy her to my sweet love,
And his to me:
But old folks, many feign as they were dead;
Unwieldy, slow, heavy and pale as lead.
O God, she comes!
[Enter Nurse and PETER]
O honey nurse, what news?
Hast thou met with him? Send thy man away.

Nurse. Peter, stay at the gate.

[Exit PETER]

Juliet. Now, good sweet nurse,—O Lord, why look'st thou sad?
Though news be sad, yet tell them merrily;
If good, thou shamest the music of sweet news
By playing it to me with so sour a face.

Nurse. I am a-weary, give me leave awhile:
Fie, how my bones ache! what a jaunt have I had!

Juliet. I would thou hadst my bones, and I thy news:
Nay, come, I pray thee, speak; good, good nurse, speak.

Nurse. Jesu, what haste? can you not stay awhile?
Do you not see that I am out of breath?

Juliet. How art thou out of breath, when thou hast breath
To say to me that thou art out of breath?
The excuse that thou dost make in this delay
Is longer than the tale thou dost excuse.
Is thy news good, or bad? answer to that;
Say either, and I'll stay the circumstance:
Let me be satisfied, is't good or bad?

Nurse. Well, you have made a simple choice; you know not how to choose a man: Romeo! no, not he; though his face be better than any man's, yet his leg excels all men's; and for a hand, and a foot, and a body, though they be not to be talked on, yet they are past compare: he is not the flower of courtesy, but, I'll warrant him, as gentle as a lamb. Go thy ways, wench; serve God. What, have you dined at home?

Juliet. No, no: but all this did I know before.
What says he of our marriage? what of that?

Nurse. Lord, how my head aches! what a head have I!
It beats as it would fall in twenty pieces.
My back o' t' other side,—O, my back, my back!
Beshrew your heart for sending me about,
To catch my death with jaunting up and down!

Juliet. I' faith, I am sorry that thou art not well.
Sweet, sweet, sweet nurse, tell me, what says my love?

Nurse. Your love says, like an honest gentleman, and a courteous, and a kind, and a handsome, and, I warrant, a virtuous,—Where is your mother?

Juliet. Where is my mother! why, she is within;
Where should she be? How oddly thou repliest!
'Your love says, like an honest gentleman,
Where is your mother?'

Nurse. O God's lady dear!
Are you so hot? marry, come up, I trow;
Is this the poultice for my aching bones?
Henceforward do your messages yourself.

Juliet. Here's such a coil! come, what says Romeo?

Nurse. Have you got leave to go to shrift to-day?

Juliet. I have.

Nurse. Then hie you hence to Friar Laurence' cell;
There stays a husband to make you a wife:
Now comes the wanton blood up in your cheeks,
They'll be in scarlet straight at any news.
Hie you to church; I must another way,
To fetch a ladder, by the which your love
Must climb a bird's nest soon when it is dark:
I am the drudge and toil in your delight,
But you shall bear the burden soon at night.
Go; I'll to dinner: hie you to the cell.

Juliet. Hie to high fortune! Honest nurse, farewell.

[Exeunt]

Act 2, Scene 6
Friar Laurence's cell

[Enter FRIAR LAURENCE and ROMEO]

Friar Laurence. So smile the heavens upon this holy act,
That after hours with sorrow chide us not!

Romeo. Amen, amen! but come what sorrow can,
It cannot countervail the exchange of joy
That one short minute gives me in her sight:
Do thou but close our hands with holy words,
Then love-devouring death do what he dare;
It is enough I may but call her mine.

Friar Laurence. These violent delights have violent ends
And in their triumph die, like fire and powder,
Which as they kiss consume: the sweetest honey

Is loathsome in his own deliciousness
And in the taste confounds the appetite:
Therefore love moderately; long love doth so;
Too swift arrives as tardy as too slow.
[Enter JULIET]
Here comes the lady: O, so light a foot
Will ne'er wear out the everlasting flint:
A lover may bestride the gossamer
That idles in the wanton summer air,
And yet not fall; so light is vanity.

Juliet. Good even to my ghostly confessor.

Friar Laurence. Romeo shall thank thee, daughter, for us both.

Juliet. As much to him, else is his thanks too much.

Romeo. Ah, Juliet, if the measure of thy joy
Be heap'd like mine and that thy skill be more
To blazon it, then sweeten with thy breath
This neighbour air, and let rich music's tongue
Unfold the imagined happiness that both
Receive in either by this dear encounter.

Juliet. Conceit, more rich in matter than in words,
Brags of his substance, not of ornament:
They are but beggars that can count their worth;
But my true love is grown to such excess
I cannot sum up sum of half my wealth.

Friar Laurence. Come, come with me, and we will make short work;
For, by your leaves, you shall not stay alone
Till holy church incorporate two in one.

[Exeunt]

Lesson 51

- Read Act 3, Scene 1 of *Romeo and Juliet.*

Act 3, Scene 1
A public place

[Enter MERCUTIO, BENVOLIO, Page, and Servants]

Benvolio. I pray thee, good Mercutio, let's retire:
The day is hot, the Capulets abroad,
And, if we meet, we shall not scape a brawl;
For now, these hot days, is the mad blood stirring.

Mercutio. Thou art like one of those fellows that when he enters the confines of a tavern claps me his sword upon the table and says 'God send me no need of thee!' and by the operation of the second cup draws it on the drawer, when indeed there is no need.

Benvolio. Am I like such a fellow?

Mercutio. Come, come, thou art as hot a Jack in thy mood as any in Italy, and as soon moved to be moody, and as soon moody to be moved.

Benvolio. And what to?

Mercutio. Nay, an there were two such, we should have none shortly, for one would kill the other. Thou! why, thou wilt quarrel with a man that hath a hair more, or a hair less, in his beard, than thou hast: thou wilt quarrel with a man for cracking nuts, having no other reason but because thou hast hazel eyes: what eye but such an eye would spy out such a quarrel? Thy head is as fun of quarrels as an egg is full of meat, and yet thy head hath been beaten as addle as an egg for quarrelling: thou hast quarrelled with a man for coughing in the street, because he hath wakened thy dog that hath lain asleep in the sun: didst thou not fall out with a tailor for wearing his new doublet before Easter? with another, for tying his new shoes with old riband? and yet thou wilt tutor me from quarrelling!

Benvolio. An I were so apt to quarrel as thou art, any man should buy the fee-simple of my life for an hour and a quarter.

Mercutio. The fee-simple! O simple!

Benvolio. By my head, here come the Capulets.

Mercutio. By my heel, I care not.

[Enter TYBALT and others]

Tybalt. Follow me close, for I will speak to them. Gentlemen, good den: a word with one of you.

Mercutio. And but one word with one of us? couple it with something; make it a word and a blow.

Tybalt. You shall find me apt enough to that, sir, an you will give me occasion.

Mercutio. Could you not take some occasion without giving?

Tybalt. Mercutio, thou consort'st with Romeo,—

Mercutio. Consort! what, dost thou make us minstrels? an thou make minstrels of us, look to hear nothing but

discords: here's my fiddlestick; here's that shall
make you dance. 'Zounds, consort!

Benvolio. We talk here in the public haunt of men:
Either withdraw unto some private place,
And reason coldly of your grievances,
Or else depart; here all eyes gaze on us.

Mercutio. Men's eyes were made to look, and let them gaze;
I will not budge for no man's pleasure, I.

[Enter ROMEO]

Tybalt. Well, peace be with you, sir: here comes my man.

Mercutio. But I'll be hanged, sir, if he wear your livery:
Marry, go before to field, he'll be your follower;
Your worship in that sense may call him 'man.'

Tybalt. Romeo, the hate I bear thee can afford
No better term than this,—thou art a villain.

Romeo. Tybalt, the reason that I have to love thee
Doth much excuse the appertaining rage
To such a greeting: villain am I none;
Therefore farewell; I see thou know'st me not.

Tybalt. Boy, this shall not excuse the injuries
That thou hast done me; therefore turn and draw.

Romeo. I do protest, I never injured thee,
But love thee better than thou canst devise,
Till thou shalt know the reason of my love:
And so, good Capulet,—which name I tender
As dearly as my own,—be satisfied.

Mercutio. O calm, dishonourable, vile submission!
Alla stoccata carries it away.
[Draws]
Tybalt, you rat-catcher, will you walk?

Tybalt. What wouldst thou have with me?

Mercutio. Good king of cats, nothing but one of your nine lives; that I mean to make bold withal, and as you shall use me hereafter, drybeat the rest of the eight. Will you pluck your sword out of his pitcher by the ears? make haste, lest mine be about your ears ere it be out.

Tybalt. I am for you.

[Drawing]

Romeo. Gentle Mercutio, put thy rapier up.

Mercutio. Come, sir, your passado.

[They fight]

Romeo. Draw, Benvolio; beat down their weapons.
Gentlemen, for shame, forbear this outrage!
Tybalt, Mercutio, the prince expressly hath
Forbidden bandying in Verona streets:
Hold, Tybalt! good Mercutio!

[TYBALT under ROMEO's arm stabs MERCUTIO, and flies with his followers]

Mercutio. I am hurt.
A plague o' both your houses! I am sped.
Is he gone, and hath nothing?

Benvolio. What, art thou hurt?

Mercutio. Ay, ay, a scratch, a scratch; marry, 'tis enough.
Where is my page? Go, villain, fetch a surgeon.

[Exit Page]

Romeo. Courage, man; the hurt cannot be much.

Mercutio. No, 'tis not so deep as a well, nor so wide as a church-door; but 'tis enough, 'twill serve: ask for me to-morrow, and you shall find me a grave man. I am peppered, I warrant, for this world. A plague o' both your houses! 'Zounds, a dog, a rat, a mouse, a cat, to scratch a man to death! a braggart, a rogue, a villain, that fights by the book of arithmetic! Why the devil came you between us? I was hurt under your arm.

Romeo. I thought all for the best.

Mercutio. Help me into some house, Benvolio,
Or I shall faint. A plague o' both your houses!
They have made worms' meat of me: I have it,
And soundly too: your houses!

[Exeunt MERCUTIO and BENVOLIO]

Romeo. This gentleman, the prince's near ally,
My very friend, hath got his mortal hurt
In my behalf; my reputation stain'd
With Tybalt's slander,—Tybalt, that an hour
Hath been my kinsman! O sweet Juliet,
Thy beauty hath made me effeminate
And in my temper soften'd valour's steel!

[Re-enter BENVOLIO]

Benvolio. O Romeo, Romeo, brave Mercutio's dead!
That gallant spirit hath aspired the clouds,
Which too untimely here did scorn the earth.

Romeo. This day's black fate on more days doth depend;
This but begins the woe, others must end.

Benvolio. Here comes the furious Tybalt back again.

Romeo. Alive, in triumph! and Mercutio slain!
Away to heaven, respective lenity,
And fire-eyed fury be my conduct now!
[Re-enter TYBALT]
Now, Tybalt, take the villain back again,
That late thou gavest me; for Mercutio's soul
Is but a little way above our heads,
Staying for thine to keep him company:
Either thou, or I, or both, must go with him.

Tybalt. Thou, wretched boy, that didst consort him here,
Shalt with him hence.

Romeo. This shall determine that.

[They fight; TYBALT falls]

Benvolio. Romeo, away, be gone!
The citizens are up, and Tybalt slain.
Stand not amazed: the prince will doom thee death,
If thou art taken: hence, be gone, away!

Romeo. O, I am fortune's fool!

Benvolio. Why dost thou stay?

[Exit ROMEO]

[Enter Citizens, &c]

First Citizen. Which way ran he that kill'd Mercutio?
Tybalt, that murderer, which way ran he?

Benvolio. There lies that Tybalt.

First Citizen. Up, sir, go with me;
I charge thee in the princes name, obey.
[Enter Prince, attended; MONTAGUE, CAPULET, their wives, and others]

Prince Escalus. Where are the vile beginners of this fray?

Benvolio. O noble prince, I can discover all
The unlucky manage of this fatal brawl:
There lies the man, slain by young Romeo,
That slew thy kinsman, brave Mercutio.

Lady Capulet. Tybalt, my cousin! O my brother's child!
O prince! O cousin! husband! O, the blood is spilt
O my dear kinsman! Prince, as thou art true,
For blood of ours, shed blood of Montague.
O cousin, cousin!

Prince Escalus. Benvolio, who began this bloody fray?

Benvolio. Tybalt, here slain, whom Romeo's hand did slay;
Romeo that spoke him fair, bade him bethink
How nice the quarrel was, and urged withal
Your high displeasure: all this uttered
With gentle breath, calm look, knees humbly bow'd,
Could not take truce with the unruly spleen
Of Tybalt deaf to peace, but that he tilts
With piercing steel at bold Mercutio's breast,
Who all as hot, turns deadly point to point,
And, with a martial scorn, with one hand beats

Cold death aside, and with the other sends
It back to Tybalt, whose dexterity,
Retorts it: Romeo he cries aloud,
'Hold, friends! friends, part!' and, swifter than
his tongue,
His agile arm beats down their fatal points,
And 'twixt them rushes; underneath whose arm
An envious thrust from Tybalt hit the life
Of stout Mercutio, and then Tybalt fled;
But by and by comes back to Romeo,
Who had but newly entertain'd revenge,
And to 't they go like lightning, for, ere I
Could draw to part them, was stout Tybalt slain.
And, as he fell, did Romeo turn and fly.
This is the truth, or let Benvolio die.

Lady Capulet. He is a kinsman to the Montague;
Affection makes him false; he speaks not true:
Some twenty of them fought in this black strife,
And all those twenty could but kill one life.
I beg for justice, which thou, prince, must give;
Romeo slew Tybalt, Romeo must not live.

Prince Escalus. Romeo slew him, he slew Mercutio;
Who now the price of his dear blood doth owe?

Montague. Not Romeo, prince, he was Mercutio's friend;
His fault concludes but what the law should end,
The life of Tybalt.

Prince Escalus. And for that offence
Immediately we do exile him hence:
I have an interest in your hate's proceeding,
My blood for your rude brawls doth lie a-bleeding;
But I'll amerce you with so strong a fine
That you shall all repent the loss of mine:
I will be deaf to pleading and excuses;

Nor tears nor prayers shall purchase out abuses:
Therefore use none: let Romeo hence in haste,
Else, when he's found, that hour is his last.
Bear hence this body and attend our will:
Mercy but murders, pardoning those that kill.

[Exeunt]

Lesson 52

- Read Act 3, Scenes 2, 3, and 4 of *Romeo and Juliet.*

Act 3, Scene 2
Capulet's orchard

[Enter JULIET]

Juliet. Gallop apace, you fiery-footed steeds,
Towards Phoebus' lodging: such a wagoner
As Phaethon would whip you to the west,
And bring in cloudy night immediately.
Spread thy close curtain, love-performing night,
That runaway's eyes may wink and Romeo
Leap to these arms, untalk'd of and unseen.
Lovers can see to do their amorous rites
By their own beauties; or, if love be blind,
It best agrees with night. Come, civil night,
Thou sober-suited matron, all in black,
And learn me how to lose a winning match,
Play'd for a pair of stainless maidenhoods:
Hood my unmann'd blood, bating in my cheeks,
With thy black mantle; till strange love, grown bold,
Think true love acted simple modesty.

Come, night; come, Romeo; come, thou day in night;
For thou wilt lie upon the wings of night
Whiter than new snow on a raven's back.
Come, gentle night, come, loving, black-brow'd night,
Give me my Romeo; and, when he shall die,
Take him and cut him out in little stars,
And he will make the face of heaven so fine
That all the world will be in love with night
And pay no worship to the garish sun.
O, I have bought the mansion of a love,
But not possess'd it, and, though I am sold,
Not yet enjoy'd: so tedious is this day
As is the night before some festival
To an impatient child that hath new robes
And may not wear them. O, here comes my nurse,
And she brings news; and every tongue that speaks
But Romeo's name speaks heavenly eloquence.
[Enter Nurse, with cords]
Now, nurse, what news? What hast thou there? the cords
That Romeo bid thee fetch?

Nurse. Ay, ay, the cords.

[Throws them down]

Juliet. Ay me! what news? why dost thou wring thy hands?

Nurse. Ah, well-a-day! he's dead, he's dead, he's dead!
We are undone, lady, we are undone!
Alack the day! he's gone, he's kill'd, he's dead!

Juliet. Can heaven be so envious?

Nurse. Romeo can,
Though heaven cannot: O Romeo, Romeo!
Who ever would have thought it? Romeo!

Juliet. What devil art thou, that dost torment me thus?
This torture should be roar'd in dismal hell.
Hath Romeo slain himself? say thou but 'I,'
And that bare vowel 'I' shall poison more
Than the death-darting eye of cockatrice:
I am not I, if there be such an I;
Or those eyes shut, that make thee answer 'I.'
If he be slain, say 'I'; or if not, no:
Brief sounds determine of my weal or woe.

Nurse. I saw the wound, I saw it with mine eyes,—
God save the mark!—here on his manly breast:
A piteous corse, a bloody piteous corse;
Pale, pale as ashes, all bedaub'd in blood,
All in gore-blood; I swounded at the sight.

Juliet. O, break, my heart! poor bankrupt, break at once!
To prison, eyes, ne'er look on liberty!
Vile earth, to earth resign; end motion here;
And thou and Romeo press one heavy bier!

Nurse. O Tybalt, Tybalt, the best friend I had!
O courteous Tybalt! honest gentleman!
That ever I should live to see thee dead!

Juliet. What storm is this that blows so contrary?
Is Romeo slaughter'd, and is Tybalt dead?
My dear-loved cousin, and my dearer lord?
Then, dreadful trumpet, sound the general doom!
For who is living, if those two are gone?

Nurse. Tybalt is gone, and Romeo banished;
Romeo that kill'd him, he is banished.

Juliet. O God! did Romeo's hand shed Tybalt's blood?

Nurse. It did, it did; alas the day, it did!

Juliet. O serpent heart, hid with a flowering face!
Did ever dragon keep so fair a cave?
Beautiful tyrant! fiend angelical!
Dove-feather'd raven! wolvish-ravening lamb!
Despised substance of divinest show!
Just opposite to what thou justly seem'st,
A damned saint, an honourable villain!
O nature, what hadst thou to do in hell,
When thou didst bower the spirit of a fiend
In moral paradise of such sweet flesh?
Was ever book containing such vile matter
So fairly bound? O that deceit should dwell
In such a gorgeous palace!

Nurse. There's no trust,
No faith, no honesty in men; all perjured,
All forsworn, all naught, all dissemblers.
Ah, where's my man? give me some aqua vitae:
These griefs, these woes, these sorrows make me old.
Shame come to Romeo!

Juliet. Blister'd be thy tongue
For such a wish! he was not born to shame:
Upon his brow shame is ashamed to sit;
For 'tis a throne where honour may be crown'd
Sole monarch of the universal earth.
O, what a beast was I to chide at him!

Nurse. Will you speak well of him that kill'd your cousin?

Juliet. Shall I speak ill of him that is my husband?
Ah, poor my lord, what tongue shall smooth thy name,
When I, thy three-hours wife, have mangled it?
But, wherefore, villain, didst thou kill my cousin?
That villain cousin would have kill'd my husband:
Back, foolish tears, back to your native spring;
Your tributary drops belong to woe,

Which you, mistaking, offer up to joy.
My husband lives, that Tybalt would have slain;
And Tybalt's dead, that would have slain my husband:
All this is comfort; wherefore weep I then?
Some word there was, worser than Tybalt's death,
That murder'd me: I would forget it fain;
But, O, it presses to my memory,
Like damned guilty deeds to sinners' minds:
'Tybalt is dead, and Romeo—banished;'
That 'banished,' that one word 'banished,'
Hath slain ten thousand Tybalts. Tybalt's death
Was woe enough, if it had ended there:
Or, if sour woe delights in fellowship
And needly will be rank'd with other griefs,
Why follow'd not, when she said 'Tybalt's dead,'
Thy father, or thy mother, nay, or both,
Which modern lamentations might have moved?
But with a rear-ward following Tybalt's death,
'Romeo is banished,' to speak that word,
Is father, mother, Tybalt, Romeo, Juliet,
All slain, all dead. 'Romeo is banished!'
There is no end, no limit, measure, bound,
In that word's death; no words can that woe sound.
Where is my father, and my mother, nurse?

Nurse. Weeping and wailing over Tybalt's corse:
Will you go to them? I will bring you thither.

Juliet. Wash they his wounds with tears: mine shall be spent,
When theirs are dry, for Romeo's banishment.
Take up those cords: poor ropes, you are beguiled,
Both you and I; for Romeo is exiled:
He made you for a highway to my bed;
But I, a maid, die maiden-widowed.
Come, cords, come, nurse; I'll to my wedding-bed;
And death, not Romeo, take my maidenhead!

Nurse. Hie to your chamber: I'll find Romeo
To comfort you: I wot well where he is.
Hark ye, your Romeo will be here at night:
I'll to him; he is hid at Laurence' cell.

Juliet. O, find him! give this ring to my true knight,
And bid him come to take his last farewell.

[Exeunt]

Act 3, Scene 3
Friar Laurence's cell

[Enter FRIAR LAURENCE]

Friar Laurence. Romeo, come forth; come forth, thou fearful man:
Affliction is enamour'd of thy parts,
And thou art wedded to calamity.

[Enter ROMEO]

Romeo. Father, what news? what is the prince's doom?
What sorrow craves acquaintance at my hand,
That I yet know not?

Friar Laurence. Too familiar
Is my dear son with such sour company:
I bring thee tidings of the prince's doom.

Romeo. What less than dooms-day is the prince's doom?

Friar Laurence. A gentler judgment vanish'd from his lips,
Not body's death, but body's banishment.

Romeo. Ha, banishment! be merciful, say 'death;'
For exile hath more terror in his look,
Much more than death: do not say 'banishment.'

Friar Laurence. Hence from Verona art thou banished:
Be patient, for the world is broad and wide.

Romeo. There is no world without Verona walls,
But purgatory, torture, hell itself.
Hence-banished is banish'd from the world,
And world's exile is death: then banished,
Is death mis-term'd: calling death banishment,
Thou cutt'st my head off with a golden axe,
And smilest upon the stroke that murders me.

Friar Laurence. O deadly sin! O rude unthankfulness!
Thy fault our law calls death; but the kind prince,
Taking thy part, hath rush'd aside the law,
And turn'd that black word death to banishment:
This is dear mercy, and thou seest it not.

Romeo. 'Tis torture, and not mercy: heaven is here,
Where Juliet lives; and every cat and dog
And little mouse, every unworthy thing,
Live here in heaven and may look on her;
But Romeo may not: more validity,
More honourable state, more courtship lives
In carrion-flies than Romeo: they may seize
On the white wonder of dear Juliet's hand
And steal immortal blessing from her lips,
Who even in pure and vestal modesty,
Still blush, as thinking their own kisses sin;
But Romeo may not; he is banished:
Flies may do this, but I from this must fly:
They are free men, but I am banished.
And say'st thou yet that exile is not death?
Hadst thou no poison mix'd, no sharp-ground knife,
No sudden mean of death, though ne'er so mean,
But 'banished' to kill me?—'banished'?
O friar, the damned use that word in hell;
Howlings attend it: how hast thou the heart,

Being a divine, a ghostly confessor,
A sin-absolver, and my friend profess'd,
To mangle me with that word 'banished'?

Friar Laurence. Thou fond mad man, hear me but speak a word.

Romeo. O, thou wilt speak again of banishment.

Friar Laurence. I'll give thee armour to keep off that word:
Adversity's sweet milk, philosophy,
To comfort thee, though thou art banished.

Romeo. Yet 'banished'? Hang up philosophy!
Unless philosophy can make a Juliet,
Displant a town, reverse a prince's doom,
It helps not, it prevails not: talk no more.

Friar Laurence. O, then I see that madmen have no ears.

Romeo. How should they, when that wise men have no eyes?

Friar Laurence. Let me dispute with thee of thy estate.

Romeo. Thou canst not speak of that thou dost not feel:
Wert thou as young as I, Juliet thy love,
An hour but married, Tybalt murdered,
Doting like me and like me banished,
Then mightst thou speak, then mightst thou tear thy hair,
And fall upon the ground, as I do now,
Taking the measure of an unmade grave.

[Knocking within]

Friar Laurence. Arise; one knocks; good Romeo, hide thyself.

Romeo. Not I; unless the breath of heartsick groans,
Mist-like, infold me from the search of eyes.

[Knocking]

Friar Laurence. Hark, how they knock! Who's there? Romeo, arise;
Thou wilt be taken. Stay awhile! Stand up;
[Knocking]
Run to my study. By and by! God's will,
What simpleness is this! I come, I come!
[Knocking]
Who knocks so hard? whence come you? what's your will?

Nurse. *[Within]* Let me come in, and you shall know
my errand;
I come from Lady Juliet.

Friar Laurence. Welcome, then.

[Enter Nurse]

Nurse. O holy friar, O, tell me, holy friar,
Where is my lady's lord, where's Romeo?

Friar Laurence. There on the ground, with his own tears made drunk.

Nurse. O, he is even in my mistress' case,
Just in her case! O woful sympathy!
Piteous predicament! Even so lies she,
Blubbering and weeping, weeping and blubbering.
Stand up, stand up; stand, and you be a man:
For Juliet's sake, for her sake, rise and stand;
Why should you fall into so deep an O?

Romeo. Nurse!

Nurse. Ah sir! ah sir! Well, death's the end of all.

Romeo. Spakest thou of Juliet? how is it with her?
Doth she not think me an old murderer,

Now I have stain'd the childhood of our joy
With blood removed but little from her own?
Where is she? and how doth she? and what says
My conceal'd lady to our cancell'd love?

Nurse. O, she says nothing, sir, but weeps and weeps;
And now falls on her bed; and then starts up,
And Tybalt calls; and then on Romeo cries,
And then down falls again.

Romeo. As if that name,
Shot from the deadly level of a gun,
Did murder her; as that name's cursed hand
Murder'd her kinsman. O, tell me, friar, tell me,
In what vile part of this anatomy
Doth my name lodge? tell me, that I may sack
The hateful mansion.

[Drawing his sword]

Friar Laurence. Hold thy desperate hand:
Art thou a man? thy form cries out thou art:
Thy tears are womanish; thy wild acts denote
The unreasonable fury of a beast:
Unseemly woman in a seeming man!
Or ill-beseeming beast in seeming both!
Thou hast amazed me: by my holy order,
I thought thy disposition better temper'd.
Hast thou slain Tybalt? wilt thou slay thyself?
And slay thy lady too that lives in thee,
By doing damned hate upon thyself?
Why rail'st thou on thy birth, the heaven, and earth?
Since birth, and heaven, and earth, all three do meet
In thee at once; which thou at once wouldst lose.
Fie, fie, thou shamest thy shape, thy love, thy wit;
Which, like a usurer, abound'st in all,
And usest none in that true use indeed

Which should bedeck thy shape, thy love, thy wit:
Thy noble shape is but a form of wax,
Digressing from the valour of a man;
Thy dear love sworn but hollow perjury,
Killing that love which thou hast vow'd to cherish;
Thy wit, that ornament to shape and love,
Misshapen in the conduct of them both,
Like powder in a skilless soldier's flask,
Is set afire by thine own ignorance,
And thou dismember'd with thine own defence.
What, rouse thee, man! thy Juliet is alive,
For whose dear sake thou wast but lately dead;
There art thou happy: Tybalt would kill thee,
But thou slew'st Tybalt; there are thou happy too:
The law that threaten'd death becomes thy friend
And turns it to exile; there art thou happy:
A pack of blessings lights up upon thy back;
Happiness courts thee in her best array;
But, like a misbehaved and sullen wench,
Thou pout'st upon thy fortune and thy love:
Take heed, take heed, for such die miserable.
Go, get thee to thy love, as was decreed,
Ascend her chamber, hence and comfort her:
But look thou stay not till the watch be set,
For then thou canst not pass to Mantua;
Where thou shalt live, till we can find a time
To blaze your marriage, reconcile your friends,
Beg pardon of the prince, and call thee back
With twenty hundred thousand times more joy
Than thou went'st forth in lamentation.
Go before, nurse: commend me to thy lady;
And bid her hasten all the house to bed,
Which heavy sorrow makes them apt unto:
Romeo is coming.

Nurse. O Lord, I could have stay'd here all the night
To hear good counsel: O, what learning is!
My lord, I'll tell my lady you will come.

Romeo. Do so, and bid my sweet prepare to chide.

Nurse. Here, sir, a ring she bid me give you, sir:
Hie you, make haste, for it grows very late.

[Exit]

Romeo. How well my comfort is revived by this!

Friar Laurence. Go hence; good night; and here stands all your state:
Either be gone before the watch be set,
Or by the break of day disguised from hence:
Sojourn in Mantua; I'll find out your man,
And he shall signify from time to time
Every good hap to you that chances here:
Give me thy hand; 'tis late: farewell; good night.

Romeo. But that a joy past joy calls out on me,
It were a grief, so brief to part with thee: Farewell.

[Exeunt]

Act 3, Scene 4
A room in Capulet's house

[Enter CAPULET, LADY CAPULET, and PARIS]

Capulet. Things have fall'n out, sir, so unluckily,
That we have had no time to move our daughter:
Look you, she loved her kinsman Tybalt dearly,
And so did I:—Well, we were born to die.
'Tis very late, she'll not come down to-night:

I promise you, but for your company,
I would have been a-bed an hour ago.

Paris. These times of woe afford no time to woo.
Madam, good night: commend me to your daughter.

Lady Capulet. I will, and know her mind early to-morrow;
To-night she is mew'd up to her heaviness.

Capulet. Sir Paris, I will make a desperate tender
Of my child's love: I think she will be ruled
In all respects by me; nay, more, I doubt it not.
Wife, go you to her ere you go to bed;
Acquaint her here of my son Paris' love;
And bid her, mark you me, on Wednesday next—
But, soft! what day is this?

Paris. Monday, my lord,

Capulet. Monday! ha, ha! Well, Wednesday is too soon,
O' Thursday let it be: o' Thursday, tell her,
She shall be married to this noble earl.
Will you be ready? do you like this haste?
We'll keep no great ado,—a friend or two;
For, hark you, Tybalt being slain so late,
It may be thought we held him carelessly,
Being our kinsman, if we revel much:
Therefore we'll have some half a dozen friends,
And there an end. But what say you to Thursday?

Paris. My lord, I would that Thursday were to-morrow.

Capulet. Well get you gone: o' Thursday be it, then.
Go you to Juliet ere you go to bed,
Prepare her, wife, against this wedding-day.
Farewell, my lord. Light to my chamber, ho!
Afore me! it is so very very late,

That we may call it early by and by.
Good night.

[Exeunt]

Lesson 53

- Read Act 3, Scene 5 of *Romeo and Juliet.*

Act 3, Scene 5
Capulet's orchard

[Enter ROMEO and JULIET above, at the window]

Juliet. Wilt thou be gone? it is not yet near day:
It was the nightingale, and not the lark,
That pierced the fearful hollow of thine ear;
Nightly she sings on yon pomegranate-tree:
Believe me, love, it was the nightingale.

Romeo. It was the lark, the herald of the morn,
No nightingale: look, love, what envious streaks
Do lace the severing clouds in yonder east:
Night's candles are burnt out, and jocund day
Stands tiptoe on the misty mountain tops.
I must be gone and live, or stay and die.

Juliet. Yon light is not day-light, I know it, I:
It is some meteor that the sun exhales,
To be to thee this night a torch-bearer,
And light thee on thy way to Mantua:
Therefore stay yet; thou need'st not to be gone.

Romeo. Let me be ta'en, let me be put to death;
I am content, so thou wilt have it so.
I'll say yon grey is not the morning's eye,
'Tis but the pale reflex of Cynthia's brow;
Nor that is not the lark, whose notes do beat
The vaulty heaven so high above our heads:
I have more care to stay than will to go:
Come, death, and welcome! Juliet wills it so.
How is't, my soul? Let's talk; it is not day.

Juliet. It is, it is: hie hence, be gone, away!
It is the lark that sings so out of tune,
Straining harsh discords and unpleasing sharps.
Some say the lark makes sweet division;
This doth not so, for she divideth us:
Some say the lark and loathed toad change eyes,
O, now I would they had changed voices too!
Since arm from arm that voice doth us affray,
Hunting thee hence with hunt's-up to the day,
O, now be gone; more light and light it grows.

Romeo. More light and light; more dark and dark our woes!

[Enter Nurse, to the chamber]

Nurse. Madam!

Juliet. Nurse?

Nurse. Your lady mother is coming to your chamber:
The day is broke; be wary, look about.

[Exit]

Juliet. Then, window, let day in, and let life out.

Romeo. Farewell, farewell! one kiss, and I'll descend.

[He goeth down]

Juliet. Art thou gone so? love, lord, ay, husband, friend!
I must hear from thee every day in the hour,
For in a minute there are many days:
O, by this count I shall be much in years
Ere I again behold my Romeo!

Romeo. Farewell!
I will omit no opportunity
That may convey my greetings, love, to thee.

Juliet. O think'st thou we shall ever meet again?

Romeo. I doubt it not; and all these woes shall serve
For sweet discourses in our time to come.

Juliet. O God, I have an ill-divining soul!
Methinks I see thee, now thou art below,
As one dead in the bottom of a tomb:
Either my eyesight fails, or thou look'st pale.

Romeo. And trust me, love, in my eye so do you:
Dry sorrow drinks our blood. Adieu, adieu!

[Exit]

Juliet. O fortune, fortune! all men call thee fickle:
If thou art fickle, what dost thou with him.
That is renown'd for faith? Be fickle, fortune;
For then, I hope, thou wilt not keep him long,
But send him back.

Lady Capulet. *[Within]* Ho, daughter! are you up?

Juliet. Who is't that calls? is it my lady mother?
Is she not down so late, or up so early?
What unaccustom'd cause procures her hither?

[Enter LADY CAPULET]

Lady Capulet. Why, how now, Juliet!

Juliet. Madam, I am not well.

Lady Capulet. Evermore weeping for your cousin's death?
What, wilt thou wash him from his grave with tears?
An if thou couldst, thou couldst not make him live;
Therefore, have done: some grief shows much of love;
But much of grief shows still some want of wit.

Juliet. Yet let me weep for such a feeling loss.

Lady Capulet. So shall you feel the loss, but not the friend
Which you weep for.

Juliet. Feeling so the loss,
Cannot choose but ever weep the friend.

Lady Capulet. Well, girl, thou weep'st not so much for his death,
As that the villain lives which slaughter'd him.

Juliet. What villain madam?

Lady Capulet. That same villain, Romeo.

Juliet. *[Aside]* Villain and he be many miles asunder.—
God Pardon him! I do, with all my heart;
And yet no man like he doth grieve my heart.

Lady Capulet. That is, because the traitor murderer lives.

Juliet. Ay, madam, from the reach of these my hands:
Would none but I might venge my cousin's death!

Lady Capulet. We will have vengeance for it, fear thou not:
Then weep no more. I'll send to one in Mantua,
Where that same banish'd runagate doth live,
Shall give him such an unaccustom'd dram,
That he shall soon keep Tybalt company:
And then, I hope, thou wilt be satisfied.

Juliet. Indeed, I never shall be satisfied
With Romeo, till I behold him—dead—
Is my poor heart for a kinsman vex'd.
Madam, if you could find out but a man
To bear a poison, I would temper it;
That Romeo should, upon receipt thereof,
Soon sleep in quiet. O, how my heart abhors
To hear him named, and cannot come to him.
To wreak the love I bore my cousin
Upon his body that slaughter'd him!

Lady Capulet. Find thou the means, and I'll find such a man.
But now I'll tell thee joyful tidings, girl.

Juliet. And joy comes well in such a needy time:
What are they, I beseech your ladyship?

Lady Capulet. Well, well, thou hast a careful father, child;
One who, to put thee from thy heaviness,
Hath sorted out a sudden day of joy,
That thou expect'st not nor I look'd not for.

Juliet. Madam, in happy time, what day is that?

Lady Capulet. Marry, my child, early next Thursday morn,
The gallant, young and noble gentleman,

The County Paris, at Saint Peter's Church,
Shall happily make thee there a joyful bride.

Juliet. Now, by Saint Peter's Church and Peter too,
He shall not make me there a joyful bride.
I wonder at this haste; that I must wed
Ere he, that should be husband, comes to woo.
I pray you, tell my lord and father, madam,
I will not marry yet; and, when I do, I swear,
It shall be Romeo, whom you know I hate,
Rather than Paris. These are news indeed!

Lady Capulet. Here comes your father; tell him so yourself,
And see how he will take it at your hands.

[Enter CAPULET and Nurse]

Capulet. When the sun sets, the air doth drizzle dew;
But for the sunset of my brother's son
It rains downright.
How now! a conduit, girl? what, still in tears?
Evermore showering? In one little body
Thou counterfeit'st a bark, a sea, a wind;
For still thy eyes, which I may call the sea,
Do ebb and flow with tears; the bark thy body is,
Sailing in this salt flood; the winds, thy sighs;
Who, raging with thy tears, and they with them,
Without a sudden calm, will overset
Thy tempest-tossed body. How now, wife!
Have you deliver'd to her our decree?

Lady Capulet. Ay, sir; but she will none, she gives you thanks.
I would the fool were married to her grave!

Capulet. Soft! take me with you, take me with you, wife.
How! will she none? doth she not give us thanks?
Is she not proud? doth she not count her blest,

Unworthy as she is, that we have wrought
So worthy a gentleman to be her bridegroom?

Juliet. Not proud, you have; but thankful, that you have:
Proud can I never be of what I hate;
But thankful even for hate, that is meant love.

Capulet. How now, how now, chop-logic! What is this?
'Proud,' and 'I thank you,' and 'I thank you not;'
And yet 'not proud,' mistress minion, you,
Thank me no thankings, nor, proud me no prouds,
But fettle your fine joints 'gainst Thursday next,
To go with Paris to Saint Peter's Church,
Or I will drag thee on a hurdle thither.
Out, you green-sickness carrion! out, you baggage!
You tallow-face!

Lady Capulet. Fie, fie! what, are you mad?

Juliet. Good father, I beseech you on my knees,
Hear me with patience but to speak a word.

Capulet. Hang thee, young baggage! disobedient wretch!
I tell thee what: get thee to church o' Thursday,
Or never after look me in the face:
Speak not, reply not, do not answer me;
My fingers itch. Wife, we scarce thought us blest
That God had lent us but this only child;
But now I see this one is one too much,
And that we have a curse in having her:
Out on her, hilding!

Nurse. God in heaven bless her!
You are to blame, my lord, to rate her so.

Capulet. And why, my lady wisdom? hold your tongue,
Good prudence; smatter with your gossips, go.

Nurse. I speak no treason.

Capulet. O, God ye god-den.

Nurse. May not one speak?

Capulet. Peace, you mumbling fool!
Utter your gravity o'er a gossip's bowl;
For here we need it not.

Lady Capulet. You are too hot.

Capulet. God's bread! it makes me mad:
Day, night, hour, tide, time, work, play,
Alone, in company, still my care hath been
To have her match'd: and having now provided
A gentleman of noble parentage,
Of fair demesnes, youthful, and nobly train'd,
Stuff'd, as they say, with honourable parts,
Proportion'd as one's thought would wish a man;
And then to have a wretched puling fool,
A whining mammet, in her fortune's tender,
To answer 'I'll not wed; I cannot love,
I am too young; I pray you, pardon me.'
But, as you will not wed, I'll pardon you:
Graze where you will you shall not house with me:
Look to't, think on't, I do not use to jest.
Thursday is near; lay hand on heart, advise:
An you be mine, I'll give you to my friend;
And you be not, hang, beg, starve, die in
the streets,
For, by my soul, I'll ne'er acknowledge thee,
Nor what is mine shall never do thee good:
Trust to't, bethink you; I'll not be forsworn.

[Exit]

Juliet. Is there no pity sitting in the clouds,
That sees into the bottom of my grief?
O, sweet my mother, cast me not away!
Delay this marriage for a month, a week;
Or, if you do not, make the bridal bed
In that dim monument where Tybalt lies.

Lady Capulet. Talk not to me, for I'll not speak a word:
Do as thou wilt, for I have done with thee.

[Exit]

Juliet. O God!—O nurse, how shall this be prevented?
My husband is on earth, my faith in heaven;
How shall that faith return again to earth,
Unless that husband send it me from heaven
By leaving earth? comfort me, counsel me.
Alack, alack, that heaven should practise stratagems
Upon so soft a subject as myself!
What say'st thou? hast thou not a word of joy?
Some comfort, nurse.

Nurse. Faith, here it is.
Romeo is banish'd; and all the world to nothing,
That he dares ne'er come back to challenge you;
Or, if he do, it needs must be by stealth.
Then, since the case so stands as now it doth,
I think it best you married with the county.
O, he's a lovely gentleman!
Romeo's a dishclout to him: an eagle, madam,
Hath not so green, so quick, so fair an eye
As Paris hath. Beshrew my very heart,
I think you are happy in this second match,
For it excels your first: or if it did not,
Your first is dead; or 'twere as good he were,
As living here and you no use of him.

Juliet. Speakest thou from thy heart?

Nurse. And from my soul too;
Or else beshrew them both.

Juliet. Amen!

Nurse. What?

Juliet. Well, thou hast comforted me marvellous much.
Go in: and tell my lady I am gone,
Having displeased my father, to Laurence' cell,
To make confession and to be absolved.

Nurse. Marry, I will; and this is wisely done.

[Exit]

Juliet. Ancient damnation! O most wicked fiend!
Is it more sin to wish me thus forsworn,
Or to dispraise my lord with that same tongue
Which she hath praised him with above compare
So many thousand times? Go, counsellor;
Thou and my bosom henceforth shall be twain.
I'll to the friar, to know his remedy:
If all else fail, myself have power to die.

[Exit]

Lesson 54

- Read Act 4, Scenes 1 through 4 of *Romeo and Juliet.*

Act 4, Scene 1
Friar Laurence's cell

[Enter FRIAR LAURENCE and PARIS]

Friar Laurence. On Thursday, sir? the time is very short.

Paris. My father Capulet will have it so;
And I am nothing slow to slack his haste.

Friar Laurence. You say you do not know the lady's mind:
Uneven is the course, I like it not.

Paris. Immoderately she weeps for Tybalt's death,
And therefore have I little talk'd of love;
For Venus smiles not in a house of tears.
Now, sir, her father counts it dangerous
That she doth give her sorrow so much sway,
And in his wisdom hastes our marriage,
To stop the inundation of her tears;
Which, too much minded by herself alone,
May be put from her by society:
Now do you know the reason of this haste.

Friar Laurence. *[Aside]* I would I knew not why it should be slow'd.
Look, sir, here comes the lady towards my cell.

[Enter JULIET]

Paris. Happily met, my lady and my wife!

Juliet. That may be, sir, when I may be a wife.

Paris. That may be must be, love, on Thursday next.

Juliet. What must be shall be.

Friar Laurence. That's a certain text.

Paris. Come you to make confession to this father?

Juliet. To answer that, I should confess to you.

Paris. Do not deny to him that you love me.

Juliet. I will confess to you that I love him.

Paris. So will ye, I am sure, that you love me.

Juliet. If I do so, it will be of more price,
Being spoke behind your back, than to your face.

Paris. Poor soul, thy face is much abused with tears.

Juliet. The tears have got small victory by that;
For it was bad enough before their spite.

Paris. Thou wrong'st it, more than tears, with that report.

Juliet. That is no slander, sir, which is a truth;
And what I spake, I spake it to my face.

Paris. Thy face is mine, and thou hast slander'd it.

Juliet. It may be so, for it is not mine own.
Are you at leisure, holy father, now;
Or shall I come to you at evening mass?

Friar Laurence. My leisure serves me, pensive daughter, now.
My lord, we must entreat the time alone.

Paris. God shield I should disturb devotion!
Juliet, on Thursday early will I rouse ye:
Till then, adieu; and keep this holy kiss.

[Exit]

Juliet. O shut the door! and when thou hast done so,
Come weep with me; past hope, past cure, past help!

Friar Laurence. Ah, Juliet, I already know thy grief;
It strains me past the compass of my wits:
I hear thou must, and nothing may prorogue it,
On Thursday next be married to this county.

Juliet. Tell me not, friar, that thou hear'st of this,
Unless thou tell me how I may prevent it:
If, in thy wisdom, thou canst give no help,
Do thou but call my resolution wise,
And with this knife I'll help it presently.
God join'd my heart and Romeo's, thou our hands;
And ere this hand, by thee to Romeo seal'd,
Shall be the label to another deed,
Or my true heart with treacherous revolt
Turn to another, this shall slay them both:
Therefore, out of thy long-experienced time,
Give me some present counsel, or, behold,
'Twixt my extremes and me this bloody knife
Shall play the umpire, arbitrating that
Which the commission of thy years and art
Could to no issue of true honour bring.
Be not so long to speak; I long to die,
If what thou speak'st speak not of remedy.

Friar Laurence. Hold, daughter: I do spy a kind of hope,
Which craves as desperate an execution.
As that is desperate which we would prevent.
If, rather than to marry County Paris,
Thou hast the strength of will to slay thyself,
Then is it likely thou wilt undertake
A thing like death to chide away this shame,

That copest with death himself to scape from it:
And, if thou darest, I'll give thee remedy.

Juliet. O, bid me leap, rather than marry Paris,
From off the battlements of yonder tower;
Or walk in thievish ways; or bid me lurk
Where serpents are; chain me with roaring bears;
Or shut me nightly in a charnel-house,
O'er-cover'd quite with dead men's rattling bones,
With reeky shanks and yellow chapless skulls;
Or bid me go into a new-made grave
And hide me with a dead man in his shroud;
Things that, to hear them told, have made me tremble;
And I will do it without fear or doubt,
To live an unstain'd wife to my sweet love.

Friar Laurence. Hold, then; go home, be merry, give consent
To marry Paris: Wednesday is to-morrow:
To-morrow night look that thou lie alone;
Let not thy nurse lie with thee in thy chamber:
Take thou this vial, being then in bed,
And this distilled liquor drink thou off;
When presently through all thy veins shall run
A cold and drowsy humour, for no pulse
Shall keep his native progress, but surcease:
No warmth, no breath, shall testify thou livest;
The roses in thy lips and cheeks shall fade
To paly ashes, thy eyes' windows fall,
Like death, when he shuts up the day of life;
Each part, deprived of supple government,
Shall, stiff and stark and cold, appear like death:
And in this borrow'd likeness of shrunk death
Thou shalt continue two and forty hours,
And then awake as from a pleasant sleep.
Now, when the bridegroom in the morning comes
To rouse thee from thy bed, there art thou dead:
Then, as the manner of our country is,

In thy best robes uncover'd on the bier
Thou shalt be borne to that same ancient vault
Where all the kindred of the Capulets lie.
In the mean time, against thou shalt awake,
Shall Romeo by my letters know our drift,
And hither shall he come: and he and I
Will watch thy waking, and that very night
Shall Romeo bear thee hence to Mantua.
And this shall free thee from this present shame;
If no inconstant toy, nor womanish fear,
Abate thy valour in the acting it.

Juliet. Give me, give me! O, tell not me of fear!

Friar Laurence. Hold; get you gone, be strong and prosperous
In this resolve: I'll send a friar with speed
To Mantua, with my letters to thy lord.

Juliet. Love give me strength! and strength shall help afford.
Farewell, dear father!

[Exeunt]

Act 4, Scene 2
Hall in Capulet's house

[Enter CAPULET, LADY CAPULET, Nurse, and two Servingmen]

Capulet. So many guests invite as here are writ.
[Exit First Servant]
Sirrah, go hire me twenty cunning cooks.

Second Servant. You shall have none ill, sir; for I'll try if they
can lick their fingers.

Capulet. How canst thou try them so?

Second Servant. Marry, sir, 'tis an ill cook that cannot lick his
own fingers: therefore he that cannot lick his
fingers goes not with me.

Capulet. Go, be gone.
[Exit Second Servant]
We shall be much unfurnished for this time.
What, is my daughter gone to Friar Laurence?

Nurse. Ay, forsooth.

Capulet. Well, he may chance to do some good on her:
A peevish self-will'd harlotry it is.

Nurse. See where she comes from shrift with merry look.

[Enter JULIET]

Capulet. How now, my headstrong! where have you been gadding?

Juliet. Where I have learn'd me to repent the sin
Of disobedient opposition
To you and your behests, and am enjoin'd
By holy Laurence to fall prostrate here,
And beg your pardon: pardon, I beseech you!
Henceforward I am ever ruled by you.

Capulet. Send for the county; go tell him of this:
I'll have this knot knit up to-morrow morning.

Juliet. I met the youthful lord at Laurence' cell;
And gave him what becomed love I might,
Not step o'er the bounds of modesty.

Capulet. Why, I am glad on't; this is well: stand up:
This is as't should be. Let me see the county;
Ay, marry, go, I say, and fetch him hither.

Now, afore God! this reverend holy friar,
Our whole city is much bound to him.

Juliet. Nurse, will you go with me into my closet,
To help me sort such needful ornaments
As you think fit to furnish me to-morrow?

Lady Capulet. No, not till Thursday; there is time enough.

Capulet. Go, nurse, go with her: we'll to church to-morrow.

[Exeunt JULIET and Nurse]

Lady Capulet. We shall be short in our provision:
'Tis now near night.

Capulet. Tush, I will stir about,
And all things shall be well, I warrant thee, wife:
Go thou to Juliet, help to deck up her;
I'll not to bed to-night; let me alone;
I'll play the housewife for this once. What, ho!
They are all forth. Well, I will walk myself
To County Paris, to prepare him up
Against to-morrow: my heart is wondrous light,
Since this same wayward girl is so reclaim'd.

[Exeunt]

Act 4, Scene 3
Juliet's chamber

[Enter JULIET and Nurse]

Juliet. Ay, those attires are best: but, gentle nurse,
I pray thee, leave me to myself to-night,
For I have need of many orisons

To move the heavens to smile upon my state,
Which, well thou know'st, is cross, and full of sin.

[Enter LADY CAPULET]

Lady Capulet. What, are you busy, ho? need you my help?

Juliet. No, madam; we have cull'd such necessaries
As are behoveful for our state to-morrow:
So please you, let me now be left alone,
And let the nurse this night sit up with you;
For, I am sure, you have your hands full all,
In this so sudden business.

Lady Capulet. Good night:
Get thee to bed, and rest; for thou hast need.

[Exeunt LADY CAPULET and Nurse]

Juliet. Farewell! God knows when we shall meet again.
I have a faint cold fear thrills through my veins,
That almost freezes up the heat of life:
I'll call them back again to comfort me:
Nurse! What should she do here?
My dismal scene I needs must act alone.
Come, vial.
What if this mixture do not work at all?
Shall I be married then to-morrow morning?
No, no: this shall forbid it: lie thou there.
[Laying down her dagger]
What if it be a poison, which the friar
Subtly hath minister'd to have me dead,
Lest in this marriage he should be dishonour'd,
Because he married me before to Romeo?
I fear it is: and yet, methinks, it should not,
For he hath still been tried a holy man.
How if, when I am laid into the tomb,

I wake before the time that Romeo
Come to redeem me? there's a fearful point!
Shall I not, then, be stifled in the vault,
To whose foul mouth no healthsome air breathes in,
And there die strangled ere my Romeo comes?
Or, if I live, is it not very like,
The horrible conceit of death and night,
Together with the terror of the place,—
As in a vault, an ancient receptacle,
Where, for these many hundred years, the bones
Of all my buried ancestors are packed:
Where bloody Tybalt, yet but green in earth,
Lies festering in his shroud; where, as they say,
At some hours in the night spirits resort;—
Alack, alack, is it not like that I,
So early waking, what with loathsome smells,
And shrieks like mandrakes' torn out of the earth,
That living mortals, hearing them, run mad:—
O, if I wake, shall I not be distraught,
Environed with all these hideous fears?
And madly play with my forefather's joints?
And pluck the mangled Tybalt from his shroud?
And, in this rage, with some great kinsman's bone,
As with a club, dash out my desperate brains?
O, look! methinks I see my cousin's ghost
Seeking out Romeo, that did spit his body
Upon a rapier's point: stay, Tybalt, stay!
Romeo, I come! this do I drink to thee.

[She falls upon her bed, within the curtains]

Act 4, Scene 4
Hall in Capulet's house

[Enter LADY CAPULET and Nurse]

Lady Capulet. Hold, take these keys, and fetch more spices, nurse.

Nurse. They call for dates and quinces in the pastry.

[Enter CAPULET]

Capulet. Come, stir, stir, stir! the second cock hath crow'd,
The curfew-bell hath rung, 'tis three o'clock:
Look to the baked meats, good Angelica:
Spare not for the cost.

Nurse. Go, you cot-quean, go,
Get you to bed; faith, You'll be sick to-morrow
For this night's watching.

Capulet. No, not a whit: what! I have watch'd ere now
All night for lesser cause, and ne'er been sick.

Lady Capulet. Ay, you have been a mouse-hunt in your time;
But I will watch you from such watching now.

[Exeunt LADY CAPULET and Nurse]

Capulet. A jealous hood, a jealous hood!

[Enter three or four Servingmen, with spits, logs, and baskets]

Capulet. Now, fellow,
What's there?

First Servant. Things for the cook, sir; but I know not what.

Capulet. Make haste, make haste.
[Exit First Servant]
Sirrah, fetch drier logs:
Call Peter, he will show thee where they are.

Second Servant. I have a head, sir, that will find out logs,
And never trouble Peter for the matter.

[Exit]

Capulet. Mass, and well said; a merry whoreson, ha!
Thou shalt be logger-head. Good faith, 'tis day:
The county will be here with music straight,
For so he said he would: I hear him near.
[Music within]
Nurse! Wife! What, ho! What, nurse, I say!
[Re-enter Nurse]
Go waken Juliet, go and trim her up;
I'll go and chat with Paris: hie, make haste,
Make haste; the bridegroom he is come already:
Make haste, I say.

[Exeunt]

Lesson 55

- Read Act 4, Scene 5 of *Romeo and Juliet.*

Act 4, Scene 5
Juliet's chamber

[Enter Nurse]

Nurse. Mistress! what, mistress! Juliet! fast, I warrant her, she:
Why, lamb! why, lady! fie, you slug-a-bed!
Why, love, I say! madam! sweet-heart! why, bride!
What, not a word? you take your pennyworths now;
Sleep for a week; for the next night, I warrant,
The County Paris hath set up his rest,
That you shall rest but little. God forgive me,
Marry, and amen, how sound is she asleep!

I must needs wake her. Madam, madam, madam!
Ay, let the county take you in your bed;
He'll fright you up, i' faith. Will it not be?
[Undraws the curtains]
What, dress'd! and in your clothes! and down again!
I must needs wake you; Lady! lady! lady!
Alas, alas! Help, help! my lady's dead!
O, well-a-day, that ever I was born!
Some aqua vitae, ho! My lord! my lady!

[Enter LADY CAPULET]

Lady Capulet. What noise is here?

Nurse. O lamentable day!

Lady Capulet. What is the matter?

Nurse. Look, look! O heavy day!

Lady Capulet. O me, O me! My child, my only life,
Revive, look up, or I will die with thee!
Help, help! Call help.

[Enter CAPULET]

Capulet. For shame, bring Juliet forth; her lord is come.

Nurse. She's dead, deceased, she's dead; alack the day!

Lady Capulet. Alack the day, she's dead, she's dead, she's dead!

Capulet. Ha! let me see her: out, alas! she's cold:
Her blood is settled, and her joints are stiff;
Life and these lips have long been separated:
Death lies on her like an untimely frost
Upon the sweetest flower of all the field.

Nurse. O lamentable day!

Lady Capulet. O woeful time!

Capulet. Death, that hath ta'en her hence to make me wail,
Ties up my tongue, and will not let me speak.

[Enter FRIAR LAURENCE and PARIS, with Musicians]

Friar Laurence. Come, is the bride ready to go to church?

Capulet. Ready to go, but never to return.
O son! the night before thy wedding-day
Hath Death lain with thy wife. There she lies,
Flower as she was, deflowered by him.
Death is my son-in-law, Death is my heir;
My daughter he hath wedded: I will die,
And leave him all; life, living, all is Death's.

Paris. Have I thought long to see this morning's face,
And doth it give me such a sight as this?

Lady Capulet. Accursed, unhappy, wretched, hateful day!
Most miserable hour that e'er time saw
In lasting labour of his pilgrimage!
But one, poor one, one poor and loving child,
But one thing to rejoice and solace in,
And cruel death hath catch'd it from my sight!

Nurse. O woe! O woeful, woeful, woeful day!
Most lamentable day, most woeful day,
That ever, ever, I did yet behold!
O day! O day! O day! O hateful day!
Never was seen so black a day as this:
O woeful day, O woeful day!

Paris. Beguiled, divorced, wronged, spited, slain!
Most detestable death, by thee beguil'd,
By cruel cruel thee quite overthrown!
O love! O life! not life, but love in death!

Capulet. Despised, distressed, hated, martyr'd, kill'd!
Uncomfortable time, why camest thou now
To murder, murder our solemnity?
O child! O child! my soul, and not my child!
Dead art thou! Alack! my child is dead;
And with my child my joys are buried.

Friar Laurence. Peace, ho, for shame! confusion's cure lives not
In these confusions. Heaven and yourself
Had part in this fair maid; now heaven hath all,
And all the better is it for the maid:
Your part in her you could not keep from death,
But heaven keeps his part in eternal life.
The most you sought was her promotion;
For 'twas your heaven she should be advanced:
And weep ye now, seeing she is advanced
Above the clouds, as high as heaven itself?
O, in this love, you love your child so ill,
That you run mad, seeing that she is well:
She's not well married that lives married long;
But she's best married that dies married young.
Dry up your tears, and stick your rosemary
On this fair corse; and, as the custom is,
In all her best array bear her to church:
For though fond nature bids us an lament,
Yet nature's tears are reason's merriment.

Capulet. All things that we ordained festival,
Turn from their office to black funeral;
Our instruments to melancholy bells,
Our wedding cheer to a sad burial feast,
Our solemn hymns to sullen dirges change,

Our bridal flowers serve for a buried corse,
And all things change them to the contrary.

Friar Laurence. Sir, go you in; and, madam, go with him;
And go, Sir Paris; every one prepare
To follow this fair corse unto her grave:
The heavens do lour upon you for some ill;
Move them no more by crossing their high will.

[Exeunt CAPULET, LADY CAPULET, PARIS, and FRIAR LAURENCE]

First Musician. Faith, we may put up our pipes, and be gone.

Nurse. Honest goodfellows, ah, put up, put up;
For, well you know, this is a pitiful case.

[Exit]

First Musician. Ay, by my troth, the case may be amended.

[Enter PETER]

Peter. Musicians, O, musicians, 'Heart's ease, Heart's ease:' O, an you will have me live, play 'Heart's ease.'

First Musician. Why 'Heart's ease?'

Peter. O, musicians, because my heart itself plays 'My heart is full of woe:' O, play me some merry dump, to comfort me.

First Musician. Not a dump we; 'tis no time to play now.

Peter. You will not, then?

First Musician. No.

Peter. I will then give it you soundly.

First Musician. What will you give us?

Peter. No money, on my faith, but the gleek;
I will give you the minstrel.

First Musician. Then I will give you the serving-creature.

Peter. Then will I lay the serving-creature's dagger on
your pate. I will carry no crotchets: I'll re you,
I'll fa you; do you note me?

First Musician. An you re us and fa us, you note us.

Second Musician. Pray you, put up your dagger, and put out your wit.

Peter. Then have at you with my wit! I will dry-beat you
with an iron wit, and put up my iron dagger. Answer
me like men:
'When griping grief the heart doth wound,
And doleful dumps the mind oppress,
Then music with her silver sound'—
why 'silver sound'? why 'music with her silver
sound'? What say you, Simon Catling?

First Musician. Marry, sir, because silver hath a sweet sound.

Peter. Pretty! What say you, Hugh Rebeck?

Second Musician. I say 'silver sound,' because musicians sound for silver.

Peter. Pretty too! What say you, James Soundpost?

Third Musician. Faith, I know not what to say.

Peter. O, I cry you mercy; you are the singer: I will say
for you. It is 'music with her silver sound,'
because musicians have no gold for sounding:
'Then music with her silver sound
With speedy help doth lend redress.'

[Exit]

First Musician. What a pestilent knave is this same!

Second Musician. Hang him, Jack! Come, we'll in here; tarry for the mourners, and stay dinner.

[Exeunt]

Lesson 56

- Read Act 5, Scenes 1 and 2 of *Romeo and Juliet.*

Act 5, Scene 1
Mantua. A street

[Enter ROMEO]

Romeo. If I may trust the flattering truth of sleep,
My dreams presage some joyful news at hand:
My bosom's lord sits lightly in his throne;
And all this day an unaccustom'd spirit
Lifts me above the ground with cheerful thoughts.
I dreamt my lady came and found me dead—
Strange dream, that gives a dead man leave
to think!—
And breathed such life with kisses in my lips,

That I revived, and was an emperor.
Ah me! how sweet is love itself possess'd,
When but love's shadows are so rich in joy!
[Enter BALTHASAR, booted]
News from Verona!—How now, Balthasar!
Dost thou not bring me letters from the friar?
How doth my lady? Is my father well?
How fares my Juliet? that I ask again;
For nothing can be ill, if she be well.

Balthasar. Then she is well, and nothing can be ill:
Her body sleeps in Capel's monument,
And her immortal part with angels lives.
I saw her laid low in her kindred's vault,
And presently took post to tell it you:
O, pardon me for bringing these ill news,
Since you did leave it for my office, sir.

Romeo. Is it even so? then I defy you, stars!
Thou know'st my lodging: get me ink and paper,
And hire post-horses; I will hence to-night.

Balthasar. I do beseech you, sir, have patience:
Your looks are pale and wild, and do import
Some misadventure.

Romeo. Tush, thou art deceived:
Leave me, and do the thing I bid thee do.
Hast thou no letters to me from the friar?

Balthasar. No, my good lord.

Romeo. No matter: get thee gone,
And hire those horses; I'll be with thee straight.
[Exit BALTHASAR]
Well, Juliet, I will lie with thee to-night.
Let's see for means: O mischief, thou art swift

To enter in the thoughts of desperate men!
I do remember an apothecary,—
And hereabouts he dwells,—which late I noted
In tatter'd weeds, with overwhelming brows,
Culling of simples; meagre were his looks,
Sharp misery had worn him to the bones:
And in his needy shop a tortoise hung,
An alligator stuff'd, and other skins
Of ill-shaped fishes; and about his shelves
A beggarly account of empty boxes,
Green earthen pots, bladders and musty seeds,
Remnants of packthread and old cakes of roses,
Were thinly scatter'd, to make up a show.
Noting this penury, to myself I said
'An if a man did need a poison now,
Whose sale is present death in Mantua,
Here lives a caitiff wretch would sell it him.'
O, this same thought did but forerun my need;
And this same needy man must sell it me.
As I remember, this should be the house.
Being holiday, the beggar's shop is shut.
What, ho! apothecary!

[Enter Apothecary]

Apothecary. Who calls so loud?

Romeo. Come hither, man. I see that thou art poor:
Hold, there is forty ducats: let me have
A dram of poison, such soon-speeding gear
As will disperse itself through all the veins
That the life-weary taker may fall dead
And that the trunk may be discharged of breath
As violently as hasty powder fired
Doth hurry from the fatal cannon's womb.

Apothecary. Such mortal drugs I have; but Mantua's law
Is death to any he that utters them.

Romeo. Art thou so bare and full of wretchedness,
And fear'st to die? famine is in thy cheeks,
Need and oppression starveth in thine eyes,
Contempt and beggary hangs upon thy back;
The world is not thy friend nor the world's law;
The world affords no law to make thee rich;
Then be not poor, but break it, and take this.

Apothecary. My poverty, but not my will, consents.

Romeo. I pay thy poverty, and not thy will.

Apothecary. Put this in any liquid thing you will,
And drink it off; and, if you had the strength
Of twenty men, it would dispatch you straight.

Romeo. There is thy gold, worse poison to men's souls,
Doing more murders in this loathsome world,
Than these poor compounds that thou mayst not sell.
I sell thee poison; thou hast sold me none.
Farewell: buy food, and get thyself in flesh.
Come, cordial and not poison, go with me
To Juliet's grave; for there must I use thee.

[Exeunt]

Act 5, Scene 2
Friar Laurence's cell

[Enter FRIAR JOHN]

Friar John. Holy Franciscan friar! brother, ho!

[Enter FRIAR LAURENCE]

Friar Laurence. This same should be the voice of Friar John.
Welcome from Mantua: what says Romeo?
Or, if his mind be writ, give me his letter.

Friar John. Going to find a bare-foot brother out
One of our order, to associate me,
Here in this city visiting the sick,
And finding him, the searchers of the town,
Suspecting that we both were in a house
Where the infectious pestilence did reign,
Seal'd up the doors, and would not let us forth;
So that my speed to Mantua there was stay'd.

Friar Laurence. Who bare my letter, then, to Romeo?

Friar John. I could not send it,—here it is again,—
Nor get a messenger to bring it thee,
So fearful were they of infection.

Friar Laurence. Unhappy fortune! by my brotherhood,
The letter was not nice but full of charge
Of dear import, and the neglecting it
May do much danger. Friar John, go hence;
Get me an iron crow, and bring it straight
Unto my cell.

Friar John. Brother, I'll go and bring it thee.

[Exit]

Friar Laurence. Now must I to the monument alone;
Within three hours will fair Juliet wake:
She will beshrew me much that Romeo
Hath had no notice of these accidents;
But I will write again to Mantua,
And keep her at my cell till Romeo come;
Poor living corse, closed in a dead man's tomb!

[Exit]

Lesson 57

- Read Act 5, Scene 3 of *Romeo and Juliet.*

Act 5, Scene 3
A churchyard; in it a tomb belonging to the Capulets

[Enter PARIS, and his Page bearing flowers and a torch]

Paris. Give me thy torch, boy: hence, and stand aloof:
Yet put it out, for I would not be seen.
Under yond yew-trees lay thee all along,
Holding thine ear close to the hollow ground;
So shall no foot upon the churchyard tread,
Being loose, unfirm, with digging up of graves,
But thou shalt hear it: whistle then to me,
As signal that thou hear'st something approach.
Give me those flowers. Do as I bid thee, go.

Page. *[Aside]* I am almost afraid to stand alone
Here in the churchyard; yet I will adventure.

[Retires]

Paris. Sweet flower, with flowers thy bridal bed I strew,—
O woe! thy canopy is dust and stones;—
Which with sweet water nightly I will dew,
Or, wanting that, with tears distill'd by moans:
The obsequies that I for thee will keep
Nightly shall be to strew thy grave and weep.
[The Page whistles]

The boy gives warning something doth approach.
What cursed foot wanders this way to-night,
To cross my obsequies and true love's rite?
What with a torch! muffle me, night, awhile.

[Retires]

[Enter ROMEO and BALTHASAR, with a torch, mattock, &c]

Romeo. Give me that mattock and the wrenching iron.
Hold, take this letter; early in the morning
See thou deliver it to my lord and father.
Give me the light: upon thy life, I charge thee,
Whate'er thou hear'st or seest, stand all aloof,
And do not interrupt me in my course.
Why I descend into this bed of death,
Is partly to behold my lady's face;
But chiefly to take thence from her dead finger
A precious ring, a ring that I must use
In dear employment: therefore hence, be gone:
But if thou, jealous, dost return to pry
In what I further shall intend to do,
By heaven, I will tear thee joint by joint
And strew this hungry churchyard with thy limbs:
The time and my intents are savage-wild,
More fierce and more inexorable far
Than empty tigers or the roaring sea.

Balthasar. I will be gone, sir, and not trouble you.

Romeo. So shalt thou show me friendship. Take thou that:
Live, and be prosperous: and farewell, good fellow.

Balthasar. *[Aside]* For all this same, I'll hide me hereabout:
His looks I fear, and his intents I doubt.

[Retires]

Romeo. Thou detestable maw, thou womb of death,
Gorged with the dearest morsel of the earth,
Thus I enforce thy rotten jaws to open,
And, in despite, I'll cram thee with more food!

[Opens the tomb]

Paris. This is that banish'd haughty Montague,
That murder'd my love's cousin, with which grief,
It is supposed, the fair creature died;
And here is come to do some villanous shame
To the dead bodies: I will apprehend him.
[Comes forward]
Stop thy unhallow'd toil, vile Montague!
Can vengeance be pursued further than death?
Condemned villain, I do apprehend thee:
Obey, and go with me; for thou must die.

Romeo. I must indeed; and therefore came I hither.
Good gentle youth, tempt not a desperate man;
Fly hence, and leave me: think upon these gone;
Let them affright thee. I beseech thee, youth,
Put not another sin upon my head,
By urging me to fury: O, be gone!
By heaven, I love thee better than myself;
For I come hither arm'd against myself:
Stay not, be gone; live, and hereafter say,
A madman's mercy bade thee run away.

Paris. I do defy thy conjurations,
And apprehend thee for a felon here.

Romeo. Wilt thou provoke me? then have at thee, boy!

[They fight]

Page. O Lord, they fight! I will go call the watch.

[Exit]

Paris. O, I am slain!
[Falls]
If thou be merciful,
Open the tomb, lay me with Juliet.

[Dies]

Romeo. In faith, I will. Let me peruse this face.
Mercutio's kinsman, noble County Paris!
What said my man, when my betossed soul
Did not attend him as we rode? I think
He told me Paris should have married Juliet:
Said he not so? or did I dream it so?
Or am I mad, hearing him talk of Juliet,
To think it was so? O, give me thy hand,
One writ with me in sour misfortune's book!
I'll bury thee in a triumphant grave;
A grave? O no! a lantern, slaughter'd youth,
For here lies Juliet, and her beauty makes
This vault a feasting presence full of light.
Death, lie thou there, by a dead man interr'd.
[Laying PARIS in the tomb]
How oft when men are at the point of death
Have they been merry! which their keepers call
A lightning before death: O, how may I
Call this a lightning? O my love! my wife!
Death, that hath suck'd the honey of thy breath,
Hath had no power yet upon thy beauty:
Thou art not conquer'd; beauty's ensign yet
Is crimson in thy lips and in thy cheeks,
And death's pale flag is not advanced there.
Tybalt, liest thou there in thy bloody sheet?
O, what more favour can I do to thee,
Than with that hand that cut thy youth in twain
To sunder his that was thine enemy?

Forgive me, cousin! Ah, dear Juliet,
Why art thou yet so fair? shall I believe
That unsubstantial death is amorous,
And that the lean abhorred monster keeps
Thee here in dark to be his paramour?
For fear of that, I still will stay with thee;
And never from this palace of dim night
Depart again: here, here will I remain
With worms that are thy chamber-maids; O, here
Will I set up my everlasting rest,
And shake the yoke of inauspicious stars
From this world-wearied flesh. Eyes, look your last!
Arms, take your last embrace! and, lips, O you
The doors of breath, seal with a righteous kiss
A dateless bargain to engrossing death!
Come, bitter conduct, come, unsavoury guide!
Thou desperate pilot, now at once run on
The dashing rocks thy sea-sick weary bark!
Here's to my love!
[Drinks]
O true apothecary!
Thy drugs are quick. Thus with a kiss I die.
[Dies]
[Enter, at the other end of the churchyard, FRIAR LAURENCE, with a lantern, crow, and spade]

Friar Laurence. Saint Francis be my speed! how oft to-night
Have my old feet stumbled at graves! Who's there?

Balthasar. Here's one, a friend, and one that knows you well.

Friar Laurence. Bliss be upon you! Tell me, good my friend,
What torch is yond, that vainly lends his light
To grubs and eyeless skulls? as I discern,
It burneth in the Capel's monument.

Balthasar. It doth so, holy sir; and there's my master,
One that you love.

Friar Laurence. Who is it?

Balthasar. Romeo.

Friar Laurence. How long hath he been there?

Balthasar. Full half an hour.

Friar Laurence. Go with me to the vault.

Balthasar. I dare not, sir
My master knows not but I am gone hence;
And fearfully did menace me with death,
If I did stay to look on his intents.

Friar Laurence. Stay, then; I'll go alone. Fear comes upon me:
O, much I fear some ill unlucky thing.

Balthasar. As I did sleep under this yew-tree here,
I dreamt my master and another fought,
And that my master slew him.

Friar Laurence. Romeo!
[Advances]
Alack, alack, what blood is this, which stains
The stony entrance of this sepulchre?
What mean these masterless and gory swords
To lie discolour'd by this place of peace?
[Enters the tomb]
Romeo! O, pale! Who else? what, Paris too?
And steep'd in blood? Ah, what an unkind hour
Is guilty of this lamentable chance!
The lady stirs.

[JULIET wakes]

Juliet. O comfortable friar! where is my lord?
I do remember well where I should be,
And there I am. Where is my Romeo?

[Noise within]

Friar Laurence. I hear some noise. Lady, come from that nest
Of death, contagion, and unnatural sleep:
A greater power than we can contradict
Hath thwarted our intents. Come, come away.
Thy husband in thy bosom there lies dead;
And Paris too. Come, I'll dispose of thee
Among a sisterhood of holy nuns:
Stay not to question, for the watch is coming;
Come, go, good Juliet,
[Noise again]
I dare no longer stay.

Juliet. Go, get thee hence, for I will not away.
[Exit FRIAR LAURENCE]
What's here? a cup, closed in my true love's hand?
Poison, I see, hath been his timeless end:
O churl! drunk all, and left no friendly drop
To help me after? I will kiss thy lips;
Haply some poison yet doth hang on them,
To make die with a restorative.
[Kisses him]
Thy lips are warm.

First Watchman. *[Within]* Lead, boy: which way?

Juliet. Yea, noise? then I'll be brief. O happy dagger!
[Snatching ROMEO's dagger]
This is thy sheath;

[Stabs herself]
there rust, and let me die.

[Falls on ROMEO's body, and dies]

[Enter Watch, with the Page of PARIS]

Page. This is the place; there, where the torch doth burn.

First Watchman. The ground is bloody; search about the churchyard:
Go, some of you, whoe'er you find attach.
Pitiful sight! here lies the county slain,
And Juliet bleeding, warm, and newly dead,
Who here hath lain these two days buried.
Go, tell the prince: run to the Capulets:
Raise up the Montagues: some others search:
We see the ground whereon these woes do lie;
But the true ground of all these piteous woes
We cannot without circumstance descry.

[Re-enter some of the Watch, with BALTHASAR]

Second Watchman. Here's Romeo's man; we found him in the churchyard.

First Watchman. Hold him in safety, till the prince come hither.

[Re-enter others of the Watch, with FRIAR LAURENCE]

Third Watchman. Here is a friar, that trembles, sighs and weeps:
We took this mattock and this spade from him,
As he was coming from this churchyard side.

First Watchman. A great suspicion: stay the friar too.

[Enter the PRINCE and Attendants]

Prince Escalus. What misadventure is so early up,
That calls our person from our morning's rest?

[Enter CAPULET, LADY CAPULET, and others]

Capulet. What should it be, that they so shriek abroad?

Lady Capulet. The people in the street cry Romeo,
Some Juliet, and some Paris; and all run,
With open outcry toward our monument.

Prince Escalus. What fear is this which startles in our ears?

First Watchman. Sovereign, here lies the County Paris slain;
And Romeo dead; and Juliet, dead before,
Warm and new kill'd.

Prince Escalus. Search, seek, and know how this foul murder comes.

First Watchman. Here is a friar, and slaughter'd Romeo's man;
With instruments upon them, fit to open
These dead men's tombs.

Capulet. O heavens! O wife, look how our daughter bleeds!
This dagger hath mista'en—for, lo, his house
Is empty on the back of Montague,—
And it mis-sheathed in my daughter's bosom!

Lady Capulet. O me! this sight of death is as a bell,
That warns my old age to a sepulchre.

[Enter MONTAGUE and others]

Prince Escalus. Come, Montague; for thou art early up,
To see thy son and heir more early down.

Montague. Alas, my liege, my wife is dead to-night;
Grief of my son's exile hath stopp'd her breath:
What further woe conspires against mine age?

Prince Escalus. Look, and thou shalt see.

Montague. O thou untaught! what manners is in this?
To press before thy father to a grave?

Prince Escalus. Seal up the mouth of outrage for a while,
Till we can clear these ambiguities,
And know their spring, their head, their
true descent;
And then will I be general of your woes,
And lead you even to death: meantime forbear,
And let mischance be slave to patience.
Bring forth the parties of suspicion.

Friar Laurence. I am the greatest, able to do least,
Yet most suspected, as the time and place
Doth make against me of this direful murder;
And here I stand, both to impeach and purge
Myself condemned and myself excused.

Prince Escalus. Then say at once what thou dost know in this.

Friar Laurence. I will be brief, for my short date of breath
Is not so long as is a tedious tale.
Romeo, there dead, was husband to that Juliet;
And she, there dead, that Romeo's faithful wife:
I married them; and their stol'n marriage-day
Was Tybalt's dooms-day, whose untimely death
Banish'd the new-made bridegroom from the city,
For whom, and not for Tybalt, Juliet pined.
You, to remove that siege of grief from her,
Betroth'd and would have married her perforce
To County Paris: then comes she to me,

And, with wild looks, bid me devise some mean
To rid her from this second marriage,
Or in my cell there would she kill herself.
Then gave I her, so tutor'd by my art,
A sleeping potion; which so took effect
As I intended, for it wrought on her
The form of death: meantime I writ to Romeo,
That he should hither come as this dire night,
To help to take her from her borrow'd grave,
Being the time the potion's force should cease.
But he which bore my letter, Friar John,
Was stay'd by accident, and yesternight
Return'd my letter back. Then all alone
At the prefixed hour of her waking,
Came I to take her from her kindred's vault;
Meaning to keep her closely at my cell,
Till I conveniently could send to Romeo:
But when I came, some minute ere the time
Of her awaking, here untimely lay
The noble Paris and true Romeo dead.
She wakes; and I entreated her come forth,
And bear this work of heaven with patience:
But then a noise did scare me from the tomb;
And she, too desperate, would not go with me,
But, as it seems, did violence on herself.
All this I know; and to the marriage
Her nurse is privy: and, if aught in this
Miscarried by my fault, let my old life
Be sacrificed, some hour before his time,
Unto the rigour of severest law.

Prince Escalus. We still have known thee for a holy man.
Where's Romeo's man? what can he say in this?

Balthasar. I brought my master news of Juliet's death;
And then in post he came from Mantua
To this same place, to this same monument.

This letter he early bid me give his father,
And threatened me with death, going in the vault,
I departed not and left him there.

Prince Escalus. Give me the letter; I will look on it.
Where is the county's page, that raised the watch?
Sirrah, what made your master in this place?

Page. He came with flowers to strew his lady's grave;
And bid me stand aloof, and so I did:
Anon comes one with light to ope the tomb;
And by and by my master drew on him;
And then I ran away to call the watch.

Prince Escalus. This letter doth make good the friar's words,
Their course of love, the tidings of her death:
And here he writes that he did buy a poison
Of a poor 'pothecary, and therewithal
Came to this vault to die, and lie with Juliet.
Where be these enemies? Capulet! Montague!
See, what a scourge is laid upon your hate,
That heaven finds means to kill your joys with love.
And I for winking at your discords too
Have lost a brace of kinsmen: all are punish'd.

Capulet. O brother Montague, give me thy hand:
This is my daughter's jointure, for no more
Can I demand.

Montague. But I can give thee more:
For I will raise her statue in pure gold;
That while Verona by that name is known,
There shall no figure at such rate be set
As that of true and faithful Juliet.

Capulet. As rich shall Romeo's by his lady's lie;
Poor sacrifices of our enmity!

Prince Escalus. A glooming peace this morning with it brings;
The sun, for sorrow, will not show his head:
Go hence, to have more talk of these sad things;
Some shall be pardon'd, and some punished:
For never was a story of more woe
Than this of Juliet and her Romeo.

[Exeunt]

Lesson 60 (no reading for Lessons 58-59)

- Read this summary of *The Pilgrim's Progress* written by an 8th grade student going through Literature and Composition I, Jessica Rutherford.

The Pilgrim's Progress by John Bunyan is an allegory. It is a story that tells about a pilgrim seeking comfort. It's a tale of sorrow and joy, peace and anxiety, life and death, and God's truth.

As the story begins, you are in a dream with a man named Christian. Christian has this big burden on his back which is slowing him down, but it is so heavy no one can take it off! He seeks the help of God. His family doesn't understand what he is saying when he tells them that they have to leave the town they live in, called the City of Destruction. Christian leaves without them, because he is deeply troubled with his burden. He goes on while everyone in the city is calling him back. Two men, Pliable and Obstinate, actually run to bring him back. They ask why he is leaving. Christian says that he is seeking help from God, and he explains that he read that the city where they live will be destroyed. Pliable stays with Christian, and they go on their way. Christian is told which way to go by a man named Evangelist. He tells Christian to go to the wicket gate, and there he will be put on the path to the Celestial City, or Heaven.

As they continue on, Christian tells Pliable more about God and about Heaven, where they are going. But soon they come to The Slough of Despond. The men slide into it, and are stuck. Pliable says he doesn't want to be killed, and that he doesn't think any of what Christian has been saying is true, because he can't see them. Pliable gets out and goes back to his house, but Christian is stuck, sinking because of his burden. But someone pulls him out, and Christian goes on his way.

He comes upon a man named Mr. Worldly Wiseman. This man tells Christian that he need not go to the wicket gate as it will be too dangerous, but he should rather go to the house of Legality. Christian goes, but stands at the bottom of the hill that leads to Legality's house and fears of being burned by the fire or crushed by the mountain. Christian doesn't know what to do, when he sees Evangelist walking toward him. Evangelist asks Christian if he did not tell him which way to go, and if he did not tell him to be very wary of anyone turning him from his path. Christian asks forgiveness from God before walking with Evangelist back to where he had met Worldly Wiseman.

Christian goes on his way again and makes it to the little wicket gate. He is rushed inside when he knocks on the gate, and the gate is closed as the gatekeeper explains that people try to kill pilgrims as they enter the gate. He tells Christian that he should be cautious, as these killers can be anywhere. He guides Christian to the house of the Interpreter. The Interpreter shows Christian all sorts of good things, and some bad. He warns Christian that he should never become like the man who goes to hell, and Christian doesn't forget how horrible the experience is. The Interpreter hands Christian a note and tells him this is the key to get into the Celestial City, and he should not hope to get in without it.

He sends Christian on his way, and Christian walks for days, ascending a hill that has a little shelter halfway up. Christian, being very weary, falls asleep. As he wakes, he cries, for he has sinned, having slept where he shouldn't have. He doesn't notice his note from The Interpreter fall from his bosom. Christian is almost to the top of the hill before realizing his note has gone. He rushes back to get it, hoping no one has taken it, and finds it quickly. He turns back to go up the hill, asking God to forgive his sin. He meets someone in the way, and he tells him "My name is now Christian, but my name used to be Graceless." His name has changed as his faith has changed.

Christian takes much longer in his journey, and has the company of one named Faithful. But they came to a town where Faithful is burned alive. So Christian walks alone for a little ways before coming into the company of Hopeful. Christian and

Hopeful walk together the rest of the way. It's a long, winding road, but they get there. What Christian doesn't know is his wife is getting ready to take the same journey he just completed.

Christian's wife, Christiana, leaves with her children and her friend, Mercy. They go to the wicket gate and are let in. They journey to the house of the Interpreter, from which they leave with a bodyguard and food to eat. They stop where Christian had fallen into a sinful slumber, but they know what happened to Christian the whole way he went, and they keep alert.

Christiana and her children have a much shorter journey, and are reunited with Christian, who is surprised and overjoyed to see them. They live in Heaven for eternity.

So, what is *The Pilgrim's Progress* about? It's about a pilgrim searching for truth, and seeking God with such a passion that he influences others to go, too! It's about a pilgrim finding God's comfort and making sacrifices to get to Him. It's about sorrow and joy, peace and anxiety, life and death, and God's truth. That's what the Pilgrim's Progress is about.

- Read about the author, John Bunyan.

John Bunyan was born in the 1600s, though the exact date of his birth is unknown. There are records of his christening on November 22, 1628, and one would assume he was an infant at that time, so 1628 is generally regarded as his birth year. Bunyan lived in south-central England. His father was a tinker, one who mended and made pots and pans. It was not a well-thought of position, but it was one Bunyan grew up learning. It also allowed him to explore the surrounding countryside and get a feel for how others outside his tiny country surroundings lived and acted. This would serve him later as he began writing of the journeys of Christian in *The Pilgrim's Progress.*

Bunyan likely wasn't overly educated, but he did learn to read and write. Most of England was uneducated and illiterate, so learning to read and write was a bigger deal than it seems. John Bunyan loved to read, leaning heavily toward stories with monsters, villains, and heroes.

From a young boy, Bunyan was obsessed with whether or not he was going to face eternal damnation as a sinner. He felt guilty whenever he enjoyed himself playing games or doing other leisure activities. His spirit was tormented and he was sent into deep depression at times. He was plagued by John Calvin's doctrine of predestination, wondering how anyone could know if they were part of the "elect" or if everything they did on earth was for naught because they weren't part of the elect. Thankfully, Reverend John Gifford ministered to him and over time, Bunyan came to peace with his place in the family of God. He joined Gifford's congregation, and eventually began preaching, and then writing.

During John Bunyan's lifetime, England was in a state of turmoil. It was required at the time for everyone to belong to the Church of England with other forms of worship being prohibited. (You might know from studies of history that a group of people known as Pilgrims left England around that time to head for a new start in the so-called New World, America.) Bunyan refused to stop preaching or go into hiding, and he was eventually arrested for holding religious meetings and not attending services of the Church of England. He was sent to jail for twelve years. Despite the horrific conditions of the jail, this period of his life proved to be his most creative. It was during this time that he wrote and published many books, and it was also when the idea of *The Pilgrim's Progress* was concocted.

There was peace for a time where prisoners who had been arrested for "dissenting" were released and John Bunyan returned to preaching. But a short three years later, the laws were reversed and Bunyan found himself back in jail. He was only there for six months this time, but he was able to complete his masterpiece, *The Pilgrim's Progress*, which was published in 1678. It was so popular that many people requested a sequel, leading to Part II and the story of Christian's wife. Part II was published in 1684.

Throughout his life, John Bunyan ended up publishing around sixty different writings, from sermons to books. However, none comes close to the popularity of *The Pilgrim's Progress*. Bunyan's life ended abruptly when he caught a cold traveling to London in a heavy downpour. His cold developed into pneumonia, and he died August 31, 1688, having left his mark on England and the world.

Lesson 61

- Read some more about the book.

After John Bunyan wrote Part I of *The Pilgrim's Progress* while in prison, he began to show his manuscript to friends, asking for their feedback. Some of his friends encouraged him to publish, but others said he shouldn't, and that he had been too casual with such sacred topics as he addressed in his book. He decided to publish anyway.

The book was an instant success. The first edition, one very cheaply made so Bunyan could reach the humble and poor people he had grown up around, sold out quickly, prompting a second edition before the year was out. By the third edition, Bunyan had revised the book and added several scenes. This was the last edition personally revised by Bunyan and is the one that is the most popular today. All told, more than 100,000 copies were sold during Bunyan's lifetime, a huge number for the time period and printing methods available. The book was translated into many different languages.

Bunyan believed in real, rather than symbolic, angels and demons. He had seen them vividly during hallucinations and nightmares in his youth. He thought dreams were real as well as prophetic. All of these things led to him being able to describe them in vivid detail. This and other attention to detail in his books made his writing easy for the reader to get into. Despite grammar, spelling, and syntax mistakes, Bunyan was able to capture and keep the attention of his readers, and they demanded more.

As such, six years after the first edition of *The Pilgrim's Progress*, a sequel was published, (now generally published with the first book and simply called Part 2). In this sequel, John Bunyan tells the story of Christian's wife, Christiana, and their children as they make the journey to the Desired Country. The sequel was not nearly as popular as the first part, and is considered by many to be an inferior work. But it still has its merit and is worth the read.

- Read a character list.

Part 1

Christian: The main character of Part 1. He flees the City of Destruction and journeys toward the Celestial City where he desires to live for eternity with God.

Evangelist: A preacher who wants to help people find the way to Heaven.

Obstinate: Doesn't like change and thinks Christian is crazy for wanting to make his pilgrimage.

Pliant: He wants to join Christian on his journey, but turns back at the first sign of trial.

Mr. Worldly Wiseman: A pious individual who is held in high regard by his friends. He obeys the Commandments and occupies the moral high ground. He tries to convince Christian to set up camp in the village of Morality instead of going to the Celestial City.

Good-will: The keeper of the Wicket Gate, the entrance to the King's Highway on the way to the Celestial City

Interpreter: The Holy Spirit Christian encounters in a house where he is given much direction in his journey.

Three Shining Ones: Angels whom Christian meets at the Cross.

Formalist: He knows the outward signs of religion, but not the inner workings.

Hypocrisy: He is all things to all men.

Discretion, Prudence, Piety, and Charity: Virgins in charge of Palace Beautiful.

Apollyon: A monster in the Valley of Humiliation. He has the scales of a fish, the feet of a bear, the mouth of a lion, and the wings of a dragon. Apollyon attacks and nearly kills Christian.

Faithful: Another inhabitant of the City of Destruction who meets up with Christian coming out of the Valley of the Shadow of Death. He is one (of two) who shares part of the journey with Christian.

Mr. Talkative: He likes to talk about things but not do anything.

Lord Hate-good: He sentences Faithful to death.

Hopeful: The other one (of two) who shares part of the journey with Christian. He accompanies Christian from Vanity Fair to the Celestial City.

By-ends: He likes the sunny side of religion. He got his name from his friends due to his ability to take on all opportunities for profit he comes across.

Giant Despair: He pounces on Christian and Hopeful when they are asleep and throws them in the dungeon of his Doubting Castle for trespassing. He almost kills them before Christian remembers his magic key that will let them escape.

Knowledge, Experience, Watchful, and Sincere: Helpful shepherds of the flocks of the lords on the Delectable Mountains. They give Christian and Hopeful directions to the Celestial City.

Ignorance: He comes from the County of Conceit and trails Christian and Hopeful all the way to the gates of the Celestial City. They disagree with his ideas but he tells them to worry about themselves. He is cast into Hell by the King of the Celestial City.

Turn-away: He has been seized by seven devils and is being carried away to be thrown into Hell.

Flatterer: He gets Christian and Hopeful to follow him and leads them into capture by a net. They are rescued by a Shining One and led back to the Holy Way.

Atheist: He tells Christian and Hopeful that there is no such place as the Celestial City and laughs at them for believing in such.

Part 2

Christiana: Christian's wife, the main character of Part 2. She regrets having remained behind when Christian left on his journey so she sets out on her own with Matthew, James, Samuel, and Joseph (referred to as "the children").

Mercy: A friend who joins Christiana on her journey and ends up marrying Christiana's son, Matthew.

Great-heart: A Christian solider assigned to lead Christiana to the Celestial Gate.

Old Honest: He is from the Town of Stupidity, but he joins Christiana on her journey.

Gaius: He is an innkeeper at an inn between the Valley of the Shadow of Death and Vanity Fair. He tells Christiana of Christian's heritage, tracing it back to Peter, Paul, and others.

Mnason: The group stays at his house in Vanity Fair. His daughters Grace and Martha marry Christiana's sons Samuel and Joseph.

Feeble-mind: He is rescued from Slay-good the giant by Great-heart and joins the traveling group.

Ready-to-halt: A crippled man who hobbles along on crutches, but joins the party on their travels.

Mr. Despondency and his daughter Much-afraid: They are rescued from the dungeon of Doubting Castle by Great-heart. They join the party but complain the whole way.

Valiant-for-truth: Like Great-heart, he is a mighty giant killer. He likes to talk.

Stand-fast: The group meets him in the Enchanted Ground. He is praying that God would save him from a witch trying to seduce him.

Madam Bubble: The witch trying to seduce Stand-fast, preying on his weaknesses of exhaustion and poverty by offering a bed and purse of money.

There are also various monsters and giants the group encounters on the way.

- What do you notice about the character names? The characters represent the names they are given. This book is an **allegory**. The whole book is a metaphor. It has a meaning beyond the setting, characters, and plot. Each part of the story means something more than what's before your eyes. There is a man named Christian. He is going on a journey. But the allegory, or metaphor, is that he represents someone who recognizes his sin and need for saving and seeks God and salvation through Jesus Christ.

Lesson 62

- Read this summary of section 1 of *The Pilgrim's Progress* written by 8th grade Literature and Composition I student, Jessica Rutherford.

In the beginning, the Narrator is walking through the wilderness, sees a cabin, and lays down to sleep. As he sleeps, he has a dream. And this is where our story begins.

A man named Christian is at his house with a book in his hand and a heavy burden on his back. In his book, he reads that the city he lives in with his wife and children will be burned by fire from heaven, and they need to escape. Everyone thinks he is crazy, and they don't believe him. But Christian is very troubled. So on the word of a man named Evangelist, he flees to seek the way to the Celestial City.

As Christian walks away from his town, people call him back, and two of them go out to bring him back: Obstinate and Pliable. Christian tells the men to come with him. Pliable comes, but Obstinate returns to his home. Christian tells Pliable about the Celestial City as they walk along on the path Evangelist told Christian to take.

Pliable and Christian are talking about the wonders of the Celestial City and what might happen when they get there when they both suddenly fall into the Slough of Despond. Pliable gets up easily, but Christian begins to sink under his heavy burden. Pliable says that Christian has lied about the Celestial City and its wonders, so he climbs out on the side close to his home and leaves Christian to sink as he returns home. Christian yells and asks for someone to help, and Help comes. Help grabs Christian, pulls him out of the slough, and Christian thanks him and walks on.

As Christian continues walking, he runs into Mr. Worldly Wiseman. Christian tells him about his burden and asks for help. Mr. Worldly Wiseman tells Christian that Evangelist was wrong and that Christian needs to seek help from Legality in the village of Morality. Christian goes, but at the foot of the mountain he stops. He sees the mountain about to collapse on top of him and sees fire around the base. Christian cries out and walks away. He then sees Evangelist, who asks Christian why he walked away from the path he was told to follow. Christian ashamedly tells Evangelist about the Slough of Despond, and Mr. Worldly Wiseman. Christian prays and asks God to forgive him for sinning and walking off of the path to Him. And Christian walks on the path to the little wicket gate once more.

- Look at the map of the book's setting on the next three pages. They make the map by fitting side by side with the first page on the left, the second page in the middle, and the third page on the right.

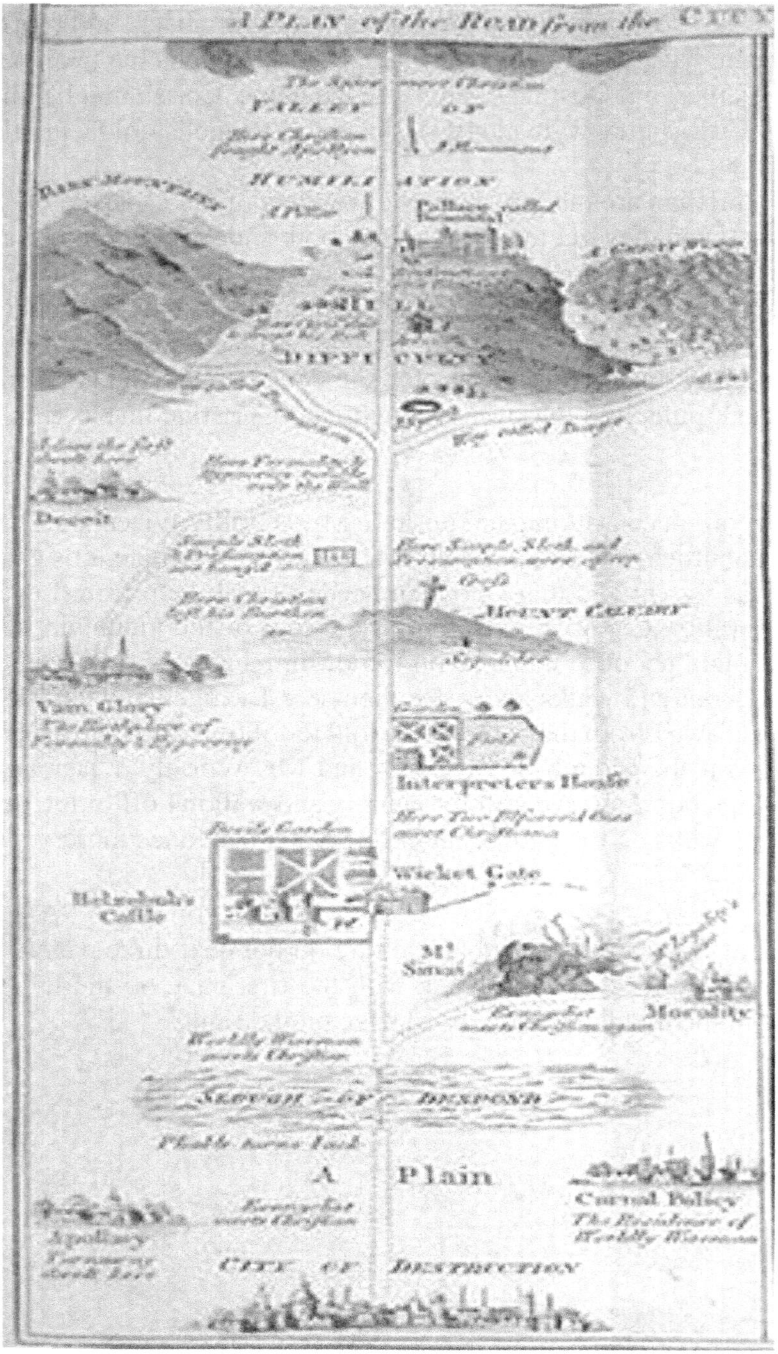
A PLAN of the ROAD from the CITY
VALLEY OF
HUMILIATION
DIFFICULTY
Deceit
MOUNT CALVARY
Vain Glory
Interpreters House
Wicket Gate
Mt Sinai
Morality
SLOUGH OF DESPOND
A Plain
Carnal Policy
CITY OF DESTRUCTION

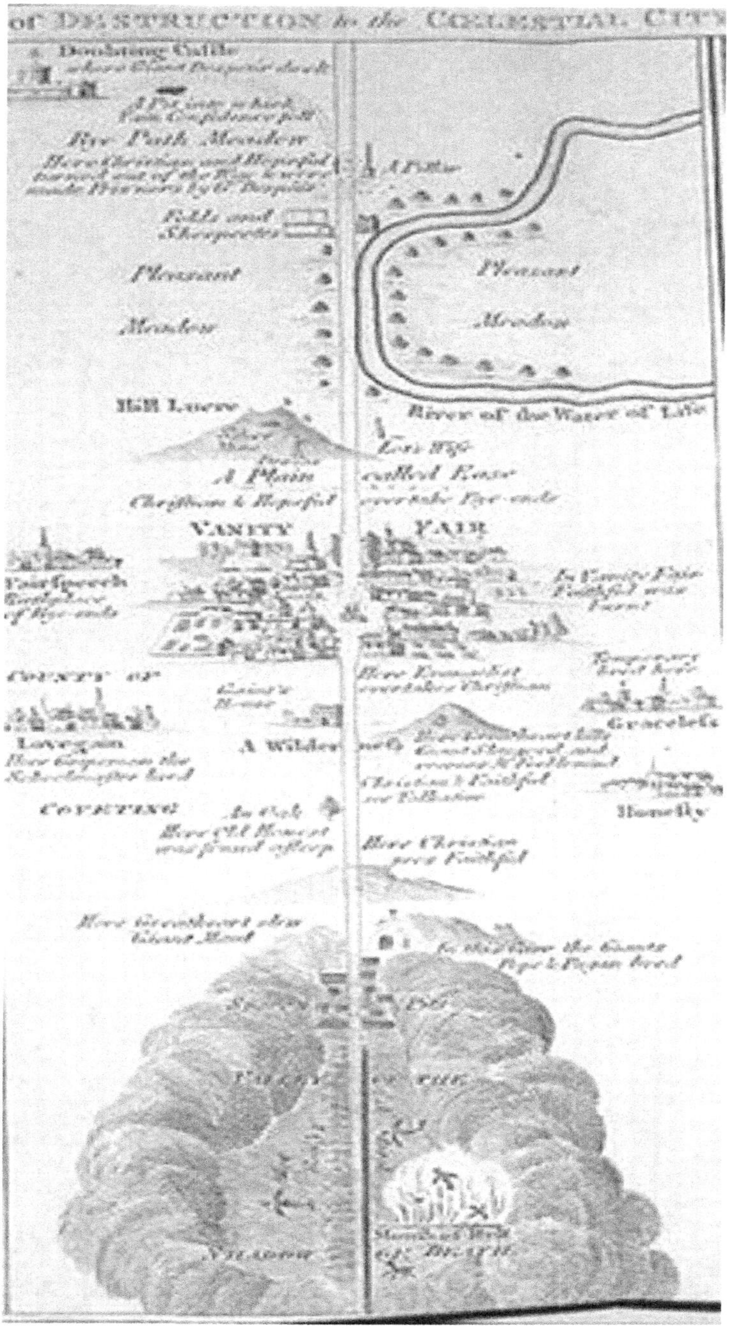
of DESTRUCTION to the CELESTIAL CITY
Doubting Castle
By-Path Meadow
A Pillar
Pleasant
Meadow
Pleasant
Meadow
Hill Lucre
River of the Water of Life
A Plain called Ease
VANITY FAIR
A Wilderness
COVETING
Lovegain

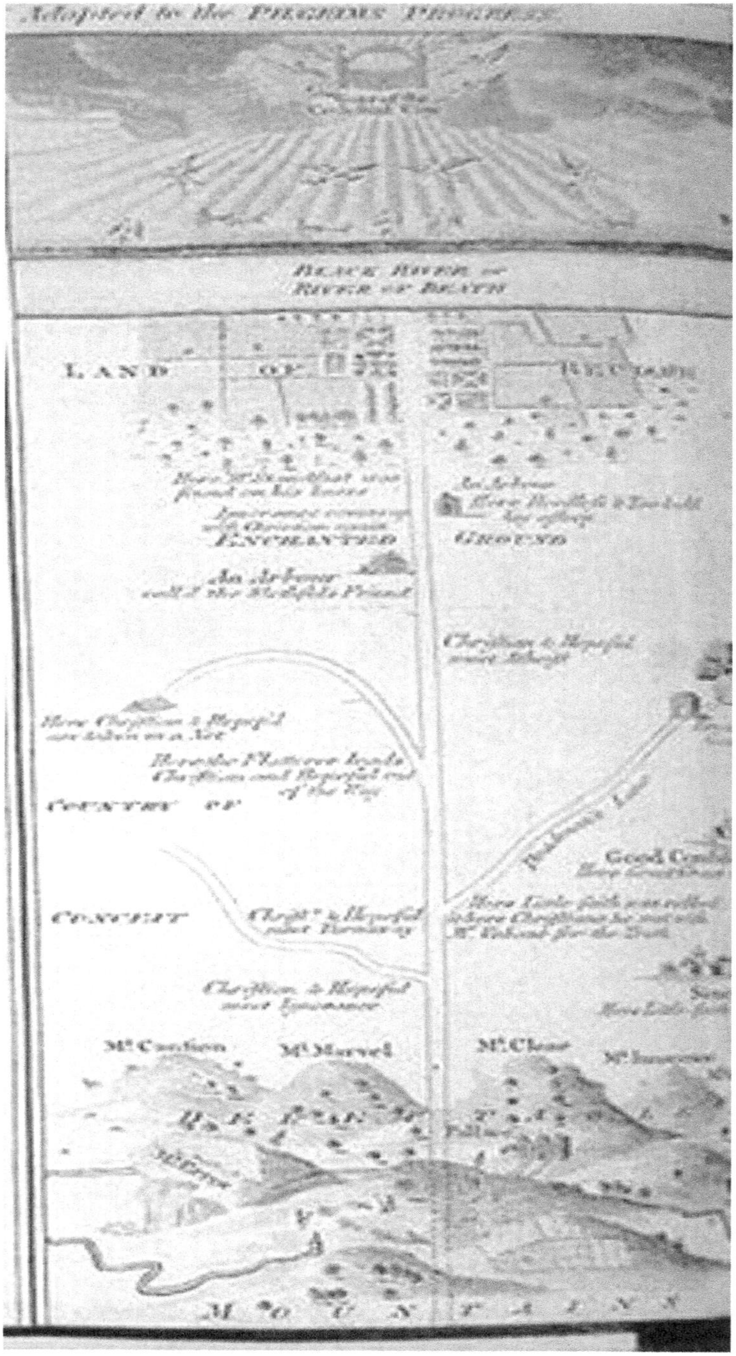
LAND OF
ENCHANTED
GROUND
An Arbour
COUNTRY OF
Mt. Marvel

Lesson 63

- Read Book 1, Section 1 of *The Pilgrim's Progress.*

The Pilgrim's Progress
John Bunyan
Book 1, Section 1
Flight from the City of Destruction

As I walk'd through the wilderness of this world, I lighted on a certain place, where was a Denn; And I laid me down in that place to sleep: And as I slept I dreamed a Dream. I dreamed, and behold I saw a Man cloathed with Raggs, standing in a certain place, with his face from his own House, a Book in his hand, and a great burden upon his Back. I looked and saw him open the Book, and Read therein; and as he read, he wept and trembled: and not being able longer to contain, he brake out with a lamentable cry; saying, what shall I do?

In this plight therefore he went home, and refrained himself as long as he could, that his Wife and Children should not perceive his distress; but he could not be silent long, because that his trouble increased: wherefore at length he brake his mind to his Wife and Children; and thus he began to talk to them, O my dear Wife, said he, and you the Children of my bowels, I your dear friend am in my self undone, by reason of a burden that lieth hard upon me: moreover, I am for certain informed, that this our City will be burned with fire from Heaven, in which fearful overthrow, both my self, with thee, my Wife, and you my sweet babes, shall miserably come to ruine; except (the which, yet I see not) some way of escape can be found, whereby we may be delivered. At this his Relations were sore amazed; not for that they believed, that what he had said to them was true, but because they thought, that some frenzy distemper had got into his head: therefore, it drawing towards night, and they hoping that sleep might settle his brains, with all haste they got him to bed; but the night was as troublesome to him as the day: wherefore instead of sleeping, he spent it in sighs and tears. So when the morning was come, they would know how he did; and he told them worse and worse. He also set to talking to them again, but they began to be hardened; they also thought to drive away his distemper by harsh and surly carriages to him: sometimes they would deride, sometimes they would chide, and sometimes they would quite neglect him:

wherefore he began to retire himself to his Chamber to pray for, and pity them; and also to condole his own misery: he would also walk solitarily in the Fields, sometimes reading, and sometimes praying: and thus for some days he spent his time.

Now, I saw upon a time, when he was walking in the Fields, that he was (as he was wont) reading in his Book, and greatly distressed in his mind; and as he read, he burst out, as he had done before, crying, What shall I do to be saved?

I saw also that he looked this way, and that way, as if he would run; yet he stood still, because, as I perceived, he could not tell which way to go. I looked then, and saw a man named Evangelist coming to him, and he asked, Wherefore dost thou cry? He answered, Sir, I perceive, by the Book in my hand, that I am Condemned to die, and after that to come to Judgment; and I find that I am not willing to do the first, nor able to do the second.

Then said Evangelist, Why not willing to die? since this life is attended with so many evils? The Man answered, Because, I fear that this burden that is upon my back, will sink me lower than the Grave; and I shall fall into Tophet. And Sir, if I be not fit to go to Prison, I am not fit (I am sure) to go to Judgement, and from thence to Execution; and the thoughts of these things make me cry.

Then said Evangelist, If this be thy condition, why standest thou still? He answered, Because I know not whither to go, Then he gave him a Parchment-Roll, and there was written within, Fly from the wrath to come.

The Man therefore Read it, and looking upon Evangelist very carefully; said, Whither must I fly? Then said Evangelist, pointing with his finger over a very wide Field, Do you see yonder Wicket-gate? The Man said, No. Then said the other, Do you see yonder shining light? He said, I think I do. Then said Evangelist, Keep that light in your eye, and go up directly thereto, so shalt thou see the Gate; at which when thou knockest, it shall be told thee what thou shalt do.

So I saw in my Dream that the Man began to run; Now he had not run far from his own door, but his Wife and Children perceiving it, began to cry after him to return: but the Man put his fingers in his Ears, and ran on crying, Life, life, Eternal Life: so he looked not behind him, but fled towards the middle of the Plain.

The Neighbors also came out to see him run, and as he ran, some mocked, others threatned; and some cried after him to return: Now among those that did so, there were two that were resolved to fetch him back by force. The name of the one was Obstinate, and the name of the other Pliable. Now by this time the Man was got a good distance from them; But however they were resolved to pursue him; which they did and in a little time they over-took him. Then said the Man, Neighbours, Wherefore are you come? They said, To perswade you to go back with us; but he said, That can by no means be: You dwell, said he, in the City of Destruction, (the place also where I was born) I see it to be so; and dying there, sooner or later, you will sink lower than the Grave, into a place that burns with Fire and Brimstone: Be content good Neighbours, and go along with me.

What! said Obstinate, and leave our Friends, and our Comforts behind us!

Yes, said Christian, (for that was his name) because that all, which you shall forsake, is not worthy to be compared with a little of that that I am seeking to enjoy, and if you will go along with me, and hold it, you shall fare as I myself; for there where I go, is enough, and to spare; Come away, and prove my words.

Obstinate: What are the things you seek, since you leave all the world to find them?

Christian: I seek an Inheritance, incorruptible, undefiled, and that fadeth not away; and it is laid up in Heaven, and fast there, to be bestowed at the time appointed, on them that diligently seek it. Read it so, if you will, in my Book.

Obstinate: Tush, said Obstinate, away with your Book; will you go back with us, or no?

Christian: No, not I, said the other; because I have laid my hand to the Plow.

Obstinate: Come then, Neighbour Pliable, let us turn again, and go home without him; there is a company of these Craz'd-headed Coxcombs, that when they take a fancy by the end, are wiser in their own eyes then seven men that can render a reason.

Pliable: Then said Pliable, Don't revile; if what the good Christian says is true, the things he looks after are better than ours; my heart inclines to go with my Neighbour.

Obstinate: What! more Fools still? be ruled by me and go back; who knows whither such a brain- sick fellow will lead you? Go back, go back, and be wise.

Christian: Come with me Neighbour Pliable, there are such things to be had which I spoke of, and many more Glories besides; If you believe not me, read here in this Book; and for the truth of what is exprest therein, behold, all is confirmed by the blood of him that made it.

Pliable: Well Neighbour Obstinate (said Pliable) I begin to come to a point; I intend to go along with this good man, and to cast in my lot with him: But my good Companion, do you know the way to this desired place?

Christian: I am directed by a man whose name is Evangelist, to speed me to a little Gate that is before us, where we shall receive instruction about the way.

Pliable: Come then, good Neighbour, let us be going: Then they went both together.

Obstinate: And I will go back to my place, said Obstinate: I will be no Companion of such mis-led, fantastical Fellows.

Now I saw in my Dream, that when Obstinate was gon back, Christian and Pliable went talking over the Plain; and thus they began their discourse,

Christian: Come Neighbour Pliable, how do you do? I am glad you are perswaded to go along with me; and had even Obstinate himself, but felt what I have felt of the Powers, and Terrours of what is yet unseen, he would not thus lightly have given us the back.

Pliable: Come Neighbour Christian, since there is none but us two here, tell me now further, what the things are, and how to be enjoyed, whither we are going.

Christian: I can better conceive of them with my Mind, then speak of them with my Tongue: But yet since you are desirous to know, I will read of them in my Book.

Pliable: And do you think that the words of your Book are certainly true?

Christian: Yes verily, for it was made by him that cannot lye.

Pliable: Well said; what things are they?

Christian: There is an endless Kingdom to be Inhabited, and everlasting life to be given us; that we may Inhabit that Kingdom for ever.

Pliable: Well said, and what else?

Christian: There are Crowns of Glory to be given us; and Garments that will make us shine like the Sun in the Firmament of Heaven.

Pliable: This is excellent; And what else?

Christian: There shall be no more crying, nor sorrow; For he that is owner of the place, will wipe all tears from our eyes.

Pliable: And what company shall we have there?

Christian: There we shall be with Seraphims, and Cherubins, Creatures that will dazle your eyes to look on them: There also you shall meet with thousands, and ten thousands that have gone before us to that place; none of them are hurtful, but loving, and holy; every one walking in the sight of God; and standing in his presence with acceptance for ever: In a word, there we shall see the Elders with their Golden Crowns: There we shall see the Holy Virgins with their Golden Harps. There we shall see Men that by the World were cut in pieces, burnt in flames, eaten of Beasts, drownded in the Seas, for the love that they bare to the Lord of the place; all well, and cloathed with Immortality, as with a Garment.

Pliable: The hearing of this is enough to ravish ones heart; but are these things to be enjoyed? how shall we get to be Sharers hereof?

Christian: The Lord, the Governour of that Countrey, hath Recorded that in this Book: The substance of which is, If we be truly willing to have it, he will bestow it upon us freely.

Pliable: Well, my good Companion, glad am I to hear of these things: Come on, let us mend our pace.

Christian: I cannot go as fast as I would, by reason of this burden that is upon my back.

The Slough of Despond

Now I saw in my Dream, that just as they had ended this talk, they drew near to a very Miry Slow that was in the midst of the Plain, and they being heedless, did both fall suddenly into the bogg. The name of the Slow was Dispond. Here therefore they wallowed for a time, being grievously bedaubed with the dirt; And Christian, because of the burden that was on his back, began to sink in the Mire.

Pliable: Then said Pliable, Ah, Neighbour Christian, where are you now?

Christian: Truly, said Christian, I do not know.

Pliable: At that Pliable began to be offended; and angerly, said to his Fellow, Is this the happiness you have told me all this while of? if we have such ill speed at our first setting out, What may we expect, 'twixt this and our Journeys end? May I get out again with my life, you shall possess the brave Country alone for me. And with that he gave a desperate struggle or two, and got out of the Mire, on that side of the Slow which was next to his own House: So away he went, and Christian saw him no more.

Wherefore Christian was left to tumble in the Slough of Despond alone; but still he endeavored to struggle to that side of the slough that was farthest from his own house, and next to the wicket-gate; the which he did, but could not get out because of the burden that was upon his back: but I beheld in my dream, that a man came to him, whose name was Help, and asked him what he did there.

Christian: Sir, said Christian, I was bid to go this way by a man called Evangelist, who directed me also to yonder gate, that I might escape the wrath to come. And as I was going thither, I fell in here.

Help: But why did not you look for the steps?

Christian: Fear followed me so hard that I fled the next way, and fell in.

Help: Then, said he, Give me thine hand: so he gave him his hand, and he drew him out, and he set him upon sound ground, and bid him go on his way.

Then I stepped to him that plucked him out, and said, "Sir, wherefore, since over this place is the way from the city of Destruction to yonder gate, is it, that this plat is not mended, that poor travellers might go thither with more security?" And he said unto me, "This miry slough is such a place as cannot be mended: it is the descent whither the scum and filth that attends conviction for sin doth continually run, and therefore it is called the Slough of Despond; for still, as the sinner is awakened about his lost condition, there arise in his soul many fears and doubts, and discouraging apprehensions, which all of them get together, and settle in this place: and this is the reason of the badness of this ground.

"It is not the pleasure of the King that this place should remain so bad. His laborers also have, by the direction of his Majesty's surveyors, been for above this sixteen hundred years employed about this patch of ground, if perhaps it might have been mended: yea, and to my knowledge," said he, "there have been swallowed up at least twenty thousand cart loads, yea, millions of wholesome instructions, that have at all seasons been brought from all places of the King's dominions, (and they that can tell, say, they are the best materials to make good ground of the place,) if so be it might have been mended; but it is the Slough of Despond still, and so will be when they have done what they can.

"True, there are, by the direction of the Lawgiver, certain good and substantial steps, placed even through the very midst of this slough; but at such time as this place doth much spew out its filth, as it doth against change of weather, these steps are hardly seen; or if they be, men, through the dizziness of their heads, step beside, and then they are bemired to purpose, notwithstanding the steps be there: but the ground is good when they are once got in at the gate."

Now I saw in my dream, that by this time Pliable was got home to his house. So his neighbors came to visit him; and some of them called him wise man for coming back, and some called him fool for hazarding himself with Christian: others again did mock at his cowardliness, saying, "Surely, since you began to venture, I would not have been so base as to have given out for a few difficulties:" so Pliable sat sneaking among them. But at last he got more confidence, and then they all turned their tales, and began to deride poor Christian behind his back. And thus much concerning Pliable.

Mr. Worldly Wiseman

Now as Christian was walking solitary by himself, he espied one afar off come crossing over the field to meet him; and their hap was to meet just as they were crossing the way of each other. The gentleman's name that met him was Mr. Wordly Wiseman: he dwelt in the town of Carnal Policy, a very great town, and also hard by from whence Christian came. This man then, meeting with Christian, and having some inkling of him, (for Christian's setting forth from the city of Destruction was much noised abroad, not only in the town where he dwelt, but also it began to be the town-talk in some other places) - Mr. Worldly Wiseman, therefore, having some guess of him, by beholding his laborious going, by observing his sighs and groans, and the like, began thus to enter into some talk with Christian.

Mr. Worldly Wiseman: How now, good fellow, whither away after this burdened manner?

Christian: A burdened manner indeed, as ever I think poor creature had! And whereas you ask me, Whither away? I tell you, sir, I am going to yonder wicket-gate before me; for there, as I am informed, I shall be put into a way to be rid of my heavy burden.

Mr. Worldly Wiseman: Hast thou a wife and children?

Christian: Yes; but I am so laden with this burden, that I cannot take that pleasure in them as formerly: methinks I am as if I had none.

Mr. Worldly Wiseman: Wilt thou hearken to me, if I give thee counsel?

Christian: If it be good, I will; for I stand in need of good counsel.

Mr. Worldly Wiseman: I would advise thee, then, that thou with all speed get thyself rid of thy burden; for thou wilt never be settled in thy mind till then: nor canst thou enjoy the benefits of the blessings which God hath bestowed upon thee till then.

Christian: That is that which I seek for, even to be rid of this heavy burden: but get it off myself I cannot, nor is there any man in our country that can take it off my shoulders; therefore am I going this way, as I told you, that I may be rid of my burden.

Mr. Worldly Wiseman: Who bid thee go this way to be rid of thy burden?

Christian: A man that appeared to me to be a very great and honorable person: his name, as I remember, is Evangelist.

Mr. Worldly Wiseman: I beshrew him for his counsel! there is not a more dangerous and troublesome way in the world than is that into which he hath directed thee; and that thou shalt find, if thou wilt be ruled by his counsel. Thou hast met with something, as I perceive, already; for I see the dirt of the Slough of Despond is upon thee: but that slough is the beginning of the sorrows that do attend those that go on in that way. Hear me; I am older than thou: thou art like to meet with, in the way which thou goest, wearisomeness, painfulness, hunger, perils, nakedness, sword, lions, dragons, darkness, and, in a word, death, and what not. These things are certainly true, having been confirmed by many testimonies. And should a man so carelessly cast away himself, by giving heed to a stranger?

Christian: Why, sir, this burden on my back is more terrible to me than are all these things which you have mentioned: nay, methinks I care not what I meet with in the way, if so be I can also meet with deliverance from my burden.

Mr. Worldly Wiseman: How camest thou by thy burden at first?

Christian: By reading this book in my hand.

Mr. Worldly Wiseman: I thought so; and it has happened unto thee as to other weak men, who, meddling with things too high for them, do suddenly fall into thy distractions; which distractions do not only unman men, as thine I perceive have done thee, but they run them upon desperate ventures, to obtain they know not what.

Christian: I know what I would obtain; it is ease from my heavy burden.

Mr. Worldly Wiseman: But why wilt thou seek for ease this way, seeing so many dangers attend it? Especially since (hadst thou but patience to hear me) I could direct thee to the obtaining of what thou desirest, without the dangers that thou in this way wilt run thyself into. Yea, and the remedy is at hand. Besides, I will add, that instead of those dangers, thou shalt meet with much safety, friendship, and content.

Christian: Sir, I pray open this secret to me.

Mr. Worldly Wiseman: Why, in yonder village (the village is named Morality) there dwells a gentleman whose name is Legality, a very judicious man, and a man of a very good name, that has skill to help men off with such burdens as thine is from their shoulders; yea to my knowledge, he hath done a great deal of good this way; aye, and besides, he hath skill to cure those that are somewhat crazed in their wits with their burdens. To him, as I said, thou mayest go, and be helped presently. His house is not quite a mile from this place; and if he should not be at home himself, he hath a pretty young man to his son, whose name is Civility, that can do it (to speak on) as well as the old gentleman himself: there, I say, thou mayest be eased of thy burden; and if thou art not minded to go back to thy former habitation, (as indeed I would not wish thee,) thou mayest send for thy wife and children to this village, where there are houses now standing empty, one of which thou mayest have at a reasonable rate: provision is there also cheap and good; and that which will make thy life the more happy is, to be sure there thou shalt live by honest neighbors, in credit and good fashion.

Now was Christian somewhat at a stand; but presently he concluded, If this be true which this gentleman hath said, my wisest course is to take his advice: and with that he thus farther spake.

Christian: Sir, which is my way to this honest man's house?

Mr. Worldly Wiseman: Do you see yonder high hill?

Christian: Yes, very well.

Mr. Worldly Wiseman: By that hill you must go, and the first house you come at is his.

So Christian turned out of his way to go to Mr. Legality's house for help: but, behold, when he was got now hard by the hill, it seemed so high, and also that side of it that was next the way- side did hang so much over, that Christian was afraid to venture further, lest the hill should fall on his head; wherefore there he stood still, and wotted not what to do. Also his burden now seemed heavier to him than while he was in his way. There came also flashes of fire, out of the hill, that made Christian afraid that he should be burnt: here therefore he did sweat and quake for fear. And now he began to be sorry that he had taken Mr. Worldly Wiseman's counsel; and with that he saw Evangelist coming to meet him, at the sight also of whom he began to blush for shame. So Evangelist drew nearer and nearer; and coming up to him, he looked upon him, with a severe and dreadful countenance, and thus began to reason with Christian.

Evangelist: What doest thou here, Christian? said he: at which words Christian knew not what to answer; wherefore at present he stood speechless before him. Then said Evangelist farther, Art not thou the man that I found crying without the walls of the city of Destruction?

Christian: Yes, dear sir, I am the man.

Evangelist: Did not I direct thee the way to the little wicket-gate?

Christian: Yes, dear sir, said Christian.

Evangelist: How is it then thou art so quickly turned aside? For thou art now out of the way.

Christian: I met with a gentleman so soon as I had got over the Slough of Despond, who persuaded me that I might, in the village before me, find a man that could take off my burden.

Evangelist: What was he?

Christian: He looked like a gentleman, and talked much to me, and got me at last to yield: so I came hither; but when I beheld this hill, and how it hangs over the way, I suddenly made a stand, lest it should fall on my head.

Evangelist: What said that gentleman to you?

Christian: Why, he asked me whither I was going; and I told him.

Evangelist: And what said he then?

Christian: He asked me if I had a family; and I told him. But, said I, I am so laden with the burden that is on my back, that I cannot take pleasure in them as formerly.

Evangelist: And what said he then?

Christian: He bid me with speed get rid of my burden; and I told him it was ease that I sought. And, said I, I am therefore going to yonder gate, to receive farther direction how I may get to the place of deliverance. So he said that he would show me a better way, and short, not so attended with difficulties as the way, sir, that you set me in; which way, said he, will direct you to a gentleman's house that hath skill to take off these burdens: so I believed him, and turned out of that way into this, if haply I might be soon eased of my burden. But when I came to this place, and beheld things as they are, I stopped, for fear (as I said) of danger: but I now know not what to do.

Evangelist: Then said Evangelist, Stand still a little, that I show thee the words of God. So he stood trembling. Then said Evangelist, "See that ye refuse not Him that speaketh; for if they escaped not who refused him that spake on earth, much more shall not we escape, if we turn away from Him that speaketh from heaven." He said, moreover, "Now the just shall live by faith; but if any man draw back, my soul shall have no pleasure in him." He also did thus apply them: Thou art the man that art running into this misery; thou hast begun to reject the counsel of the Most High, and to draw back thy foot from the way of peace, even almost to the hazarding of thy perdition.

Then Christian fell down at his feet as dead, crying, Woe is me, for I am undone! At the sight of which Evangelist caught him by the right hand, saying, "All manner of sin and blasphemies shall be forgiven unto men." "Be not faithless, but believing." Then did Christian again a little revive, and stood up trembling, as at first, before Evangelist.

Then Evangelist proceeded, saying, Give more earnest heed to the things that I shall tell thee of. I will now show thee who it was that deluded thee, and who it was also to whom he sent thee. The man that met thee is one Worldly Wiseman, and rightly is he so called; partly because he savoreth only the doctrine of this world, (therefore he always goes to the town of Morality to church;) and partly because he loveth that doctrine best, for it saveth him best from the cross, and because he is of this carnal temper, therefore he seeketh to pervert my ways, though right. Now there are three things in this man's counsel that thou must utterly abhor.

1. His turning thee out of the way. 2. His laboring to render the cross odious to thee. 3. And his setting thy feet in that way that leadeth unto the administration of death. First, Thou must abhor his turning thee out of the way; yea, and thine own consenting thereto; because this is to reject the counsel of God for the sake of the counsel of a Worldly Wiseman. The Lord says, "Strive to enter in at the straight gate," the gate to which I send thee; "for strait is the gate that leadeth unto life, and few there be that find it." From this little wicket-gate, and from the way thereto, hath this wicked man turned thee, to the bringing of thee almost to destruction: hate, therefore, his turning thee out of the way, and abhor thyself for hearkening to him.

Secondly, Thou must abhor his laboring to render the cross odious unto thee; for thou art to prefer it before the treasures of Egypt. Besides, the King of glory hath told thee, that he that will save his life shall lose it. And he that comes after him, and hates not his father, and mother, and wife, and children, and brethren, and sisters, yea, and his own life also, he cannot be his disciple. I say, therefore, for a man to labor to persuade thee that that shall be thy death, without which, the truth hath said, thou canst not have eternal life, this doctrine thou must abhor.

Thirdly, Thou must hate his setting of thy feet in the way that leadeth to the ministration of death. And for this thou must consider to whom he sent thee, and also how unable that person was to deliver thee from thy burden.

He to whom thou wast sent for ease, being by name Legality, is the son of the bond-woman which now is, and is in bondage with her children, and is, in a mystery, this Mount Sinai, which thou hast feared will fall on thy head. Now if she with her children are in bondage, how canst thou expect by them to be made free? This Legality, therefore, is not able to set thee free from thy burden. No man was as yet ever rid of his burden by him; no, nor ever is like to be: ye cannot be justified by the works of the law; for by the deeds of the law no man living can be rid of his burden: Therefore Mr. Worldly Wiseman is an alien, and Mr. Legality is a cheat; and for his son Civility, notwithstanding his simpering looks, he is but a hypocrite, and cannot help thee. Believe me, there is nothing in all this noise that thou hast heard of these sottish men, but a design to beguile thee of thy salvation, by turning thee from the way in which I had set thee. After this, Evangelist called aloud to the heavens for confirmation of what he had said; and with that there came words and fire out of the mountain under which poor Christian stood, which made the hair of his flesh stand up. The words were pronounced: "As many as are of the works of the law, are under the curse; for it is written, Cursed is every one that continueth not in all things which are written in the book of the law to do them."

Now Christian looked for nothing but death, and began to cry out lamentably; even cursing the time in which he met with Mr. Worldly Wiseman; still calling himself a thousand fools for hearkening to his counsel. He also was greatly ashamed to think that this gentleman's arguments, flowing only from the flesh, should have the prevalency with him so far as to cause him to forsake the right way. This done, he applied himself again to Evangelist in words and sense as follows.

Christian: Sir, what think you? Is there any hope? May I now go back, and go up to the wicket- gate? Shall I not be abandoned for this, and sent back from thence ashamed? I am sorry I have hearkened to this man's counsel; but may my sin be forgiven?

Evangelist: Then said Evangelist to him, Thy sin is very great, for by it thou hast committed two evils: thou hast forsaken the way that is good, to tread in forbidden paths. Yet will the man at the gate receive thee, for he has good-will for men; only, said he, take heed that thou turn not aside again, lest thou "perish from the way, when his wrath is kindled but a little."

Lesson 64

- Read this summary of section 2 of *The Pilgrim's Progress*, written with help from 8th grade Literature and Composition I student, Ashlyn Rutherford.

As Christian journeys to the Wicket Gate, he feels like he's walking along forbidden ground because he knows he's a sinner. He walks for some time but finally arrives at the gate. Over the gate is written, "Knock, and it shall be opened to you" (from Matthew 7:7). He knocks and knocks and the gate is finally opened by Goodwill who, (upon finding out who Christian is, why he has come, where he is going, and why no one has followed him on his journey), allows Christian to set off again to The House of the Interpreter along a straight and narrow path.

Christian arrives and The Interpreter lets Christian in. Christian asks so many questions, but The Interpreter answers them all as though he is asked these very questions every day. Christian sees many things here that stick with him. Among them are a horribly dusty room that is swept clean, explained to Christian to represent the heart of a person being cleaned of original sin so the King of Glory can enter in. Another is when he sees a man in an iron cage. He learns that this man used to be a Christian on his way to the Celestial City. But along the way, he renounced the faith and must suffer the tortures of Hell.

Finally, The Interpreter shows him a man who is shaking in terror from a dream he had had about the Heavens becoming dark with storms and a fierce man sitting on a cloud surrounded by flaming attendants. The fierce man calls the world to Judgment. Christian inquires what is so terrifying about that, and the dreamer explains how he tried to hide from the man on the cloud but that he could not hide from him. He is terrified of judgment.

Christian understands from these things that if he continues on his way he will get rid of his burden, and if he turns back he will never get rid of it. He knows he cannot hide because he will always be found again. So Christian thanks The Interpreter and leaves him while telling himself that he's seen things he wanted to see and things that he didn't want to see, things that made him hopeful for what might happen on the road ahead and some that made him terrified to carry on. But carry on he does.

Lesson 65

- Read Book 1, Section 2 of *The Pilgrim's Progress*.

Book 1, Section 2
The Wicket Gate

Then did Christian address himself to go back; and Evangelist, after he had kissed him, gave him one smile, and bid him God speed; So he went on with haste, neither spake he to any man by the way; nor if any asked him, would he vouchsafe them an answer. He went like one that was all the while treading on forbidden ground, and could by no means think himself safe, till again he was got into the way which he had left to follow Mr. Worldly Wiseman's counsel. So, in process of time, Christian got up to the gate. Now, over the gate there was written, "Knock, and it shall be opened unto you."

He knocked, therefore, more than once or twice, saying,
"May I now enter here? Will he within
Open to sorry me, though I have been
An undeserving rebel? Then shall I
Not fail to sing his lasting praise on high."

At last there came a grave person to the gate, named Goodwill, who asked who was there, and whence he came, and what he would have.

Christian: Here is a poor burdened sinner. I come from the city of Destruction, but am going to Mount Zion, that I may be delivered from the wrath to come; I would therefore, sir, since I am informed that by this gate is the way thither, know if you are willing to let me in.

Goodwill: I am willing with all my heart, said he; and with that he opened the gate. So when Christian was stepping in, the other gave him a pull. Then said Christian, What means that? The other told him, A little distance from this gate there is erected a strong castle, of which Beelzebub is the captain: from thence both he and they that are with him shoot arrows at those that come up to this gate, if haply they may die before they can enter in. Then said Christian, I rejoice and tremble. So when he was got in, the man of the Gate asked him who directed him thither.

Christian: Evangelist bid me come hither and knock, as I did: and he said, that you, sir, would tell me what I must do.

Goodwill: An open door is set before thee, and no man can shut it.

Christian: Now I begin to reap the benefits of my hazards.

Goodwill: But how is it that you came alone?

Christian: Because none of my neighbors saw their danger as I saw mine.

Goodwill: Did any of them know of your coming?

Christian: Yes, my wife and children saw me at the first, and called after me to turn again: also, some of my neighbors stood crying and calling after me to return; but I put my fingers in my ears, and so came on my way.

Goodwill: But did none of them follow you, to persuade you to go back?

Christian: Yes, both Obstinate and Pliable; but when they saw that they could not prevail, Obstinate went railing back; but Pliable came with me a little way.

Goodwill: But why did he not come through?

Christian: We indeed came both together until we came to the Slough of Despond, into the which we also suddenly fell. And then was my neighbor Pliable discouraged, and would not venture farther. Wherefore, getting out again on the side next to his own house, he told me I should possess the brave country alone for him: so he went his way, and I came mine; he after Obstinate, and I to this gate.

Goodwill: Then said Goodwill, Alas, poor man; is the celestial glory of so little esteem with him, that he counteth it not worth running the hazard of a few difficulties to obtain it?

Christian: Truly, said Christian, I have said the truth of Pliable; and if I should also say all the truth of myself, it will appear there is no betterment betwixt him and myself. It is true, he went back to his own house, but I also turned aside to go in the way of death, being persuaded thereto by the carnal arguments of one Mr. Worldly Wiseman.

Goodwill: Oh, did he light upon you? What, he would have had you have seek for ease at the hands of Mr. Legality! They are both of them a very cheat. But did you take his counsel?

Christian: Yes, as far as I durst. I went to find out Mr. Legality, until I thought that the mountain that stands by his house would have fallen upon my head; wherefore there I was forced to stop.

Goodwill: That mountain has been the death of many, and will be the death of many more: it is well you escaped being by it dashed in pieces.

Christian: Why truly I do not know what had become of me there, had not Evangelist happily met me again as I was musing in the midst of my dumps; but it was God's mercy that he came to me again, for else I had never come hither. But now I am come, such a one as I am, more fit indeed for death by that mountain, than thus to stand talking with my Lord. But O, what a favor is this to me, that yet I am admitted entrance here!

Goodwill: We make no objections against any, notwithstanding all that they have done before they come hither; they in no wise are cast out. And therefore good Christian, come a little way with me, and I will teach thee about the way thou must go. Look before thee; dost thou see this narrow way? That is the way thou must go. It was cast up by the patriarchs, prophets, Christ, and his apostles, and it is as strait as a rule can make it; this is the way thou must go.

Christian: But, said Christian, are there no turnings nor windings, by which a stranger may lose his way?

Goodwill: Yes, there are many ways butt down upon this, and they are crooked and wide: but thus thou mayest distinguish the right from the wrong, the right only being strait and narrow.

Then I saw in my dream, that Christian asked him further, if he could not help him off with his burden that was upon his back. For as yet he had not got rid thereof; nor could he by any means get it off without help.

He told him, "As to thy burden, be content to bear it until thou comest to the place of deliverance; for there it will fall from thy back of itself."

Then Christian began to gird up his loins, and to address himself to his journey. So the other told him, that by that he was gone some distance from the gate, he would come to the house of the Interpreter, at whose door he should knock, and he would show him excellent things. Then Christian took his leave of his friend, and he again bid him God speed.

The House of the Interpreter

Then he went on till he came at the house of the Interpreter, where he knocked over and over. At last one came to the door, and asked who was there.

Christian: Sir, here is a traveller, who was bid by an acquaintance of the good man of this house to call here for my profit; I would therefore speak with the master of the house.

So he called for the master of the house, who, after a little time, came to Christian, and asked him what he would have.

Christian: Sir, said Christian, I am a man that am come from the city of Destruction, and am going to the Mount Zion; and I was told by the man that stands at the gate at the head of this way, that if I called here you would show me excellent things, such as would be helpful to me on my journey.

Interpreter: Then said Interpreter, Come in; I will show thee that which will be profitable to thee. So he commanded his man to light the candle, and bid Christian follow him; so he had him into a private room, and bid his man open a door; the which when he had done, Christian saw the picture a very grave person hang up against the wall; and this was the fashion of it: It had eyes lifted up to heaven, the best of books in his hand, the law of truth was written upon its lips, the world was behind its back; it stood as if it pleaded with men, and a crown of gold did hang over its head.

Christian: Then said Christian, What means this?

Interpreter: The man whose picture this is, is one of a thousand: he can beget children, travail in birth with children, and nurse them himself when they are born. And whereas thou seest him with his eyes lift up to heaven, the best of books in his hand, and the law of truth writ on his lips: it is to show thee, that his work is to know, and unfold dark things to sinners; even as also thou seest him stand as if he pleaded with men. And whereas thou seest the world as cast behind him, and that a crown hangs over his head; that is to show thee, that slighting and despising the things that are present, for the love that he hath to his Master's service, he is sure in the world that comes next, to have glory for his reward. Now, said the Interpreter, I have showed thee this picture first, because the man whose picture this is, is the only man whom the Lord of the place whither thou art going hath authorized to be thy guide in all difficult places thou mayest meet with in the way: wherefore take good heed to what I have showed thee, and bear well in thy mind what thou hast seen, lest in thy journey thou meet with some that pretend to lead thee right, but their way goes down to death.

Then he took him by the hand, and led him into a very large parlor that was full of dust, because never swept; the which after he had reviewed it a little while, the Interpreter called for a man to sweep. Now, when he began to sweep, the dust began so abundantly to fly about, that Christian had almost therewith been choked. Then said the Interpreter to a damsel that stood by, "Bring hither water, and sprinkle the room;" the which when she had done, it was swept and cleansed with pleasure.

Christian: Then said Christian, What means this?

Interpreter: The Interpreter answered, This parlor is the heart of a man that was never sanctified by the sweet grace of the Gospel. The dust is his original sin, and inward corruptions, that have defiled the whole man. He that began to sweep at first, is the law; but she that brought water, and did sprinkle it, is the Gospel. Now whereas thou sawest, that so soon as the first began to sweep, the dust did so fly about that the room by him could not be cleansed, but that thou wast almost choked therewith; this is to show thee, that the law, instead of cleansing the heart (by its working) from sin, doth revive, put strength into, and increase it in the soul, even as it doth discover and forbid it; for it doth not give power to subdue. Again, as thou sawest the damsel sprinkle the room with water, upon which it was cleansed with pleasure, this is to show thee, that when the Gospel comes in the sweet and precious influences thereof to the heart, then, I say, even as thou sawest the damsel lay the dust by sprinkling the floor with water, so is sin vanquished and subdued, and the soul made clean, through the faith of it, and consequently fit for the King of glory to inhabit.

I saw moreover in my dream, that the Interpreter took him by the hand, and had him into a little room, where sat two little children, each one in his chair. The name of the eldest was Passion, and the name of the other Patience. Passion seemed to be much disconted, but Patience was very quiet. Then Christian asked, "What is the reason of the discontent of Passion?" The Interpreter answered, "The governor of them would have him stay for his best things till the beginning of the next year, but he will have all now; but Patience is willing to wait." Then I saw that one came to Passion, and brought him a bag of treasure, and poured it down at his feet: the which he took up, and rejoiced therein, and withal laughed Patience to scorn. But I beheld but a while, and he had lavished all away, and had nothing left him but rags.

Christian: Then said Christian to the Interpreter, Expound this matter more fully to me.

Interpreter: So he said, These two lads are figures; Passion of the men of this world, and Patience of the men of that which is to come; for, as here thou seest, passion will have all now, this year, that is to say, in this world; so are the men of this world: They must have all their good things now; they cannot stay till the next year, that is, until the next world, for their portion of good. That proverb, "A bird in the hand is worth two in the bush," is of more authority with them than are all the divine testimonies of the good of the world to come. But as thou sawest that he had quickly lavished all away, and had presently left him nothing but rags, so will it be with all such men at the end of this world.

Christian: Then said Christian, Now I see that Patience has the best wisdom, and that upon many accounts. 1. Because he stays for the best things. 2. And also because he will have the glory of his, when the other has nothing but rags.

Interpreter: Nay, you may add another, to wit, the glory of the next world will never wear out; but these are suddenly gone. Therefore Passion had not so much reason to laugh at Patience because he had his good things first, as Patience will have to laugh at Passion because he had his best things last; for first must give place to last, because last must have his time to come: but last gives place to nothing, for there is not another to succeed. He, therefore, that hath his portion first, must needs have a time to spend it; but he that hath his portion last, must have it lastingly: therefore it is said of Dives, "In thy lifetime thou receivedst thy good things, and likewise Lazarus evil things; but now he is comforted, and thou art tormented."

Christian: Then I perceive it is not best to cover things that are now, but to wait for things to come.

Interpreter: You say truth: for the things that are seen are temporal, but the things that are not seen are eternal. But though this be so, yet since things present and our fleshly appetite are such near neighbors one to another; and again, because things to come and carnal sense are such strangers one to another; therefore it is, that the first of these so suddenly fall into amity, and that distance is so continued between the second.

Then I saw in my dream, that the Interpreter took Christian by the hand, and led him into a place where was a fire burning against a wall, and one standing by it, always casting much water upon it, to quench it; yet did the fire burn higher and hotter.

Then said Christian, What means this?

The Interpreter answered, This fire is the work of grace that is wrought in the heart; he that casts water upon it, to extinguish and put it out, is the devil: but in that thou seest the fire, notwithstanding, burn higher and hotter, thou shalt also see the reason of that. So he had him about to the back side of the wall, where he saw a man with a vessel of oil in his hand, of the which he did also continually cast (but secretly) into the fire.

Then said Christian, What means this?

The Interpreter answered, This is Christ, who continually, with the oil of his grace, maintains the work already begun in the heart; by the means of which, notwithstanding what the devil can do, the souls of his people prove gracious still. And in that thou sawest that the man stood behind the wall to maintain the fire; this is to teach thee, that it is hard for the tempted to see how this work of grace is maintained in the soul.

I saw also, that the Interpreter took him again by the hand, and led him into a pleasant place, where was built a stately palace, beautiful to behold; at the sight of which Christian was greatly delighted. He saw also upon the top thereof certain persons walking, who were clothed all in gold.

Then said Christian may we go in thither?

Then the Interpreter took him, and led him up towards the door of the palace; and behold, at the door stood a great company of men, as desirous to go in, but durst not. There also sat a man at a little distance from the door, at a table-side, with a book and his inkhorn before him, to take the names of them that should enter therein; he saw also that in the doorway stood many men in armor to keep it, being resolved to do to the men that would enter, what hurt and mischief they could. Now was Christian somewhat in amaze. At last, when every man started back for fear of the armed men, Christian saw a man of a very stout countenance come up to the man that sat there to write, saying, "Set down my name, sir;" the which when he had done, he saw the man draw his sword, and put a helmet on his head, and rush towards the door upon the armed men, who laid upon him with deadly force; but the man, not at all discouraged, fell to cutting and hacking most fiercely. So after he had received and given many wounds to those that attempted to keep him out; he cut his way through them all, and pressed forward into the palace; at which there was a pleasant voice heard from those that were within, even of those that walked upon the top of the palace, saying,

"Come in, come in,
Eternal glory thou shalt win."

So he went in, and was clothed with such garments as they. Then Christian smiled, and said, I think verily I know the meaning of this.

Now, said Christian, let me go hence. Nay, stay, said the Interpreter, till I have showed thee a little more, and after that thou shalt go on thy way. So he took him by the hand again, and led him into a very dark room, where there sat a man in an iron cage.

Now the man, to look on, seemed very sad; he sat with his eyes looking down to the ground, his hands folded together, and he sighed as if he would break his heart. Then said Christian, What means this? At which the Interpreter bid him talk with the man.

Then said Christian to the man, What art thou? The man answered, I am what I was not once.

Christian: What wast thou once?

The Man: The man said, I was once a fair and flourishing professor, both in mine own eyes, and also in the eyes of others: I once was, as I thought, fair for the celestial city, and had then even joy at the thoughts that I should get thither.

Christian: Well, but what art thou now?

The Man: I am now a man of despair, and am shut up in it, as in this iron cage. I cannot get out; Oh now I cannot!

Christian: But how camest thou into this condition?

The Man: I left off to watch and be sober: I laid the reins upon the neck of my lusts; I sinned against the light of the word, and the goodness of God; I have grieved the Spirit, and he is gone; I tempted the devil, and he is come to me; I have provoked God to anger, and he has left me: I have so hardened my heart, that I cannot repent.

Then said Christian to the Interpreter, But is there no hope for such a man as this? Ask him, said the Interpreter.

Christian: Then said Christian, Is there no hope, but you must be kept in the iron cage of despair?

The Man: No, none at all.

Christian: Why, the Son of the Blessed is very pitiful.

The Man: I have crucified him to myself afresh; I have despised his person; I have despised his righteousness; I have counted his blood an unholy thing; I have done despite to the spirit of grace, therefore I have shut myself out of all the promises and there now remains to me nothing but threatenings, dreadful threatenings, faithful threatenings of certain judgment and fiery indignation, which shall devour me as an adversary.

Christian: For what did you bring yourself into this condition?

The Man: For the lusts, pleasures, and profits of this world; in the enjoyment of which I did then promise myself much delight: but now every one of those things also bite me, and gnaw me like a burning worm.

Christian: But canst thou not now repent and turn?

The Man: God hath denied me repentance. His word gives me no encouragement to believe; yea, himself hath shut me up in this iron cage: nor can all the men in the world let me out. Oh eternity! eternity! how shall I grapple with the misery that I must meet with in eternity?

Interpreter: Then said the Interpreter to Christian, Let this man's misery be remembered by thee, and be an everlasting caution to thee.

Christian: Well, said Christian, this is fearful! God help me to watch and to be sober, and to pray that I may shun the cause of this man's misery. Sir, is it not time for me to go on my way now?

Interpreter: Tarry till I shall show thee one thing more, and then thou shalt go on thy way. So he took Christian by the hand again and led him into a chamber where there was one rising out of bed; and as he put on his raiment, he shook and trembled. Then said Christian, Why doth this man thus tremble? The Interpreter then bid him tell to Christian the reason of his so doing.

So he began, and said, "This night, as I was in my sleep, I dreamed, and behold the heavens grew exceeding black; also it thundered and lightened in most fearful wise, that it put me into an agony. So I looked up in my dream, and saw the clouds rack at an unusual rate; upon which I heard a great sound of a trumpet, and saw also a man sitting upon a cloud, attended with the thousands of heaven: they were all in flaming fire; also the heavens were in a burning flame. I heard then a voice, saying, 'rise, ye dead, and come to judgment.'And with that the rocks rent, the graves opened, and the dead that were therein came forth: some of them were exceeding glad, and looked upward; and some sought to hide themselves under the mountains. Then I saw the man that sat upon the cloud open the book, and bid the world draw near. Yet there was, by reason of a fierce flame that issued out and came from before him, a convenient distance between him and them, as between the judge and the prisoners at the bar. I heard it also proclaimed to them that attended on the man that sat on the cloud, 'Gather together the tares, the chaff, and stubble, and cast them into the burning Lake.' And with that the bottomless pit opened, just whereabout I stood; out of the mouth of which there came, in an abundant manner, smoke, and coals of fire, with hideous noises. It was also said to the same persons, Gather my wheat into my Garner. And with that I saw many catched up and carried away into the clouds, but I was left behind. I also sought to hide myself, but I could not, for the man that sat upon the cloud still kept his eye upon me; my sins also came into my mind, and my conscience did accuse me on every side. Upon this I awakened from my sleep."

Christian: But what was it that made you so afraid of this sight?

The Man: Why, I thought that the day of judgment was come, and that I was not ready for it: but this frightened me most, that the angels gathered up several, and left me behind; also the pit of hell opened her mouth just where I stood. My conscience too afflicted me; and, as I thought, the Judge had always his eye upon me, showing indignation in his countenance.

Then said the Interpreter to Christian, "Hast thou considered all these things?"

Christian: Yes, and they put me in hope and fear.

Interpreter: Well, keep all things so in thy mind, that they may be as a goad in thy sides, to prick thee forward in the way thou must go. Then Christian began to gird up his loins, and to address himself to his journey. Then said the Interpreter, "The Comforter be always with thee, good Christian, to guide thee in the way that leads to the city."

So Christian went on his way, saying,
"Here I have seen things rare and profitable,
Things pleasant, dreadful, things to make me stable
In what I have begun to take in hand:
Then let me think on them, and understand
Wherefore they showed me were, and let me be
Thankful, O good Interpreter, to thee."

Lesson 66

- Read this summary of section 3 of *The Pilgrim's Progress* written by 8th grade Literature and Composition I student, Jessica Rutherford.

Christian is walking down a path fenced up by the wall Salvation. Christian runs down the road with difficulty because of his burden. The end of the path leads to a cross. The burden falls from his back, and Christian praises God. He says "He hath given me rest by his sorrow, and life by his death."

Now three Shining Ones come down upon Christian. The first says to him "Peace be to thee. Thy sins be forgiven thee," the second gives him spectacular new clothes to replace his rags, and the third puts a mark on his head and gives him a scroll with a seal. Christian goes from that place, singing loudly.
`

As Christian walks along the path again, in time he comes across three men: Simple, Sloth, and Presumption. They are all fast asleep. Christian tries to get them to wake and tells them about dangers in the area, but they just fall asleep once more. So Christian walks on, troubled. Now he sees two men jump over the wall onto the path: Formalist and Hypocrisy. Christian tries to explain to them that they have to get in through the wicket gate to be given passage into the Celestial City. They both shrug their shoulders and walk on without a care. They tell Christian that they wanted to cut short the path they had to take, and so climbed over the wall. Christian explains that what they did violated God's law. But they walk on and so the three men part ways.

Christian now walks on to the foot of a hill which has a spring from which he drinks and refreshes himself. Then he sees that he must climb up the hill and does so with difficulty. He comes across a shack halfway up the hill, and he rests there. He falls asleep, although it is a sin. He doesn't realize that he has fallen asleep until he awakes at dusk. His scroll has fallen from his bosom, but he doesn't realize until he makes it to the top of the hill, a much easier journey than the first half. After rushing back to grab the scroll, he weeps and asks God to forgive his sin. Still mad at himself, he continues.

Christian comes across lions on the path and is frightened. He is wondering how he is to get past them when a man calls out to him. A Porter named Watchful walks past the lions without them attacking, so they walk back the way that The Porter had come. The Porter asks Christian to stay at the house Beautiful, as it was dark and Christian couldn't continue his journey. Christian is taken into the house, while The Porter calls to one of the virgins of the house to see if Christian would be welcome to stay. The woman, named Discretion, says he is welcome. He is introduced to the other virgins of the house. They are named Piety, Charity, and Prudence. All four of them question him about his journey, and Christian tells them everything that has happened thus far in his journey. Then he eats with the family and sleeps in their home. When Christian wakes, he sings to God and thanks him for the family taking him in for the night. Soon he finds he has stayed with the family for many more days. When Christian leaves, all of the women bid him farewell, and wish him well on his journey.

Lesson 67

- Read the first part Book 1, Section 3 of *The Pilgrim's Progress*.

Book 1, Section 3
Cross and Sepulchre

Now I saw in my dream, that the highway up which Christian was to go, was fenced on either side with a wall, and that wall was called Salvation. Up this way, therefore, did burdened Christian run, but not without great difficulty, because of the load on his back. He ran thus till he came at a place somewhat ascending; and upon that place stood a cross, and a little below, in the bottom, a sepulchre. So I saw in my dream, that just as Christian came up with the cross, his burden loosed from off his shoulders, and fell from off his back, and began to tumble, and so continued to do till it came to the mouth of the sepulchre, where it fell in, and I saw it no more.

Then was Christian glad and lightsome, and said with a merry heart, "He hath given me rest by his sorrow, and life by his death." Then he stood still a while, to look and wonder; for it was very surprising to him that the sight of the cross should thus ease him of his burden. He looked, therefore, and looked again, even till the springs that were in his head sent the waters down his cheeks. Now as he stood looking and weeping, behold, three Shining Ones came to him, and saluted him with, "Peace be to thee." So the first said to him, "Thy sins be forgiven thee;" the second stripped him of his rags, and clothed him with change of raiment; the third also set a mark on his forehead, and gave him a roll with a seal upon it, which he bid him look on as he ran, and that he should give it in at the celestial gate: so they went their way. Then Christian gave three leaps for joy, and went on singing,

"Thus far did I come laden with my sin,
Nor could aught ease the grief that I was in,

Till I came hither. What a place is this!
Must here be the beginning of my bliss?
Must here the burden fall from off my back?
Must here the strings that bound it to me crack?
Blest cross! blest sepulchre! blest rather be
The Man that there was put to shame for me!"

Simple, Sloth, and Presumption; Formalist and Hypocrisy

I saw then in my dream, that he went on thus, even until he came at the bottom, where he saw, a little out of the way, three men fast asleep, with fetters upon their heels. The name of the one was Simple, of another Sloth, and of the third Presumption.

Christian then seeing them lie in this case, went to them, if peradventure he might awake them, and cried, you are like them that sleep on the top of a mast, for the Dead Sea is under you, a gulf that hath no bottom: awake, therefore, and come away; be willing also, and I will help you off with your irons. He also told them, If he that goeth about like a roaring lion, comes by, you will certainly become a prey to his teeth. With that they looked upon him, and began to reply in this sort: Simple said, I see no danger; Sloth said, Yet a little more sleep; and Presumption said, Every tub must stand upon its own bottom. And so they lay down to sleep again, and Christian went on his way.

Yet he was troubled to think that men in that danger should so little esteem the kindness of him that so freely offered to help them, both by awakening of them, counselling of them, and proffering to help them off with their irons. And as he was troubled thereabout, he espied two men come tumbling over the wall, on the left hand of the narrow way; and they made up apace to him. The name of the one was Formalist, and the name of the other Hypocrisy. So, as I said, they drew up unto him, who thus entered with them into discourse.

Christian: Gentlemen, whence came you, and whither do you go?

Formalist and Hypocrisy: We were born in the land of Vain-glory, and are going, for praise, to Mount Zion.

Christian: Why came you not in at the gate which standeth at the beginning of the way? Know ye not that it is written, that "he that cometh not in by the door, but climbeth up some other way, the same is a thief and a robber"?

Formalist and Hypocrisy: They said, that to go to the gate for entrance was by all their countrymen counted too far about; and that therefore their usual way was to make a short cut of it, and to climb over the wall, as they had done.

Christian: But will it not be counted a trespass against the Lord of the city whither we are bound, thus to violate his revealed will?

Formalist and Hypocrisy: They told him, that as for that, he needed not to trouble his head thereabout: for what they did they had custom for, and could produce, if need were, testimony that would witness it for more than a thousand years.

Christian: But, said Christian, will you stand a trial at law?

Formalist and Hypocrisy: They told him, that custom, it being of so long standing as above a thousand years, would doubtless now be admitted as a thing legal by an impartial judge: and besides, said they, if we get into the way, what matter is it which way we get in? If we are in, we are in: thou art but in the way, who, as we perceive, came in at the gate; and we also are in the way, that came tumbling over the wall: wherein now is thy condition better than ours?

Christian: I walk by the rule of my Master: you walk by the rude working of your fancies. You are counted thieves already by the Lord of the way: therefore I doubt you will not be found true men at the end of the way. You come in by yourselves without his direction, and shall go out by yourselves without his mercy.

To this they made him but little answer; only they bid him look to himself. Then I saw that they went on, every man in his way, without much conference one with another, save that these two men told Christian, that as to laws and ordinances, they doubted not but that they should as conscientiously do them as he. Therefore, said they, we see not wherein thou differest from us, but by the coat that is on thy back, which was, as we trow, given thee by some of thy neighbors, to hide the shame of thy nakedness.

Christian: By laws and ordinances you will not be saved, since you came not in by the door. And as for this coat that is on my back, it was given me by the Lord of the place whither I go; and that, as you say, to cover my nakedness with. And I take it as a token of kindness to me; for I had nothing but rags before. And besides, thus I comfort myself as I go. Surely, think I, when I come to the gate of the city, the Lord thereof will know me for good, since I have his coat on my back; a coat that he gave me freely in the day that he stripped me of my rags. I have, moreover, a mark in my forehead, of which perhaps you have taken no notice, which one of my Lord's most intimate associates fixed there in the day that my burden fell off my shoulders. I will tell you, moreover, that I had then given me a roll sealed, to comfort me by reading as I go on the way; I was also bid to give it in at the celestial gate, in token of my certain going in after it: all which things I doubt you want, and want them because you came not in at the gate.

To these things they gave him no answer; only they looked upon each other, and laughed. Then I saw that they went all on, save that Christian kept before, who had no more talk but with himself, and that sometimes sighingly, and sometimes comfortably: also he would be often reading in the roll that one of the Shining Ones gave him, by which he was refreshed.

The Three Ways: Difficulty, Danger, and Destruction

I believe then, that they all went on till they came to the foot of an Hill, at the bottom of which was a Spring. There was also in the same place two other ways besides that which came straight from the Gate; one turned to the left hand, and the other to the right, at the bottom of the Hill: but the narrow way lay right up the Hill, (and the name of the going up the side of the Hill, is called Difficulty.) Christian now went to the Spring and drank thereof to refresh himself, and then began to go up the Hill; saying,

This Hill, though high, I covet to ascend,
The difficulty will not me offend:
For I perceive the way to life lies here;
Come, pluck up, Heart; lets neither faint nor fear:
Better, tho *difficult*, th' right way to go,
Then wrong, though *easie*, where the end is wo.

The other two also came to the foot of the hill. But when they saw that the hill was steep and high, and that there were two other ways to go; and supposing also that these two ways might meet again with that up which Christian went, on the other side of the hill; therefore they were resolved to go in those ways. Now the name of one of those ways was Danger, and the name of the other Destruction. So the one took the way which is called Danger, which led him into a great wood; and the other took directly up the way to Destruction, which led him into a wide field, full of dark mountains, where he stumbled and fell, and rose no more.

I looked then after Christian, to see him go up the hill, where I perceived he fell from running to going, and from going to clambering upon his hands and his knees, because of the steepness of the place. Now about the midway to the top of the hill was a pleasant Arbor, made by the Lord of the hill for the refreshment of weary travellers. Thither, therefore, Christian got, where also he sat down to rest him: then he pulled his roll out of his bosom, and read therein to his comfort; he also now began afresh to take a review of the coat or garment that was given to him as he stood by the cross. Thus pleasing himself awhile, he at last fell into a slumber, and thence into a fast sleep, which detained him in that place until it was almost night; and in his sleep his roll fell out of his hand. Now, as he was sleeping, there came one to him, and awaked him, saying, "Go to the ant, thou sluggard; consider her ways, and be wise.". And with that, Christian suddenly started up, and sped him on his way, and went apace till he came to the top of the hill.

Timorous and Mistrust

Now when he was got up to the top of the hill, there came two men running amain; the name of the one was Timorous, and of the other Mistrust: to whom Christian said, Sirs, what's the matter? you run the wrong way. Timorous answered, that they were going to the city of Zion, and had got up that difficult place: but, said he, the farther we go, the more danger we meet with; wherefore we turned, and are going back again.

Yes, said Mistrust, for just before us lie a couple of lions in the way, whether sleeping or waking we know not; and we could not think, if we came within reach, but they would presently pull us in pieces.

Christian: Then said Christian, You make me afraid; but whither shall I fly to be safe? If I go back to mine own country, that is prepared for fire and brimstone, and I shall certainly perish there; if I can get to the celestial city, I am sure to be in safety there: I must venture. To go back is nothing but death: to go forward is fear of death, and life everlasting beyond it: I will yet go forward. So Mistrust and Timorous ran down the hill, and Christian went on his way. But thinking again of what he had heard from the men, he felt in his bosom for his roll, that he might read therein and be comforted; but he felt, and found it not. Then was Christian in great distress, and knew not what to do; for he wanted that which used to relieve him, and that which should have been his pass into the celestial city. Here, therefore, he began to be much perplexed, and knew not what to do. At last he bethought himself that he had slept in the arbor that is on the side of the hill; and falling down upon his knees, he asked God forgiveness for that foolish act, and then went back to look for his roll. But all the way he went back, who can sufficiently set forth the sorrow of Christian's heart? Sometimes he sighed, sometimes he wept, and oftentimes he chid himself for being so foolish to fall asleep in that place, which was erected only for a little refreshment from his weariness. Thus, therefore, he went back, carefully looking on this side and on that, all the way as he went, if happily he might find his roll, that had been his comfort so many times in his journey. He went thus till he came again in sight of the arbor where he sat and slept; but that sight renewed his sorrow the more, by bringing again, even afresh, his evil of sleeping unto his mind. Thus, therefore, he now went on, bewailing his sinful sleep, saying, O wretched man that I am, that I should sleep in the daytime! that I should sleep in the midst of difficulty! that I should so indulge the flesh as to use that rest for ease to my flesh which the Lord of the hill hath erected only for the relief of the spirits of pilgrims! How many steps have I taken in vain! Thus it happened to Israel; for their sin they were sent back again by the way of the Red Sea; and I am made to tread those steps with sorrow, which I might have trod with delight, had it not been for this sinful sleep. How far might I have been on my way by this time! I am made to tread those steps thrice over, which I needed not to have trod but once: yea, now also I am like to be benighted, for the day is almost spent. O that I had not slept!

Lesson 68

- Read the rest of Book 1, Section 3 of *The Pilgrim's Progress.*

The House Beautiful

Now by this time he was come to the arbor again, where for a while he sat down and wept; but at last, (as Providence would have it,) looking sorrowfully down under the settle, there he espied his roll, the which he with trembling and haste catched up, and put it into his bosom. But who can tell how joyful this man was when he had gotten his roll again? For this roll was the assurance of his life, and acceptance at the desired haven. Therefore he laid it up in his bosom, gave thanks to God for directing his eye to the place where it lay, and with joy and tears betook himself again to his journey. But O how nimbly did he go up the rest of the hill! Yet before he got up, the sun went down upon Christian; and this made him again recall the vanity of his sleeping to his remembrance; and thus he again began to condole with himself: Oh thou sinful sleep! how for thy sake am I like to be benighted in my journey! I must walk without the sun, darkness must cover the path of my feet, and I must hear the noise of the doleful creatures, because of my sinful sleep! Now also he remembered the story that Mistrust and Timorous told him of, how they were frighted with the sight of the lions. Then said Christian to himself again, These beasts range in the night for their prey; and if they should meet with me in the dark, how should I shift them? how should I escape being by them torn in pieces? Thus he went on his way. But while he was bewailing his unhappy miscarriage, he lift up his eyes, and behold there was a very stately palace before him, the name of which was Beautiful, and it stood by the highway-side.

So I saw in my dream that he made haste, and went forward, that if possible he might get lodging there. Now before he had gone far, he entered into a very narrow passage, which was about a furlong off the Porter's lodge, and looking very narrowly before him as he went, he espied two lions in the way. Now, thought he, I see the dangers that Mistrust and Timorous were driven back by. (The lions were chained, but he saw not the chains.) Then he was afraid, and thought also himself to go back after them; for he thought nothing but death was before him. But the Porter at the lodge, whose name is Watchful, perceiving that Christian made a halt, as if he would go back, cried unto him, saying, Is thy strength so small? Fear not the lions, for they are chained, and are placed there for trial of faith where it is, and for discovery of those that have none: keep in the midst of the path, and no hurt shall come unto thee.

Then I saw that he went on, trembling for fear of the lions, but taking good heed to the directions of the Porter; he heard them roar, but they did him no harm. Then he clapped his hands, and went on till he came and stood before the gate where the Porter was. Then said Christian to the Porter, Sir, what house is this? and may I lodge here to-night? The Porter answered, This house was built by the Lord of the hill, and he built it for the relief and security of pilgrims. The Porter also asked whence he was, and whither he was going.

Christian: I am come from the city of Destruction, and am going to Mount Zion: but because the sun is now set, I desire, if I may, to lodge here to-night.

The Porter: What is your name?

Christian: My name is now Christian, but my name at the first was Graceless: I came of the race of Japheth, whom God will persuade to dwell in the tents of Shem.

The Porter: But how does it happen that you come so late? The sun is set.

Christian: I had been here sooner, but that, wretched man that I am, I slept in the arbor that stands on the hill-side! Nay, I had, notwithstanding that, been here much sooner, but that in my sleep I lost my evidence, and came without it to the brow of the hill; and then feeling for it, and not finding it, I was forced with sorrow of heart to go back to the place where I slept my sleep, where I found it; and now I am come.

The Porter: Well, I will call out one of the virgins of this place, who will, if she likes your talk, bring you in to the rest of the family, according to the rules of the house. So Watchful the Porter rang a bell, at the sound of which came out of the door of the house a grave and beautiful damsel, named Discretion, and asked why she was called.

The Porter answered, This man is on a journey from the city of Destruction to Mount Zion; but being weary and benighted, he asked me if he might lodge here to-night: so I told him I would call for thee, who, after discourse had with him, mayest do as seemeth thee good, even according to the law of the house.

Then she asked him whence he was, and whither he was going; and he told her. She asked him also how he got into the way; and he told her. Then she asked him what he had seen and met with in the way, and he told her. And at last she asked his name. So he said, It is Christian; and I have so much the more a desire to lodge here to-night, because, by what I perceive, this place was built by the Lord of the hill for the relief and security of pilgrims. So she smiled, but the water stood in her eyes; and after a little pause she said, I will call forth two or three more of the family. So she ran to the door, and called out Prudence, Piety, and Charity, who, after a little more discourse with him, had him into the family; and many of them meeting him at the threshold of the house, said, Come in, thou blessed of the Lord; this house was built by the Lord of the hill on purpose to entertain such pilgrims in. Then he bowed his head, and followed them into the house. So when he was come in and sat down, they gave him something to drink, and consented together that, until supper was ready, some of them should have some particular discourse with Christian, for the best improvement of time; and they appointed Piety, Prudence, and Charity to discourse with him: and thus they began.

Piety: Come, good Christian, since we have been so loving to you as to receive you into our house this night, let us, if perhaps we may better ourselves thereby, talk with you of all things that have happened to you in your pilgrimage.

Christian: With a very good will; and I am glad that you are so well disposed.

Piety: What moved you at first to betake yourself to a pilgrim's life?

Christian: I was driven out of my native country by a dreadful sound that was in mine ears; to wit, that unavoidable destruction did attend me, if I abode in that place where I was.

Christian: But how did it happen that you came out of your country this way?

Christian: It was as God would have it; for when I was under the fears of destruction, I did not know whither to go; but by chance there came a man, even to me, as I was trembling and weeping, whose name is Evangelist, and he directed me to the Wicket-gate, which else I should never have found, and so set me into the way that hath led me directly to this house.

Piety: But did you not come by the house of the Interpreter?

Christian: Yes, and did see such things there, the remembrance of which will stick by me as long as I live, especially three things: to wit, how Christ, in despite of Satan, maintains his work of grace in the heart; how the man had sinned himself quite out of hopes of God's mercy; and also the dream of him that thought in his sleep the day of judgment was come.

Piety: Why, did you hear him tell his dream?

Christian: Yes, and a dreadful one it was, I thought; it made my heart ache as he was telling of it, but yet I am glad I heard it.

Piety: Was this all you saw at the house of the Interpreter?

Christian: No; he took me, and had me where he showed me a stately palace, and how the people were clad in gold that were in it; and how there came a venturous man, and cut his way through the armed men that stood in the door to keep him out; and how he was bid to come in, and win eternal glory. Methought those things did ravish my heart. I would have stayed at that good man's house a twelvemonth, but that I knew I had farther to go.

Piety: And what saw you else in the way?

Christian: Saw? Why, I went but a little farther, and I saw One, as I thought in my mind, hang bleeding upon a tree; and the very sight of him made my burden fall off my back; for I groaned under a very heavy burden, but then it fell down from off me. It was a strange thing to me, for I never saw such a thing before: yea, and while I stood looking up, (for then I could not forbear looking,) three Shining Ones came to me. One of them testified that my sins were forgiven me; another stripped me of my rags, and gave me this broidered coat which you see; and the third set the mark which you see in my forehead, and gave me this sealed roll, (and with that he plucked it out of his bosom.)

Piety: But you saw more than this, did you not?

Christian: The things that I have told you were the best: yet some other I saw, as, namely, I saw three men, Simple, Sloth, and Presumption, lie asleep, a little out of the way, as I came, with irons upon their heels; but do you think I could awake them? I also saw Formality and Hypocrisy come tumbling over the wall, to go, as they pretended, to Zion; but they were quickly lost, even as I myself did tell them, but they would not believe. But, above all, I found it hard work to get up this hill, and as hard to come by the lions' mouths; and, truly, if it had not been for the good man, the porter that stands at the gate, I do not know but that, after all, I might have gone back again; but I thank God I am here, and thank you for receiving me.

Then Prudence thought good to ask him a few questions, and desired his answer to them.

Prudence: Do you not think sometimes of the country from whence you came?

Christian: Yea, but with much shame and detestation. Truly, if I had been mindful of that country from whence I came out, I might have had opportunity to have returned; but now I desire a better country, that is, a heavenly one.

Prudence: Do you not yet bear away with you some of the things that then you were conversant withal?

Christian: Yes, but greatly against my will; especially my inward and carnal cogitations, with which all my countrymen, as well as myself, were delighted. But now all those things are my grief; and might I but choose mine own things, I would choose never to think of those things more: but when I would be a doing that which is best, that which is worst is with me.

Prudence: Do you not find sometimes as if those things were vanquished, which at other times are your perplexity?

Christian: Yes, but that is but seldom; but they are to me golden hours in which such things happen to me.

Prudence: Can you remember by what means you find your annoyances at times as if they were vanquished?

Christian: Yes: when I think what I saw at the cross, that will do it; and when I look upon my broidered coat, that will do it; and when I look into the roll that I carry in my bosom, that will do it; and when my thoughts wax warm about whither I am going, that will do it.

Prudence: And what is it that makes you so desirous to go to Mount Zion?

Christian: Why, there I hope to see Him alive that did hang dead on the cross; and there I hope to be rid of all those things that to this day are in me an annoyance to me: there they say there is no death, and there I shall dwell with such company as I like best. For, to tell you the truth, I love Him because I was by Him eased of my burden; and I am weary of my inward sickness. I would fain be where I shall die no more, and with the company that shall continually cry, *Holy, holy, holy*.

Then said Charity to Christian, Have you a family; Are you a married man?

Christian: I have a wife and four small children.

Charity: And why did you not bring them along with you?

Christian: Then Christian wept, and said, Oh, how willingly would I have done it! but they were all of them utterly averse to my going on pilgrimage.

Charity: But you should have talked to them, and have endeavored to show them the danger of staying behind.

Christian: So I did; and told them also what God had shown to me of the destruction of our city; but I seemed to them as one that mocked, and they believed me not.

Charity: And did you pray to God that he would bless your counsel to them?

Christian: Yes, and that with much affection; for you must think that my wife and poor children were very dear to me.

Charity: But did you tell them of your own sorrow, and fear of destruction? for I suppose that destruction was visible enough to you.

Christian: Yes, over, and over, and over. They might also see my fears in my countenance, in my tears, and also in my trembling under the apprehension of the judgment that did hang over our heads; but all was not sufficient to prevail with them to come with me.

Charity: But what could they say for themselves, why they came not?

Christian: Why, my wife was afraid of losing this world, and my children were given to the foolish delights of youth; so, what by one thing, and what by another, they left me to wander in this manner alone.

Charity: But did you not, with your vain life, damp all that you, by words, used by way of persuasion to bring them away with you?

Christian: Indeed, I cannot commend my life, for I am conscious to myself of many failings therein. I know also, that a man, by his conversation, may soon overthrow what, by argument or persuasion, he doth labor to fasten upon others for their good. Yet this I can say, I was very wary of giving them occasion, by any unseemly action, to make them averse to going on pilgrimage. Yea, for this very thing, they would tell me I was too precise, and that I denied myself of things (for their sakes) in which they saw no evil. Nay, I think I may say, that if what they saw in me did hinder them, it was my great tenderness in sinning against God, or of doing any wrong to my neighbor.

Charity: Indeed, Cain hated his brother, because his own works were evil, and his brother's righteous, and if thy wife and children have been offended with thee for this, they thereby show themselves to be implacable to good; thou hast delivered thy soul from their blood.

Now I saw in my dream, that thus they sat talking together until supper was ready. So when they had made ready, they sat down to meat. Now the table was furnished with fat things, and with wine that was well refined; and all their talk at the table was about the Lord of the hill; as, namely, about what he had done, and wherefore he did what he did, and why he had builded that house; and by what they said, I perceived that he had been a great warrior, and had fought with and slain him that had the power of death, but not without great danger to himself, which made me love him the more.

For, as they said, and as I believe, said Christian, he did it with the loss of much blood. But that which put the glory of grace into all he did, was, that he did it out of pure love to his country. And besides, there were some of them of the household that said they had been and spoke with him since he did die on the cross; and they have attested that they had it from his own lips, that he is such a lover of poor pilgrims, that the like is not to be found from the east to the west. They, moreover, gave an instance of what they affirmed; and that was, he had stripped himself of his glory that he might do this for the poor; and that they heard him say and affirm, that he would not dwell in the mountain of Zion alone. They said, moreover, that he had made many pilgrims princes, though by nature they were beggars born, and their original had been the dunghill.

Thus they discoursed together till late at night; and after they had committed themselves to their Lord for protection, they betook themselves to rest. The pilgrim they laid in a large upper chamber, whose window opened towards the sun-rising. The name of the chamber was Peace, where he slept till break of day, and then he awoke and sang,

"Where am I now? Is this the love and care
Of Jesus, for the men that pilgrims are,
Thus to provide that I should be forgiven,
And dwell already the next door to heaven!"

So in the morning they all got up; and, after some more discourse, they told him that he should not depart till they had shown him the rarities of that place. And first they had him into the study, where they showed him records of the greatest antiquity; in which, as I remember my dream, they showed him the pedigree of the Lord of the hill, that he was the Son of the Ancient of days, and came by eternal generation. Here also was more fully recorded the acts that he had done, and the names of many hundreds that he had taken into his service; and how he had placed them in such habitations that could neither by length of days, nor decays of nature, be dissolved.

Then they read to him some of the worthy acts that some of his servants had done; as how they had subdued kingdoms, wrought righteousness, obtained promises, stopped the mouths of lions, quenched the violence of fire, escaped the edge of the sword, out of weakness were made strong, waxed valiant in fight, and turned to flight the armies of the aliens. Then they read again another part of the records of the house, where it was shown how willing their Lord was to receive into his favor any, even any, though they in time past had offered great affronts to his person and proceedings. Here also were several other histories of many other famous things, of all which Christian had a view; as of things both ancient and modern, together with prophecies and predictions of things that have their certain accomplishment, both to the dread and amazement of enemies, and the comfort and solace of pilgrims.

The next day they took him, and had him into the armory, where they showed him all manner of furniture which their Lord had provided for pilgrims, as sword, shield, helmet, breastplate, all-prayer, and shoes that would not wear out. And there was here enough of this to harness out as many men for the service of their Lord as there be stars in the heaven for multitude. They also showed him some of the engines with which some of his servants had done wonderful things. They showed him Moses' rod; the hammer and nail with which Jael slew Sisera; the pitchers, trumpets, and lamps too, with which Gideon put to flight the armies of Midian. Then they showed him the ox-goad wherewith Shamgar slew six hundred men. They showed him also the jawbone with which Samson did such mighty feats. They showed him moreover the sling and stone with which David slew Goliath of Gath; and the sword also with which their Lord will kill the man of sin, in the day that he shall rise up to the prey. They showed him besides many excellent things, with which Christian was much delighted. This done, they went to their rest again.

Then I saw in my dream, that on the morrow he got up to go forward, but they desired him to stay till the next day also; and then, said they, we will, if the day be clear, show you the Delectable Mountains; which, they said, would yet farther add to his comfort, because they were nearer the desired haven than the place where at present he was; so he consented and stayed. When the morning was up, they had him to the top of the house, and bid him look south. So he did, and behold, at a great distance, he saw a most pleasant mountainous country, beautified with woods, vineyards, fruits of all sorts, flowers also, with springs and fountains, very delectable to behold. Then he asked the name of the country. They said it was

Immanuel's land; and it is as common, said they, as this hill is, to and for all the pilgrims. And when thou comest there, from thence thou mayest see to the gate of the celestial city, as the shepherds that live there will make appear.

Now he bethought himself of setting forward, and they were willing he should. But first, said they, let us go again into the armory. So they did; and when he came there, they harnessed him from head to foot with what was of proof, lest perhaps he should meet with assaults in the way. He being therefore thus accoutred, walked out with his friends to the gate; and there he asked the Porter if he saw any pilgrim pass by.

Then the Porter answered, Yes.

Christian: Pray, did you know him? said he.

The Porter: I asked his name, and he told me it was Faithful.

Christian: O, said Christian, I know him; he is my townsman, my near neighbor; he comes from the place where I was born. How far do you think he may be before?

The Porter: He is got by this time below the hill.

Christian: Well, said Christian, good Porter, the Lord be with thee, and add to all thy plain blessings much increase for the kindness that thou hast showed me.

Lesson 69

- Read this summary of section 4 of *The Pilgrim's Progress* written with help from 8th grade Literature and Composition I student, Ashlyn Rutherford.

Christian continues his journey with his four companions, Discretion, Piety, Charity, and Prudence, in the Valley of Humiliation. But, along the valley, he sees a fiend in the distance, a monster by the name of Apollyon. He asks Christian why they are traveling along this path. Christian tells him where he came from and where he is going. Apollyon attacks Christian with flaming darts. After a long fight where Christian thinks he is defeated, he grabs his sword and stabs Apollyon, who flies away, threatening revenge.

Leaving the Valley of Humiliation, Christian enters the Valley of the Shadow of Death. In the middle of the Valley, Christian comes to the mouth of Hell with flames and huge plumes of smoke emanating from it. He uses All-prayer, a blanket prayer that protects him, and journeys on through the Valley, terrified of the many demons he can hear, but not see due to the smoke.

Finally, he hears a voice say, "Though I walk through the Valley of the Shadow of Death, I will fear no evil, for Thou art with me." He knows that no spiritual foe would utter those words, so he finds the strength to continue through the valley. Morning arrives and Christian looks back to see the path he has traveled rather blindly. He sees he has passed pits, ditches, and deep holes without even getting close to falling into them. God had helped him through the night and been by his side through the Valley.

Lesson 70

- Read Book 1, Section 4 of *The Pilgrim's Progress.*

The Valley of Humiliation and Apollyon

Then he began to go forward; but Discretion, Piety, Charity, and Prudence would accompany him down to the foot of the hill. So they went on together, reiterating their former discourses, till they came to go down the hill. Then said Christian, As it was difficult coming up, so, so far as I can see, it is dangerous going down. Yes, said Prudence, so it is; for it is a hard matter for a man to go down into the valley of Humiliation, as thou art now, and to catch no slip by the way; therefore, said they, we are come out to accompany thee down the hill. So he began to go down, but very warily; yet he caught a slip or two.

Then I saw in my dream, that these good companions, when Christian was got down to the bottom of the hill, gave him a loaf of bread, a bottle of wine, and a cluster of raisins; and then he went on his way,

"Whilst Christian is among his godly friends,
Their golden mouths make him sufficient mends
For all his griefs; and when they let him go,
He's clad with northern steel from top to toe."

But now, in this valley of Humiliation, poor Christian was hard put to it; for he had gone but a little way before he espied a foul fiend coming over the field to meet him: his name is Apollyon. Then did Christian begin to be afraid, and to cast in his mind whether to go back, or to stand his ground. But he considered again, that he had no armor for his back, and therefore thought that to turn the back to him might give him greater advantage with ease to pierce him with his darts; therefore he resolved to venture and stand his ground: for, thought he, had I no more in mine eye than the saving of my life, it would be the best way to stand.

So he went on, and Apollyon met him. Now the monster was hideous to behold: he was clothed with scales like a fish, and they are his pride; he had wings like a dragon, and feet like a bear, and out of his belly came fire and smoke; and his mouth was as the mouth of a lion. When he was come up to Christian, he beheld him with a disdainful countenance, and thus began to question him.

Apollyon: Whence came you, and whither are you bound?

Christian: I am come from the city of Destruction, which is the place of all evil, and I am going to the city of Zion.

Apollyon: By this I perceive thou art one of my subjects; for all that country is mine, and I am the prince and god of it. How is it, then, that thou hast run away from thy king? Were it not that I hope thou mayest do me more service, I would strike thee now at one blow to the ground.

Christian: I was, indeed, born in your dominions, but your service was hard, and your wages such as a man could not live on; for the wages of sin is death; therefore, when I was come to years, I did, as other considerate persons do, look out if perhaps I might mend myself.

Apollyon: There is no prince that will thus lightly lose his subjects, neither will I as yet lose thee; but since thou complainest of thy service and wages, be content to go back, and what our country will afford I do here promise to give thee.

Christian: But I have let myself to another, even to the King of princes; and how can I with fairness go back with thee?

Apollyon: Thou hast done in this according to the proverb, "changed a bad for a worse;" but it is ordinary for those that have professed themselves his servants, after a while to give him the slip, and return again to me. Do thou so to, and all shall be well.

Christian: I have given him my faith, and sworn my allegiance to him; how then can I go back from this, and not be hanged as a traitor.

Apollyon: Thou didst the same by me, and yet I am willing to pass by all, if now thou wilt yet turn again and go back.

Christian: What I promised thee was in my non-age: and besides, I count that the Prince, under whose banner I now stand, is able to absolve me, yea, and to pardon also what I did as to my compliance with thee. And besides, O thou destroying Apollyon, to speak truth, I like his service, his wages, his servants, his government, his company, and country, better than thine; therefore leave off to persuade me farther: I am his servant, and I will follow him.

Apollyon: Consider again, when thou art in cool blood, what thou art like to meet with in the way that thou goest. Thou knowest that for the most part his servants come to an ill end, because they are transgressors against me and my ways. How many of them have been put to shameful deaths! And besides, thou countest his service better than mine; whereas he never yet came from the place where he is, to deliver any that served him out of their enemies' hands: but as for me, how many times, as all the world very well knows, have I delivered, either by power or fraud, those that have faithfully served me, from him and his, though taken by them! And so will I deliver thee.

Christian: His forbearing at present to deliver them, is on purpose to try their love, whether they will cleave to him to the end: and as for the ill end thou sayest they come to, that is most glorious in their account. For, for present deliverance, they do not much expect it; for they stay for their glory; and then they shall have it, when their Prince comes in his and the glory of the angels.

Apollyon: Thou hast already been unfaithful in thy service to him; and how dost thou think to receive wages of him?

Christian: Wherein, O Apollyon, have I been unfaithful to him?

Apollyon: Thou didst faint at first setting out, when thou wast almost choked in the gulf of Despond. Thou didst attempt wrong ways to be rid of thy burden, whereas thou shouldst have stayed till thy Prince had taken it off. Thou didst sinfully sleep, and lose thy choice things. Thou wast almost persuaded also to go back at the sight of the lions. And when thou talkest of thy journey, and of what thou hast seen and heard, thou art inwardly desirous of vainglory in all that thou sayest or doest.

Christian: All this is true, and much more which thou hast left out; but the Prince whom I serve and honor is merciful, and ready to forgive. But besides, these infirmities possessed me in thy country, for there I sucked them in, and I have groaned under them, been sorry for them, and have obtained pardon of my Prince.

Apollyon: Then Apollyon broke out into a grievous rage, saying, I am an enemy to this Prince; I hate his person, his laws, and people: I am come out on purpose to withstand thee.

Christian: Apollyon, beware what you do, for I am in the King's highway, the way of holiness; therefore take heed to yourself.

Apollyon: Then Apollyon straddled quite over the whole breadth of the way, and said, I am void of fear in this matter. Prepare thyself to die; for I swear by my infernal den, that thou shalt go no farther: here will I spill thy soul. And with that he threw a flaming dart at his breast; but Christian had a shield in his hand, with which he caught it, and so prevented the danger of that.

Then did Christian draw, for he saw it was time to bestir him; and Apollyon as fast made at him, throwing darts as thick as hail; by the which, notwithstanding all that Christian could do to avoid it, Apollyon wounded him in his head, his hand, and foot. This made Christian give a little back: Apollyon, therefore, followed his work amain, and Christian again took courage, and resisted as manfully as he could. This sore combat lasted for above half a day, even till Christian was almost quite spent: for you must know, that Christian, by reason of his wounds, must needs grow weaker and weaker.

Then Apollyon, espying his opportunity, began to gather up close to Christian, and wrestling with him, gave him a dreadful fall; and with that Christian's sword flew out of his hand. Then said Apollyon, I am sure of thee now: and with that he had almost pressed him to death, so that Christian began to despair of life. But, as God would have it, while Apollyon was fetching his last blow, thereby to make a full end of this good man, Christian nimbly reached out his hand for his sword, and caught it, saying, Rejoice not against me, O mine enemy: when I fall, I shall arise, and with that gave him a deadly thrust, which made him give back, as one that had received his mortal wound. Christian perceiving that, made at him again, saying, Nay, in all these things we are more than conquerors, through Him that loved us. And with that Apollyon spread forth his dragon wings, and sped him away, that Christian saw him no more.

In this combat no man can imagine, unless he had seen and heard, as I did, what yelling and hideous roaring Apollyon made all the time of the fight; he spake like a dragon: and on the other side, what sighs and groans burst from Christian's heart. I never saw him all the while give so much as one pleasant look, till he perceived he had wounded Apollyon with his two-edged sword; then, indeed, he did smile, and look upward! But it was the dreadfullest sight that ever I saw.

So when the battle was over, Christian said, I will here give thanks to him that hath delivered me out of the mouth of the lion, to him that did help me against Apollyon. And so he did, saying,

"Great Beelzebub, the captain of this fiend,
Designed my ruin; therefore to this end
He sent him harness'd out; and he, with rage
That hellish was, did fiercely me engage:

But blessed Michael helped me, and I,
By dint of sword, did quickly make him fly:
Therefore to Him let me give lasting praise,
And thank and bless his holy name always."

Then there came to him a hand with some of the leaves of the tree of life, the which Christian took and applied to the wounds that he had received in the battle, and was healed immediately. He also sat down in that place to eat bread, and to drink of the bottle that was given him a little before: so, being refreshed, he addressed himself to his journey with his sword drawn in his hand; for he said, I know not but some other enemy may be at hand. But he met with no other affront from Apollyon quite through this valley.

The Valley of the Shadow of Death

Now at the end of this valley was another, called the Valley of the Shadow of Death; and Christian must needs go through it, because the way to the Celestial City lay through the midst of it. Now, this valley is a very solitary place. The prophet Jeremiah thus describes it: "A wilderness, a land of deserts and pits, a land of drought, and of the Shadow of Death, a land that no man" (but a Christian) "passeth through, and where no man dwelt." Now here Christian was worse put to it than in his fight with Apollyon, as by the sequel you shall see.

I saw then in my dream, that when Christian was got to the borders of the Shadow of Death, there met him two men, children of them that brought up an evil report of the good land, making haste to go back; to whom Christian spake as follows.

Christian: Whither are you going?

The Two Men: They said, Back, back; and we would have you do so too, if either life or peace is prized by you.

Christian: Why, what's the matter? said Christian.

The Two Men: Matter! said they; we were going that way as you are going, and went as far as we durst: and indeed we were almost past coming back; for had we gone a little further, we had not been here to bring the news to thee.

Christian: But what have you met with? said Christian.

The Two Men: Why, we were almost in the Valley of the Shadow of Death, but that by good hap we looked before us, and saw the danger before we came to it.

Christian: But what have you seen? said Christian.

The Two Men: Seen! why the valley itself, which is as dark as pitch: we also saw there the hobgoblins, satyrs, and dragons of the pit: we heard also in that valley a continual howling and yelling, as of a people under unutterable misery, who there sat bound in affliction and irons: and over that valley hang the discouraging clouds of confusion: Death also doth always spread his wings over it. In a word, it is every whit dreadful, being utterly without order.

Christian: Then, said Christian, I perceive not yet, by what you have said, but that this is my way to the desired haven.

The Two Men: Be it thy way; we will not choose it for ours.

So they parted, and Christian went on his way, but still with his sword drawn in his hand, for fear lest he should be assaulted.

I saw then in my dream, so far as this valley reached, there was on the right hand a very deep ditch; that ditch is it into which the blind have led the blind in all ages, and have both there miserably perished. Again, behold, on the left hand there was a very dangerous quag, into which, if even a good man falls, he finds no bottom for his foot to stand on: into that quag king David once did fall, and had no doubt therein been smothered, had not He that is able plucked him out.

The pathway was here also exceeding narrow, and therefore good Christian was the more put to it; for when he sought, in the dark, to shun the ditch on the one hand, he was ready to tip over into the mire on the other; also, when he sought to escape the mire, without great carefulness he would be ready to fall into the ditch. Thus he went on, and I heard him here sigh bitterly; for besides the danger mentioned above, the pathway was here so dark, that ofttimes when he lifted up his foot to go forward, he knew not where, or upon what he should set it next.

About the midst of this valley I perceived the mouth of hell to be, and it stood also hard by the wayside. Now, thought Christian, what shall I do? And ever and anon the flame and smoke would come out in such abundance, with sparks and hideous noises, (things that cared not for Christian's sword, as did Apollyon before,) that he was forced to put up his sword, and betake himself to another weapon, called All-prayer; so he cried, in my hearing, O Lord, I beseech thee, deliver my soul. Thus he went on a great while, yet still the flames would be reaching towards him; also he heard doleful voices, and rushings to and fro, so that sometimes he thought he should be torn in pieces, or trodden down like mire in the streets. This frightful sight was seen, and these dreadful noises were heard by him for several miles together; and coming to a place where he thought he heard a company of fiends coming forward to meet him, he stopped, and began to muse what he had best to do. Sometimes he had half a thought to go back; then again he thought he might be half-way through the valley. He remembered also, how he had already vanquished many a danger; and that the danger of going back might be much more than for to go forward. So he resolved to go on; yet the fiends seemed to come nearer and nearer. But when they were come even almost at him, he cried out with a most vehement voice, I will walk in the strength of the Lord God. So they gave back, and came no farther.

One thing I would not let slip. I took notice that now poor Christian was so confounded that he did not know his own voice; and thus I perceived it. Just when he was come over against the mouth of the burning pit, one of the wicked ones got behind him, and stepped up softly to him, and whisperingly suggested many grievous blasphemies to him, which he verily thought had proceeded from his own mind. This put Christian more to it than any thing that he met with before, even to think that he should now blaspheme Him that he loved so much before. Yet if he could have helped it, he would not have done it; but he had not the discretion either to stop his ears, or to know from whence these blasphemies came.

When Christian had travelled in this disconsolate condition some considerable time, he thought he heard the voice of a man, as going before him, saying, Though I walk through the Valley of the Shadow of Death, I will fear no evil, for thou art with me. Then was he glad, and that for these reasons:

First, Because he gathered from thence, that some who feared God were in this valley as well as himself.

Secondly, For that he perceived God was with them, though in that dark and dismal state. And why not, thought he, with me? though by reason of the impediment that attends this place, I cannot perceive it.

Thirdly, For that he hoped (could he overtake them) to have company by and by. So he went on, and called to him that was before; but he knew not what to answer, for that he also thought himself to be alone. And by and by the day broke: then said Christian, "He hath turned the shadow of death into the morning."

Now morning being come, he looked back, not out of desire to return, but to see, by the light of the day, what hazards he had gone through in the dark. So he saw more perfectly the ditch that was on the one hand, and the quag that was on the other; also how narrow the way was which led betwixt them both. Also now he saw the hobgoblins, and satyrs, and dragons of the pit, but all afar off; for after break of day they came not nigh; yet they were discovered to him, according to that which is written, "He discovereth deep things out of darkness, and bringeth out to light the shadow of death."

Now was Christian much affected with this deliverance from all the dangers of his solitary way; which dangers, though he feared them much before, yet he saw them more clearly now, because the light of the day made them conspicuous to him. And about this time the sun was rising, and this was another mercy to Christian; for you must note, that though the first part of the Valley of the Shadow of Death was dangerous, yet this second part, which he was yet to go, was, if possible, far more dangerous; for, from the place where he now stood, even to the end of the valley, the way was all along set so full of snares, traps, gins, and nets here, and so full of pits, pitfalls, deep holes, and shelvings-down there, that had it now been dark, as it was when he came the first part of the way, had he had a thousand souls, they had in reason been cast away; but, as I said, just now the sun was rising. Then said he, "His Candle shineth on my head, and by his light I go through darkness."

In this light, therefore, he came to the end of the valley. Now I saw in my dream, that at the end of the valley lay blood, bones, ashes, and mangled bodies of men, even of pilgrims that had gone this way formerly; and while I was musing what should be the reason, I espied a little before me a cave, where two giants, Pope and Pagan, dwelt in old times; by whose power and tyranny the men whose bones, blood, ashes, etc., lay there, were cruelly put to death. But by this place Christian went without much danger, whereat I somewhat wondered; but I have learnt since, that Pagan has been dead many a day; and as for the other, though he be yet alive, he is, by reason of age, and also of the many shrewd brushes that he met with in his younger days, grown so crazy and stiff in his joints that he can now do little more than sit in his cave's mouth, grinning at pilgrims as they go by, and biting his nails because he cannot come at them. So I saw that Christian went on his way; yet, at the sight of the old man that sat at the mouth of the cave, he could not tell what to think, especially because he spoke to him, though he could not go after him, saying, You will never mend, till more of you be burned. But he held his peace, and set a good face on it; and so went by, and catched no hurt. Then sang Christian,

"O world of wonders, (I can say no less,)
That I should be preserved in that distress
That I have met with here! O blessed be
That hand that from it hath delivered me!
Dangers in darkness, devils, hell, and sin,
Did compass me, while I this vale was in;
Yea, snares, and pits, and traps, and nets did lie
My path about, that worthless, silly I
Might have been catch'd, entangled, and cast down;
But since I live, let Jesus wear the crown."

Lesson 71

- Read this summary of section 5 of *The Pilgrim's Progress* written by 8th grade Literature and Composition I student, Jessica Rutherford.

Christian is walking down the path when he sees a man walking briskly ahead of him. Christian calls out, but the man doesn't stop. Christian overtakes the man and realizes it's his friend Faithful. They walk together, talking about their own journeys.

Faithful talks about what the town was like after Christian had left and Pliable had returned. Faithful tells of the start of his journey and how he met Discontent along the way before the wicket gate, and Discontent tried to make him turn out of the way and not pursue it again. But Faithful says he just walked right past and went to the wicket gate. Faithful says he also met with Shame, Pride, Arrogancy, Self-Conceit, and Worldly-Glory. Faithful tells Christian how he walked through the Valley of the Shadow of Death briskly because he could see the very narrow path with the daylight, unlike Christian's walk through that valley.

Along the path, they meet with Talkative. He tells Faithful and Christian that he is going to the same place they are, the Celestial City. But as they converse, Christian and Faithful see that Talkative isn't going because he believes in God. They see Talkative is talking about faith, but he doesn't believe it.

Christian and Faithful try and speak to Talkative about him believing what he is saying, but Talkative finds his way around it. Christian and Faithful speak quietly to each other, knowing that Talkative will not make it into the Celestial City without him actually putting what he says into practice. They try to make him understand this fact, but he again changes the subject. Christian and Faithful know now that Talkative will never make it into the Heavenly city to which they all travel.

Talkative walks ahead of Faithful and Christian because he doesn't wish for more conversations about him putting his words into practice. So Faithful and Christian talk about what may happen to Talkative, because they know he will be rejected at the entrance of the Celestial City. They soon start singing about Talkative, saying;

"How Talkative at first lifts up his plumes!
How bravely doth he speak! How he presumes
To drive down all before him! But so soon
As Faithful talks of heart-work, like the moon
That's past the full, into the wane he goes;
And so will all but he that heart-work know."

Lesson 72

- Read the first part Book 1, Section 5 of *The Pilgrim's Progress*.

Book 1, Section 5
Faithful

Now, as Christian went on his way, he came to a little ascent, which was cast up on purpose that pilgrims might see before them: up there, therefore, Christian went; and looking forward, he saw Faithful before him upon his journey: Then said Christian aloud, Ho, ho; so-ho; stay, and I will be your companion. At that Faithful looked behind him; to whom Christian cried again, Stay, stay, till I come up to you. But Faithful answered, No, I am upon my life, and the avenger of blood is behind me.

At this Christian was somewhat moved, and putting to all his strength, he quickly got up with Faithful, and did also overrun him; so the last was first. Then did Christian vaingloriously smile, because he had gotten the start of his brother; but not taking good heed to his feet, he suddenly stumbled and fell, and could not rise again until Faithful came up to help him.

Then I saw in my dream, they went very lovingly on together, and had sweet discourse of all things that had happened to them in their pilgrimage; and thus Christian began.

Christian: My honored and well-beloved brother Faithful, I am glad that I have overtaken you, and that God has so tempered our spirits that we can walk as companions in this so pleasant a path.

Faithful: I had thought, my dear friend, to have had your company quite from our town, but you did get the start of me; wherefore I was forced to come thus much of the way alone.

Christian: How long did you stay in the city of Destruction before you set out after me on your pilgrimage?

Faithful: Till I could stay no longer; for there was a great talk presently after you were gone out, that our city would, in a short time, with fire from heaven, be burnt down to the ground.

Christian: What, did your neighbors talk so?

Faithful: Yes, it was for a while in every body's mouth.

Christian: What, and did no more of them but you come out to escape the danger?

Faithful: Though there was, as I said, a great talk thereabout, yet I do not think they did firmly believe it; for, in the heat of the discourse, I heard some of them deridingly speak of you and of your desperate journey, for so they called this your pilgrimage. But I did believe, and do still, that the end of our city will be with fire and brimstone from above; and therefore I have made my escape.

Christian: Did you hear no talk of neighbor Pliable?

Faithful: Yes, Christian, I heard that he followed you till he came to the Slough of Despond, where, as some said, he fell in; but he would not be known to have so done: but I am sure he was soundly bedabbled with that kind of dirt.

Christian: And what said the neighbors to him?

Faithful: He hath, since his going back, been had greatly in derision, and that among all sorts of people: some do mock and despise him, and scarce will any set him on work. He is now seven times worse than if he had never gone out of the city.

Christian: But why should they be so set against him, since they also despise the way that he forsook?

Faithful: O, they say, Hang him; he is a turncoat; he was not true to his profession! I think God has stirred up even His enemies to hiss at him, and make him a proverb, because he hath forsaken the way.

Christian: Had you no talk with him before you came out?

Faithful: I met him once in the streets, but he leered away on the other side, as one ashamed of what he had done; So I spake not to him.

Christian: Well, at my first setting out I had hopes of that man; but now I fear he will perish in the overthrow of the city. For it has happened to him according to the true proverb, The dog is turned to his vomit again, and the sow that was washed to her wallowing in the mire.

Faithful: These are my fears of him too; but who can hinder that which will be?

Christian: Well, neighbor Faithful, said Christian, let us leave him, and talk of things that more immediately concern ourselves. Tell me now what you have met with in the way as you came; for I know you have met with some things, or else it may be writ for a wonder.

Faithful: I escaped the slough that I perceive you fell into, and got up to the gate without that danger; only I met with one whose name was Wanton, that had like to have done me mischief.

Christian: It was well you escaped her net: Joseph was hard put to it by her, and he escaped her as you did; but it had like to have cost him his life. But what did she do to you?

Faithful: You cannot think (but that you know something) what a flattering tongue she had; she lay at me hard to turn aside with her, promising me all manner of content.

Christian: Nay, she did not promise you the content of a good conscience.

Faithful: You know what I mean; all carnal and fleshly content.

Christian: Thank God that you escaped her: the abhorred of the Lord shall fall into her pit.

Faithful: Nay, I know not whether I did wholly escape her or no.

Christian: Why, I trow you did not consent to her desires?

Faithful: No, not to defile myself; for I remembered an old writing that I had seen, which said, "Her steps take hold on Hell." So I shut mine eyes, because I would not be bewitched with her looks. Then she railed on me, and I went my way.

Christian: Did you meet with no other assault as you came?

Faithful: When I came to the foot of the hill called Difficulty, I met with a very aged man, who asked me what I was, and whither bound. I told him that I was a pilgrim, going to the Celestial City. Then said the old man, Thou lookest like an honest fellow; wilt thou be content to dwell with me for the wages that I shall give thee? Then I asked his name, and where he dwelt? He said his name was Adam the First, and that he dwelt in the town of Deceit I asked him then what was his work, and what the wages that he would give. He told me that his work was *many delights*; and his wages, that I should be his heir at last. I further asked him, what house he kept, and what other servants he had. So he told me that his house was maintained with all the dainties of the world, and that his servants were those of his own begetting. Then I asked how many children he had. He said that he had but three daughters, the Lust of the Flesh, the Lust of the Eyes, and the Pride of Life, and that I should marry them if I would. Then I asked, how long time he would have me live with him; And he told me, as long as he lived himself.

Christian: Well, and what conclusion came the old man and you to at last?

Faithful: Why, at first I found myself somewhat inclinable to go with the man, for I thought he spake very fair; but looking in his forehead, as I talked with him, I saw there written, "Put off the old man with his deeds."

Christian: And how then?

Faithful: Then it came burning hot into my mind, that, whatever he said, and however he flattered, when he got me home to his house he would sell me for a slave. So I bid him forbear to talk, for I would not come near the door of his house. Then he reviled me, and told me that he would send such a one after me that should make my way bitter to my soul. So I turned to go away from him; but just as I turned myself to go thence, I felt him take hold of my flesh, and give me such a deadly twitch back, that I thought he had pulled part of me after himself: this made me cry, "O wretched man." So I went on my way up the hill.

Now, when I had got above half-way up, I looked behind me, and saw one coming after me, swift as the wind; so he overtook me just about the place where the settle stands.

Christian: Just there, said Christian, did I sit down to rest me; but being overcome with sleep, I there lost this roll out of my bosom.

Faithful: But, good brother, hear me out. So soon as the man overtook me, it was but a word and a blow; for down he knocked me, and laid me for dead. But when I was a little come to myself again I asked him wherefore he served me so. He said because of my secret inclining to Adam the First. And with that he struck me another deadly blow on the breast, and beat me down backward; so I lay at his foot as dead as before. So when I came to myself again I cried him mercy: but he said, I know not how to show mercy; and with that he knocked me down again. He had doubtless made an end of me, but that one came by and bid him forbear.

Christian: Who was that that bid him forbear?

Faithful: I did not know him at first: but as he went by, I perceived the holes in his hands and in his side: Then I concluded that he was our Lord. So I went up the hill.

Christian: That man that overtook you was Moses. He spareth none; neither knoweth he how to shew mercy to those that transgress the law.

Faithful: I know it very well; it was not the first time that he has met with me. 'Twas he that came to me when I dwelt securely at home, and that told me he would burn my house over my head if I stayed there.

Christian: But did you not see the house that stood there on the top of the hill, on the side of which Moses met you?

Faithful: Yes, and the lions too, before I came at it. But, for the lions, I think they were asleep, for it was about noon; and because I had so much of the day before me, I passed by the Porter, and came down the hill.

Christian: He told me, indeed, that he saw you go by; but I wish you had called at the house, for they would have showed you so many rarities that you would scarce have forgot them to the day of your death. But pray tell me, Did you meet nobody in the Valley of Humility?

Faithful: Yes, I met with one Discontent, who would willingly have persuaded me to go back again with him: his reason was, for that the valley was altogether without honor. He told me, moreover, that to go there was the way to disoblige all my friends, as Pride, Arrogancy, Self-Conceit, Worldly Glory, with others, who he knew, as he said, would be very much offended if I made such a fool of myself as to wade through this valley.

Christian: Well, and how did you answer him?

Faithful: I told him, that although all these that he named, might claim a kindred of me, and that rightly, (for indeed they were my relations according to the flesh,) yet since I became a pilgrim they have disowned me, and I also have rejected them; and therefore they were to me now no more than if they had never been of my lineage. I told him, moreover, that as to this valley, he had quite misrepresented the thing; for before honor is humility, and a haughty spirit before a fall. Therefore, said I, I had rather go through this valley to the honor that was so accounted by the wisest, than choose that which he esteemed most worthy of our affections.

Christian: Met you with nothing else in that valley?

Faithful: Yes, I met with Shame; but of all the men that I met with on my pilgrimage, he, I think, bears the wrong name. The other would be said nay, after a little argumentation, and somewhat else; but this bold-faced Shame would never have done.

Christian: Why, what did he say to you?

Faithful: What? why, he objected against religion itself. He said it was a pitiful, low, sneaking business for a man to mind religion. He said, that a tender conscience was an unmanly thing; and that for a man to watch over his words and ways, so as to tie up himself from that hectoring liberty that the brave spirits of the times accustomed themselves unto, would make him the ridicule of the times. He objected also, that but few of the mighty, rich, or wise, were ever of my opinion; nor any of them neither, before they were persuaded to be fools, and to be of a voluntary fondness to venture the loss of all for nobody knows what. He, moreover, objected the base and low estate and condition of those that were chiefly the pilgrims of the times in which they lived; also their ignorance and want of understanding in all natural science. Yea, he did hold me to it at that rate also, about a great many more things than here I relate; as, that it was a shame to sit whining and mourning under a sermon, and a shame to come sighing and groaning home; that it was a shame to ask my neighbor forgiveness for petty faults, or to make restitution where I have taken from any. He said also, that religion made a man grow strange to the great, because of a few vices, which he called by finer names, and made him own and respect the base, because of the same religious fraternity: And is not this, said he, a shame?

Christian: And what did you say to him?

Faithful: Say? I could not tell what to say at first. Yea, he put me so to it, that my blood came up in my face; even this Shame fetched it up, and had almost beat me quite off. But at last I began to consider, that that which is highly esteemed among men, is had in abomination with God. And I thought again, this Shame tells me what men are; but he tells me nothing what God, or the word of God is. And I thought, moreover, that at the day of doom we shall not be doomed to death or life according to the hectoring spirits of the world, but according to the wisdom and law of the Highest. Therefore, thought I, what God says is best, is indeed best, though all the men in the world are against it. Seeing, then, that God prefers his religion; seeing God prefers a tender Conscience; seeing they that make themselves fools for the kingdom of heaven are wisest, and that the poor man that loveth Christ is richer than the greatest man in the world that hates him; Shame, depart, thou art an enemy to my salvation. Shall I entertain thee against my sovereign Lord? How then shall I look him in the face at his coming? Should I now be ashamed of his ways and servants, how can I expect the blessing? But indeed this Shame was a bold villain; I could scarcely shake him out of my company; yea, he would be haunting of me, and continually whispering me in the ear, with some one or other of the infirmities that attend religion. But at last I told him, that it was but in vain to attempt farther in this business; for those things that he disdained, in those did I see most glory: and so at last I got past this importunate one. And when I had shaken him off, then I began to sing,

"The trials that those men do meet withal,
That are obedient to the heavenly call,
Are manifold, and suited to the flesh,
And come, and come, and come again afresh;
That now, or some time else, we by them may
Be taken, overcome, and cast away.
O let the pilgrims, let the pilgrims then,
Be vigilant, and quit themselves like men."

Christian: I am glad, my brother, that thou didst withstand this villain so bravely; for of all, as thou sayest, I think he has the wrong name; for he is so bold as to follow us in the streets, and to attempt to put us to shame before all men; that is, to make us ashamed of that which is good. But if he was not himself audacious, he would never attempt to do as he does. But let us still resist him; for, notwithstanding all his bravadoes, he promoteth the fool, and none else. "The wise shall inherit glory," said Solomon; "but shame shall be the promotion of fools"?

Faithful: I think we must cry to Him for help against Shame, that would have us to be valiant for truth upon the earth.

Christian: You say true; but did you meet nobody else in that valley?

Faithful: No, not I; for I had sunshine all the rest of the way through that, and also through the Valley of the Shadow of Death.

Christian: 'Twas well for you; I am sure it fared far otherwise with me. I had for a long season, as soon almost as I entered into that valley, a dreadful combat with that foul fiend Apollyon; yea, I thought verily he would have killed me, especially when he got me down, and crushed me under him, as if he would have crushed me to pieces; for as he threw me, my sword flew out of my hand: nay, he told me he was sure of me; but I cried to God, and he heard me, and delivered me out of all my troubles. Then I entered into the Valley of the Shadow of Death, and had no light for almost half the way through it. I thought I should have been killed there over and over; but at last day brake, and the sun rose, and I went through that which was behind with far more ease and quiet.

Lesson 73

- Read the rest of Book 1, Section 5 of *The Pilgrim's Progress*.

Talkative

Moreover, I saw in my dream, that as they went on, Faithful, as he chanced to look on one side, saw a man whose name was Talkative, walking at a distance beside them; for in this place there was room enough for them all to walk. He was a tall man, and something more comely at a distance than at hand. To this man Faithful addressed himself in this manner.

Faithful: Friend, whither away? Are you going to the heavenly country?

Talkative: I am going to the same place.

Faithful: That is well; then I hope we shall have your good company?

Talkative: With a very good will, will I be your companion.

Faithful: Come on, then, and let us go together, and let us spend our time in discoursing of things that are profitable.

Talkative: To talk of things that are good, to me is very acceptable, with you or with any other; and I am glad that I have met with those that incline to so good a work; for, to speak the truth, there are but few who care thus to spend their time as they are in their travels, but choose much rather to be speaking of things to no profit; and this hath been a trouble to me.

Faithful: That is, indeed, a thing to be lamented; for what thing so worthy of the use of the tongue and mouth of men on earth, as are the things of the God of heaven?

Talkative: I like you wonderful well, for your saying is full of conviction; and I will add, What thing is so pleasant, and what so profitable, as to talk of the things of God? What things so pleasant? that is, if a man hath any delight in things that are wonderful. For instance, if a man doth delight to talk of the history, or the mystery of things; or if a man doth love to talk of miracles, wonders, or signs, where shall he find things recorded so delightful, and so sweetly penned, as in the holy Scripture?

Faithful: That is true; but to be profited by such things in our talk, should be our chief design.

Talkative: That's it that I said; for to talk of such things is most profitable; for by so doing a man may get knowledge of many things; as of the vanity of earthly things, and the benefit of things above. Thus in general; but more particularly, by this a man may learn the necessity of the new birth, the insufficiency of our works, the need of Christ's righteousness, etc. Besides, by this a man may learn what it is to repent, to believe, to pray, to suffer, or the like: by this, also, a man may learn what are the great promises and consolations of the, to his own comfort. Farther, by this a man may learn to refute false opinions, to vindicate the truth, and also to instruct the ignorant.

Faithful: All this is true; and glad am I to hear these things from you.

Talkative: Alas! the want of this is the cause that so few understand the need of faith, and the necessity of a work of grace in their soul, in order to eternal life; but ignorantly live in the works of the law, by which a man can by no means obtain the kingdom of heaven.

Faithful: But, by your leave, heavenly knowledge of these is the gift of God; no man attaineth to them by human industry, or only by the talk of them.

Talkative: All this I know very well; for a man can receive nothing, except it be given him from heaven: all is of grace, not of works. I could give you a hundred scriptures for the confirmation of this.

Faithful: Well, then, said Faithful, what is that one thing that we shall at this time found our discourse upon?

Talkative: What you will. I will talk of things heavenly, or things earthly; things moral, or things evangelical; things sacred, or things profane; things past, or things to come; things foreign, or things at home; things more essential, or things circumstantial: provided that all be done to our profit.

Faithful: Now did Faithful begin to wonder; and stepping to Christian, (for he walked all this while by himself,) he said to him, but softly, What a brave companion have we got! Surely, this man will make a very excellent pilgrim.

Christian: At this Christian modestly smiled, and said, This man, with whom you are so taken, will beguile with this tongue of his, twenty of them that know him not.

Faithful: Do you know him, then?

Christian: Know him? Yes, better than he knows himself.

Faithful: Pray what is he?

Christian: His name is Talkative: he dwelleth in our town. I wonder that you should be a stranger to him, only I consider that our town is large.

Faithful: Whose son is he? And whereabout doth he dwell?

Christian: He is the son of one Say-well. He dwelt in Prating-Row; and he is known to all that are acquainted with him by the name of Talkative of Prating-Row; and, notwithstanding his fine tongue, he is but a sorry fellow.

Faithful: Well, he seems to be a very pretty man.

Christian: That is, to them that have not a thorough acquaintance with him, for he is best abroad; near home he is ugly enough. Your saying that he is a pretty man, brings to my mind what I have observed in the work of a painter, whose pictures show best at a distance; but very near, more unpleasing.

Faithful: But I am ready to think you do but jest, because you smiled.

Christian: God forbid that I should jest (though I smiled) in this matter, or that I should accuse any falsely. I will give you a further discovery of him. This man is for any company, and for any talk; as he talketh now with you, so will he talk when he is on the ale-bench; and the more drink he hath in his crown, the more of these things he hath in his mouth. Religion hath no place in his heart, or house, or conversation; all he hath lieth in his tongue, and his religion is to make a noise therewith.

Faithful: Say you so? Then am I in this man greatly deceived.

Christian: Deceived! you may be sure of it. Remember the proverb, "They say, and do not;" but the kingdom of God is not in word, but in power. He talketh of prayer, of repentance, of faith, and of the new birth; but he knows but only to talk of them. I have been in his family, and have observed him both at home and abroad; and I know what I say of him is the truth. His house is as empty of religion as the white of an egg is of savor. There is there neither prayer, nor sign of repentance for sin; yea, the brute, in his kind, serves God far better than he. He is the very stain, reproach, and shame of religion to all that know him; it can hardly have a good word in all that end of the town where he dwells, through him. Thus say the common people that know him, "A saint abroad, and a devil at home." His poor family finds it so; he is such a churl, such a railer at, and so unreasonable with his servants, that they neither know how to do for or speak to him. Men that have any dealings with him say, It is better to deal with a Turk than with him, for fairer dealings they shall have at their hands. This Talkative (if it be possible) will go beyond them, defraud, beguile, and overreach them. Besides, he brings up his sons to follow his steps; and if he finds in any of them a foolish timorousness, (for so he calls the first appearance of a tender conscience,) he calls them fools and blockheads, and by no means will employ them in much, or speak to their commendation before others. For my part, I am of opinion that he has, by his wicked life, caused many to stumble and fall; and will be, if God prevents not, the ruin of many more.

Faithful: Well, my brother, I am bound to believe you, not only because you say you know him, but also because, like a Christian, you make your reports of men. For I cannot think that you speak these things of ill-will, but because it is even so as you say.

Christian: Had I known him no more than you, I might, perhaps, have thought of him as at the first you did; yea, had I received this report at their hands only that are enemies to religion, I should have thought it had been a slander-a lot that often falls from bad men's mouths upon good men's names and professions. But all these things, yea, and a great many more as bad, of my own knowledge, I can prove him guilty of. Besides, good men are ashamed of him; they can neither call him brother nor friend; the very naming of him among them makes them blush, if they know him.

Faithful: Well, I see that saying and doing are two things, and hereafter I shall better observe this distinction.

Christian: They are two things indeed, and are as diverse as are the soul and the body; for, as the body without the soul is but a dead carcass, so *saying*, if it be alone, is but a dead carcass also. The soul of religion is the practical part. "Pure religion and undefiled before God and the Father is this, to visit the fatherless and widows in their affliction, and to keep himself unspotted from the world." This, Talkative is not aware of; he thinks that hearing and saying will make a good Christian; and thus he deceiveth his own soul. Hearing is but as the sowing of the seed; talking is not sufficient to prove that fruit is indeed in the heart and life. And let us assure ourselves, that at the day of doom men shall be judged according to their fruits. It will not be said then, Did you believe? but, Were you doers, or talkers only? and accordingly shall they be judged. The end of the world is compared to our harvest, and you know men at harvest regard nothing but fruit. Not that any thing can be accepted that is not of faith; but I speak this to show you how insignificant the profession of Talkative will be at that day.

Faithful: This brings to my mind that of Moses, by which he describeth the beast that is clean. He is such an one that parteth the hoof, and cheweth the cud; not that parteth the hoof only, or that cheweth the cud only. The hare cheweth the cud, but yet is unclean, because he parteth not the hoof. And this truly resembleth Talkative: he cheweth the cud, he seeketh knowledge; he cheweth upon the word, but he divideth not the hoof. He parteth not with the way of sinners; but, as the hare, he retaineth the foot of the dog or bear, and therefore he is unclean.

Christian: You have spoken, for aught I know, the true gospel sense of these texts. And I will add another thing: Paul calleth some men, yea, and those great talkers too, sounding brass, and tinkling cymbals; that is, as he expounds them in another place, things without life giving sound. Things without life; that is, without the true faith and grace of the gospel; and consequently, things that shall never be placed in the kingdom of heaven among those that are the children of life; though their sound, by their talk, be as if it were the tongue or voice of an angel.

Faithful: Well, I was not so fond of his company at first, but I am as sick of it now. What shall we do to be rid of him?

Christian: Take my advice, and do as I bid you, and you shall find that he will soon be sick of your company too, except God shall touch his heart, and turn it.

Faithful: What would you have me to do?

Christian: Why, go to him, and enter into some serious discourse about the power of religion; and ask him plainly, (when he has approved of it, for that he will,) whether this thing be set up in his heart, house, or conversation.

Faithful: Then Faithful stepped forward again, and said to Talkative, Come, what cheer? How is it now?

Talkative: Thank you, well: I thought we should have had a great deal of talk by this time.

Faithful: Well, if you will, we will fall to it now; and since you left it with me to state the question, let it be this: How doth the saving grace of God discover itself when it is in the heart of man?

Talkative: I perceive, then, that our talk must be about the power of things. Well, it is a very good question, and I shall be willing to answer you. And take my answer in brief, thus: First, where the grace of God is in the heart, it causeth there a great outcry against sin. Secondly-

Faithful: Nay, hold; let us consider of one at once. I think you should rather say, it shows itself by inclining the soul to abhor its sin.

Talkative: Why, what difference is there between crying out against, and abhorring of sin?

Faithful: Oh! a great deal. A man may cry out against sin, of policy; but he cannot abhor it but by virtue of a godly antipathy against it. I have heard many cry out against sin in the pulpit, who yet can abide it well enough in the heart, house, and conversation. Joseph's mistress cried out with a loud voice, as if she had been very holy; but she would willingly, notwithstanding that, have committed uncleanness with him. Some cry out against sin, even as the mother cries out against her child in her lap, when she calleth it slut and naughty girl, and then falls to hugging and kissing it.

Talkative: You lie at the catch, I perceive.

Faithful: No, not I; I am only for setting things right. But what is the second thing whereby you would prove a discovery of a work of grace in the heart?

Talkative: Great knowledge of gospel mysteries.

Faithful: This sign should have been first: but, first or last, it is also false; for knowledge, great knowledge, may be obtained in the mysteries of the Gospel, and yet no work of grace in the soul. Yea, if a man have all knowledge, he may yet be nothing, and so, consequently, be no child of God. When Christ said, "Do you know all these things?" and the disciples answered, Yes, he added, "Blessed are ye if ye do them." He doth not lay the blessing in the knowing of them, but in the doing of them. For there is a knowledge that is not attended with doing: "He that knoweth his Master's will, and doeth it not." A man may know like an angel, and yet be no Christian: therefore your sign of it is not true. Indeed, to *know* is a thing that pleaseth talkers and boasters; but to *do* is that which pleaseth God. Not that the heart can be good without knowledge, for without that the heart is naught. There are, therefore, two sorts of knowledge, knowledge that resteth in the bare speculation of things, and knowledge that is accompanied with the grace of faith and love, which puts a man upon doing even the will of God from the heart: the first of these will serve the talker; but without the other, the true Christian is not content. "Give me understanding, and I shall keep thy law; yea, I shall observe it with my whole heart."

Talkative: You lie at the catch again: this is not for edification.

Faithful: Well, if you please, propound another sign how this work of grace discovereth itself where it is.

Talkative: Not I, for I see we shall not agree.

Faithful: Well, if you will not, will you give me leave to do it?

Talkative: You may use your liberty.

Faithful: A work of grace in the soul discovereth itself, either to him that hath it, or to standers-by.

To him that hath it, thus: It gives him conviction of sin, especially the defilement of his nature, and the sin of unbelief, for the sake of which he is sure to be damned, if he findeth not mercy at God's hand, by faith in Jesus Christ. This sight and sense of things worketh in him sorrow and shame for sin. He findeth, moreover, revealed in him the Saviour of the world, and the absolute necessity of closing with him for life; at the which he findeth hungerings and thirstings after him; to which hungerings, etc., the promise is made. Now, according to the strength or weakness of his faith in his Saviour, so is his joy and peace, so is his love to holiness, so are his desires to know him more, and also to serve him in this world. But though, I say, it discovereth itself thus unto him, yet it is but seldom that he is able to conclude that this is a work of grace; because his corruptions now, and his abused reason, make his mind to misjudge in this matter: therefore in him that hath this work there is required a very sound judgment, before he can with steadiness conclude that this is a work of grace.

To others it is thus discovered:

1. By an experimental confession of his faith in Christ. 2. By a life answerable to that confession; to wit, a life of holiness-heart-holiness, family-holiness, (if he hath a family,) and by conversation-holiness in the world; which in the general teacheth him inwardly to abhor his sin, and himself for that, in secret; to suppress it in his family, and to promote holiness in the world: not by talk only, as a hypocrite or talkative person may do, but by a practical subjection in faith and love to the power of the word. And now, sir, as to this brief description of the work of grace, and also the discovery of it, if you have aught to object, object; if not, then give me leave to propound to you a second question.

Talkative: Nay, my part is not now to object, but to hear; let me, therefore, have your second question.

Faithful: It is this: Do you experience this first part of the description of it; and doth your life and conversation testify the same? Or standeth your religion in word or tongue, and not in deed and truth? Pray, if you incline to answer me in this, say no more than you know the God above will say Amen to, and also nothing but what your conscience can justify you in; for not he that commendeth himself is approved, but whom the Lord commendeth. Besides, to say I am thus and thus, when my conversation, and all my neighbors, tell me I lie, is great wickedness.

Then Talkative at first began to blush; but, recovering himself, thus he replied: You come now to experience, to conscience, and to God; and to appeal to him for justification of what is spoken. This kind of discourse I did not expect; nor am I disposed to give an answer to such questions, because I count not myself bound thereto, unless you take upon you to be a catechiser; and though you should so do, yet I may refuse to make you my judge. But I pray, will you tell me why you ask me such questions?

Faithful: Because I saw you forward to talk, and because I knew not that you had aught else but notion. Besides, to tell you all the truth, I have heard of you that you are a man whose religion lies in talk, and that your conversation gives this your mouth-profession the lie. They say you are a spot among Christians, and that religion fareth the worse for your ungodly conversation; that some have already stumbled at your wicked ways, and that more are in danger of being destroyed thereby: your religion, and an ale-house, and covetousness, and uncleanness, and swearing, and lying, and vain company-keeping, etc., will stand together. The proverb is true of you which is said of a harlot, to wit, "That she is a shame to all women:" so are you a shame to all professors.

Talkative: Since you are so ready to take up reports, and to judge so rashly as you do, I cannot but conclude you are some peevish or melancholy man, not fit to be discoursed with; and so adieu. Then up came Christian, and said to his brother, I told you how it would happen; your words and his lusts could not agree. He had rather leave your company than reform his life. But he is gone, as I said: let him go; the loss is no man's but his own. He has saved us the trouble of going from him; for he continuing (as I suppose he will do) as he is, would have been but a blot in our company: besides, the apostle says, "From such withdraw thyself."

Faithful: But I am glad we had this little discourse with him; it may happen that he will think of it again: however, I have dealt plainly with him, and so am clear of his blood if he perisheth.

Christian: You did well to talk so plainly to him as you did. There is but little of this faithful dealing with men now-a-days, and that makes religion to stink so in the nostrils of many as it doth; for they are these talkative fools, whose religion is only in word, and who are debauched and vain in their conversation, that (being so much admitted into the fellowship of the godly) do puzzle the world, blemish Christianity, and grieve the sincere. I wish that all men would deal with such as you have done; then should they either be made more conformable to religion, or the company of saints would be too hot for them. Then did Faithful say,

"How Talkative at first lifts up his plumes!
How bravely doth he speak! How he presumes
To drive down all before him! But so soon
As Faithful talks of heart-work, like the moon
That's past the full, into the wane he goes;
And so will all but he that heart-work know."

Thus they went on, talking of what they had seen by the way, and so made that way easy, which would otherwise no doubt have been tedious to them, for now they went through a wilderness.

Lesson 74

- If the summaries have been helpful to you, you can find some at the website cliffsnotes.com/literature – click P to find *The Pilgrim's Progress* and then utilize the sidebar for the summary and analysis of each section. This section will be called section 7 (their numbering is different than this book). You can go to this site each day to read their summary. Otherwise, feel free to just read the sections in this book.
- Read Book 1, Section 6 of *The Pilgrim's Progress.*

Book 1, Section 6
Evangelist

Now when they were got almost quite out of this wilderness, Faithful chanced to cast his eye back, and espied one coming after them, and he knew him. Oh! said Faithful to his brother, who comes yonder? Then Christian looked, and said, It is my good friend Evangelist. Aye, and my good friend too, said Faithful, for 'twas he that set me on the way to the gate. Now was Evangelist come up unto them, and thus saluted them.

Evangelist: Peace be with you, dearly beloved, and peace be to your helpers.

Christian: Welcome, welcome, my good Evangelist: the sight of thy countenance brings to my remembrance thy ancient kindness and unwearied labors for my eternal good.

Faithful: And a thousand times welcome, said good Faithful, thy company, O sweet Evangelist; how desirable is it to us poor pilgrims!

Evangelist: Then said Evangelist, How hath it fared with you, my friends, since the time of our last parting? What have you met with, and how have you behaved yourselves?

Then Christian and Faithful told him of all things that had happened to them in the way; and how, and with what difficulty, they had arrived to that place.

Right glad am I, said Evangelist, not that you have met with trials, but that you have been victors, and for that you have, notwithstanding many weaknesses, continued in the way to this very day.

I say, right glad am I of this thing, and that for mine own sake and yours: I have sowed, and you have reaped; and the day is coming, when "both he that soweth, and they that reap, shall rejoice together," that is, if you hold out: "for in due season ye shall reap, if ye faint not." The crown is before you, and it is an incorruptible one; "so run that ye may obtain it." Some there be that set out for this crown, and after they have gone far for it, another comes in and takes it from them: "hold fast, therefore, that you have; let no man take your crown." You are not yet out of the gunshot of the devil; "you have not resisted unto blood, striving against sin." Let the kingdom be always before you, and believe steadfastly concerning the things that are invisible. Let nothing that is on this side the other world get within you. And, above all, look well to your own hearts and to the lusts thereof; for they are "deceitful above all things, and desperately wicked." Set your faces like a flint; you have all power in heaven and earth on your side.

Christian: Then Christian thanked him for his exhortations; but told him withal, that they would have him speak farther to them for their help the rest of the way; and the rather, for that they well knew that he was a prophet, and could tell them of things that might happen unto them, and also how they might resist and overcome them. To which request Faithful also consented. So Evangelist began as followeth.

Evangelist: My sons, you have heard in the word of the truth of the Gospel, that you must "through many tribulations enter into the kingdom of heaven;" and again, that "in every city, bonds and afflictions abide you;" and therefore you cannot expect that you should go long on your pilgrimage without them, in some sort or other. You have found something of the truth of these testimonies upon you already, and more will immediately follow: for now, as you see, you are almost out of this wilderness, and therefore you will soon come into a town that you will by and by see before you; and in that town you will be hardly beset with enemies, who will strain hard but they will kill you; and be you sure that one or both of you must seal the testimony which you hold, with blood; but "be you faithful unto death, and the King will give you a crown of life." He that shall die there, although his death will be unnatural, and his pain, perhaps, great, he will yet have the better of his fellow;

not only because he will be arrived at the Celestial City soonest, but because he will escape many miseries that the other will meet with in the rest of his journey. But when you are come to the town, and shall find fulfilled what I have here related, then remember your friend, and quit yourselves like men, and "commit the keeping of your souls to God in well doing, as unto a faithful Creator."

Vanity Fair

Then I saw in my dream, that when they were got out of the wilderness, they presently saw a town before them, and the name of that town is Vanity; and at the town there is a fair kept, called Vanity Fair. It is kept all the year long. It beareth the name of Vanity Fair, because the town where it is kept is lighter than vanity, and also because all that is there sold, or that cometh thither, is vanity; as is the saying of the wise, "All that cometh is vanity."

This fair is no new-erected business but a thing of ancient standing. I will show you the original of it.

Almost five thousand years ago there were pilgrims walking to the Celestial City, as these two honest persons are: and Beelzebub, Apollyon, and Legion, with their companions, perceiving by the path that the pilgrims made, that their way to the city lay through this town of Vanity, they contrived here to set up a fair; a fair wherein should be sold all sorts of vanity, and that it should last all the year long. Therefore, at this fair are all such merchandise sold as houses, lands, trades, places, honors, preferments, titles, countries, kingdoms, lusts, pleasures; and delights of all sorts, as harlots, wives, husbands, children, masters, servants, lives, blood, bodies, souls, silver, gold, pearls, precious stones, and what not.

And moreover, at this fair there is at all times to be seen jugglings, cheats, games, plays, fools, apes, knaves, and rogues, and that of every kind.
Here are to be seen, too, and that for nothing, thefts, murders, adulteries, false-swearers, and that of a blood-red color.

And, as in other fairs of less moment, there are the several rows and streets under their proper names, where such and such wares are vended; so here, likewise, you have the proper places, rows, streets, (namely, countries and kingdoms,) where the wares of this fair are soonest to be found. Here is the Britain Row, the French Row, the Italian Row, the Spanish Row, the German Row, where several sorts of vanities are to be sold. But, as in other fairs, some one commodity is as the chief of all the fair; so the ware of Rome and her merchandise is greatly promoted in this fair; only our English nation, with some others, have taken a dislike thereat.

Now, as I said, the way to the Celestial City lies just through this town, where this lusty fair is kept; and he that will go to the city, and yet not go through this town, "must needs go out of the world." The Prince of princes himself, when here, went through this town to his own country, and that upon a fair-day too; yea, and, as I think, it was Beelzebub, the chief lord of this fair, that invited him to buy of his vanities, yea, would have made him lord of the fair, would he but have done him reverence as he went through the town. Yea, because he was such a person of honor, Beelzebub had him from street to street, and showed him all the kingdoms of the world in a little time, that he might, if possible, allure that blessed One to cheapen and buy some of his vanities; but he had no mind to the merchandise, and therefore left the town, without laying out so much as one farthing upon these vanities. This fair, therefore, is an ancient thing, of long standing, and a very great fair.

Now, these pilgrims, as I said, must needs go through this fair. Well, so they did; but behold, even as they entered into the fair, all the people in the fair were moved; and the town itself, as it were, in a hubbub about them, and that for several reasons: for, First, The Pilgrims were clothed with such kind of raiment as was diverse from the raiment of any that traded in that fair. The people, therefore, of the fair made a great gazing upon them: some said they were fools; some, they were bedlams; and some, they were outlandish men.

Secondly, And as they wondered at their apparel, so they did likewise at their speech; for few could understand what they said. They naturally spoke the language of Canaan; but they that kept the fair were the men of this world: so that from one end of the fair to the other, they seemed barbarians each to the other.

Thirdly, But that which did not a little amuse the merchandisers was, that these pilgrims set very light by all their wares. They cared not so much as to look upon them; and if they called upon them to buy, they would put their fingers in their ears, and cry, "Turn away mine eyes from beholding vanity," and look upward, signifying that their trade and traffic was in heaven.

One chanced, mockingly, beholding the carriage of the men, to say unto them, "What will ye buy?" But they, looking gravely upon him, said, "We buy the truth." At that there was an occasion taken to despise the men the more; some mocking, some taunting, some speaking reproachfully, and some calling upon others to smite them. At last, things came to an hubbub and great stir in the fair, insomuch that all order was confounded. Now was word presently brought to the great one of the fair, who quickly came down, and deputed some of his most trusty friends to take those men into examination about whom the fair was almost overturned. So the men were brought to examination; and they that sat upon them asked them whence they came, whither they went, and what they did there in such an unusual garb. The men told them they were pilgrims and strangers in the world, and that they were going to their own country, which was the heavenly Jerusalem, and that they had given no occasion to the men of the town, nor yet to the merchandisrs, thus to abuse them, and to let them in their journey, except it was for that, when one asked them what they would buy, they said they would buy the truth. But they that were appointed to examine them did not believe them to be any other than bedlams and mad, or else such as came to put all things into a confusion in the fair. Therefore they took them and beat them, and besmeared them with dirt, and then put them into the cage, that they might be made a spectacle to all the men of the fair. There, therefore, they lay for some time, and were made the objects of any man's sport, or malice, or revenge; the great one of the fair laughing still at all that befell them. But the men being patient, and "not rendering railing for railing, but contrariwise blessing," and giving good words for bad, and kindness for injuries done, some men in the fair, that were more observing and less prejudiced than the rest, began to check and blame the baser sort for their continual abuses done by them to the men. They, therefore, in an angry manner let fly at them again, counting them as bad as the men in the cage, and telling them that they seemed confederates, and should be made partakers of their misfortunes. The others replied that, for aught they could see, the men were quiet and sober, and intended nobody any harm; and that there were many that traded in their fair that were more worthy to be put into the cage, yea, and pillory too, than were the men that they had abused. Thus, after divers words had passed on both sides, (the men behaving themselves all the while very wisely and soberly before them,) they fell to some blows among themselves, and did harm one to another. Then were these two poor men brought before their examiners again, and were charged as being guilty of the late hubbub that had been in the fair. So they beat them pitifully, and hanged irons upon them, and led them in chains up and down the fair, for an example and terror to others, lest any should speak in their behalf, or join themselves unto them. But Christian and Faithful behaved themselves yet more wisely, and received the ignominy and shame that was cast upon them with so much meekness and patience, that it won to their side (though but few in comparison of the rest) several of the men in the fair. This put the other party yet into a greater rage, insomuch that they concluded the death of these two men. Wherefore they threatened that neither cage nor irons should serve their turn, but that they should die for the abuse they had done, and for deluding the men of the fair.

Then were they remanded to the cage again, until further order should be taken with them. So they put them in, and made their feet fast in the stocks.

Here, also, they called again to mind what they had heard from their faithful friend Evangelist, and were the more confirmed in their way and sufferings by what he told them would happen to them. They also now comforted each other, that whose lot it was to suffer, even he should have the best of it: therefore each man secretly wished that he might have that preferment. But committing themselves to the all-wise disposal of Him that ruleth all things, with much content they abode in the condition in which they were, until they should be otherwise disposed of.

Then a convenient time being appointed, they brought them forth to their trial, in order to their condemnation. When the time was come, they were brought before their enemies and arraigned. The judge's name was Lord Hate-good; their indictment was one and the same in substance, though somewhat varying in form; the contents whereof was this: "That they were enemies to, and disturbers of, the trade; that they had made commotions and divisions in the town, and had won a party to their own most dangerous opinions, in contempt of the law of their prince."

Then Faithful began to answer, that he had only set himself against that which had set itself against Him that is higher than the highest. And, said he, as for disturbance, I make none, being myself a man of peace: the parties that were won to us, were won by beholding our truth and innocence, and they are only turned from the worse to the better. And as to the king you talk of, since he is Beelzebub, the enemy of our Lord, I defy him and all his angels.

Then proclamation was made, that they that had ought to say for their lord the king against the prisoner at the bar, should forthwith appear, and give in their evidence.

So there came in three witnesses, to wit, Envy, Superstition, and Pickthank. They were then asked if they knew the prisoner at the bar; and what they had to say for their lord the king against him.

Then stood forth Envy, and said to this effect: My lord, I have known this man a long time, and will attest upon my oath before this honorable bench, that he is-

Judge: Hold; give him his oath.

So they sware him. Then he said, My lord, this man, notwithstanding his plausible name, is one of the vilest men in our country; he neither regardeth prince nor people, law nor custom, but doeth all that he can to possess all men with certain of his disloyal notions, which he in the general calls principles of faith and holiness. And in particular, I heard him once myself affirm, that Christianity and the customs of our town of Vanity were diametrically opposite, and could not be reconciled. By which saying, my lord, he doth at once not only condemn all our laudable doings, but us in the doing of them.

Then did the judge say to him, Hast thou any more to say?

Envy: My lord, I could say much more, only I would not be tedious to the court. Yet if need be, when the other gentlemen have given in their evidence, rather than any thing shall be wanting that will dispatch him, I will enlarge my testimony against him. So he was bid to stand by.

Then they called Superstition, and bid him look upon the prisoner. They also asked, what he could say for their lord the king against him. Then they sware him; so he began.

Superstition: My lord, I have no great acquaintance with this man, nor do I desire to have further knowledge of him. However, this I know, that he is a very pestilent fellow, from some discourse that I had with him the other day, in this town; for then, talking with him, I heard him say, that our religion was naught, and such by which a man could by no means please God. Which saying of his, my lord, your lordship very well knows what necessarily thence will follow, to wit, that we still do worship in vain, are yet in our sins, and finally shall be damned: and this is that which I have to say.

Then was Pickthank sworn, and bid say what he knew in the behalf of their lord the king against the prisoner at the bar.

Pickthank: My lord, and you gentlemen all, this fellow I have known of a long time, and have heard him speak things that ought not to be spoken; for he hath railed on our noble prince Beelzebub, and hath spoken contemptibly of his honorable friends, whose names are, the Lord Old Man, the Lord Carnal Delight, the Lord Luxurious, the Lord Desire of Vain Glory, my old Lord Lechery, Sir Having Greedy, with all the rest of our nobility: and he hath said, moreover, that if all men were of his mind, if possible, there is not one of these noblemen should have any longer a being in this town. Besides, he hath not been afraid to rail on you, my lord, who are now appointed to be his judge, calling you an ungodly villain, with many other such like vilifying terms, with which he hath bespattered most of the gentry of our town.

When this Pickthank had told his tale, the judge directed his speech to the prisoner at the bar, saying, Thou runagate, heretic, and traitor, hast thou heard what these honest gentlemen have witnessed against thee?

Faithful: May I speak a few words in my own defence?

Judge: Sirrah, sirrah, thou deservest to live no longer, but to be slain immediately upon the place; yet, that all men may see our gentleness towards thee, let us hear what thou, vile runagate, hast to say.

Faithful: 1. I say, then, in answer to what Mr. Envy hath spoken, I never said aught but this, that what rule, or laws, or custom, or people, were flat against the word of God, are diametrically opposite to Christianity. If I have said amiss in this, convince me of my error, and I am ready here before you to make my recantation.

2. As to the second, to wit, Mr. Superstition, and his charge against me, I said only this, that in the worship of God there is required a divine faith; but there can be no divine faith without a divine revelation of the will of God. Therefore, whatever is thrust into the worship of God that is not agreeable to divine revelation, cannot be done but by a human faith; which faith will not be profitable to eternal life.

3. As to what Mr. Pickthank hath said, I say, (avoiding terms, as that I am said to rail, and the like,) that the prince of this town, with all the rabblement, his attendants, by this gentleman named, are more fit for a being in hell than in this town and country. And so the Lord have mercy upon me.
Then the judge called to the jury, (who all this while stood by to hear and observe,) Gentlemen of the jury, you see this man about whom so great an uproar hath been made in this town; you have also heard what these worthy gentlemen have witnessed against him; also, you have heard his reply and confession: it lieth now in your breasts to hang him, or save his life; but yet I think meet to instruct you in our law.

There was an act made in the days of Pharaoh the Great, servant to our prince, that, lest those of a contrary religion should multiply and grow too strong for him, their males should be thrown into the river. There was also an act made in the days of Nebuchadnezzar the Great, another of his servants, that whoever would not fall down and worship his golden image, should be thrown into a fiery furnace. There was also an act made in the days of Darius, that whoso for some time called upon any god but him, should be cast into the lion's den. Now, the substance of these laws this rebel has broken, not only in thought, (which is not to be borne,) but also in word and deed; which must, therefore, needs be intolerable.

For that of Pharaoh, his law was made upon a supposition to prevent mischief, no crime being yet apparent; but here is a crime apparent. For the second and third, you see he disputeth against our religion; and for the treason that he hath already confessed, he deserveth to die the death.

Then went the jury out, whose names were Mr. Blindman, Mr. No-good, Mr. Malice, Mr. Love-lust, Mr. Live-loose, Mr. Heady, Mr. High-mind, Mr. Enmity, Mr. Liar, Mr. Cruelty, Mr. Hate-light, and Mr. Implacable; who every one gave in his private verdict against him among themselves, and afterwards unanimously concluded to bring him in guilty before the judge. And first among themselves, Mr. Blindman, the foreman, said, I see clearly that this man is a heretic. Then said Mr. No-good, Away with such a fellow from the earth. Aye, said Mr. Malice, for I hate the very looks of him. Then said Mr. Love-lust, I could never endure him. Nor I, said Mr. Live-loose, for he would always be condemning my way. Hang him, hang him, said Mr. Heady. A sorry scrub, said Mr. High-mind. My heart riseth against him, said Mr. Enmity. He is a rogue, said Mr. Liar. Hanging is too good for him, said Mr. Cruelty. Let us dispatch him out of the way, said Mr. Hate-light. Then said Mr. Implacable, Might I have all the world given me, I could not be reconciled to him; therefore let us forthwith bring him in guilty of death.

And so they did; therefore he was presently condemned to be had from the place where he was, to the place from whence he came, and there to be put to the most cruel death that could be invented.
They therefore brought him out, to do with him according to their law; and first they scourged him, then they buffeted him, then they lanced his flesh with knives; after that, they stoned him with stones, then pricked him with their swords; and last of all, they burned him to ashes at the stake. Thus came Faithful to his end.

Now I saw, that there stood behind the multitude a chariot and a couple of horses waiting for Faithful, who (so soon as his adversaries had dispatched him) was taken up into it, and straightway was carried up through the clouds with sound of trumpet, the nearest way to the celestial gate. But as for Christian, he had some respite, and was remanded back to prison: so he there remained for a space. But he who overrules all things, having the power of their rage in his own hand, so wrought it about, that Christian for that time escaped them, and went his way.

And as he went, he sang, saying,
"Well, Faithful, thou hast faithfully profest
Unto thy Lord, with whom thou shalt be blest,
When faithless ones, with all their vain delights,
Are crying out under their hellish plights:
Sing, Faithful, sing, and let thy name survive;
For though they killed thee, thou art yet alive."

Lesson 75

- Read the first part of Book 1, Section 7 of *The Pilgrim's Progress*.

Book 1, Section 7
By-Ends and His Friends

Now I saw in my dream, that Christian went not forth alone; for there was one whose name was Hopeful, (being so made by the beholding of Christian and Faithful in their words and behavior, in their sufferings at the fair,) who joined himself unto him, and entering into a brotherly covenant, told him that he would be his companion. Thus one died to bear testimony to the truth, and another rises out of his ashes to be a companion with Christian in his pilgrimage.

This Hopeful also told Christian, that there were many more of the men in the fair that would take their time, and follow after.

So I saw, that quickly after they were got out of the fair, they overtook one that was going before them, whose name was By-ends; so they said to him, What countryman, sir? and how far go you this way? He told them, that he came from the town of Fair-speech, and he was going to the Celestial City; but told them not his name.

From Fair-speech? said Christian; is there any good that lives there?

By-Ends: Yes, said By-ends, I hope so.

Christian: Pray, sir, what may I call you? said Christian.

By-Ends: I am a stranger to you, and you to me: if you be going this way, I shall be glad of your company; if not, I must be content.

Christian: This town of Fair-speech, said Christian, I have heard of; and, as I remember, they say it's a wealthy place.

By-Ends: Yes, I will assure you that it is; and I have very many rich kindred there.

Christian: Pray, who are your kindred there, if a man may be so bold?

By-Ends: Almost the whole town; and in particular my Lord Turn-about, my Lord Time-server, my Lord Fair-speech, from whose ancestors that town first took its name; also, Mr. Smooth-man, Mr. Facing-both-ways, Mr. Any-thing; and the parson of our parish, Mr. Two-tongues, was my mother's own brother, by father's side; and, to tell you the truth, I am become a gentleman of good quality; yet my great-grandfather was but a waterman, looking one way and rowing another, and I got most of my estate by the same occupation.

Christian: Are you a married man.

By-Ends: Yes, and my wife is a very virtuous woman, the daughter of a virtuous woman; she was my Lady Feigning's daughter; therefore she came of a very honorable family, and is arrived to such a pitch of breeding, that she knows how to carry it to all, even to prince and peasant. 'Tis true, we somewhat differ in religion from those of the stricter sort, yet but in two small points: First, we never strive against wind and tide. Secondly, we are always most zealous when religion goes in his silver slippers; we love much to walk with him in the street, if the sun shines and the people applaud him.

Then Christian stepped a little aside to his fellow Hopeful, saying, it runs in my mind that this is one By-ends, of Fair-speech; and if it be he, we have as very a knave in our company as dwelleth in all these parts. Then said Hopeful, Ask him; methinks he should not be ashamed of his name. So Christian came up with him again, and said, Sir, you talk as if you knew something more than all the world doth; and, if I take not my mark amiss, I deem I have half a guess of you. Is not your name Mr. By-ends of Fair-speech?

By-Ends: This is not my name, but indeed it is a nickname that is given me by some that cannot abide me, and I must be content to bear it as a reproach, as other good men have borne theirs before me.

Christian: But did you never give an occasion to men to call you by this name?

By-Ends: Never, never! The worst that ever I did to give them an occasion to give me this name was, that I had always the luck to jump in my judgment with the present way of the times, whatever it was, and my chance was to get thereby: but if things are thus cast upon me, let me count them a blessing; but let not the malicious load me therefore with reproach.

Christian: I thought, indeed, that you were the man that I heard of; and to tell you what I think, I fear this name belongs to you more properly than you are willing we should think it doth.

By-Ends: Well if you will thus imagine, I cannot help it; you shall find me a fair company-keeper, if you will still admit me your associate.

Christian: If you will go with us, you must go against wind and tide; the which, I perceive, is against your opinion: you must also own Religion in his rags, as well as when in his silver slippers; and stand by him, too, when bound in irons, as well as when he walketh the streets with applause.

By-Ends: You must not impose, nor lord it over my faith; leave me to my liberty, and let me go with you.

Christian: Not a step farther, unless you will do, in what I propound, as we.

Then said By-ends, I shall never desert my old principles, since they are harmless and profitable. If I may not go with you, I must do as I did before you overtook me, even go by myself, until some overtake me that will be glad of my company. Now I saw in my dream, that Christian and Hopeful forsook him, and kept their distance before him; but one of them, looking back, saw three men following Mr. By-ends; and, behold, as they came up with him, he made them a very low congee; and they also gave him a compliment. The men's names were, Mr. Hold-the-world, Mr. Money-love, and Mr. Save-all, men that Mr. By-ends had formerly been acquainted with; for in their minority they were schoolfellows, and taught by one Mr. Gripeman, a schoolmaster in Lovegain, which is a market-town in the county of Coveting, in the North. This Schoolmaster taught them the art of getting, either by violence, cozenage, flattering, lying, or by putting on a guise of religion; and these four gentlemen had attained much of the art of their master, so that they could each of them have kept such a school themselves.

Well, when they had, as I said, thus saluted each other, Mr. Money-love said to Mr. By-ends, Who are they upon the road before us? For Christian and Hopeful were yet within view.

By-Ends: They are a couple of far country-men, that, after their mode, are going on pilgrimage.

Mr. Money-Love: Alas! why did they not stay, that we might have had their good company? for they, and we, and you, sir, I hope, are all going on pilgrimage.

By-Ends: We are so, indeed; but the men before us are so rigid, and love so much their own notions, and do also so lightly esteem the opinions of others, that let a man be ever so godly, yet if he jumps not with them in all things, they thrust him quite out of their company.

Mr. Save-All: That is bad; but we read of some that are righteous overmuch, and such men's rigidness prevails with them to judge and condemn all but themselves. But I pray, what, and how many, were the things wherein you differed?

By-Ends: Why, they, after their headstrong manner, conclude that it is their duty to rush on their journey all weathers, and I am for waiting for wind and tide. They are for hazarding all for God at a clap; and I am for taking all advantages to secure my life and estate. They are for holding their notions, though all other men be against them; but I am for religion in what, and so far as the times and my safety will bear it. They are for religion when in rags and contempt; but I am for him when he walks in his silver slippers, in the sunshine, and with applause.

Mr. Hold-the-World: Aye, and hold you there still, good Mr. By-ends; for, for my part, I can count him but a fool, that having the liberty to keep what he has, shall be so unwise as to lose it. Let us be wise as serpents. It is best to make hay while the sun shines. You see how the bee lieth still in winter, and bestirs her only when she can have profit with pleasure. God sends sometimes rain, and sometimes sunshine: if they be such fools to go through the first, yet let us be content to take fair weather along with us. For my part, I like that religion best that will stand with the security of God's good blessings unto us; for who can imagine, that is ruled by his reason, since God has bestowed upon us the good things of this life, but that he would have us keep them for his sake? Abraham and Solomon grew rich in religion; and Job says, that a good man shall lay up gold as dust; but he must not be such as the men before us, if they be as you have described them.

Mr. Save-All: I think that we are all agreed in this matter; and therefore there needs no more words about it.

Mr. Money-Love: No, there needs no more words about this matter, indeed; for he that believes neither Scripture nor reason, (and you see we have both on our side,) neither knows his own liberty nor seeks his own safety.

By-Ends: My brethren, we are, as you see, going all on pilgrimage; and for our better diversion from things that are bad, give me leave to propound unto you this question. Suppose a man, a minister, or a tradesman, etc., should have an advantage lie before him to get the good blessings of this life, yet so as that he can by no means come by them, except, in appearance at least, he becomes extraordinary zealous in some points of religion that he meddled not with before; may he not use this means to attain his end, and yet be a right honest man?

Mr. Money-Love: I see the bottom of your question; and with these gentlemen's good leave, I will endeavor to shape you an answer. And first, to speak to your question as it concerneth a minister himself: suppose a minister, a worthy man, possessed but of a very small benefice, and has in his eye a greater, more fat and plump by far; he has also now an opportunity of getting it, yet so as by being more studious, by preaching more frequently and zealously, and, because the temper of the people requires it, by altering of some of his principles; for my part, I see no reason why a man may not do this, provided he has a call, aye, and more a great deal besides, and yet be an honest man. For why?

1. His desire of a greater benefice is lawful, (this cannot be contradicted,) since it is set before him by Providence; so then he may get it if he can, making no question for conscience' sake.

2. Besides, his desire after that benefice makes him more studious, a more zealous preacher, etc., and so makes him a better man, yea, makes him better improve his parts, which is according to the mind of God.

3. Now, as for his complying with the temper of his people, by deserting, to serve them, some of his principles, this argueth, 1. That he is of a self-denying temper. 2. Of a sweet and winning deportment. And, 3. So more fit for the ministerial function.

4. I conclude, then, that a minister that changes a small for a great, should not, for so doing, be judged as covetous; but rather, since he is improved in his parts and industry thereby, be counted as one that pursues his call, and the opportunity put into his hand to do good.

And now to the second part of the question, which concerns the tradesman you mentioned. Suppose such an one to have but a poor employ in the world, but by becoming religious he may mend his market, perhaps get a rich wife, or more and far better customers to his shop; for my part, I see no reason but this may be lawfully done. For why?

1. To become religious is a virtue, by what means soever a man becomes so.

2. Nor is it unlawful to get a rich wife, or more custom to my shop.

3. Besides, the man that gets these by becoming religious, gets that which is good of them that are good, by becoming good himself; so then here is a good wife, and good customers, and good gain, and all these by becoming religious, which is good: therefore, to become religious to get all these is a good and profitable design.

This answer, thus made by Mr. Money-love to Mr. By-ends' question, was highly applauded by them all; wherefore they concluded, upon the whole, that it was most wholesome and advantageous. And because, as they thought, no man was able to contradict it; and because Christian and Hopeful were yet within call, they jointly agreed to assault them with the question as soon as they overtook them; and the rather, because they had opposed Mr. By-ends before. So they called after them, and they stopped and stood still till they came up to them; but they concluded, as they went, that not Mr. By-ends, but old Mr. Hold-the-world should propound the question to them, because, as they supposed, their answer to him would be without the remainder of that heat that was kindled betwixt Mr. By-ends and them at their parting a little before.

So they came up to each other, and after a short salutation, Mr. Hold-the-world propounded the question to Christian and his fellow, and then bid them to answer if they could.

Then said Christian, Even a babe in religion may answer ten thousand such questions. For if it be unlawful to follow Christ for loaves, as it is; how much more abominable is it to make of him and religion a stalking-horse to get and enjoy the world! Nor do we find any other than heathens, hypocrites, devils, and wizards, that are of this opinion.

1. Heathens: for when Hamor and Shechem had a mind to the daughter and cattle of Jacob, and saw that there was no way for them to come at them but by being circumcised, they said to their companions, If every male of us be circumcised, as they are circumcised, shall not their cattle, and their substance, and every beast of theirs be ours? Their daughters and their cattle were that which they sought to obtain, and their religion the stalking-horse they made use of to come at them. Read the whole story.

2. The hypocritical Pharisees were also of this religion: long prayers were their pretence, but to get widows' houses was their intent; and greater damnation was from God their judgment.

3. Judas the devil was also of this religion: he was religious for the bag, that he might be possessed of what was put therein; but he was lost, cast away, and the very son of perdition.

4. Simon the wizard was of this religion too; for he would have had the Holy Ghost, that he might have got money therewith: and his sentence from Peter's mouth was according.

5. Neither will it go out of my mind, but that that man who takes up religion for the world, will throw away religion for the world; for so surely as Judas designed the world in becoming religious, so surely did he also sell religion and his Master for the same. To answer the question, therefore, affirmatively, as I perceive you have done, and to accept of, as authentic, such answer, is heathenish, hypocritical, and devilish; and your reward will be according to your works.

Then they stood staring one upon another, but had not wherewith to answer Christian. Hopeful also approved of the soundness of Christian's answer; so there was a great silence among them. Mr. By-ends and his company also staggered and kept behind, that Christian and Hopeful might outgo them. Then said Christian to his fellow, If these men cannot stand before the sentence of men, what will they do with the sentence of God? And if they are mute when dealt with by vessels of clay, what will they do when they shall be rebuked by the flames of a devouring fire?

The Plain "Ease," Demas, and the Silver Mine

Then Christian and Hopeful outwent them again, and went till they came at a delicate plain, called Ease, where they went with much content; but that plain was but narrow, so they were quickly got over it. Now at the farther side of that plain was a little hill, called Lucre, and in that hill a silver-mine, which some of them that had formerly gone that way, because of the rarity of it, had turned aside to see; but going too near the brim of the pit, the ground, being deceitful under them, broke, and they were slain: some also had been maimed there, and could not, to their dying day, be their own men again.

Then I saw in my dream, that a little off the road, over against the silver-mine, stood Demas (gentleman-like) to call passengers to come and see; who said to Christian and his fellow, Ho! turn aside hither, and I will show you a thing.

Christian: What thing so deserving as to turn us out of the way to see it?

Demas: Here is a silver-mine, and some digging in it for treasure; if you will come, with a little pains you may richly provide for yourselves.

Hopeful: Then said Hopeful, let us go see.

Christian: Not I, said Christian: I have heard of this place before now, and how many there have been slain; and besides, that treasure is a snare to those that seek it, for it hindereth them in their pilgrimage.

Then Christian called to Demas, saying, Is not the place dangerous? Hath it not hindered many in their pilgrimage?

Demas: Not very dangerous, except to those that are careless; but withal he blushed as he spake.

Christian: Then said Christian to Hopeful, Let us not stir a step, but still keep on our way.

Hopeful: I will warrant you, when By-ends comes up, if he hath the same invitation as we, he will turn in thither to see.

Christian: No doubt thereof, for his principles lead him that way, and a hundred to one but he dies there.

Demas: Then Demas called again, saying, But will you not come over and see?

Christian: Then Christian roundly answered, saying, Demas, thou art an enemy to the right ways of the Lord of this way, and hast been already condemned for thine own turning aside, by one of his Majesty's judges, and why seekest thou to bring us into the like condemnation? Besides, if we at all turn aside, our Lord the King will certainly hear thereof, and will there put us to shame, where we would stand with boldness before him.

Demas cried again, that he also was one of their fraternity; and that if they would tarry a little, he also himself would walk with them.

Christian: Then said Christian, What is thy name? Is it not the same by which I have called thee?

Demas: Yes, my name is Demas; I am the son of Abraham.

Christian: I know you; Gehazi was your great-grandfather, and Judas your father, and you have trod in their steps; it is but a devilish prank that thou usest: thy father was hanged for a traitor, and thou deservest no better reward. Assure thyself, that when we come to the King, we will tell him of this thy behavior.

Thus they went their way. By this time By-ends and his companions were come again within sight, and they at the first beck went over to Demas. Now, whether they fell into the pit by looking over the brink thereof, or whether they went down to dig, or whether they were smothered in the bottom by the damps that commonly arise, of these things I am not certain; but this I observed, that they were never seen again in the way. Then sang Christian,

"By-ends and silver Demas both agree;
One calls, the other runs, that he may be
A sharer in his lucre: so these two
Take up in this world, and no farther go."

Lesson 76

- Read the rest of Book 1, Section 7 of *The Pilgrim's Progress*.

Lot's Wife

"They stood looking and looking upon it, but could not for a time tell what they should make thereof."

Now I saw that, just on the other side of this plain, the pilgrims came to a place where stood an old monument, hard by the highway-side, at the sight of which they were both concerned, because of the strangeness of the form thereof; for it seemed to them as if it had been a woman transformed into the shape of a pillar. Here, therefore, they stood looking and looking upon it, but could not for a time tell what they should make thereof. At last Hopeful espied, written above upon the head thereof, a writing in an unusual hand; but he being no scholar, called to Christian (for he was learned) to see if he could pick out the meaning: so he came, and after a little laying of letters together, he found the same to be this, "Remember Lot's wife." So he read it to his fellow; after which they both concluded that that was the pillar of salt into which Lot's wife was turned, for her looking back with a covetous heart when she was going from Sodom for safety. Which sudden and amazing sight gave them occasion for this discourse.

Christian: Ah, my brother, this is a seasonable sight: it came opportunely to us after the invitation which Demas gave us to come over to view the hill Lucre; and had we gone over, as he desired us, and as thou wast inclined to do, my brother, we had, for aught I know, been made, like this woman, a spectacle for those that shall come after to behold.

Hopeful: I am sorry that I was so foolish, and am made to wonder that I am not now as Lot's wife; for wherein was the difference betwixt her sin and mine? She only looked back, and I had a desire to go see. Let grace be adored; and let me be ashamed that ever such a thing should be in mine heart.

Christian: Let us take notice of what we see here, for our help from time to come. This woman escaped one judgment, for she fell not by the destruction of Sodom; yet she was destroyed by another, as we see: she is turned into a pillar of salt.

Hopeful: True, and she may be to us both caution and example; caution, that we should shun her sin; or a sign of what judgment will overtake such as shall not be prevented by this caution: so Korah, Dathan, and Abiram, with the two hundred and fifty men that perished in their sin, did also become a sign or example to others to beware. But above all, I muse at one thing, to wit, how Demas and his fellows can stand so confidently yonder to look for that treasure, which this woman but for looking behind her after, (for we read not that she stepped one foot out of the way,) was turned into a pillar of salt; especially since the judgment which overtook her did make her an example within sight of where they are; for they cannot choose but see her, did they but lift up their eyes.

Christian: It is a thing to be wondered at, and it argueth that their hearts are grown desperate in the case; and I cannot tell who to compare them to so fitly, as to them that pick pockets in the presence of the judge, or that will cut purses under the gallows. It is said of the men of Sodom, that they were "sinners exceedingly," because they were sinners "before the Lord," that is, in his eyesight, and notwithstanding the kindnesses that he had shown them; for the land of Sodom was now like the garden of Eden as heretofore. This, therefore, provoked him the more to jealousy, and made their plague as hot as the fire of the Lord out of heaven could make it. And it is most rationally to be concluded, that such, even such as these are, that shall sin in the sight, yea, and that too in despite of such examples that are set continually before them, to caution them to the contrary, must be partakers of severest judgments.

Hopeful: Doubtless thou hast said the truth; but what a mercy is it, that neither thou, but especially I, am not made myself this example! This ministereth occasion to us to thank God, to fear before him, and always to remember Lot's wife.

The River of the Water of Life

I saw then that they went on their way to a pleasant river, which David the king called "the river of God;" but John, "the river of the water of life." Now their way lay just upon the bank of this river: here, therefore, Christian and his companion walked with great delight; they drank also of the water of the river, which was pleasant and enlivening to their weary spirits. Besides, on the banks of this river, on either side, were green trees with all manner of fruit; and the leaves they ate to prevent surfeits, and other diseases that are incident to those that heat their blood by travel. On either side of the river was also a meadow, curiously beautified with lilies; and it was green all the year long. In this meadow they lay down and slept, for here they might lie down safely. When they awoke they gathered again of the fruit of the trees, and drank again of the water of the river, and then lay down again to sleep. Thus they did several days and nights. Then they sang;

"Behold ye, how these Crystal Streams do glide,
To comfort pilgrims by the highway-side.
The meadows green, besides their fragrant smell,
Yield dainties for them; And he that can tell
What pleasant fruit, yea, leaves these trees do yield,
Will soon sell all, that he may buy this field."

So when they were disposed to go on, (for they were not as yet at their journey's end,) they ate, and drank, and departed.

By-Path Meadow and Giant Despair

Now I beheld in my dream, that they had not journeyed far, but the river and the way for a time parted, at which they were not a little sorry; yet they durst not go out of the way. Now the way from the river was rough, and their feet tender by reason of their travels; so the souls of the pilgrims were much discouraged because of the way (*Num. 21:4*). Wherefore, still as they went on, they wished for a better way. Now, a little before them, there was on the left hand of the road a meadow, and a stile to go over into it, and that meadow is called By-path meadow. Then said Christian to his fellow, If this meadow lieth along by our wayside, let's go over into it. Then he went to the stile to see, and behold a path lay along by the way on the other side of the fence. It is according to my wish, said Christian; here is the easiest going; come, good Hopeful, and let us go over.

Hopeful: But how if this path should lead us out of the way?

Christian: That is not likely, said the other. Look, doth it not go along by the wayside? So Hopeful, being persuaded by his fellow, went after him over the stile. When they were gone over, and were got into the path, they found it very easy for their feet; and withal, they, looking before them, espied a man walking as they did, and his name was Vain-Confidence: so they called after him, and asked him whither that way led. He said, To the Celestial Gate. Look, said Christian, did not I tell you so? by this you may see we are right. So they followed, and he went before them. But behold the night came on, and it grew very dark; so that they that went behind lost the sight of him that went before.

He therefore that went before, (Vain-Confidence by name,) not seeing the way before him, fell into a deep pit, which was on purpose there made, by the prince of those grounds, to catch vain-glorious fools withal, and was dashed in pieces with his fall.

Now, Christian and his fellow heard him fall. So they called to know the matter, but there was none to answer, only they heard a groaning. Then said Hopeful, Where are we now? Then was his fellow silent, as mistrusting that he had led him out of the way; and now it began to rain, and thunder, and lighten in a most dreadful manner, and the water rose amain.

Then Hopeful groaned in himself, saying, Oh that I had kept on my way!

Christian: Who could have thought that this path should have led us out of the way?

Hopeful: I was afraid on't at the very first, and therefore gave you that gentle caution. I would have spoke plainer, but that you are older than I.

Christian: Good brother, be not offended; I am sorry I have brought thee out of the way, and that I have put thee into such imminent danger. Pray, my brother, forgive me; I did not do it of an evil intent.

Hopeful: Be comforted, my brother, for I forgive thee; and believe, too, that this shall be for our good.

Christian: I am glad I have with me a merciful brother: but we must not stand here; let us try to go back again.

Hopeful: But, good brother, let me go before.

Christian: No, if you please, let me go first, that if there be any danger, I may be first therein, because by my means we are both gone out of the way.

Hopeful: No, said Hopeful, you shall not go first, for your mind being troubled may lead you out of the way again. Then for their encouragement they heard the voice of one saying, "Let thine heart be toward the highway, even the way that thou wentest: turn again." But by this time the waters were greatly risen, by reason of which the way of going back was very dangerous. (Then I thought that it is easier going out of the way when we are in, than going in when we are out.) Yet they adventured to go back; but it was so dark, and the flood was so high, that in their going back they had like to have been drowned nine or ten times.

Neither could they, with all the skill they had, get again to the stile that night. Wherefore at last, lighting under a little shelter, they sat down there till the day brake; but being weary, they fell asleep. Now there was, not far from the place where they lay, a castle, called Doubting Castle, the owner whereof was Giant Despair, and it was in his grounds they now were sleeping: wherefore he, getting up in the morning early, and walking up and down in his fields, caught Christian and Hopeful asleep in his grounds. Then with a grim and surly voice, he bid them awake, and asked them whence they were, and what they did in his grounds. They told him they were pilgrims, and that they had lost their way.

Then said the giant, You have this night trespassed on me by trampling in and lying on my grounds, and therefore you must go along with me. So they were forced to go, because he was stronger than they. They also had but little to say, for they knew themselves in a fault. The giant, therefore, drove them before him, and put them into his castle, into a very dark dungeon, nasty and stinking to the spirits of these two men. Here, then, they lay from Wednesday morning till Saturday night, without one bit of bread, or drop of drink, or light, or any to ask how they did; they were, therefore, here in evil case, and were far from friends and acquaintance. Now in this place Christian had double sorrow, because it was through his unadvised counsel that they were brought into this distress.

Now Giant Despair had a wife, and her name was Diffidence: so when he was gone to bed he told his wife what he had done, to wit, that he had taken a couple of prisoners, and cast them into his dungeon for trespassing on his grounds. Then he asked her also what he had best do further to them. So she asked him what they were, whence they came, and whither they were bound, and he told her. Then she counseled him, that when he arose in the morning he should beat them without mercy. So when he arose, he getteth him a grievous crab-tree cudgel, and goes down into the dungeon to them, and there first falls to rating of them as if they were dogs, although they gave him never a word of distaste. Then he falls upon them, and beats them fearfully, in such sort that they were not able to help themselves, or to turn them upon the floor. This done, he withdraws and leaves them there to condole their misery, and to mourn under their distress: so all that day they spent the time in nothing but sighs and bitter lamentations. The next night, she, talking with her husband further about them, and understanding that they were yet alive, did advise him to counsel them to make away with themselves. So when morning was come, he goes to them in a surly manner, as before, and perceiving them to be very sore with the stripes that he had given them the day before, he told them, that since they were never like to come out of that place, their only way would be forthwith to make an end of themselves, either with knife, halter, or poison; for why, said he, should you choose to live, seeing it is attended with so much bitterness? But they desired him to let them go. With that he looked ugly upon them, and rushing to them, had doubtless made an end of them himself, but that he fell into one of his fits, (for he sometimes in sunshiny weather fell into fits,) and lost for a time the use of his hands; wherefore he withdrew, and left them as before to consider what to do. Then did the prisoners consult between themselves whether it was best to take his counsel or no; and thus they began to discourse:

Christian: Brother, said Christian, what shall we do? The life that we now live is miserable. For my part, I know not whether it is best to live thus, or to die out of hand. My soul chooseth strangling rather than life, and the grave is more easy for me than this dungeon. Shall we be ruled by the giant?

Hopeful: Indeed our present condition is dreadful, and death would be far more welcome to me than thus for ever to abide; but yet, let us consider, the Lord of the country to which we are going hath said, "Thou shalt do no murder," no, not to another man's person; much more, then, are we forbidden to take his counsel to kill ourselves. Besides, he that kills another, can but commit murder upon his body; but for one to kill himself, is to kill body and soul at once. And moreover, my brother, thou talkest of ease in the grave; but hast thou forgotten the hell whither for certain the murderers go? for "no murderer hath eternal life," etc. And let us consider again, that all the law is not in the hand of Giant Despair: others, so far as I can understand, have been taken by him as well as we, and yet have escaped out of his hands. Who knows but that God, who made the world, may cause that Giant Despair may die; or that, at some time or other, he may forget to lock us in; or that he may, in a short time, have another of his fits before us, and may lose the use of his limbs? And if ever that should come to pass again, for my part, I am resolved to pluck up the heart of a man, and to try my utmost to get from under his hand. I was a fool that I did not try to do it before. But, however, my brother, let us be patient, and endure a while: the time may come that may give us a happy release; but let us not be our own murderers. With these words Hopeful at present did moderate the mind of his brother; so they continued together in the dark that day, in their sad and doleful condition.

Well, towards evening the giant goes down into the dungeon again, to see if his prisoners had taken his counsel. But when he came there he found them alive; and truly, alive was all; for now, what for want of bread and water, and by reason of the wounds they received when he beat them, they could do little but breathe. But I say, he found them alive; at which he fell into a grievous rage, and told them, that seeing they had disobeyed his counsel, it should be worse with them than if they had never been born.

At this they trembled greatly, and I think that Christian fell into a swoon; but coming a little to himself again, they renewed their discourse about the giant's counsel, and whether yet they had best take it or no. Now Christian again seemed for doing it; but Hopeful made his second reply as followeth:

Hopeful: My brother, said he, rememberest thou not how valiant thou hast been heretofore? Apollyon could not crush thee, nor could all that thou didst hear, or see, or feel, in the Valley of the Shadow of Death. What hardship, terror, and amazement hast thou already gone through; and art thou now nothing but fears! Thou seest that I am in the dungeon with thee, a far weaker man by nature than thou art. Also this giant hath wounded me as well as thee, and hath also cut off the bread and water from my mouth, and with thee I mourn without the light. But let us exercise a little more patience. Remember how thou playedst the man at Vanity Fair, and wast neither afraid of the chain nor cage, nor yet of bloody death: wherefore let us (at least to avoid the shame that it becomes not a Christian to be found in) bear up with patience as well as we can. Now night being come again, and the giant and his wife being in bed, she asked him concerning the prisoners, and if they had taken his counsel: to which he replied, They are sturdy rogues; they choose rather to bear all hardships than to make away with themselves. Then said she, Take them into the castle-yard to-morrow, and show them the bones and skulls of those that thou hast already dispatched, and make them believe, ere a week comes to an end, thou wilt tear them in pieces, as thou hast done their fellows before them.

So when the morning was come, the giant goes to them again, and takes them into the castle-yard, and shows them as his wife had bidden him. These, said he, were pilgrims, as you are, once, and they trespassed on my grounds, as you have done; and when I thought fit I tore them in pieces; and so within ten days I will do you: get you down to your den again. And with that he beat them all the way thither. They lay, therefore, all day on Saturday in a lamentable case, as before. Now, when night was come, and when Mrs. Diffidence and her husband the giant was got to bed, they began to renew their discourse of their prisoners; and withal, the old giant wondered that he could neither by his blows nor counsel bring them to an end. And with that his wife replied, I fear, said she, that they live in hopes that some will come to relieve them; or that they have picklocks about them, by the means of which they hope to escape. And sayest thou so, my dear? said the giant; I will therefore search them in the morning.

Well, on Saturday, about midnight they began to pray, and continued in prayer till almost break of day.

Now, a little before it was day, good Christian, as one half amazed, brake out into this passionate speech: What a fool, quoth he, am I, thus to lie in a stinking dungeon, when I may as well walk at liberty! I have a key in my bosom, called Promise, that will, I am persuaded, open any lock in Doubting Castle. Then said Hopeful, That is good news; good brother, pluck it out of thy bosom, and try.

Then Christian pulled it out of his bosom, and began to try at the dungeon-door, whose bolt, as he turned the key, gave back, and the door flew open with ease, and Christian and Hopeful both came out. Then he went to the outward door that leads into the castle-yard, and with his key opened that door also. After he went to the iron gate, for that must be opened too; but that lock went damnable hard, yet the key did open it. They then thrust open the gate to make their escape with speed; but that gate, as it opened, made such a creaking, that it waked Giant Despair, who hastily rising to pursue his prisoners, felt his limbs to fail, for his fits took him again, so that he could by no means go after them. Then they went on, and came to the King's highway, and so were safe, because they were out of his jurisdiction.

Now, when they were gone over the stile, they began to contrive with themselves what they should do at that stile, to prevent those that shall come after from falling into the hands of Giant Despair. So they consented to erect there a pillar, and to engrave upon the side thereof this sentence: "Over this stile is the way to Doubting Castle, which is kept by Giant Despair, who despiseth the King of the Celestial country, and seeks to destroy his holy pilgrims." Many, therefore, that followed after, read what was written, and escaped the danger. This done, they sang as follows:

"Out of the way we went, and then we found
What 'twas to tread upon forbidden ground:
And let them that come after have a care,
Lest heedlessness makes them as we to fare;

Lest they, for trespassing, his prisoners are,
Whose castle's Doubting, and whose name's Despair."

Lesson 77

- Read Book 1, Section 8 of *The Pilgrim's Progress*.

Book 1, Section 8
The Delectable Mountains

They went then till they came to the Delectable Mountains, which mountains belong to the Lord of that hill of which we have spoken before. So they went up to the mountains, to behold the gardens and orchards, the vineyards and fountains of water; where also they drank and washed themselves, and did freely eat of the vineyards. Now, there were on the tops of these mountains shepherds feeding their flocks, and they stood by the highway-side. The pilgrims, therefore, went to them, and leaning upon their staffs, (as is common with weary pilgrims when they stand to talk with any by the way,) they asked, Whose Delectable Mountains are these; and whose be the sheep that feed upon them?

The Shepherds: These mountains are Emmanuel's land, and they are within sight of his city; and the sheep also are his, and he laid down his life for them.

Christian: Is this the way to the Celestial City?

The Shepherds: You are just in your way.

Christian: How far is it thither?

The Shepherds: Too far for any but those who shall get thither indeed.

Christian: Is the way safe or dangerous?

The Shepherds: Safe for those for whom it is to be safe; but transgressors shall fall therein.

Christian: Is there in this place any relief for pilgrims that are weary and faint in the way?

The Shepherds: The Lord of these mountains hath given us a charge not to be forgetful to entertain strangers; therefore the good of the place is before you.

I saw also in my dream, that when the shepherds perceived that they were wayfaring men, they also put questions to them, (to which they made answer as in other places,) as, Whence came you? and, How got you into the way? and, By what means have you so persevered therein? for but few of them that begin to come hither, do show their face on these mountains. But when the shepherds heard their answers, being pleased therewith, they looked very lovingly upon them, and said, Welcome to the Delectable Mountains.

The shepherds, I say, whose names were Knowledge, Experience, Watchful, and Sincere, took them by the hand, and had them to their tents, and made them partake of that which was ready at present. They said moreover, We would that you should stay here a while, to be acquainted with us, and yet more to solace yourselves with the good of these Delectable Mountains. Then they told them that they were content to stay. So they went to their rest that night, because it was very late.
Then I saw in my dream, that in the morning the shepherds called up Christian and Hopeful to walk with them upon the mountains. So they went forth with them, and walked a while, having a pleasant prospect on every side. Then said the shepherds one to another, Shall we show these pilgrims some wonders? So when they had concluded to do it, they had them first to the top of a hill called Error, which was very steep on the farthest side, and bid them look down to the bottom. So Christian and Hopeful looked down, and saw at the bottom several men dashed all to pieces by a fall that they had had from the top. Then said Christian, What meaneth this? The shepherds answered, Have you not heard of them that were made to err, by hearkening to Hymenius and Philetus, as concerning the faith of the resurrection of the body? They answered, Yes. Then said the shepherds, Those that you see lie dashed in pieces at the bottom of this mountain are they; and they have continued to this day unburied, as you see, for an example to others to take heed how they clamber too high, or how they come too near the brink of this mountain.

Then I saw that they had them to the top of another mountain, and the name of that is Caution, and bid them look afar off; which, when they did, they perceived, as they thought, several men walking up and down among the tombs that were there; and they perceived that the men were blind, because they stumbled sometimes upon the tombs, and because they could not get out from among them. Then said Christian, What means this?

The shepherds then answered, Did you not see, a little below these mountains, a stile that led into a meadow, on the left hand of this way? They answered, Yes. Then said the shepherds, From that stile there goes a path that leads directly to Doubting Castle, which is kept by Giant Despair; and these men (pointing to them among the tombs) came once on pilgrimage, as you do now, even until they came to that same stile. And because the right way was rough in that place, they chose to go out of it into that meadow, and there were taken by Giant Despair, and cast into Doubting Castle; where after they had a while been kept in the dungeon, he at last did put out their eyes, and led them among those tombs, where he has left them to wander to this very day, that the saying of the wise man might be fulfilled, "He that wandereth out of the way of understanding shall remain in the congregation of the dead." Then Christian and Hopeful looked upon one another, with tears gushing out, but yet said nothing to the shepherds.

Then I saw in my dream, that the shepherds had them to another place in a bottom, where was a door on the side of a hill; and they opened the door, and bid them look in. They looked in, therefore, and saw that within it was very dark and smoky; they also thought that they heard there a rumbling noise, as of fire, and a cry of some tormented, and that they smelt the scent of brimstone. Then said Christian, What means this? The shepherds told them, This is a by-way to hell, a way that hypocrites go in at; namely, such as sell their birthright, with Esau; such as sell their Master, with Judas; such as blaspheme the Gospel, with Alexander; and that lie and dissemble, with Ananias and Sapphira his wife.

Then said Hopeful to the shepherds, I perceive that these had on them, even every one, a show of pilgrimage, as we have now; had they not?

The Shepherds: Yes, and held it a long time, too.

Hopeful: How far might they go on in pilgrimage in their day, since they, notwithstanding, were miserably cast away?

The Shepherds: Some farther, and some not so far as these mountains. Then said the pilgrims one to the other, We had need to cry to the Strong for strength.

The Shepherds: Aye, and you will have need to use it, when you have it, too. By this time the pilgrims had a desire to go forward, and the shepherds a desire they should; so they walked together towards the end of the mountains. Then said the shepherds one to another, Let us here show the pilgrims the gates of the Celestial City, if they have skill to look through our perspective glass. The pilgrims lovingly accepted the motion: so they had them to the top of a high hill, called Clear, and gave them the glass to look. Then they tried to look; but the remembrance of that last thing that the shepherds had shown them made their hands shake, by means of which impediment they could not look steadily through the glass; yet they thought they saw something like the gate, and also some of the glory of the place. Then they went away, and sang,

"Thus by the shepherds secrets are reveal'd,
Which from all other men are kept concealed:
Come to the shepherds then, if you would see
Things deep, things hid, and that mysterious be."

When they were about to depart, one of the shepherds gave them a note of the way. Another of them bid them beware of the Flatterer. The third bid them take heed that they slept not upon Enchanted Ground. And the fourth bid them God speed. So I awoke from my dream.

Ignorance

And I slept, and dreamed again, and saw the same two pilgrims going down the mountains along the highway towards the city. Now, a little below these mountains, on the left hand, lieth the country of Conceit, from which country there comes into the way in which the pilgrims walked, a little crooked lane. Here, therefore, they met with a very brisk lad that came out of that country, and his name was Ignorance. So Christian asked him from what parts he came, and whither he was going.

Ignorance: Sir, I was born in the country that lieth off there, a little on the left hand, and I am going to the Celestial City.

Christian: But how do you think to get in at the gate, for you may find some difficulty there?

Ignorance: As other good people do, said he.

Christian: But what have you to show at that gate, that the gate should be opened to you?

Ignorance: I know my Lord's will, and have been a good liver; I pay every man his own; I pray, fast, pay tithes, and give alms, and have left my country for whither I am going.

Christian: But thou camest not in at the wicket-gate, that is at the head of this way; thou camest in hither through that same crooked lane, and therefore I fear, however thou mayest think of thyself, when the reckoning-day shall come, thou wilt have laid to thy charge, that thou art a thief and a robber, instead of getting admittance into the city.

Ignorance: Gentlemen, ye be utter strangers to me; I know you not: be content to follow the religion of your country, and I will follow the religion of mine. I hope all will be well. And as for the gate that you talk of, all the world knows that is a great way off of our country. I cannot think that any man in all our parts doth so much as know the way to it; nor need they matter whether they do or no, since we have, as you see, a fine, pleasant, green lane, that comes down from our country, the next way into the way.

When Christian saw that the man was wise in his own conceit, he said to Hopeful whisperingly, "There is more hope of a fool than of him." And said, moreover, "When he that is a fool walketh by the way, his wisdom faileth him, and he saith to every one that he is a fool. What, shall we talk farther with him, or outgo him at present, and so leave him to think of what he hath heard already, and then stop again for him afterwards, and see if by degrees we can do any good to him?" Then said Hopeful,

"Let Ignorance a little while now muse
On what is said, and let him not refuse
Good counsel to embrace, lest he remain
Still ignorant of what's the chiefest gain.
God saith, those that no understanding have,
(Although he made them,) them he will not save."

Hopeful: He further added, It is not good, I think, to say so to him all at once; let us pass him by, if you will, and talk to him anon, even as he is able to bear it.

The story of Little-Faith

So they both went on, and Ignorance he came after. Now, when they had passed him a little way, they entered into a very dark lane, where they met a man whom seven devils had bound with seven strong cords, and were carrying him back to the door that they saw on the side of the hill. Now good Christian began to tremble, and so did Hopeful, his companion; yet, as the devils led away the man, Christian looked to see if he knew him; and he thought it might be one Turn-away, that dwelt in the town of Apostasy. But he did not perfectly see his face, for he did hang his head like a thief that is found; but being gone past, Hopeful looked after him, and espied on his back a paper with this inscription, "Wanton professor, and damnable apostate."

Then said Christian to his fellow, Now I call to remembrance that which was told me of a thing that happened to a good man hereabout. The name of the man was Little-Faith; but a good man, and he dwelt in the town of Sincere. The thing was this. At the entering in at this passage, there comes down from Broadway-gate, a lane, called Dead-Man's lane; so called because of the murders that are commonly done there; and this Little-Faith going on pilgrimage, as we do now, chanced to sit down there and sleep. Now there happened at that time to come down the lane from Broadway-gate, three sturdy rogues, and their names were Faint-Heart, Mistrust, and Guilt, three brothers; and they, espying Little-Faith where he was, came galloping up with speed. Now the good man was just awaked from his sleep, and was getting up to go on his journey. So they came up all to him, and with threatening language bid him stand. At this, Little-Faith looked as white as a sheet, and had neither power to fight nor fly. Then said Faint-Heart, Deliver thy purse; but he making no haste to do it, (for he was loth to lose his money,) Mistrust ran up to him, and thrusting his hand into his pocket, pulled out thence a bag of silver. Then he cried out, Thieves, thieves! With that, Guilt, with a great club that was in his hand, struck Little-Faith on the head, and with that blow felled him flat to the ground, where he lay bleeding as one that would bleed to death. All this while the thieves stood by. But at last, they hearing that some were upon the road, and fearing lest it should be one Great-Grace, that dwells in the town of Good-Confidence, they betook themselves to their heels, and left this good man to shift for himself. Now, after a while, Little-Faith came to himself, and getting up, made shift to scramble on his way. This was the story.

Hopeful: But did they take from him all that ever he had?

Christian: No; the place where his jewels were they never ransacked; so those he kept still. But, as I was told, the good man was much afflicted for his loss; for the thieves got most of his spending-money. That which they got not, as I said, were jewels; also, he had a little odd money left, but scarce enough to bring him to his journey's end. Nay, (if I was not misinformed,) he was forced to beg as he went, to keep himself alive, for his jewels he might not sell; but beg and do what he could, he went, as we say, with many a hungry belly the most part of the rest of the way.

Hopeful: But is it not a wonder they got not from him his certificate, by which he was to receive his admittance at the Celestial Gate?

Christian: It is a wonder; but they got not that, though they missed it not through any good cunning of his; for he, being dismayed by their coming upon him, had neither power nor skill to hide any thing; so it was more by good providence than by his endeavor that they missed of that good thing.

Hopeful: But it must needs be a comfort to him they got not this jewel from him.

Christian: It might have been great comfort to him, had he used it as he should; but they that told me the story said that he made but little use of it all the rest of the way, and that because of the dismay that he had in their taking away his money. Indeed, he forgot it a great part of the rest of his journey; and besides, when at any time it came into his mind, and he began to be comforted therewith, then would fresh thoughts of his loss come again upon him, and these thoughts would swallow up all.

Hopeful: Alas, poor man, this could not but be a great grief to him.

Christian: Grief? Aye, a grief indeed! Would it not have been so to any of us, had we been used as he, to be robbed and wounded too, and that in a strange place, as he was? It is a wonder he did not die with grief, poor heart. I was told that he scattered almost all the rest of the way with nothing but doleful and bitter complaints; telling, also, to all that overtook him, or that he overtook in the way as he went, where he was robbed, and how; who they were that did it, and what he had lost; how he was wounded, and that he hardly escaped with life.

Hopeful: But it is a wonder that his necessity did not put him upon selling or pawning some of his jewels, that he might have wherewith to relieve himself in his journey.

Christian: Thou talkest like one upon whose head is the shell to this very day. For what should he pawn them? or to whom should he sell them? In all that country where he was robbed, his jewels were not accounted of; nor did he want that relief which could from thence be administered to him. Besides, had his jewels been missing at the gate of the Celestial City, he had (and that he knew well enough) been excluded from an inheritance there, and that would have been worse to him than the appearance and villany of ten thousand thieves.

Hopeful: Why art thou so tart, my brother? Esau sold his birthright, and that for a mess of pottage, and that birthright was his greatest jewel: and if he, why might not Little-Faith do so too?

Christian: Esau did sell his birthright indeed, and so do many besides, and by so doing exclude themselves from the chief blessing, as also that caitiff did; but you must put a difference betwixt Esau and Little-Faith, and also betwixt their estates. Esau's birthright was typical; but Little-Faith's jewels were not so. Esau's belly was his god; but Little-Faith's belly was not so. Esau's want lay in his fleshy appetite; Little-Faith's did not so. Besides, Esau could see no further than to the fulfilling of his lusts: For I am at the point to die, said he: and what good will this birthright do me? But Little-Faith, though it was his lot to have but a little faith, was by his little faith kept from such extravagances, and made to see and prize his jewels more than to sell them, as Esau did his birthright. You read not any where that Esau had faith, no, not so much as a little; therefore no marvel, where the flesh only bears sway, (as it will in that man where no faith is to resist,) if he sells his birthright and his soul and all, and that to the devil of hell; for it is with such as it is with the ass, who in her occasion cannot be turned away: when their minds are set upon their lusts, they will have them, whatever they cost. But Little-Faith was of another temper; his mind was on things divine; his livelihood was upon things that were spiritual, and from above: therefore, to what end should he that is of such a temper sell his jewels (had there been any that would have bought them) to fill his mind with empty things? Will a man give a penny to fill his belly with hay? or can you persuade the turtle-dove to live upon carrion, like the crow? Though faithless ones can, for carnal lusts, pawn, or mortgage, or sell what they have, and themselves outright to boot; yet they that have faith, saving faith, though but a little of it, cannot do so. Here, therefore, my brother, is thy mistake.

Hopeful: I acknowledge it; but yet your severe reflection had almost made me angry.

Christian: Why, I did but compare thee to some of the birds that are of the brisker sort, who will run to and fro in untrodden paths with the shell upon their heads: but pass by that, and consider the matter under debate, and all shall be well betwixt thee and me.

Hopeful: But, Christian, these three fellows, I am persuaded in my heart, are but a company of cowards: would they have run else, think you, as they did, at the noise of one that was coming on the road? Why did not Little-Faith pluck up a greater heart? He might, methinks, have stood one brush with them, and have yielded when there had been no remedy.

Christian: That they are cowards, many have said, but few have found it so in the time of trial. As for a great heart, Little-Faith had none; and I perceive by thee, my brother, hadst thou been the man concerned, thou art but for a brush, and then to yield. And verily, since this is the height of thy stomach now they are at a distance from us, should they appear to thee as they did to him, they might put thee to second thoughts.

But consider again, that they are but journeymen thieves; They serve under the king of the bottomless pit, who, if need be, will come to their aid himself, and his voice is as the roaring of a lion. I myself have been engaged as this Little-Faith was, and I found it a terrible thing. These three villains set upon me, and I beginning like a Christian to resist, they gave but a call, and in came their master. I would, as the saying is, have given my life for a penny, but that, as God would have it, I was clothed with armor of proof. Aye, and yet, though I was so harnessed, I found it hard work to quit myself like a man: no man can tell what in that combat attends us, but he that hath been in the battle himself.

Hopeful: Well, but they ran, you see, when they did but suppose that one Great-Grace was in the way.

Christian: True, they have often fled, both they and their master, when Great-Grace hath but appeared; and no marvel, for he is the King's champion. But I trow you will put some difference between Little-Faith and the King's champion. All the King's subjects are not his champions; nor can they, when tried, do such feats of war as he. Is it meet to think that a little child should handle Goliath as David did? or that there should be the strength of an ox in a wren? Some are strong, some are weak; some have great faith, some have little: this man was one of the weak, and therefore he went to the wall.

Hopeful: I would it had been Great-Grace, for their sakes.

Christian: If it had been he, he might have had his hands full: for I must tell you, that though Great-Grace is excellent good at his weapons, and has, and can, so long as he keeps them at sword's point, do well enough with them; yet if they get within him, even Faint-Heart, Mistrust, or the other, it shall go hard but they will throw up his heels. And when a man is down, you know, what can he do?

Whoso looks well upon Great-Grace's face, will see those scars and cuts there that shall easily give demonstration of what I say. Yea, once I heard that he should say, (and that when he was in the combat,) We despaired even of life. How did these sturdy rogues and their fellows make David groan, mourn, and roar! Yea, Heman, and Hezekiah too, though champions in their days, were forced to bestir them when by these assaulted; and yet, notwithstanding, they had their coats soundly brushed by them. Peter, upon a time, would go try what he could do; but though some do say of him that he is the prince of the apostles, they handled him so that they made him at last afraid of a sorry girl.

Besides, their king is at their whistle; he is never out of hearing; and if at any time they be put to the worst, he, if possible, comes in to help them; and of him it is said, "The sword of him that layeth at him cannot hold; the spear, the dart, nor the habergeon. He esteemeth iron as straw, and brass as rotten wood. The arrow cannot make him fly; sling-stones are turned with him into stubble. Darts are counted as stubble; he laugheth at the shaking of a spear." What can a man do in this case? It is true, if a man could at every turn have Job's horse, and had skill and courage to ride him, he might do notable things. "For his neck is clothed with thunder. He will not be afraid as a grasshopper: the glory of his nostrils is terrible. He paweth in the valley, and rejoiceth in his strength; he goeth on to meet the armed men. He mocketh at fear, and is not affrighted; neither turneth he back from the sword. The quiver rattleth against him, the glittering spear and the shield. He swalloweth the ground with fierceness and rage; neither believeth he that it is the sound of the trumpet. He saith among the trumpets, Ha, ha! and he smelleth the battle afar off, the thunder of the captains, and the shoutings."

But for such footmen as thee and I are, let us never desire to meet with an enemy, nor vaunt as if we could do better, when we hear of others that have been foiled, nor be tickled at the thoughts of our own manhood; for such commonly come by the worst when tried. Witness Peter, of whom I made mention before: he would swagger, aye, he would; he would, as his vain mind prompted him to say, do better and stand more for his Master than all men: but who so foiled and run down by those villains as he?

When, therefore, we hear that such robberies are done on the King's highway, two things become us to do.

1. To go out harnessed, and be sure to take a shield with us: for it was for want of that, that he who laid so lustily at Leviathan could not make him yield; for, indeed, if that be wanting, he fears us not at all. Therefore, he that had skill hath said, "Above all, take the shield of faith, wherewith ye shall be able to quench all the fiery darts of the wicked."

2. It is good, also, that we desire of the King a convoy, yea, that he will go with us himself. This made David rejoice when in the Valley of the Shadow of Death; and Moses was rather for dying where he stood, than to go one step without his God.

O, my brother, if he will but go along with us, what need we be afraid of ten thousands that shall set themselves against us? But without him, the proud helpers fall under the slain.

I, for my part, have been in the fray before now; and though (through the goodness of Him that is best) I am, as you see, alive, yet I cannot boast of any manhood. Glad shall I be if I meet with no more such brunts; though I fear we are not got beyond all danger. However, since the lion and the bear have not as yet devoured me, I hope God will also deliver us from the next uncircumcised Philistine. Then sang Christian,

"Poor Little-Faith! hast been among the thieves?
Wast robb'd? Remember this, whoso believes,
And get more faith; then shall you victors be
Over ten thousand-else scarce over three."

Lesson 78

- Read Book 1, Section 9 of *The Pilgrim's Progress*.

Book 1, Section 9

And I slept, and dreamed again, and saw the same two pilgrims going down the mountains along the highway towards the city. Now, a little below these mountains, on the left hand, lieth the country of Conceit, from which country there comes into the way in which the pilgrims walked, a little crooked lane. Here, therefore, they met with a very brisk lad that came out of that country, and his name was Ignorance. So Christian asked him from what parts he came, and whither he was going.

Ignorance: Sir, I was born in the country that lieth off there, a little on the left hand, and I am going to the Celestial City.

Christian: But how do you think to get in at the gate, for you may find some difficulty there?

Ignorance: As other good people do, said he.

Christian: But what have you to show at that gate, that the gate should be opened to you?

Ignorance: I know my Lord's will, and have been a good liver; I pay every man his own; I pray, fast, pay tithes, and give alms, and have left my country for whither I am going.

Christian: But thou camest not in at the wicket-gate, that is at the head of this way; thou camest in hither through that same crooked lane, and therefore I fear, however thou mayest think of thyself, when the reckoning-day shall come, thou wilt have laid to thy charge, that thou art a thief and a robber, instead of getting admittance into the city.

Ignorance: Gentlemen, ye be utter strangers to me; I know you not: be content to follow the religion of your country, and I will follow the religion of mine. I hope all will be well. And as for the gate that you talk of, all the world knows that is a great way off of our country. I cannot think that any man in all our parts doth so much as know the way to it; nor need they matter whether they do or no, since we have, as you see, a fine, pleasant, green lane, that comes down from our country, the next way into the way.

When Christian saw that the man was wise in his own conceit, he said to Hopeful whisperingly, "There is more hope of a fool than of him." And said, moreover, "When he that is a fool walketh by the way, his wisdom faileth him, and he saith to every one that he is a fool." What, shall we talk farther with him, or outgo him at present, and so leave him to think of what he hath heard already, and then stop again for him afterwards, and see if by degrees we can do any good to him?

Then said Hopeful,

"Let Ignorance a little while now muse
On what is said, and let him not refuse

Good counsel to embrace, lest he remain
Still ignorant of what's the chiefest gain.
God saith, those that no understanding have,
(Although he made them,) them he will not save."

Hopeful: He further added, It is not good, I think, to say so to him all at once; let us pass him by, if you will, and talk to him anon, even as he is able to bear it.

So they both went on, and Ignorance he came after. Now, when they had passed him a little way, they entered into a very dark lane, where they met a man whom seven devils had bound with seven strong cords, and were carrying him back to the door that they saw on the side of the hill. Now good Christian began to tremble, and so did Hopeful, his companion; yet, as the devils led away the man, Christian looked to see if he knew him; and he thought it might be one Turn-away, that dwelt in the town of Apostacy. But he did not perfectly see his face, for he did hang his head like a thief that is found; but being gone past, Hopeful looked after him, and espied on his back a paper with this inscription, "Wanton professor, and damnable apostate."

Then said Christian to his fellow, Now I call to remembrance that which was told me of a thing that happened to a good man hereabout. The name of the man was Little-Faith; but a good man, and he dwelt in the town of Sincere. The thing was this. At the entering in at this passage, there comes down from Broadway-gate, a lane, called Dead-Man's lane; so called because of the murders that are commonly done there; and this Little-Faith going on pilgrimage, as we do now, chanced to sit down there and sleep. Now there happened at that time to come down the lane from Broadway-gate, three sturdy rogues, and their names were Faint-Heart, Mistrust, and Guilt, three brothers; and they, espying Little-Faith where he was, came galloping up with speed. Now the good man was just awaked from his sleep, and was getting up to go on his journey. So they came up all to him, and with threatening language bid him stand. At this, Little-Faith looked as white as a sheet, and had neither power to fight nor fly. Then said Faint-Heart, Deliver thy purse; but he making no haste to do it, (for he was loth to lose his money,) Mistrust ran up to him, and thrusting his hand into his pocket, pulled out thence a bag of silver. Then he cried out, Thieves, thieves! With that, Guilt, with a great club that was in his hand, struck Little-Faith on the head, and with that blow felled him flat to the ground, where he lay bleeding as one that would bleed to death. All this while the thieves stood by. But at last, they hearing that some were upon the road, and fearing lest it should be one Great-Grace, that dwells in the town of Good-Confidence, they betook themselves to their heels, and left this good man to shift for himself. Now, after a while, Little-Faith came to himself, and getting up, made shift to scramble on his way. This was the story.

Hopeful: But did they take from him all that ever he had?

Christian: No; the place where his jewels were they never ransacked; so those he kept still. But, as I was told, the good man was much afflicted for his loss; for the thieves got most of his spending-money. That which they got not, as I said, were jewels; also, he had a little odd money left, but scarce enough to bring him to his journey's end. Nay, (if I was not misinformed,) he was forced to beg as he went, to keep himself alive, for his jewels he might not sell; but beg and do what he could, he went, as we say, with many a hungry belly the most part of the rest of the way.

Hopeful: But is it not a wonder they got not from him his certificate, by which he was to receive his admittance at the Celestial Gate?

Christian: It is a wonder; but they got not that, though they missed it not through any good cunning of his; for he, being dismayed by their coming upon him, had neither power nor skill to hide any thing; so it was more by good providence than by his endeavor that they missed of that good thing.

Hopeful: But it must needs be a comfort to him they got not this jewel from him.

Christian: It might have been great comfort to him, had he used it as he should; but they that told me the story said that he made but little use of it all the rest of the way, and that because of the dismay that he had in their taking away his money. Indeed, he forgot it a great part of the rest of his journey; and besides, when at any time it came into his mind, and he began to be comforted therewith, then would fresh thoughts of his loss come again upon him, and these thoughts would swallow up all.

Hopeful: Alas, poor man, this could not but be a great grief to him.

Christian: Grief? Aye, a grief indeed! Would it not have been so to any of us, had we been used as he, to be robbed and wounded too, and that in a strange place, as he was? It is a wonder he did not die with grief, poor heart. I was told that he scattered almost all the rest of the way with nothing but doleful and bitter complaints; telling, also, to all that overtook him, or that he overtook in the way as he went, where he was robbed, and how; who they were that did it, and what he had lost; how he was wounded, and that he hardly escaped with life.

Hopeful: But it is a wonder that his necessity did not put him upon selling or pawning some of his jewels, that he might have wherewith to relieve himself in his journey.

Christian: Thou talkest like one upon whose head is the shell to this very day. For what should he pawn them? or to whom should he sell them? In all that country where he was robbed, his jewels were not accounted of; nor did he want that relief which could from thence be administered to him. Besides, had his jewels been missing at the gate of the Celestial City, he had (and that he knew well enough) been excluded from an inheritance there, and that would have been worse to him than the appearance and villany of ten thousand thieves.

Hopeful: Why art thou so tart, my brother? Esau sold his birthright, and that for a mess of pottage, and that birthright was his greatest jewel: and if he, why might not Little-Faith do so too?

Christian: Esau did sell his birthright indeed, and so do many besides, and by so doing exclude themselves from the chief blessing, as also that caitiff did; but you must put a difference betwixt Esau and Little-Faith, and also betwixt their estates. Esau's birthright was typical; but Little-Faith's jewels were not so. Esau's belly was his god; but Little-Faith's belly was not so. Esau's want lay in his fleshy appetite; Little-Faith's did not so. Besides, Esau could see no further than to the fulfilling of his lusts: For I am at the point to die, said he: and what good will this birthright do me? But Little-Faith, though it was his lot to have but a little faith, was by his little faith kept from such extravagances, and made to see and prize his jewels more than to sell them, as Esau did his birthright. You read not any where that Esau had faith, no, not so much as a little; therefore no marvel, where the flesh only bears sway, (as it will in that man where no faith is to resist,) if he sells his birthright and his soul and all, and that to the devil of hell; for it is with such as it is with the ass, who in her occasion cannot be turned away, when their minds are set upon their lusts, they will have them, whatever they cost. But Little-Faith was of another temper; his mind was on things divine; his livelihood was upon things that were spiritual, and from above: therefore, to what end should he that is of such a temper sell his jewels (had there been any that would have bought them) to fill his mind with empty things? Will a man give a penny to fill his belly with hay? or can you persuade the turtle-dove to live upon carrion, like the crow? Though faithless ones can, for carnal lusts, pawn, or mortgage, or sell what they have, and themselves outright to boot; yet they that have faith, saving faith, though but a little of it, cannot do so. Here, therefore, my brother, is thy mistake.

Hopeful: I acknowledge it; but yet your severe reflection had almost made me angry.

Christian: Why, I did but compare thee to some of the birds that are of the brisker sort, who will run to and fro in untrodden paths with the shell upon their heads: but pass by that, and consider the matter under debate, and all shall be well betwixt thee and me.

Hopeful: But, Christian, these three fellows, I am persuaded in my heart, are but a company of cowards: would they have run else, think you, as they did, at the noise of one that was coming on the road? Why did not Little-Faith pluck up a greater heart? He might, methinks, have stood one brush with them, and have yielded when there had been no remedy.

Christian: That they are cowards, many have said, but few have found it so in the time of trial. As for a great heart, Little-Faith had none; and I perceive by thee, my brother, hadst thou been the man concerned, thou art but for a brush, and then to yield. And verily, since this is the height of thy stomach now they are at a distance from us, should they appear to thee as they did to him, they might put thee to second thoughts.

But consider again, that they are but journeymen thieves; They serve under the king of the bottomless pit, who, if need be, will come to their aid himself, and his voice is as the roaring of a lion. I myself have been engaged as this Little-Faith was, and I found it a terrible thing. These three villains set upon me, and I beginning like a Christian to resist, they gave but a call, and in came their master. I would, as the saying is, have given my life for a penny, but that, as God would have it, I was clothed with armor of proof. Aye, and yet, though I was so harnessed, I found it hard work to quit myself like a man: no man can tell what in that combat attends us, but he that hath been in the battle himself.

Hopeful: Well, but they ran, you see, when they did but suppose that one Great-Grace was in the way.

Christian: True, they have often fled, both they and their master, when Great-Grace hath but appeared; and no marvel, for he is the King's champion. But I trow you will put some difference between Little-Faith and the King's champion. All the King's subjects are not his champions; nor can they, when tried, do such feats of war as he. Is it meet to think that a little child should handle Goliath as David did? or that there should be the strength of an ox in a wren? Some are strong, some are weak; some have great faith, some have little: this man was one of the weak, and therefore he went to the wall.

Hopeful: I would it had been Great-Grace, for their sakes.

Christian: If it had been he, he might have had his hands full: for I must tell you, that though Great-Grace is excellent good at his weapons, and has, and can, so long as he keeps them at sword's point, do well enough with them; yet if they get within him, even Faint-Heart, Mistrust, or the other, it shall go hard but they will throw up his heels. And when a man is down, you know, what can he do?

Whoso looks well upon Great-Grace's face, will see those scars and cuts there that shall easily give demonstration of what I say. Yea, once I heard that he should say, (and that when he was in the combat,) We despaired even of life. How did these sturdy rogues and their fellows make David groan, mourn, and roar! Yea, Heman, Psa. 88, and Hezekiah too, though champions in their days, were forced to bestir them when by these assaulted; and yet, notwithstanding, they had their coats soundly brushed by them. Peter, upon a time, would go try what he could do; but though some do say of him that he is the prince of the apostles, they handled him so that they made him at last afraid of a sorry girl.

Besides, their king is at their whistle; he is never out of hearing; and if at any time they be put to the worst, he, if possible, comes in to help them; and of him it is said,

"The sword of him that layeth at him cannot hold; the spear, the dart, nor the habergeon. He esteemeth iron as straw, and brass as rotten wood. The arrow cannot make him fly; sling-stones are turned with him into stubble. Darts are counted as stubble; he laugheth at the shaking of a spear." What can a man do in this case? It is true, if a man could at every turn have Job's horse, and had skill and courage to ride him, he might do notable things. "For his neck is clothed with thunder. He will not be afraid as a grasshopper: the glory of his nostrils is terrible. He paweth in the valley, and rejoiceth in his strength; he goeth on to meet the armed men. He mocketh at fear, and is not affrighted; neither turneth he back from the sword. The quiver rattleth against him, the glittering spear and the shield. He swalloweth the ground with fierceness and rage; neither believeth he that it is the sound of the trumpet. He saith among the trumpets, Ha, ha! and he smelleth the battle afar off, the thunder of the captains, and the shoutings."

But for such footmen as thee and I are, let us never desire to meet with an enemy, nor vaunt as if we could do better, when we hear of others that have been foiled, nor be tickled at the thoughts of our own manhood; for such commonly come by the worst when tried. Witness Peter, of whom I made mention before: he would swagger, aye, he would; he would, as his vain mind prompted him to say, do better and stand more for his Master than all men: but who so foiled and run down by those villains as he?

When, therefore, we hear that such robberies are done on the King's highway, two things become us to do.

1. To go out harnessed, and be sure to take a shield with us: for it was for want of that, that he who laid so lustily at Leviathan could not make him yield; for, indeed, if that be wanting, he fears us not at all. Therefore, he that had skill hath said, "Above all, take the shield of faith, wherewith ye shall be able to quench all the fiery darts of the wicked."

2. It is good, also, that we desire of the King a convoy, yea, that he will go with us himself. This made David rejoice when in the Valley of the Shadow of Death; and Moses was rather for dying where he stood, than to go one step without his God.

O, my brother, if he will but go along with us, what need we be afraid of ten thousands that shall set themselves against us? But without him, the proud helpers fall under the slain.

I, for my part, have been in the fray before now; and though (through the goodness of Him that is best) I am, as you see, alive, yet I cannot boast of any manhood. Glad shall I be if I meet with no more such brunts; though I fear we are not got beyond all danger. However, since the lion and the bear have not as yet devoured me, I hope God will also deliver us from the next uncircumcised Philistine. Then sang Christian,

"Poor Little-Faith! hast been among the thieves?
Wast robb'd? Remember this, whoso believes,
And get more faith; then shall you victors be
Over ten thousand-else scarce over three."

So they went on, and Ignorance followed. They went then till they came at a place where they saw a way put itself into their way, and seemed withal to lie as strait as the way which they should go; and here they knew not which of the two to take, for both seemed strait before them: therefore here they stood still to consider. And as they were thinking about the way, behold a man black of flesh, but covered with a very light robe, come to them, and asked them why they stood there. They answered, they were going to the Celestial City, but knew not which of these ways to take. "Follow me," said the man, "it is thither that I am going." So they followed him in the way that but now came into the road, which by degrees turned, and turned them so far from the city that they desired to go to, that in a little time their faces were turned away from it; yet they follow him. But by and by, before they were aware, he led them both within the compass of a net, in which they were both so entangled that they knew not what to do; and with that the white robe fell off the black man's back. Then they saw where they were. Wherefore there they lay crying some time, for they could not get themselves out.

Christian: Then said Christian to his fellow, Now do I see myself in an error. Did not the shepherds bid us beware of the Flatterer? As is the saying of the wise man, so we have found it this day: "A man that flattereth his neighbor, spreadeth a net for his feet."

Hopeful: They also gave us a note of directions about the way, for our more sure finding thereof; but therein we have also forgotten to read, and have not kept ourselves from the paths of the destroyer. Here David was wiser than we; for saith he, "Concerning the works of men, by the word of thy lips I have kept me from the paths of the Destroyer." Thus they lay bewailing themselves in the net. At last they espied a Shining One coming towards them with a whip of small cords in his hand. When he was come to the place where they were, he asked them whence they came, and what they did there. They told him that they were poor pilgrims going to Zion, but were led out of their way by a black man clothed in white, who bid us, said they, follow him, for he was going thither too. Then said he with the whip, It is Flatterer, a false apostle, that hath transformed himself into an angel of light. So he rent the net, and let the men out. Then said he to them, Follow me, that I may set you in your way again. So he led them back to the way which they had left to follow the Flatterer. Then he asked them, saying, Where did you lie the last night? They said, With the shepherds upon the Delectable Mountains. He asked them then if they had not of the shepherds a note of direction for the way. They answered, Yes. But did you not, said he, when you were at a stand, pluck out and read your note? They answered, No. He asked them, Why? They said they forgot. He asked, moreover, if the shepherds did not bid them beware of the Flatterer. They answered, Yes; but we did not imagine, said they, that this fine-spoken man had been he.

Then I saw in my dream, that he commanded them to lie down; which when they did, he chastised them sore, to teach them the good way wherein they should walk, and as he chastised them, he said, "As many as I love, I rebuke and chasten; be zealous, therefore, and repent." This done, he bids them to go on their way, and take good heed to the other directions of the shepherds. So they thanked him for all his kindness, and went softly along the right way, singing,

"Come hither, you that walk along the way,
See how the pilgrims fare that go astray:
They catched are in an entangling net,
Cause they good counsel lightly did forget:
'Tis true, they rescued were; but yet, you see,
They're scouged to boot; let this your caution be."

Now, after awhile, they perceived afar off, one coming softly, and alone, all along the highway, to meet them. Then said Christian to his fellow, Yonder is a man with his back towards Zion, and he is coming to meet us.

Hopeful: I see him; let us take heed to ourselves now, lest he should prove a Flatterer also. So he drew nearer and nearer, and at last came up to them. His name was Atheist, and he asked them whither they were going.

Christian: We are going to Mount Zion.

Then Atheist fell into a very great laughter.

Christian: What's the meaning of your laughter?

Atheist: I laugh to see what ignorant persons you are, to take upon you so tedious a journey, and yet are like to have nothing but your travel for your pains.

Christian: Why, man, do you think we shall not be received?

Atheist: Received! There is not such a place as you dream of in all this world.

Christian: But there is in the world to come.

Atheist: When I was at home in mine own country I heard as you now affirm, and from that hearing went out to see, and have been seeking this city these twenty years, but find no more of it than I did the first day I set out.

Christian: We have both heard, and believe, that there is such a place to be found.

Atheist: Had not I, when at home, believed, I had not come thus far to seek; but finding none, (and yet I should, had there been such a place to be found, for I have gone to seek it farther than you,) I am going back again, and will seek to refresh myself with the things that I then cast away for hopes of that which I now see is not.

Christian: Then said Christian to Hopeful his companion, Is it true which this man hath said?

Hopeful: Take heed, he is one of the Flatterers. Remember what it cost us once already for our hearkening to such kind of fellows. What! no Mount Zion? Did we not see from the Delectable Mountains the gate of the city? Also, are we not now to walk by faith?

Let us go on, lest the man with the whip overtake us again. You should have taught me that lesson, which I will sound you in the ears withal: "Cease, my son, to hear the instruction that causeth to err from the words of knowledge." I say, my brother, cease to hear him, and let us believe to the saving of the soul.

Christian: My brother, I did not put the question to thee, for that I doubted of the truth of our belief myself, but to prove thee, and to fetch from thee a fruit of the honesty of thy heart. As for this man, I know that he is blinded by the God of this world. Let thee and me go on, knowing that we have belief of the truth; and no lie is of the truth.

Hopeful: Now do I rejoice in hope of the glory of God. So they turned away from the man; and he, laughing at them, went his way.

I then saw in my dream, that they went on until they came into a certain country whose air naturally tended to make one drowsy, if he came a stranger into it. And here Hopeful began to be very dull, and heavy to sleep: wherefore he said unto Christian, I do now begin to grow so drowsy that I can scarcely hold open mine eyes; let us lie down here, and take one nap.

Christian: By no means, said the other; lest, sleeping, we never awake more.

Hopeful: Why, my brother? sleep is sweet to the laboring man; we may be refreshed, if we take a nap.

Christian: Do you not remember that one of the shepherds bid us beware of the Enchanted Ground? He meant by that, that we should beware of sleeping; wherefore "let us not sleep, as do others; but let us watch and be sober."

Hopeful: I acknowledge myself in a fault; and had I been here alone, I had by sleeping run the danger of death. I see it is true that the wise man saith, "Two are better than one." Hitherto hath thy company been my mercy; and thou shalt have a good reward for thy labor.

Christian: Now, then, said Christian, to prevent drowsiness in this place, let us fall into good discourse.

Hopeful: With all my heart, said the other.

Christian: Where shall we begin?

Hopeful: Where God began with us. But do you begin, if you please.

Christian: I will sing you first this song:

"When saints do sleepy grow, let them come hither,
And hear how these two pilgrims talk together;
Yea, let them learn of them in any wise,
Thus to keep open their drowsy, slumb'ring eyes.
Saints' fellowship, if it be managed well,
Keeps them awake, and that in spite of hell."

Then Christian began, and said, I will ask you a question. How came you to think at first of doing what you do now?

Hopeful: Do you mean, how came I at first to look after the good of my soul?

Christian: Yes, that is my meaning.

Hopeful: I continued a great while in the delight of those things which were seen and sold at our fair; things which I believe now would have, had I continued in them still, drowned me in perdition and destruction.

Christian: What things were they?

Hopeful: All the treasures and riches of the world. Also I delighted much in rioting, reveling, drinking, swearing, lying, uncleanness, Sabbath-breaking, and what not, that tended to destroy the soul. But I found at last, by hearing and considering of things that are divine, which, indeed, I heard of you, as also of beloved Faithful, that was put to death for his faith and good living in Vanity Fair, that the end of these things is death, and that for these things' sake, the wrath of God cometh upon the children of disobedience.

Christian: And did you presently fall under the power of this conviction?

Hopeful: No, I was not willing presently to know the evil of sin, nor the damnation that follows upon the commission of it; but endeavored, when my mind at first began to be shaken with the word, to shut mine eyes against the light thereof.

Christian: But what was the cause of your carrying of it thus to the first workings of God's blessed Spirit upon you?

Hopeful: The causes were, 1. I was ignorant that this was the work of God upon me. I never thought that by awakenings for sin, God at first begins the conversion of a sinner. 2. Sin was yet very sweet to my flesh, and I was loth to leave it. 3. I could not tell how to part with mine old companions, their presence and actions were so desirable unto me. 4. The hours in which convictions were upon me, were such troublesome and such heart-affrighting hours, that I could not bear, no not so much as the remembrance of them upon my heart.

Christian: Then, as it seems, sometimes you got rid of your trouble?

Hopeful: Yes, verily, but it would come into my mind again; and then I should be as bad, nay, worse than I was before.

Christian: Why, what was it that brought your sins to mind again?

Hopeful: Many things; as,

1. If I did but meet a good man in the streets; or,

2. If I have heard any read in the Bible; or,

3. If mine head did begin to ache; or,

4. If I were told that some of my neighbors were sick; or,

5. If I heard the bell toll for some that were dead; or,

6. If I thought of dying myself; or,

7. If I heard that sudden death happened to others.

8. But especially when I thought of myself, that I must quickly come to judgment.

Christian: And could you at any time, with ease, get off the guilt of sin, when by any of these ways it came upon you?

Hopeful: No, not I; for then they got faster hold of my conscience; and then, if I did but think of going back to sin, (though my mind was turned against it,) it would be double torment to me.

Christian: And how did you do then?

Hopeful: I thought I must endeavor to mend my life; for else, thought I, I am sure to be damned.

Christian: And did you endeavor to mend?

Hopeful: Yes, and fled from, not only my sins, but sinful company too, and betook me to religious duties, as praying, reading, weeping for sin, speaking truth to my neighbors, etc. These things did I, with many others, too much here to relate.

Christian: And did you think yourself well then?

Hopeful: Yes, for a while; but at the last my trouble came tumbling upon me again, and that over the neck of all my reformations.

Christian: How came that about, since you were now reformed?

Hopeful: There were several things brought it upon me, especially such sayings as these: "All our righteousnesses are as filthy rags." "By the works of the law shall no flesh be justified." "When ye have done all these things, say, We are unprofitable," with many more such like. From whence I began to reason with myself thus: If all my righteousnesses are as filthy rags; if by the deeds of the law no man can be justified; and if, when we have done all, we are yet unprofitable, then is it but a folly to think of heaven by the law. I farther thought thus: If a man runs a hundred pounds into the shopkeeper's debt, and after that shall pay for all that he shall fetch; yet if his old debt stands still in the book uncrossed, the shopkeeper may sue him for it, and cast him into prison, till he shall pay the debt.

Christian: Well, and how did you apply this to yourself?

Hopeful: Why, I thought thus with myself: I have by my sins run a great way into God's book, and my now reforming will not pay off that score; therefore I should think still, under all my present amendments, But how shall I be freed from that damnation that I brought myself in danger of by my former transgressions?

Christian: A very good application: but pray go on.

Hopeful: Another thing that hath troubled me ever since my late amendments, is, that if I look narrowly into the best of what I do now, I still see sin, new sin, mixing itself with the best of that I do; so that now I am forced to conclude, that notwithstanding my former fond conceits of myself and duties, I have committed sin enough in one day to send me to hell, though my former life had been faultless.

Christian: And what did you do then?

Hopeful: Do! I could not tell what to do, until I broke my mind to Faithful; for he and I were well acquainted. And he told me, that unless I could obtain the righteousness of a man that never had sinned, neither mine own, nor all the righteousness of the world, could save me.

Christian: And did you think he spake true?

Hopeful: Had he told me so when I was pleased and satisfied with my own amendments, I had called him fool for his pains; but now, since I see my own infirmity, and the sin which cleaves to my best performance, I have been forced to be of his opinion.

Christian: But did you think, when at first he suggested it to you, that there was such a man to be found, of whom it might justly be said, that he never committed sin?

Hopeful: I must confess the words at first sounded strangely; but after a little more talk and company with him, I had full conviction about it.

Christian: And did you ask him what man this was, and how you must be justified by him?

Hopeful: Yes, and he told me it was the Lord Jesus, that dwelleth on the right hand of the Most High. And thus, said he, you must be justified by him, even by trusting to what he hath done by himself in the days of his flesh, and suffered when he did hang on the tree. I asked him further, how that man's righteousness could be of that efficacy, to justify another before God. And he told me he was the mighty God, and did what he did, and died the death also, not for himself, but for me; to whom his doings, and the worthiness of them, should be imputed, if I believed on him.

Christian: And what did you do then?

Hopeful: I made my objections against my believing, for that I thought he was not willing to save me.

Christian: And what said Faithful to you then?

Hopeful: He bid me go to him and see. Then I said it was presumption. He said, No; for I was invited to come. Then he gave me a book of Jesus' inditing, to encourage me the more freely to come; and he said concerning that book, that every jot and tittle thereof stood firmer than heaven and earth. Then I asked him what I must do when I came; and he told me I must entreat upon my knees, with all my heart and soul, the Father to reveal him to me. Then I asked him further, how I must make my supplications to him; and he said, Go, and thou shalt find him upon a mercy-seat, where he sits all the year long to give pardon and forgiveness to them that come. I told him, that I knew not what to say when I came; and he bid say to this effect: God be merciful to me a sinner, and make me to know and believe in Jesus Christ; for I see, that if his righteousness had not been, or I have not faith in that righteousness, I am utterly cast away. Lord, I have heard that thou art a merciful God, and hast ordained that thy Son Jesus Christ should be the Saviour of the world; and moreover, that thou art willing to bestow him upon such a poor sinner as I am- and I am a sinner indeed. Lord, take therefore this opportunity, and magnify thy grace in the salvation of my soul, through thy Son Jesus Christ. Amen.

Christian: And did you do as you were bidden?

Hopeful: Yes, over, and over, and over.

Christian: And did the Father reveal the Son to you?

Hopeful: Not at the first, nor second, nor third, nor fourth, nor fifth, no, nor at the sixth time neither.

Christian: What did you do then?

Hopeful: What? why I could not tell what to do.

Christian: Had you not thoughts of leaving off praying?

Hopeful: Yes; an hundred times twice told.

Christian: And what was the reason you did not?

Hopeful: I believed that it was true which hath been told me, to wit, that without the righteousness of this Christ, all the world could not save me; and therefore, thought I with myself, if I leave off, I die, and I can but die at the throne of grace. And withal this came into my mind, "If it tarry, wait for it; because it will surely come, and will not tarry." So I continued praying until the Father showed me his Son.

Christian: And how was he revealed unto you?

Hopeful: I did not see him with my bodily eyes, but with the eyes of my understanding, and thus it was. One day I was very sad, I think sadder than at any one time in my life; and this sadness was through a fresh sight of the greatness and vileness of my sins. And as I was then looking for nothing but hell, and the everlasting damnation of my soul, suddenly, as I thought, I saw the Lord Jesus looking down from heaven upon me, and saying, "Believe on the Lord Jesus Christ, and thou shalt be saved."

But I replied, Lord, I am a great, a very great sinner: and he answered, "My grace is sufficient for thee." Then I said, But, Lord, what is believing? And then I saw from that saying, "He that cometh to me shall never hunger, and he that believeth on me shall never thirst," that believing and coming was all one; and that he that came, that is, that ran out in his heart and affections after salvation by Christ, he indeed believed in Christ. Then the water stood in mine eyes, and I asked further, But, Lord, may such a great sinner as I am be indeed accepted of thee, and be saved by thee? And I heard him say, "And him that cometh to me, I will in no wise cast out." Then I said, But how, Lord, must I consider of thee in my coming to thee, that my faith may be placed aright upon thee? Then he said, "Christ Jesus came into the world to save sinners." He is the end of the law for righteousness to every one that believes. He died for our sins, and rose again for our justification. He loved us, and washed us from our sins in his own blood. He is the Mediator between God and us. He ever liveth to make intercession for us. From all which I gathered, that I must look for righteousness in his person, and for satisfaction for my sins by his blood: that what he did in obedience to his Father's law, and in submitting to the penalty thereof, was not for himself, but for him that will accept it for his salvation, and be thankful. And now was my heart full of joy, mine eyes full of tears, and mine affections running over with love to the name, people, and ways of Jesus Christ.

Christian: This was a revelation of Christ to your soul indeed. But tell me particularly what effect this had upon your spirit.

Hopeful: It made me see that all the world, notwithstanding all the righteousness thereof, is in a state of condemnation. It made me see that God the Father, though he be just, can justly justify the coming sinner. It made me greatly ashamed of the vileness of my former life, and confounded me with the sense of mine own ignorance; for there never came a thought into my heart before now that showed me so the beauty of Jesus Christ. It made me love a holy life, and long to do something for the honor and glory of the name of the Lord Jesus. Yea, I thought that had I now a thousand gallons of blood in my body, I could spill it all for the sake of the Lord Jesus.

I saw then in my dream, that Hopeful looked back, and saw Ignorance, whom they had left behind, coming after. Look, said he to Christian, how far yonder youngster loitereth behind.

Christian: Aye, aye, I see him: he careth not for our company.

Hopeful: But I trow it would not have hurt him, had he kept pace with us hitherto.

Christian: That is true; but I warrant you he thinketh otherwise.

Hopeful: That I think he doth; but, however, let us tarry for him. (So they did.)

Then Christian said to him, Come away, man; why do you stay so behind?

Ignorance: I take my pleasure in walking alone, even more a great deal than in company, unless I like it the better.

Then said Christian to Hopeful, (but softly,) Did I not tell you he cared not for our company? But, however, said he, come up, and let us talk away the time in this solitary place. Then, directing his speech to Ignorance, he said, Come, how do you do? How stands it between God and your soul now?

Ignorance: I hope, well; for I am always full of good motions, that come into my mind to comfort me as I walk.

Christian: What good motions? Pray tell us.

Ignorance: Why, I think of God and heaven.

Christian: So do the devils and damned souls.

Ignorance: But I think of them, and desire them.

Christian: So do many that are never like to come there. "The soul of the sluggard desireth, and hath nothing."

Ignorance: But I think of them, and leave all for them.

Christian: That I doubt: for to leave all is a very hard matter; yea, a harder matter than many are aware of. But why, or by what, art thou persuaded that thou hast left all for God and heaven?

Ignorance: My heart tells me so.

Christian: The wise man says, "He that trusteth in his own heart is a fool."

Ignorance: That is spoken of an evil heart; but mine is a good one.

Christian: But how dost thou prove that?

Ignorance: It comforts me in hopes of heaven.

Christian: That may be through its deceitfulness; for a man's heart may minister comfort to him in the hopes of that thing for which he has yet no ground to hope.

Ignorance: But my heart and life agree together; and therefore my hope is well-grounded.

Christian: Who told thee that thy heart and life agree together?

Ignorance: My heart tells me so.

Christian: "Ask my fellow if I be a thief." Thy heart tells thee so! Except the word of God beareth witness in this matter, other testimony is of no value.

Ignorance: But is it not a good heart that hath good thoughts? and is not that a good life that is according to God's commandments?

Christian: Yes, that is a good heart that hath good thoughts, and that is a good life that is according to God's commandments; but it is one thing indeed to have these, and another thing only to think so.

Ignorance: Pray, what count you good thoughts, and a life according to God's commandments?

Christian: There are good thoughts of divers kinds; some respecting ourselves, some God, some Christ, and some other things.

Ignorance: What be good thoughts respecting ourselves?

Christian: Such as agree with the word of God.

Ignorance: When do our thoughts of ourselves agree with the word of God?

Christian: When we pass the same judgment upon ourselves which the word passes. To explain myself: the word of God saith of persons in a natural condition, "There is none righteous, there is none that doeth good." It saith also, that, "every imagination of the heart of man is only evil, and that continually." And again, "The imagination of man's heart is evil from his youth." Now, then, when we think thus of ourselves, having sense thereof, then are our thoughts good ones, because according to the word of God.

Ignorance: I will never believe that my heart is thus bad.

Christian: Therefore thou never hadst one good thought concerning thyself in thy life. But let me go on. As the word passeth a judgment upon our hearts, so it passeth a judgment upon our ways; and when the thoughts of our hearts and ways agree with the judgment which the word giveth of both, then are both good, because agreeing thereto.

Ignorance: Make out your meaning.

Christian: Why, the word of God saith, that man's ways are crooked ways, not good but perverse; it saith, they are naturally out of the good way, that they have not known it. Now, when a man thus thinketh of his ways, I say, when he doth sensibly, and with heart-humiliation, thus think, then hath he good thoughts of his own ways, because his thoughts now agree with the judgment of the word of God.

Ignorance: What are good thoughts concerning God?

Christian: Even, as I have said concerning ourselves, when our thoughts of God do agree with what the word saith of him; and that is, when we think of his being and attributes as the word hath taught, of which I cannot now discourse at large. But to speak of him with reference to us: then have we right thoughts of God when we think that he knows us better than we know ourselves, and can see sin in us when and where we can see none in ourselves; when we think he knows our inmost thoughts, and that our heart, with all its depths, is always open unto his eyes; also when we think that all our righteousness stinks in his nostrils, and that therefore he cannot abide to see us stand before him in any confidence, even in all our best performances.

Ignorance: Do you think that I am such a fool as to think that God can see no further than I; or that I would come to God in the best of my performances?

Christian: Why, how dost thou think in this matter?

Ignorance: Why, to be short, I think I must believe in Christ for justification.

Christian: How! think thou must believe in Christ, when thou seest not thy need of him! Thou neither seest thy original nor actual infirmities; but hast such an opinion of thyself, and of what thou doest, as plainly renders thee to be one that did never see the necessity of Christ's personal righteousness to justify thee before God. How, then, dost thou say, I believe in Christ?

Ignorance: I believe well enough, for all that.

Christian: How dost thou believe?

Ignorance: I believe that Christ died for sinners; and that I shall be justified before God from the curse, through his gracious acceptance of my obedience to his laws. Or thus, Christ makes my duties, that are religious, acceptable to his Father by virtue of his merits, and so shall I be justified.

Christian: Let me give an answer to this confession of thy faith.

1. Thou believest with a fantastical faith; for this faith is nowhere described in the word.

2. Thou believest with a false faith; because it taketh justification from the personal righteousness of Christ, and applies it to thy own.

3. This faith maketh not Christ a justifier of thy person, but of thy actions; and of thy person for thy action's sake, which is false.

4. Therefore this faith is deceitful, even such as will leave thee under wrath in the day of God Almighty: for true justifying faith puts the soul, as sensible of its lost condition by the law, upon flying for refuge unto Christ's righteousness; (which righteousness of his is not an act of grace by which he maketh, for justification, thy obedience accepted with God, but his personal obedience to the law, in doing and suffering for us what that required at our hands;) this righteousness, I say, true faith accepteth; under the skirt of which the soul being shrouded, and by it presented as spotless before God, it is accepted, and acquitted from condemnation.

Ignorance: What! would you have us trust to what Christ in his own person has done without us? This conceit would loosen the reins of our lust, and tolerate us to live as we list: for what matter how we live, if we may be justified by Christ's personal righteousness from all, when we believe it?

Christian: Ignorance is thy name, and as thy name is, so art thou: even this thy answer demonstrateth what I say. Ignorant thou art of what justifying righteousness is, and as ignorant how to secure thy soul, through the faith of it, from the heavy wrath of God. Yea, thou also art ignorant of the true effects of saving faith in this righteousness of Christ, which is to bow and win over the heart to God in Christ, to love his name, his word, ways, and people, and not as thou ignorantly imaginest.

Hopeful: Ask him if ever he had Christ revealed to him from heaven.

Ignorance: What! you are a man for revelations! I do believe, that what both you and all the rest of you say about that matter, is but the fruit of distracted brains.

Hopeful: Why, man, Christ is so hid in God from the natural apprehensions of the flesh, that he cannot by any man be savingly known, unless God the Father reveals him to him.

Ignorance: That is your faith, but not mine, yet mine, I doubt not, is as good as yours, though I have not in my head so many whimsies as you.

Christian: Give me leave to put in a word. You ought not so slightly to speak of this matter: for this I will boldly affirm, even as my good companion hath done, that no man can know Jesus Christ but by the revelation of the Father: yea, and faith too, by which the soul layeth hold upon Christ, (if it be right,) must be wrought by the exceeding greatness of his mighty power, the working of which faith, I perceive, poor Ignorance, thou art ignorant of. Be awakened, then, see thine own wretchedness, and fly to the Lord Jesus; and by his righteousness, which is the righteousness of God, (for he himself is God,) thou shalt be delivered from condemnation.

Ignorance: You go so fast I cannot keep pace with you; do you go on before: I must stay a while behind.

Then they said,

"Well, Ignorance, wilt thou yet foolish be,
To slight good counsel, ten times given thee?
And if thou yet refuse it, thou shalt know,
Ere long, the evil of thy doing so.
Remember, man, in time: stoop, do not fear:
Good counsel, taken well, saves; therefore hear.
But if thou yet shalt slight it, thou wilt be
The loser, Ignorance, I'll warrant thee."

Lesson 79

- Read the rest of Book 1 by reading Section 10 of *The Pilgrim's Progress*.

Book 1, Section 10

Then Christian addressed himself thus to his fellow:

Christian: Well, come, my good Hopeful, I perceive that thou and I must walk by ourselves again.

So I saw in my dream, that they went on apace before, and Ignorance he came hobbling after. Then said Christian to his companion, I much pity this poor man: it will certainly go ill with him at last.

Hopeful: Alas! there are abundance in our town in his condition, whole families, yea, whole streets, and that of pilgrims too; and if there be so many in our parts, how many, think you, must there be in the place where he was born?

Christian: Indeed, the word saith, "He hath blinded their eyes, lest they should see," etc. But, now we are by ourselves, what do you think of such men? Have they at no time, think you, convictions of sin, and so, consequently, fears that their state is dangerous?

Hopeful: Nay, do you answer that question yourself, for you are the elder man.

Christian: Then I say, sometimes (as I think) they may; but they being naturally ignorant, understand not that such convictions tend to their good; and therefore they do desperately seek to stifle them, and presumptuously continue to flatter themselves in the way of their own hearts.

Hopeful: I do believe, as you say, that fear tends much to men's good, and to make them right at their beginning to go on pilgrimage.

Christian: Without all doubt it doth, if it be right; for so says the word, "The fear of the Lord is the beginning of wisdom."

Hopeful: How will you describe right fear?

Christian: True or right fear is discovered by three things:

1. By its rise; it is caused by saving convictions for sin.

2. It driveth the soul to lay fast hold of Christ for salvation.

3. It begetteth and continueth in the soul a great reverence of God, his word, and ways; keeping it tender, and making it afraid to turn from them, to the right hand or to the left, to any thing that may dishonor God, break its peace, grieve the Spirit, or cause the enemy to speak reproachfully.

Hopeful: Well said; I believe you have said the truth. Are we now almost got past the Enchanted Ground?

Christian: Why? are you weary of this discourse?

Hopeful: No, verily, but that I would know where we are.

Christian: We have not now above two miles further to go thereon. But let us return to our matter. Now, the ignorant know not that such conviction as tend to put them in fear, are for their good, and therefore they seek to stifle them.

Hopeful: How do they seek to stifle them?

Christian: 1. They think that those fears are wrought by the devil, (though indeed they are wrought of God,) and thinking so, they resist them, as things that directly tend to their overthrow. 2. They also think that these fears tend to the spoiling of their faith; when, alas for them, poor men that they are, they have none at all; and therefore they harden their hearts against them. 3. They presume they ought not to fear, and therefore, in despite of them, wax presumptuously confident. 4. They see that those fears tend to take away from them their pitiful old self-holiness, and therefore they resist them with all their might.

Hopeful: I know something of this myself; for before I knew myself it was so with me.

Christian: Well, we will leave, at this time, our neighbor Ignorance by himself, and fall upon another profitable question.

Hopeful: With all my heart; but you shall still begin.

Christian: Well then, did you not know, about ten years ago, one Temporary in your parts, who was a forward man in religion then?

Hopeful: Know him! yes; he dwelt in Graceless, a town about two miles off of Honesty, and he dwelt next door to one Turnback.

Christian: Right; he dwelt under the same roof with him. Well, that man was much awakened once: I believe that then he had some sight of his sins, and of the wages that were due thereto.

Hopeful: I am of your mind, for (my house not being above three miles from him) he would oft-times come to me, and that with many tears. Truly I pitied the man, and was not altogether without hope of him; but one may see, it is not every one that cries, "Lord, Lord!"

Christian: He told me once that he was resolved to go on pilgrimage, as we go now; but all of a sudden he grew acquainted with one Save-self, and then he became a stranger to me.

Hopeful: Now, since we are talking about him, let us a little inquire into the reason of the sudden backsliding of him and such others.

Christian: It may be very profitable; but do you begin.

Hopeful: Well, then, there are, in my judgment, four reasons for it:

1. Though the consciences of such men are awakened, yet their minds are not changed: therefore, when the power of guilt weareth away, that which provoked them to be religious ceaseth; wherefore they naturally turn to their own course again; even as we see the dog that is sick of what he hath eaten, so long as his sickness prevails, he vomits and casts up all; not that he doth this of a free mind, (if we may say a dog has a mind,) but because it troubleth his stomach: but now, when his sickness is over, and so his stomach eased, his desires being not at all alienated from his vomit, he turns him about, and licks up all; and so it is true which is written,

"The dog is turned to his own vomit again." Thus, I say, being hot for heaven, by virtue only of the sense and fear of the torments of hell, as their sense and fear of damnation chills and cools, so their desires for heaven and salvation cool also. So then it comes to pass, that when their guilt and fear is gone, their desires for heaven and happiness die, and they return to their course again.

2. Another reason is, they have slavish fears that do overmaster them: I speak now of the fears that they have of men; "For the fear of man bringeth a snare." So then, though they seem to be hot for heaven so long as the flames of hell are about their ears, yet, when that terror is a little over, they betake themselves to second thoughts, namely, that it is good to be wise and not to run (for they know not what) the hazard of losing all, or at least of bringing themselves into unavoidable and unnecessary troubles; and so they fall in with the world again.

3. The shame that attends religion lies also as a block in their way: they are proud and haughty, and religion in their eye is low and contemptible: therefore when they have lost their sense of hell and the wrath to come, they return again to their former course.

4. Guilt, and to meditate terror, are grievous to them; they like not to see their misery before they come into it; though perhaps the sight of at it first, if they loved that sight, might make them fly whither the righteous fly and are safe; but because they do, as I hinted before, even shun the thoughts of guilt and terror, therefore, when once they are rid of their awakenings about the terrors and wrath of God, they harden their hearts gladly, and choose such ways as will harden them more and more.

Christian: You are pretty near the business, for the bottom of all is for want of a change in their mind and will. And therefore they are but like the felon that standeth before the judge: he quakes and trembles, and seems to repent most heartily, but the bottom of all is the fear of the halter: not that he hath any detestation of the offence, as it is evident; because, let but this man have his liberty, and he will be a thief, and so a rogue still; whereas, if his mind was changed, he would be otherwise.

Hopeful: Now I have showed you the reason of their going back, do you show me the manner thereof.

Christian: So I will willingly.

1. They draw off their thoughts, all that they may, from the remembrance of God, death, and judgment to come.

2. Then they cast off by degrees private duties, as closet prayer, curbing their lusts, watching, sorrow for sin, and the like.

3. Then they shun the company of lively and warm Christians.

4. After that, they grow cold to public duty, as hearing, reading, godly conference, and the like.

5. They then begin to pick holes, as we say, in the coats of some of the godly, and that devilishly, that they may have a seeming color to throw religion (for the sake of some infirmities they have espied in them) behind their backs.

6. Then they begin to adhere to, and associate themselves with, carnal, loose, and wanton men.

7. Then they give way to carnal and wanton discourses in secret; and glad are they if they can see such things in any that are counted honest, that they may the more boldly do it through their example.

8. After this they begin to play with little sins openly.

9. And then, being hardened, they show themselves as they are. Thus, being launched again into the gulf of misery, unless a miracle of grace prevent it, they everlastingly perish in their own deceivings.

Now I saw in my dream, that by this time the pilgrims were got over the Enchanted Ground, and entering into the country of Beulah, whose air was very sweet and pleasant, the way lying directly through it, they solaced themselves there for a season. Yea, here they heard continually the singing of birds, and saw every day the flowers appear in the earth, and heard the voice of the turtle in the land. In this country the sun shineth night and day: wherefore this was beyond the Valley of the Shadow of Death, and also out of the reach of Giant Despair; neither could they from this place so much as see Doubting Castle. Here they were within sight of the city they were going to; also here met them some of the inhabitants thereof; for in this land the shining ones commonly walked, because it was upon the borders of heaven. In this land also the contract between the Bride and the Bridegroom was renewed; yea, here, "as the bridegroom rejoiceth over the bride, so doth God rejoice over them." Here they had no want of corn and wine; for in this place they met with abundance of what they had sought for in all their pilgrimage. Here they heard voices from out of the city, loud voices, saying, "Say ye to the daughter of Zion, Behold, thy salvation cometh! Behold, his reward is with him!" Here all the inhabitants of the country called them "the holy People, the redeemed of the Lord, sought out," etc.

Now, as they walked in this land, they had more rejoicing than in parts more remote from the kingdom to which they were bound; and drawing near to the city, they had yet a more perfect view thereof: It was builded of pearls and precious stones, also the streets thereof were paved with gold; so that, by reason of the natural glory of the city, and the reflection of the sunbeams upon it, Christian with desire fell sick; Hopeful also had a fit or two of the same disease: wherefore here they lay by it a while, crying out because of their pangs, "If you see my Beloved, tell him that I am sick of love."

But, being a little strengthened, and better able to bear their sickness, they walked on their way, and came yet nearer and nearer, where were orchards, vineyards, and gardens, and their gates opened into the highway. Now, as they came up to these places, behold the gardener stood in the way; to whom the pilgrims said, Whose goodly vineyards and gardens are these? He answered, they are the King's, and are planted here for his own delight, and also for the solace of pilgrims. So the gardener had them into the vineyards, and bid them refresh themselves with the dainties, he also showed them there the King's walks and arbors where he delighted to be: And here they tarried and slept.

Now I beheld in my dream, that they talked more in their sleep at this time than ever they did in all their journey; and, being in a muse thereabout, the gardener said even to me, Wherefore musest thou at the matter? It is the nature of the fruit of the grapes of these vineyards, "to go down so sweetly as to cause the lips of them that are asleep to speak."

So I saw that when they awoke, they addressed themselves to go up to the city. But, as I said, the reflection of the sun upon the city (for the city was pure gold,) was so extremely glorious, that they could not as yet with open face behold it, but through an instrument made for that purpose. So I saw, that as they went on, there met them two men in raiment that shone like gold, also their faces shone as the light.

These men asked the pilgrims whence they came; and they told them. They also asked them where they had lodged, what difficulties and dangers, what comforts and pleasures, they had met with in the way; and they told them. Then said the men that met them, You have but two difficulties more to meet with, and then you are in the City.

Christian then and his companion asked the men to go along with them: so they told them that they would; But, said they, you must obtain it by your own faith. So I saw in my dream, that they went on together till they came in sight of the gate.

Now I further saw, that betwixt them and the gate was a river; but there was no bridge to go over, and the river was very deep. At the sight, therefore, of this river the pilgrims were much stunned; but the men that went with them said, You must go through, or you cannot come at the gate.

The pilgrims then began to inquire if there was no other way to the gate. To which they answered, Yes; but there hath not any, save two, to wit, Enoch and Elijah, been permitted to tread that path since the foundation of the world, nor shall until the last trumpet shall sound. The pilgrims then, especially Christian, began to despond in their mind, and looked this way and that, but no way could be found by them by which they might escape the river. Then they asked the men if the waters were all of a depth. They said, No; yet they could not help them in that case; for, said they, you shall find it deeper or shallower as you believe in the King of the place.

Then they addressed themselves to the water, and entering, Christian began to sink, and crying out to his good friend Hopeful, he said, I sink in deep waters; the billows go over my head; all his waves go over me. Selah.

Then said the other, Be of good cheer, my brother: I feel the bottom, and it is good. Then said Christian, Ah! my friend, the sorrows of death have compassed me about, I shall not see the land that flows with milk and honey. And with that a great darkness and horror fell upon Christian, so that he could not see before him. Also here he in a great measure lost his senses, so that he could neither remember nor orderly talk of any of those sweet refreshments that he had met with in the way of his pilgrimage. But all the words that he spoke still tended to discover that he had horror of mind, and heart-fears that he should die in that river, and never obtain entrance in at the gate. Here also, as they that stood by perceived, he was much in the troublesome thoughts of the sins that he had committed, both since and before he began to be a pilgrim. It was also observed that he was troubled with apparitions of hobgoblins and evil spirits; for ever and anon he would intimate so much by words.

Hopeful therefore here had much ado to keep his brother's head above water; yea, sometimes he would be quite gone down, and then, ere a while, he would rise up again half dead. Hopeful did also endeavor to comfort him, saying, Brother, I see the gate, and men standing by to receive us; but Christian would answer, It is you, it is you they wait for; for you have been hopeful ever since I knew you. And so have you, said he to Christian. Ah, brother, (said he,) surely if I was right he would now arise to help me; but for my sins he hath brought me into the snare, and hath left me. Then said Hopeful, My brother, you have quite forgot the text where it is said of the wicked, "There are no bands in their death, but their strength is firm; they are not troubled as other men, neither are they plagued like other men." These troubles and distresses that you go through in these waters, are no sign that God hath forsaken you; but are sent to try you, whether you will call to mind that which heretofore you have received of his goodness, and live upon him in your distresses.

Then I saw in my dream, that Christian was in a muse a while. To whom also Hopeful added these words, Be of good cheer, Jesus Christ maketh thee whole. And with that Christian brake out with a loud voice, Oh, I see him again; and he tells me, "When thou passest through the waters, I will be with thee; and through the rivers, they shall not overflow thee." Then they both took courage, and the enemy was after that as still as a stone, until they were gone over. Christian, therefore, presently found ground to stand upon, and so it followed that the rest of the river was but shallow. Thus they got over.

Now, upon the bank of the river, on the other side, they saw the two shining men again, who there waited for them. Wherefore, being come out of the river, they saluted them, saying, We are ministering spirits, sent forth to minister for those that shall be the heirs of salvation. Thus they went along towards the gate.

Now you must note, that the city stood upon a mighty hill; but the pilgrims went up that hill with ease, because they had these two men to lead them up by the arms: they had likewise left their mortal garments behind them in the river; for though they went in with them, they came out without them. They therefore went up here with much agility and speed, though the foundation upon which the city was framed was higher than the clouds; they therefore went up through the region of the air, sweetly talking as they went, being comforted because they safely got over the river, and had such glorious companions to attend them.

The talk that they had with the shining ones was about the glory of the place; who told them that the beauty and glory of it was inexpressible. There, said they, is "Mount Sion, the heavenly Jerusalem, the innumerable company of angels, and the spirits of just men made perfect." You are going now, said they, to the paradise of God, wherein you shall see the tree of life, and eat of the never-fading fruits thereof: and when you come there you shall have white robes given you, and your walk and talk shall be every day with the King, even all the days of eternity. There you shall not see again such things as you saw when you were in the lower region upon earth; to wit, sorrow, sickness, affliction, and death; "For the former things are passed away." You are going now to Abraham, to Isaac, and Jacob, and to the prophets, men that God hath taken away from the evil to come, and that are now "resting upon their beds, each one walking in his righteousness." The men then asked, What must we do in the holy place? To whom it was answered, You must there receive the comfort of all your toil, and have joy for all your sorrow; you must reap what you have sown, even the fruit of all your prayers, and tears, and sufferings for the King by the way. In that place you must wear crowns of gold, and enjoy the perpetual sight and vision of the Holy One; for "there you shall see him as he is." There also you shall serve him continually with praise, with shouting and thanksgiving, whom you desired to serve in the world, though with much difficulty, because of the infirmity of your flesh. There your eyes shall be delighted with seeing, and your ears with hearing the pleasant voice of the Mighty One. There you shall enjoy your friends again that are gone thither before you; and there you shall with joy receive even every one that follows into the holy place after you. There also you shall be clothed with glory and majesty, and put into an equipage fit to ride out with the King of Glory. When he shall come with sound of trumpet in the clouds, as upon the wings of the wind, you shall come with him; and when he shall sit upon the throne of judgment, you shall sit by him; yea, and when he shall pass sentence upon all the workers of iniquity, let them be angels or men, you also shall have a voice in that judgment, because they were his and your enemies. Also, when he shall again return to the city, you shall go too with sound of trumpet, and be ever with him.

Now, while they were thus drawing towards the gate, behold a company of the heavenly host came out to meet them: to whom it was said by the other two shining ones, These are the men that have loved our Lord when they were in the world, and that have left all for his holy name; and he hath sent us to fetch them, and we have brought them thus far on their desired journey, that they may go in and look their Redeemer in the face with joy. Then the heavenly host gave a great shout, saying, "Blessed are they that are called to the marriage-supper of the Lamb." There came out also at this time to meet them several of the King's trumpeters, clothed in white and shining raiment, who, with melodious noises and loud, made even the heavens to echo with their sound. These trumpeters saluted Christian and his fellow with ten thousand welcomes from the world; and this they did with shouting and sound of trumpet.

This done, they compassed them round on every side; some went before, some behind, and some on the right hand, and some on the left, (as it were to guard them through the upper regions,) continually sounding as they went, with melodious noise, in notes on high; so that the very sight was to them that could behold it as if heaven itself was come down to meet them. Thus, therefore, they walked on together; and, as they walked, ever and anon these trumpeters, even with joyful sound, would, by mixing their music with looks and gestures, still signify to Christian and his brother how welcome they were into their company, and with what gladness they came to meet them. And now were these two men, as it were, in heaven, before they came to it, being swallowed up with the sight of angels, and with hearing of their melodious notes. Here also they had the city itself in view; and they thought they heard all the bells therein to ring, to welcome them thereto. But, above all, the warm and joyful thoughts that they had about their own dwelling there with such company, and that for ever and ever; oh, by what tongue or pen can their glorious joy be expressed! Thus they came up to the gate.

Now when they were come up to the gate, there was written over it, in letters of gold,

> "blessed are they that do his commandments, that they may have right to the tree of life, and may enter in through the gates into the city."

Then I saw in my dream, that the shining men bid them call at the gate: the which when they did, some from above looked over the gate, to wit, Enoch, Moses, and Elijah, etc., to whom it was said, These pilgrims are come from the City of Destruction, for the love that they bear to the King of this place; and then the pilgrims gave in unto them each man his certificate, which they had received in the beginning: those therefore were carried in unto the King, who, when he had read them, said, Where are the men? To whom it was answered, They are standing without the gate. The King then commanded to open the gate, "That the righteous nation (said he) that keepeth the truth may enter in."

Now I saw in my dream, that these two men went in at the gate; and lo, as they entered, they were transfigured; and they had raiment put on that shone like gold. There were also that met them with harps and crowns, and gave them to them; the harps to praise withal, and the crowns in token of honor. Then I heard in my dream, that all the bells in the city rang again for joy, and that it was said unto them,

> "enter ye into the joy of your lord."

I also heard the men themselves, that they sang with a loud voice, saying,

> "blessing, and honor, and glory, and power, be unto him that sitteth upon the throne, and unto the lamb, for ever and ever."

Now, just as the gates were opened to let in the men, I looked in after them, and behold the city shone like the sun; the streets also were paved with gold; and in them walked many men, with crowns on their heads, palms in their hands, and golden harps, to sing praises withal.

There were also of them that had wings, and they answered one another without intermission, saying, Holy, holy, holy is the Lord. And after that they shut up the gates; which, when I had seen, I wished myself among them.

Now, while I was gazing upon all these things, I turned my head to look back, and saw Ignorance come up to the river side; but he soon got over, and that without half the difficulty which the other two men met with. For it happened that there was then in that place one Vain-Hope, a ferryman, that with his boat helped him over; so he, as the other I saw, did ascend the hill, to come up to the gate; only he came alone, neither did any man meet him with the least encouragement. When he was come up to the gate, he looked up to the writing that was above, and then began to knock, supposing that entrance should have been quickly administered to him; but he was asked by the men that looked over the top of the gate, Whence come you? and what would you have? He answered, I have ate and drank in the presence of the King, and he has taught in our streets. Then they asked him for his certificate, that they might go in and show it to the King: so he fumbled in his bosom for one, and found none. Then said they, Have you none? but the man answered never a word. So they told the King, but he would not come down to see him, but commanded the two shining ones, that conducted Christian and Hopeful to the city, to go out and take Ignorance, and bind him hand and foot, and have him away. Then they took him up, and carried him through the air to the door that I saw in the side of the hill, and put him in there. Then I saw that there was a way to hell, even from the gate of heaven, as well as from the City of Destruction. So I awoke, and behold it was a dream.

Lesson 80

- Now you're going to read the second part of the book. Read Book 2, Stage 1 of *The Pilgrim's Progress*.

Book 2, Stage 1

By this time Christiana was got on her way, and Mercy went along with her: so as they went, her children being there also, Christiana began to discourse. And, Mercy, said Christiana, I take this as an unexpected favor, that thou shouldest set forth out of doors with me to accompany me a little in the way.

Mercy: Then said young Mercy, (for she was but young,) If I thought it would be to purpose to go with you, I would never go near the town any more.

Christiana: Well, Mercy, said Christiana, cast in thy lot with me: I well know what will be the end of our pilgrimage: my husband is where he would not but be for all the gold in the Spanish mines. Nor shalt thou be rejected, though thou goest but upon my invitation. The King, who hath sent for me and my children, is one that delighteth in mercy. Besides, if thou wilt, I will hire thee, and thou shalt go along with me as my servant. Yet we will have all things in common betwixt thee and me: only go along with me.

Mercy: But how shall I be ascertained that I also should be entertained? Had I this hope but from one that can tell, I would make no stick at all, but would go, being helped by Him that can help, though the way was never so tedious.

Christiana: Well, loving Mercy, I will tell thee what thou shalt do: go with me to the Wicket-gate, and there I will further inquire for thee; and if there thou shalt not meet with encouragement, I will be content that thou return to thy place: I will also pay thee for thy kindness which thou showest to me and my children, in the accompanying of us in the way that thou dost.

Mercy: Then will I go thither, and will take what shall follow; and the Lord grant that my lot may there fall, even as the King of heaven shall have his heart upon me.

Christiana then was glad at heart, not only that she had a companion, but also for that she had prevailed with this poor maid to fall in love with her own salvation. So they went on together, and Mercy began to weep. Then said Christiana, Wherefore weepeth my sister so?

Mercy: Alas! said she, who can but lament, that shall but rightly consider what a state and condition my poor relations are in, that yet remain in our sinful town? And that which makes my grief the more heavy is, because they have no instructor, nor any to tell them what is to come.

Christiana: Pity becomes pilgrims; and thou dost weep for thy friends, as my good Christian did for me when he left me: he mourned for that I would not heed nor regard him; but his Lord and ours did gather up his tears, and put them into his bottle; and now both I and thou, and these my sweet babes, are reaping the fruit and benefit of them. I hope, Mercy, that these tears of thine will not be lost; for the truth hath said, that "they that sow in tears shall reap in joy." And "he that goeth forth and weepeth, bearing precious seed, shall doubtless come again with rejoicing, bringing his sheaves with him."

Then said Mercy,

"Let the Most Blessed be my guide,
  If it be his blessed will,
Unto his gate, into his fold,
  Up to his holy hill.

And let him never suffer me
  To swerve, or turn aside
From his free-grace and holy ways,
  Whate'er shall me betide.

And let him gather them of mine
  That I have left behind;
Lord, make them pray they may be thine,
  With all their heart and mind."

Now my old friend proceeded, and said, But when Christiana came to the Slough of Despond, she began to be at a stand; For, said she, this is the place in which my dear husband had like to have been smothered with mud. She perceived, also, that notwithstanding the command of the King to make this place for pilgrims good, yet it was rather worse than formerly. So I asked if that was true. Yes, said the old gentleman, too true; for many there be that pretend to be the King's laborers, and that say they are for mending the King's highways, who bring dirt and dung instead of stones, and so mar instead of mending. Here Christiana therefore, with her boys, did make a stand. But said Mercy, Come, let us venture; only let us be wary. Then they looked well to their steps, and made a shift to get staggering over.

Yet Christiana had like to have been in, and that not once or twice. Now they had no sooner got over, but they thought they heard words that said unto them, "Blessed is she that believeth; for there shall be a performance of those things which were told her from the Lord."

Then they went on again; and said Mercy to Christiana, had I as good ground to hope for a loving reception at the Wicket-gate as you, I think no Slough of Despond would discourage me.

Well, said the other, you know your sore, and I know mine; and, good friend, we shall all have enough evil before we come to our journey's end. For can it be imagined that the people who design to attain such excellent glories as we do, and who are so envied that happiness as we are, but that we shall meet with what fears and snares, with what troubles and afflictions they can possibly assault us with that hate us?

And now Mr. Sagacity left me to dream out my dream by myself. Wherefore, methought I saw Christiana, and Mercy, and the boys, go all of them up to the gate: to which, when they were come, they betook themselves to a short debate about how they must manage their calling at the gate, and what should be said unto him that did open to them: so it was concluded, since Christiana was the eldest, that she should knock for entrance, and that she should speak to him that did open, for the rest. So Christiana began to knock, and as her poor husband did, she knocked and knocked again. But instead of any that answered, they all thought they heard as if a dog came barking upon them; a dog, and a great one too; and this made the women and children afraid. Nor durst they for a while to knock any more, for fear the mastiff should fly upon them. Now, therefore, they were greatly tumbled up and down in their minds, and knew not what to do: knock they durst not, for fear of the dog; go back they durst not, for fear the keeper of that gate should espy them as they so went, and should be offended with them; at last they thought of knocking again, and knocked more vehemently than they did at first. Then said the keeper of the gate, Who is there? So the dog left off to bark, and he opened unto them.

Then Christiana made low obeisance, and said, Let not our Lord be offended with his handmaidens, for that we have knocked at his princely gate. Then said the keeper, Whence come ye? And what is it that you would have?

Christiana answered, We are come from whence Christian did come, and upon the same errand as he; to wit, to be, if it shall please you, graciously admitted by this gate into the way that leads unto the Celestial City. And I answer, my Lord, in the next place, that I am Christiana, once the wife of Christian, that now is gotten above.

With that the keeper of the gate did marvel, saying, What, is she now become a pilgrim that but a while ago abhorred that life? Then she bowed her head, and said, Yea; and so are these my sweet babes also.

Then he took her by the hand and led her in, and said also, Suffer little children to come unto me; and with that he shut up the gate. This done, he called to a trumpeter that was above, over the gate, to entertain Christiana with shouting, and the sound of trumpet for joy. So he obeyed, and sounded, and filled the air with his melodious notes.

Now all this while poor Mercy did stand without, trembling and crying, for fear that she was rejected. But when Christiana had got admittance for herself and her boys, then she began to make intercession for Mercy.

Christiana: And she said, My Lord, I have a companion that stands yet without, that is come hither upon the same account as myself: one that is much dejected in her mind, for that she comes, as she thinks, without sending for; whereas I was sent for by my husband's King to come.

Now Mercy began to be very impatient, and each minute was as long to her as an hour; wherefore she prevented Christiana from a fuller interceding for her, by knocking at the gate herself. And she knocked then so loud that she made Christiana to start. Then said the keeper of the gate, Who is there? And Christiana said, It is my friend.

So he opened the gate, and looked out, but Mercy was fallen down without in a swoon, for she fainted, and was afraid that no gate should be opened to her.

Then he took her by the hand, and said, Damsel, I bid thee arise.

Oh, sir, said she, I am faint; there is scarce life left in me. But he answered, that one once said, "When my soul fainted within me I remembered the Lord: and my prayer came unto thee, into thy holy temple." Fear not, but stand upon thy feet, and tell me wherefore thou art come.

Mercy: I am come for that unto which I was never invited, as my friend Christiana was. Hers was from the King, and mine was but from her. Wherefore I fear I presume.

Keep: Did she desire thee to come with her to this place?

Mercy: Yes; and, as my Lord sees, I am come. And if there is any grace and forgiveness of sins to spare, I beseech that thy poor handmaid may be a partaker thereof.

Then he took her again by the hand, and led her gently in, and said, I pray for all them that believe on me, by what means soever they come unto me. Then said he to those that stood by, Fetch something and give it to Mercy to smell on, thereby to stay her faintings; so they fetched her a bundle of myrrh, and a while after she was revived.

And now were Christiana and her boys, and Mercy, received of the Lord at the head of the way, and spoken kindly unto by him. Then said they yet further unto him, We are sorry for our sins, and beg of our Lord his pardon, and further information what we must do.

I grant pardon, said he, by word and deed; by word in the promise of forgiveness, by deed in the way I obtained it. Take the first from my lips with a kiss, and the other as it shall be revealed.

Now I saw in my dream, that he spake many good words unto them, whereby they were greatly gladdened. He also had them up to the top of the gate, and showed them by what deed they were saved; and told them withal, that that sight they would have again as they went along in the way, to their comfort.

So he left them awhile in a summer parlor below, where they entered into talk by themselves; and thus Christiana began. O how glad am I that we are got in hither.

Mercy: So you well may; but I, of all, have cause to leap for joy.

Christiana: I thought one time, as I stood at the gate, because I had knocked and none did answer, that all our labor had been lost, especially when that ugly cur made such a heavy barking against us.

Mercy: But my worst fear was after I saw that you was taken into his favor, and that I was left behind. Now, thought I, it is fulfilled which is written, "Two women shall be grinding at the mill; the one shall be taken, and the other left." I had much ado to forbear crying out, Undone! And afraid I was to knock any more; but when I looked up to what was written over the gate, I took courage. I also thought that I must either knock again, or die; so I knocked, but I cannot tell how, for my spirit now struggled between life and death.

Christiana: Can you not tell how you knocked? I am sure your knocks were so earnest that the very sound of them made me start; I thought I never heard such knocking in all my life; I thought you would come in by a violent hand, or take the kingdom by storm.

Mercy: Alas! to be in my case, who that so was could but have done so? You saw that the door was shut upon me, and there was a most cruel dog thereabout. Who, I say, that was so faint-hearted as I, would not have knocked with all their might? But pray, what said my Lord to my rudeness? Was he not angry with me?

Christiana: When he heard your lumbering noise, he gave a wonderful innocent smile; I believe what you did pleased him well, for he showed no sign to the contrary. But I marvel in my heart why he keeps such a dog: had I known that before, I should not have had heart enough to have ventured myself in this manner. But now we are in, we are in, and I am glad with all my heart.

Mercy: I will ask, if you please, next time he comes down, why he keeps such a filthy cur in his yard; I hope he will not take it amiss.

Do so, said the children, and persuade him to hang him; for we are afraid he will bite us when we go hence.

So at last he came down to them again, and Mercy fell to the ground on her face before him, and worshiped, and said, "Let my Lord accept the sacrifice of praise which I now offer unto him with the calves of my lips."

So he said unto her, Peace be to thee; stand up. But she continued upon her face, and said, "Righteous art thou, O Lord, when I plead with thee; yet let me talk with thee of thy judgments." Wherefore dost thou keep so cruel a dog in thy yard, at the sight of which such women and children as we are ready to fly from thy gate for fear?

He answered and said, That dog has another owner; he also is kept close in another man's ground, only my pilgrims hear his barking; he belongs to the castle which you see there at a distance, but can come up to the walls of this place. He has frighted many an honest pilgrim from worse to better, by the great voice of his roaring. Indeed, he that owneth him doth not keep him out of any good-will to me or mine, but with intent to keep the pilgrims from coming to me, and that they may be afraid to come and knock at this gate for entrance. Sometimes also he has broken out, and has worried some that I loved; but I take all at present patiently. I also give my pilgrims timely help, so that they are not delivered to his power, to do with them what his doggish nature would prompt him to. But what my purchased one, I trow, hadst thou known never so much beforehand, thou wouldest not have been afraid of a dog. The beggars that go from door to door, will, rather than lose a supposed alms, run the hazard of the bawling, barking, and biting too of a dog; and shall a dog, a dog in another man's yard, a dog whose barking I turn to the profit of pilgrims, keep any from coming to me? I deliver them from the lions, and my darling from the power of the dog.

Mercy: Then said Mercy, I confess my ignorance; I spake what I understood not; I acknowledge that thou doest all things well.

Christiana: Then Christiana began to talk of their journey, and to inquire after the way. So he fed them and washed their feet, and set them in the way of his steps, according as he had dealt with her husband before.

Lesson 81

- Read Book 2, Stage 2 of *The Pilgrim's Progress.*

Book 2, Stage 2

So I saw in my dream, that they walked on their way, and had the weather very comfortable to them.

Then Christiana began to sing, saying,

Blessed be the day that I began
  A pilgrim for to be;
And blessed also be the man
  That thereto moved me.

'Tis true, 't was long ere I began
  To seek to live for ever;
But now I run fast as I can:
  'Tis better late than never.

Our tears to joy, our fears to faith,
  Are turned, as we see;
Thus our beginning (as one saith)
  Shows what our end will be.

Now there was, on the other side of the wall that fenced in the way up which Christiana and her companions were to go, a garden, and that garden belonged to him whose was that barking dog, of whom mention was made before. And some of the fruit-trees that grew in that garden shot their branches over the wall; and being mellow, they that found them did gather them up, and eat of them to their hurt. So Christiana's boys, as boys are apt to do, being pleased with the trees, and with the fruit that hung thereon, did pluck them, and began to eat. Their mother did also chide them for so doing, But still the boys went on.

Well, said she, my sons, you transgress, for that fruit is none of ours; but she did not know that it belonged to the enemy: I'll warrant you, if she had she would have been ready to die for fear. But that passed, and they went on their way. Now, by that they were gone about two bow-shots from the place that led them into the way, they espied two very ill-favored ones coming down apace to meet them. With that,

Christiana and Mercy her friend covered themselves with their veils, and so kept on their journey: the children also went on before; so that at last they met together. Then they that came down to meet them, came just up to the women, as if they would embrace them; but Christiana said, stand back, or go peaceably as you should. Yet these two, as men that are deaf, regarded not Christiana's words, but began to lay hands upon them: at that Christiana waxing very wroth, spurned at them with her feet. Mercy also, as well as she could, did what she could to shift them. Christiana again said to them, Stand back, and be gone, for we have no money to lose, being pilgrims, as you see, and such too as live upon the charity of our friends.

Ill-Favored Ones: Then said one of the two men, We make no assault upon you for money, but are come out to tell you, that if you will but grant one small request which we shall ask, we will make women of you for ever.

Christiana: Now Christiana, imagining what they should mean, made answer again, We will neither hear, nor regard, nor yield to what you shall ask. We are in haste, and cannot stay; our business is a business of life and death. So again she and her companion made a fresh essay to go past them; but they letted them in their way.

Ill-Favored Ones: And they said, We intend no hurt to your lives; it is another thing we would have.

Christiana: Aye, quoth Christiana, you would have us body and soul, for I know it is for that you are come; but we will die rather upon the spot, than to suffer ourselves to be brought into such snares as shall hazard our well-being hereafter. And with that they both shrieked out, and cried, Murder! murder! and so put themselves under those laws that are provided for the protection of women. But the men still made their approach upon them, with design to prevail against them. They therefore cried out again.

Now they being, as I said, not far from the gate in at which they came, their voice was heard from whence they were, thither: wherefore some of the house came out, and knowing that it was Christiana's tongue, they made haste to her relief. But by that they were got within sight of them, the women were in a very great scuffle; the children also stood crying by. Then did he that came in for their relief call out to the ruffians, saying, What is that thing you do? Would you make my Lord's people to transgress? He also attempted to take them, but they did make their escape over the wall into the garden of the man to whom the great dog belonged; so the dog became their protector. This Reliever then came up to the women, and asked them how they did. So they answered, We thank thy Prince, pretty well, only we have been somewhat affrighted: we thank thee also for that thou camest in to our help, otherwise we had been overcome.

Reliever: So, after a few more words, this Reliever said as followeth: I marveled much, when you were entertained at the gate above, seeing ye knew that ye were but weak women, that you petitioned not the Lord for a conductor; then might you have avoided these troubles and dangers; for he would have granted you one.

Christiana: Alas! said Christiana, we were so taken with our present blessing, that dangers to come were forgotten by us. Besides, who could have thought, that so near the King's palace there could have lurked such naughty ones? Indeed, it had been well for us had we asked our Lord for one; but since our Lord knew it would be for our profit, I wonder he sent not one along with us.

Reliever: It is not always necessary to grant things not asked for, lest by so doing they become of little esteem; but when the want of a thing is felt, it then comes under, in the eyes of him that feels it, that estimate that properly is its due, and so consequently will be thereafter used. Had my Lord granted you a conductor, you would not either so have bewailed that oversight of yours, in not asking for one, as now you have occasion to do. So all things work for good, and tend to make you more wary.

Christiana: Shall we go back again to my Lord, and confess our folly, and ask one?

Reliever: Your confession of your folly I will present him with. To go back again, you need not, for in all places where you shall come, you will find no want at all; for in every one of my Lord's lodgings, which he has prepared for the reception of his pilgrims, there is sufficient to furnish them against all attempts whatsoever. But, as I said, He will be inquired of by them, to do it for them. And 'tis a poor thing that is not worth asking for. When he had thus said, he went back to his place, and the pilgrims went on their way.

Mercy: Then said Mercy, What a sudden blank is here! I made account that we had been past all danger, and that we should never see sorrow more.

Christiana: Thy innocency, my sister, said Christiana to Mercy, may excuse thee much; but as for me, my fault is so much the greater, for that I saw this danger before I came out of the doors, and yet did not provide for it when provision might have been had. I am much to be blamed.

Mercy: Then said Mercy, How knew you this before you came from home? Pray open to me this riddle.

Christiana: Why, I will tell you. Before I set foot out of doors, one night as I lay in my bed I had a dream about this; for methought I saw two men, as like these as ever any in the world could look, stand at my bed's feet, plotting how they might prevent my salvation. I will tell you their very words. They said, (it was when I was in my troubles,) What shall we do with this woman? for she cries out, waking and sleeping, for forgiveness: if she be sufferet do go on as she begins, we shall lose her as we have lost her husband. This you know might have made me take heed, and have provided when provision might have been had.

Mercy: Well, said Mercy, as by this neglect we have an occasion ministered unto us to behold our own imperfections, so our Lord has taken occasion thereby to make manifest the riches of his grace; for he, as we see, has followed us with unasked kindness, and has delivered us from their hands that were stronger than we, of his mere good pleasure.

Thus now, when they had talked away a little more time, they drew near to a house which stood in the way, which house was built for the relief of pilgrims, as you will find more fully related in the first part of these records of the Pilgrim's Progress. So they drew on towards the house, (the house of the Interpreter;) and when they came to the door, they heard a great talk in the house. Then they gave ear, and heard, as they thought, Christiana mentioned by name; for you must know that there went along, even before her, a talk of her and her children's going on pilgrimage. And this was the most pleasing to them, because they had heard that she was Christian's wife, that woman who was some time ago so unwilling to hear of going on pilgrimage. Thus, therefore, they stood still, and heard the good people within commending her who they little thought stood at the door. At last Christiana knocked, as she had done at the gate before. Now, when she had knocked, there came to the door a young damsel, and opened the door, and looked, and behold, two women were there.

The Damsel: Then said the damsel to them, With whom would you speak in this place?

Christiana: Christiana answered, We understand that this is a privileged place for those that are become pilgrims, and we now at this door are such: wherefore we pray that we may be partakers of that for which we at this time are come; for the day, as thou seest, is very far spent, and we are loth to-night to go any further.

The Damsel: Pray, what may I call your name, that I may tell it to my Lord within.

Christiana: My name is Christiana; I was the wife of that pilgrim that some years ago did travel this way, and these be his four children. This maiden also is my companion, and is going on pilgrimage too.

Innocent: Then Innocent ran in, (for that was her name,) and said to those within, Can you think who is at the door? There is Christiana and her children, and her companion, all waiting for entertainment here. Then they leaped for joy, and went and told their Master. So he came to the door and looking upon her, he said, Art thou that Christiana whom Christian the good man left behind him when he betook himself to a pilgrim's life.

Christiana: I am that woman that was so hard-hearted as to slight my husband's troubles, and that left him to go on in his journey alone, and these are his four children; but now I also am come, for I am convinced that no way is right but this.

Interpreter: Then is fulfilled that which is written of the man that said to his son, "Go work to-day in my vineyard; and he said to his father, I will not: but afterwards repented and went."

Christiana: Then said Christiana, So be it: Amen. God made it a true saying upon me, and grant that I may be found at the last of him in peace, without spot, and blameless.

Interpreter: But why standest thou thus at the door? Come in, thou daughter of Abraham; we were talking of thee but now, for tidings have come to us before how thou art become a pilgrim. Come, children, come in; come, maiden, come in. So he had them all into the house.

So when they were within, they were bidden to sit down and rest them; the which when they had done, those that attended upon the pilgrims in the house came into the room to see them. And one smiled, and another smiled, and they all smiled for joy that Christiana was become a pilgrim: They also looked upon the boys; they stroked them over their faces with the hand, in token of their kind reception of them: they also carried it lovingly to Mercy, and bid them all welcome into their Master's house.

After a while, because supper was not ready, the Interpreter took them into his Significant Rooms, and showed them what Christian, Christiana's husband, had seen some time before. Here, therefore, they saw the man in the cage, the man and his dream, the man that cut his way through his enemies, and the picture of the biggest of them all, together with the rest of those things that were then so profitable to Christian.

This done, and after those things had been somewhat digested by Christiana and her company, the Interpreter takes them apart again, and has them first into a room where was a man that could look no way but downwards, with a muck-rake in his hand. There stood also one over his head with a celestial crown in his hand, and proffered him that crown for his muck-rake; but the man did neither look up nor regard, but raked to himself the straws, the small sticks, and dust of the floor.

Then said Christiana, I persuade myself that I know somewhat the meaning of this; for this is a figure of a man of this world: is it not, good sir?

Interpreter: Thou hast said right, said he; and his muck-rake doth show his carnal mind. And whereas thou seest him rather give heed to rake up straws and sticks, and the dust of the floor, than to do what He says that calls to him from above with the celestial crown in his hand; it is to show, that heaven is but as a fable to some, and that things here are counted the only things substantial. Now, whereas it was also showed thee that the man could look no way but downwards, it is to let thee know that earthly things, when they are with power upon men's minds, quite carry their hearts away from God.

Christiana: Then said Christiana, O deliver me from this muck-rake.

Interpreter: That prayer, said the Interpreter, has lain by till it is almost rusty: "Give me not riches," is scarce the prayer of one in ten thousand. Straws, and sticks, and dust, with most, are the great things now looked after.

With that Christiana and Mercy wept, and said, It is, alas! too true.

When the Interpreter had shown them this, he had them into the very best room in the house; a very brave room it was. So he bid them look round about, and see if they could find any thing profitable there. Then they looked round and round; for there was nothing to be seen but a very great spider on the wall, and that they overlooked.

Mercy: Then said Mercy, Sir, I see nothing; but Christiana held her peace.

Interpreter: But, said the Interpreter, look again. She therefore looked again, and said, Here is not any thing but an ugly spider, who hangs by her hands upon the wall. Then said he, Is there but one spider in all this spacious room? Then the water stood in Christiana's eyes, for she was a woman quick of apprehension; and she said, Yea, Lord, there are more here than one; yea, and spiders whose venom is far more destructive than that which is in her. The Interpreter then looked pleasantly on her, and said, Thou hast said the truth. This made Mercy to blush, and the boys to cover their faces; for they all began now to understand the riddle.

Then said the Interpreter again, "The spider taketh hold with her hands," as you see, "and is in kings' palaces." And wherefore is this recorded, but to show you, that, how full of the venom of sin soever you be, yet you may, by the hand of Faith, lay hold of and dwell in the best room that belongs to the King's house above?

Christiana: I thought, said Christiana, of something of this; but I could not imagine it at all. I thought that we were like spiders, and that we looked like ugly creatures, in what fine room soever we were: but that by this spider, that venomous and ill-favored creature, we were to learn how to act faith, that came not into my thoughts;

and yet she had taken hold with her hands, and, as I see, dwelleth in the best room in the house. God has made nothing in vain.

Then they seemed all to be glad; but the water stood in their eyes; yet they looked one upon another, and also bowed before the Interpreter.

He had them into another room, where were a hen and chickens, and bid them observe a while. So one of the chickens went to the trough to drink, and every time she drank she lifted up her head and her eyes towards heaven. See, said he, what this little chick doth, and learn of her to acknowledge whence your mercies come, by receiving them with looking up. Yet again, said he, observe and look: so they gave heed, and perceived that the hen did walk in a fourfold method towards her chickens: 1. She had a common call, and that she hath all the day long. 2. She had a special call, and that she had but sometimes. 3. She had a brooding note. And, 4. She had an outcry.

Now, said he, compare this hen to your King and these chickens to his obedient ones; for, answerable to her, he himself hath his methods which he walketh in towards his people. By his common call, he gives nothing; by his special call, he always has something to give; he has also a brooding voice, for them that are under his wing; and he has an outcry, to give the alarm when he seeth the enemy come. I choose, my darlings, to lead you into the room where such things are, because you are women, and they are easy for you.

Christiana: And, sir, said Christiana, pray let us see some more. So he had them into the slaughter-house, where was a butcher killing a sheep; and behold, the sheep was quiet, and took her death patiently. Then said the Interpreter, You must learn of this sheep to suffer and to put up with wrongs without murmurings and complaints. Behold how quietly she takes her death, and, without objecting, she suffereth her skin to be pulled over her ears. Your King doth call you his sheep.

After this he led them into his garden, where was great variety of flowers; and he, said, Do you see all these? So Christiana said, Yes. Then said he again, Behold, the flowers are diverse in stature, in quality, and color, and smell, and virtue; and some are better than others; also, where the gardener has set them, there they stand, and quarrel not one with another.

Again, he had them into his field, which he had sown with wheat and corn: but when they beheld, the tops of all were cut off, and only the straw remained. He said again, This ground was dunged, and ploughed, and sowed, but what shall we do with the crop? Then said Christiana, Burn some, and make muck of the rest. Then said the Interpreter again, Fruit, you see, is that thing you look for; and for want of that you condemn it to the fire, and to be trodden under foot of men: beware that in this you condemn not yourselves.

Then, as they were coming in from abroad, they espied a little robin with a great spider in his mouth. So the Interpreter said, Look here. So they looked, and Mercy wondered, but Christiana said, What a disparagement is it to such a pretty little bird as the robin-red-breast; he being also a bird above many, that loveth to maintain a kind of sociableness with men! I had thought they had lived upon crumbs of bread, or upon other such harmless matter: I like him worse than I did.

The Interpreter then replied, This robin is an emblem, very apt to set forth some professors by; for to sight they are, as this robin, pretty of note, color, and carriage. They seem also to have a very great love for professors that are sincere; and, above all others, to desire to associate with them, and to be in their company, as if they could live upon the good man's crumbs. They pretend also, that therefore it is that they frequent the house of the godly, and the appointments of the Lord: but when they are by themselves, as the robin, they can catch and gobble up spiders; they can change their diet, drink iniquity, and swallow down sin like water.

So, when they were come again into the house, because supper as yet was not ready, Christiana again desired that the Interpreter would either show or tell some other things that are profitable.

Then the Interpreter began, and said, The fatter the sow is, the more she desires the mire; the fatter the ox is, the more gamesomely he goes to the slaughter; and the more healthy the lustful man is, the more prone he is unto evil. There is a desire in women to go neat and find; and it is a comely thing to be adorned with that which in God's sight is of great price. 'T is easier watching a night or two, than to sit up a whole year together: so 't is easier for one to begin to profess well, than to hold out as he should to the end. Every shipmaster, when in a storm, will willingly cast that overboard which is of the smallest value in the vessel; but who will throw the best out first? None but he that feareth not God. One leak will sink a ship, and one sin will destroy a sinner. He that forgets his friend is ungrateful unto him; but he that forgets his Saviour is unmerciful to himself. He that lives in sin, and looks for happiness hereafter, is like him that soweth cockle, and thinks to fill his barn with wheat or barley. If a man would live well, let him fetch his last day to him, and make it always his company-keeper. Whispering, and change of thoughts, prove that sin is in the world. If the world, which God sets light by, is counted a thing of that worth with men, what is heaven, that God commendeth? If the life that is attended with so many troubles, is so loth to be let go by us, what is the life above? Every body will cry up the goodness of men; but who is there that is, as he should be, affected with the goodness of God? We seldom sit down to meat, but we eat, and leave. So there is in Jesus Christ more merit and righteousness than the whole world has need of.

When the Interpreter had done, he takes them out into his garden again, and had them to a tree whose inside was all rotten and gone, and yet it grew and had leaves. Then said Mercy, What means this? This tree, said he, whose outside is fair, and whose inside is rotten, is that to which many may be compared that are in the garden of God; who with their mouths speak high in behalf of God, but indeed will do nothing for him; whose leaves are fair, but their heart good for nothing but to be tinder for the devil's tinder-box.

Now supper was ready, the table spread, and all things set on the board: so they sat down, and did eat, when one had given thanks. And the Interpreter did usually entertain those that lodged with him with music at meals; so the minstrels played. There was also one that did sing, and a very fine voice he had. His song was this:

"The Lord is only my support,
  And he that doth me feed;
How can I then want any thing
  Whereof I stand in need?"

When the song and music were ended, the Interpreter asked Christiana what it was that at first did move her thus to betake herself to a pilgrim's life. Christiana answered, First, the loss of my husband came into my mind, at which I was heartily grieved; but all that was but natural affection. Then after that came the troubles and pilgrimage of my husband into my mind, and also how like a churl I had carried it to him as to that. So guilt took hold of my mind, and would have drawn me into the pond, but that opportunely I had a dream of the well-being of my husband, and a letter sent me by the King of that country where my husband dwells, to come to him. The dream and the letter together so wrought upon my mind that they forced me to this way.

Interpreter: But met you with no opposition before you set out of doors?

Christiana: Yes, a neighbor of mine, one Mrs. Timorous: she was akin to him that would have persuaded my husband to go back, for fear of the lions. She also befooled me, for, as she called it, my intended desperate adventure; she also urged what she could to dishearten me from it, the hardships and troubles that my husband met with in the way; but all this I got over pretty well. But a dream that I had of two ill-looking ones, that I thought did plot how to make me miscarry in my journey, that hath troubled me much: yea, it still runs in my mind, and makes me afraid of every one that I meet, lest they should meet me to do me a mischief, and to turn me out of my way. Yea, I may tell my Lord, though I would not have every body know of it, that between this and the gate by which we got into the way, we were both so sorely assaulted that we were made to cry out murder; and the two that made this assault upon us, were like the two that I saw in my dream.

Then said the Interpreter, Thy beginning is good; thy latter end shall greatly increase. So he addressed himself to Mercy, and said unto her, And what moved thee to come hither, sweet heart?

Mercy: Then Mercy blushed and trembled, and for a while continued silent.

Interpreter: Then said he, Be not afraid; only believe, and speak thy mind.

Mercy: So she began, and said, Truly, sir, my want of experience is that which makes me covet to be in silence, and that also that fills me with fears of coming short at last. I cannot tell of visions and dreams, as my friend Christiana can; nor know I what it is to mourn for my refusing the counsel of those that were good relations.

Interpreter: What was it, then, dear heart, that hath prevailed with thee to do as thou hast done?

Mercy: Why, when our friend here was packing up to be gone from our town, I and another went accidentally to see her. So we knocked at the door and went in. When we were within, and seeing what she was doing, we asked her what was her meaning. She said she was sent for to go to her husband; and then she up and told us how she had seen him in a dream, dwelling in a curious place, among immortals, wearing a crown, playing upon a harp, eating and drinking at his Prince's table, and singing praises to him for bringing him thither, etc. Now, methought, while she was telling these things unto us, my heart burned within me. And I said in my heart, If this be true, I will leave my father and my mother, and the land of my nativity, and will, if I may, go along with Christiana. So I asked her further of the truth of these things, and if she would let me go with her; for I saw now that there was no dwelling, but with the danger of ruin, any longer in our town. But yet I came away with a heavy heart; not for that I was unwilling to come away, but for that so many of my relations were left behind. And I am come with all the desire of my heart, and will go, if I may, with Christiana unto her husband and his King.

Interpreter: Thy setting out is good, for thou hast given credit to the truth; thou art a Ruth, who did, for the love she bare to Naomi and to the Lord her God, leave father and mother, and the land of her nativity, to come out and go with a people she knew not heretofore. "The Lord recompense thy work, and a full reward be given thee of the Lord God of Israel, under whose wings thou art come to trust."

Now supper was ended, and preparation was made for bed; the women were laid singly alone, and the boys by themselves. Now when Mercy was in bed, she could not sleep for joy, for that now her doubts of missing at last were removed further from her than ever they were before. So she lay blessing and praising God, who had such favor for her.

In the morning they arose with the sun, and prepared themselves for their departure; but the Interpreter would have them tarry a while; For, said he, you must orderly go from hence. Then said he to the damsel that first opened unto them, Take them and have them into the garden to the bath, and there wash them and make them clean from the soil which they had gathered by traveling. Then Innocent the damsel took them and led them into the garden, and brought them to the bath; so she told them that there they must wash and be clean, for so her Master would have the women to do that called at his house as they were going on pilgrimage. Then they went in and washed, yea, they and the boys, and all; and they came out of that bath, not only sweet and clean, but also much enlivened and strengthened in their joints. So when they came in, they looked fairer a deal than when they went out to the washing.

When they were returned out of the garden from the bath, the Interpreter took them and looked upon them, and said unto them, "Fair as the moon." Then he called for the seal wherewith they used to be sealed that were washed in his bath. So the seal was brought, and he set his mark upon them, that they might be known in the places whither they were yet to go. Now the seal was the contents and sum of the passover which the children of Israel did eat, when they came out of the land of Egypt; and the mark was set between their eyes. This seal greatly added to their beauty, for it was an ornament to their faces. It also added to their gravity, and made their countenance more like those of angels.

Then said the Interpreter again to the damsel that waited upon these women, Go into the vestry, and fetch out garments for these people. So she went and fetched out white raiment, and laid it down before him; so he commanded them to put it on: it was fine linen, white and clean. When the women were thus adorned, they seemed to be a terror one to the other; for that they could not see that glory each one had in herself, which they could see in each other. Now therefore they began to esteem each other better than themselves. For, You are fairer than I am, said one; and, You are more comely than I am, said another. The children also stood amazed, to see into what fashion they were brought.

Lesson 82

- Read Book 2, Stage 3 of *The Pilgrim's Progress.*

Book 2, Stage 3

The Interpreter then called for a man-servant of his, one Great-heart, and bid him take A sword, and helmet, and shield; and, Take these my daughters, said he, conduct them to the house called Beautiful, at which place they will rest next. So he took his weapons, and went before them; and the Interpreter said, God speed.

Those also that belonged to the family, sent them away with many a good wish. So they went on their way, and sang,

This place hath been our second stage:
  Here we have heard, and seen
Those good things, that from age to age
  To others hid have been.

The dunghill-raker, spider, hen,
  The chicken, too, to me
Have taught a lesson: let me then
  Conformed to it be.

The butcher, garden, and the field,
  The robin and his bait,
Also the rotten tree, doth yield
  Me argument of weight,

To move me for to watch and pray,
  To strive to be sincere;
To take my cross up day by day,
  And serve the Lord with fear.

Now I saw in my dream, that they went on, and Great-Heart before them. So they went, and came to the place where Christian's burden fell off his back and tumbled into a sepulchre. Here then they made a pause; and here also they blessed God. Now, said Christiana, it comes to my mind what was said to us at the gate, to wit, that we should have pardon by word and deed: by word, that is, by the promise; by deed, to wit, in the way it was obtained. What the promise is, of that I know something; but what is it to have pardon by deed, or in the way that it was obtained, Mr. Great-Heart, I suppose you know; wherefore, if you please, let us hear your discourse thereof.

Mr. Great-Heart: Pardon by the deed done, is pardon obtained by some one for another that hath need thereof; not by the person pardoned, but in the way, saith another, in which I have obtained it. So then, to speak to the question more at large, the pardon that you, and Mercy, and these boys have attained, was obtained by another; to wit, by him that let you in at the gate. And he hath obtained it in this double way; he hath performed righteousness to cover you, and spilt his blood to wash you in.

Christiana: But if he parts with his righteousness to us, what will he have for himself?

Mr. Great-Heart: He has more righteousness than you have need of, or than he needeth himself.

Christiana: Pray make that appear.

Mr. Great-Heart: With all my heart: but first I must premise, that he of whom we are now about to speak, is one that has not his fellow: He has two natures in one person, plain to be distinguished, impossible to be divided. Unto each of these natures a righteousness belongeth, and each righteousness is essential to that nature; so that one may as easily cause that nature to be extinct, as to separate its justice or righteousness from it. Of these righteousnesses therefore, we are not made partakers, so as that they, or any of them, should be put upon us, that we might be made just, and live thereby. Besides these, there is a righteousness which this person has, as these two natures are joined in one. And this is not the righteousness of the Godhead, as distinguished from the manhood; nor the righteousness of the manhood, as distinguished from the Godhead; but a righteousness which standeth in the union of both natures, and may properly be called the righteousness that is essential to his being prepared of God to the capacity of the mediatory office, which he was to be entrusted with. If he parts with his first righteousness, he parts with his Godhead; if he parts with his second righteousness, he parts with the purity of his manhood; if he parts with his third, he parts with that perfection that capacitates him to the office of mediation. He has therefore another righteousness, which standeth in performance, or obedience to a revealed will; and that is what he puts upon sinners, and that by which their sins are covered. Wherefore he saith, "As by one man's disobedience many were made sinners, so by the obedience of one shall many be made righteous."

Christiana: But are the other righteousnesses of no use to us?

Mr. Great-Heart: Yes; for though they are essential to his natures and office, and cannot be communicated unto another, yet it is by virtue of them that the righteousness that justifies is for that purpose efficacious. The righteousness of his Godhead gives virtue to his obedience; the righteousness of his manhood giveth capability to his obedience to justify; and the righteousness that standeth in the union of these two natures to his office, giveth authority to that righteousness to do the work for which it was ordained.

So then here is a righteousness that Christ, as God, has no need of; for he is God without it: Here is a righteousness that Christ, as man, has no need of to make him so; for he is perfect man without it. Again, here is a righteousness that Christ, as God-man, has no need of; for he is perfectly so without it. Here then is a righteousness that Christ, as God, and as God-man, has no need of, with reference to himself, and therefore he can spare it; a justifying righteousness, that he for himself wanteth not, and therefore giveth it away: Hence it is called the gift of righteousness. This righteousness, since Christ Jesus the Lord has made himself under the law, must be given away; for the law doth not only bind him that is under it, to do justly, but to use charity. Wherefore he must, or ought by the law, if he hath two coats, to give one to him that hath none. Now, our Lord indeed hath two coats, one for himself, and one to spare; wherefore he freely bestows one upon those that have none. And thus, Christiana and Mercy, and the rest of you that are here, doth your pardon come by deed, or by the work of another man. Your Lord Christ is he that worked, and hath given away what he wrought for, to the next poor beggar he meets.

But again, in order to pardon by deed, there must something be paid to God as a price, as well as something prepared to cover us withal. Sin has delivered us up to the just curse of a righteous law: now from this curse we must be justified by way of redemption, a price being paid for the harms we have done; and this is by the blood of your Lord, who came and stood in your place and stead, and died your death for your transgressions: Thus has he ransomed you from your transgressions by blood, and covered your polluted and deformed souls with righteousness, for the sake of which, God passeth by you and will not hurt you when he comes to judge the world.

Christiana: This is brave! Now I see that there was something to be learned by our being pardoned by word and deed. Good Mercy, let us labor to keep this in mind:

and, my children, do you remember it also. But, sir, was not this it that made my good Christian's burden fall from off his shoulder, and that made him give three leaps for joy?

Mr. Great-Heart: Yes, it was the belief of this that cut those strings that could not be cut by other means; and it was to give him a proof of the virtue of this, that he was suffered to carry his burden to the cross.

Christiana: I thought so; for though my heart was lightsome and joyous before, yet it is ten times more lightsome and joyous now. And I am persuaded by what I have felt, though I have felt but little as yet, that if the most burdened man in the world was here, and did see and believe as I now do, it would make his heart the more merry and blithe.

Mr. Great-Heart: There is not only comfort and the ease of a burden brought to us by the sight and consideration of these, but an endeared affection begot in us by it: for who can, if he doth but once think that pardon comes not only by promise but thus, but be affected with the way and means of his redemption, and so with the man that hath wrought it for him?

Christiana: True; methinks it makes my heart bleed to think that he should bleed for me. Oh, thou loving One: Oh, thou blessed One. Thou deservest to have me; thou hast bought me. Thou deservest to have me all: thou hast paid for me ten thousand times more than I am worth. No marvel that this made the tears stand in my husband's eyes, and that it made him trudge so nimbly on. I am persuaded he wished me with him: but, vile wretch that I was, I let him come all alone. Oh, Mercy, that thy father and mother were here; yea, and Mrs. Timorous also: nay, I wish now with all my heart that here was Madam Wanton too. Surely, surely, their hearts would be affected; nor could the fear of the one, nor the powerful lusts of the other, prevail with them to go home again, and to refuse to become good pilgrims.

Mr. Great-Heart: You speak now in the warmth of your affections; will it, think you, be always thus with you? Besides, this is not communicated to every one, nor to every one that did see your Jesus bleed. There were that stood by, and that saw the blood run from the heart to the ground, and yet were so far off this, that instead of lamenting, they laughed at him, and, instead of becoming his disciples, did harden their hearts against him. So that all that you have, my daughters, you have by peculiar impression made by a divine contemplating upon what I have spoken to you. Remember, that 'twas told you, that the hen, by her common call, gives no meat to her chickens. This you have therefore by a special grace.

Now I saw in my dream, that they went on until they were come to the place that Simple, and Sloth, and Presumption, lay and slept in when Christian went by on pilgrimage: and behold, they were hanged up in irons a little way off on the other side.

Mercy: Then said Mercy to him that was their guide and conductor, what are these three men; and for what are they hanged there?

Mr. Great-Heart: These three men were men of very bad qualities; they had no mind to be pilgrims themselves, and whomsoever they could, they hindered. They were sloth and folly themselves, and whomsoever they could persuade they made so too, and withal taught them to presume that they should do well at last. They were asleep when Christian went by; and now you go by, they are hanged.

Mercy: But could they persuade any to be of their opinion?

Mr. Great-Heart: Yes, they turned several out of the way. There was Slow-pace that they persuaded to do as they. They also prevailed with one Short-wind, with one No-heart, with one Linger-after-Lust, and with one Sleepy-head, and with a young woman, her name was Dull, to turn out of the way and become as they. Besides, they brought up an ill report of your Lord, persuading others that he was a hard taskmaster. They also brought up an evil report of the good Land, saying, it was not half so good as some pretended it was. They also began to vilify his servants, and to count the best of them meddlesome, troublesome busybodies. Further, they would call the bread of God husks; the comforts of his children, fancies; the travel and labor of pilgrims, things to no purpose.

Christiana: Nay, said Christiana, if they were such, they shall never be bewailed by me: they have but what they deserve; and I think it is well that they stand so near the highway, that others may see and take warning. But had it not been well if their crimes had been engraven in some plate of iron or brass, and left here where they did their mischiefs, for a caution to other bad men?

Mr. Great-Heart: So it is, as you may well perceive, if you will go a little to the wall.

Mercy: No, no; let them hang, and their names rot, and their crimes live forever against them. I think it a high favor that they were hanged before we came hither: who knows else what they might have done to such poor women as we are? Then she turned it into a song, saying,

"Now then you three hang there, and be a sign
To all that shall against the truth combine.
And let him that comes after, fear this end,
If unto pilgrims he is not a friend.
And thou, my soul, of all such men beware,
That unto holiness opposers are."

Thus they went on till they came to the foot of the hill Difficulty, where again the good Mr. Great-Heart took an occasion to tell them what happened there when Christian himself went by. So he had them first to the spring. Lo, saith he, this is the spring that Christian drank of before he went up this hill: and then it was clear and good; but now it is dirty with the feet of some that are not desirous that pilgrims here should quench their thirst. Thereat Mercy said, And why so envious, trow? But, said their guide, it will do, if taken up and put into a vessel that is sweet and good; for then the dirt will sink to the bottom, and the water come out by itself more clear. Thus therefore Christiana and her companions were compelled to do. They took it up, and put it into an earthen pot, and so let it stand till the dirt was gone to the bottom, and then they drank thereof.

Next he showed them the two by-ways that were at the foot of the hill, where Formality and Hypocrisy lost themselves. And, said he, these are dangerous paths. Two were here cast away when Christian came by; and although, as you see these ways are since stopped up with chains, posts, and a ditch, yet there are those that will choose to adventure here rather than take the pains to go up this hill.

Christiana: "The way of transgressors is hard." It is a wonder that they can get into these ways without danger of breaking their necks.

Mr. Great-Heart: They will venture: yea, if at any time any of the King's servants do happen to see them, and do call upon them, and tell them that they are in the wrong way, and do bid them beware of the danger, then they railingly return them answer, and say, "As for the word that thou hast spoken unto us in the name of the King, we will not hearken unto thee; but we will certainly do whatsoever thing goeth out of our own mouths." Nay, if you look a little further, you shall see that these ways are made cautionary enough, not only by these posts, and ditch, and chain, but also by being hedged up: yet they will choose to go there.

Christiana: They are idle; they love not to take pains; up-hill way is unpleasant to them. So it is fulfilled unto them as it is written, "The way of the slothful man is full of thorns." Yea, they will rather choose to walk upon a snare than to go up this hill, and the rest of this way to the city.

Then they set forward, and began to go up the hill, and up the hill they went. But before they got to the top, Christiana began to pant, and said, I dare say this is a breathing hill; no marvel if they that love their ease more than their souls choose to themselves a smoother way.

Then said Mercy, I must sit down: also the least of the children began to cry. Come, come, said Great-Heart, sit not down here; for a little above is the Prince's arbor. Then he took the little boy by the hand, and led him up thereto.

When they were come to the arbor, they were very willing to sit down, for they were all in a pelting heat. Then said Mercy, "How sweet is rest to them that labor." and how good is the Prince of pilgrims to provide such resting-places for them! Of this arbor I have heard much; but I never saw it before. But here let us beware of sleeping; for, as I have heard, it cost poor Christian dear.

Then said Mr. Great-Heart to the little ones, Come, my pretty boys, how do you do? What think you now of going on pilgrimage? Sir, said the least, I was almost beat out of heart; but I thank you for lending me a hand at my need. And I remember now what my mother hath told me, namely, that the way to heaven is as a ladder, and the way to hell is as down a hill. But I had rather go up the ladder to life, than down the hill to death.

Then said Mercy, But the proverb is, "To go down the hill is easy." But James said, (for that was his name,) The day is coming when, in my opinion, when going down the hill will be the hardest of all. 'Tis a good boy, said his master; thou hast given her a right answer. Then Mercy smiled, but the little boy did blush.

Christiana: Come, said Christiana, will you eat a bit to sweeten your mouths, while you sit here to rest your legs? for I have here a piece of pomegranate which Mr. Interpreter put into my hand just when I came out of his door; he gave me also a piece of an honeycomb, and a little bottle of spirits. I thought he gave you something, said Mercy, because he called you aside. Yes, so he did, said the other; but, said Christiana, it shall be still as I said it should, when at first we came from home; thou shalt be a sharer in all the good that I have, because thou so willingly didst become my companion. Then she gave to them, and they did eat, both Mercy and the boys. And said Christiana to Mr. Great-Heart, Sir, will you do as we? But he answered, You are going on pilgrimage, and presently I shall return; much good may what you have do you: at home I eat the same every day.

Lesson 84 (no reading for Lesson 83)

- Read Book 2, Stage 4 of *The Pilgrim's Progress*.

Book 2, Stage 4

Now when they had eaten and drank, and had chatted a little longer, their guide said to them, The day wears away; if you think good, let us prepare to be going. So they got up to go, and the little boys went before; But Christiana forgot to take her bottle of spirits with her, so she sent her little boy back to fetch it. Then said Mercy, I think this is a losing place: here Christian lost his roll, and here Christiana left her bottle behind her. Sir, what is the cause of this? So their guide made answer, and said, The cause is sleep, or forgetfulness: some sleep when they should keep awake, and some forget when they should remember; and this is the very cause why often, at the resting-places, some pilgrims in some things come off losers. Pilgrims should watch, and remember what they have already received, under their greatest enjoyments; but for want of doing so, oftentimes their rejoicing ends in tears, and their sunshine in a cloud: witness the story of Christian at this place.

When they were come to the place where Mistrust and Timorous met Christian, to persuade him to go back for fear of the lions, they perceived as it were a stage, and before it, towards the road, a broad plate with a copy of verses written thereon, and underneath the reason of raising up that stage in that place rendered. The verses were,

"Let him that sees this stage, take heed
  Unto his heart and tongue;
Lest, if he do not, here he speed
  As some have long agone."

The words underneath the verses were, "This stage was built to punish those upon, who, through timorousness or mistrust, shall be afraid to go further on pilgrimage. Also, on this stage both Mistrust and Timorous were burned through the tongue with a hot iron, for endeavoring to hinder Christian on his journey."

Then said Mercy, This is much like to the saying of the Beloved: "What shall be given unto thee, or what shall be done unto thee, thou false tongue? Sharp arrows of the mighty, with coals of juniper.

So they went on till they came within sight of the lions. Now Mr. Great-Heart was a strong man, so he was not afraid of a lion: But yet when they were come up to the place where the lions were, the boys, that went before, were now glad to cringe behind, for they were afraid of the lions; so they stepped back, and went behind. At this their guide smiled, and said, How now, my boys; do you love to go before when no danger doth approach, and love to come behind so soon as the lions appear?

Now, as they went on, Mr. Great-heart drew his sword, with intent to make a way for the pilgrims in spite of the lions. Then there appeared one that, it seems, had taken upon him to back the lions; and he said to the pilgrims' guide, What is the cause of your coming hither? Now the name of that man was Grim, or Bloody-man because of his slaying of pilgrims; and he was of the race of the giants.

Mr. Great-Heart: Then said the pilgrims' guide, These women and children are going on pilgrimage, and this is the way they must go; and go it they shall, in spite of thee and the lions.

Grim: This is not their way, neither shall they go therein. I am come forth to withstand them, and to that end will back the lions.

Now, to say the truth, by reason of the fierceness of the lions, and of the grim carriage of him that did back them, this way had of late lain much unoccupied, and was almost grown over with grass.

Christiana: Then said Christiana, Though the highways have been unoccupied heretofore, and though the travellers have been made in times past to walk through by-paths, it must not be so now I am risen, now I am risen a mother in Israel.

Grim: Then he swore by the lions that it should; and therefore bid them turn aside, for they should not have passage there.

But Great-Heart their guide made first his approach unto Grim, and laid so heavily on him with his sword that he forced him to retreat.

Grim: Then said he that attempted to back the lions, Will you slay me upon mine own ground?

Mr. Great-Heart: It is the King's highway that we are in, and in this way it is that thou hast placed the lions; but these women, and these children, though weak, shall hold on their way in spite of thy lions. And with that he gave him again a downright blow, and brought him upon his knees. With this blow also he broke his helmet, and with the next he cut off an arm. Then did the giant roar so hideously that his voice frightened the women, and yet they were glad to see him lie sprawling upon the ground. Now the lions were chained, and so of themselves could do nothing. Wherefore, when old Grim, that intended to back them, was dead, Mr. Great-Heart said to the pilgrims, Come now, and follow me, and no hurt shall happen to you from the lions. They therefore went on, but the women trembled as they passed by them; the boys also looked as if they would die; but they all got by without further hurt.

Now, when they were within sight of the Porter's lodge, they soon came up unto it; but they made the more haste after this to go thither, because it is dangerous traveling there in the night. So when they were come to the gate, the guide knocked, and the Porter cried, Who is there? But as soon as the guide had said, It is I, he knew his voice, and came down, for the guide had oft before that come thither as a conductor of pilgrims. When he was come down, he opened the gate; and seeing the guide standing just before it, (for he saw not the women, for they were behind him,) he said unto him, How now, Mr. Great-Heart, what is your business here so late at night? I have brought, said he, some pilgrims hither, where, by my Lord's commandment, they must lodge: I had been here some time ago, had I not been opposed by the giant that did use to back the lions. But I, after a long and tedious combat with him, have cut him off, and have brought the pilgrims hither in safety.

The Porter: Will you not go in, and stay till morning?

Mr. Great-Heart: No, I will return to my Lord to-night.

Christiana: O, sir, I know not how to be willing you should leave us in our pilgrimage: you have been so faithful and loving to us, you have fought so stoutly for us, you have been so hearty in counselling of us, that I shall never forget your favor towards us.

Mercy: Then said Mercy, O that we might have thy company to our journey's end! How can such poor women as we hold out in a way so full of troubles as this way is, without a friend and defender?

James: Then said James, the youngest of the boys, Pray, sir, be persuaded to go with us, and help us, because we are so weak, and the way so dangerous as it is.

Mr. Great-Heart: I am at my Lord's commandment; if he shall allot me to be your guide quite through, I will willingly wait upon you. But here you failed at first; for when he bid me come thus far with you, then you should have begged me of him to have gone quite through with you, and he would have granted your request. However, at present I must withdraw; and so, good Christiana, Mercy, and my brave children, adieu.

Then the Porter, Mr. Watchful, asked Christiana of her country, and of her kindred. And she said, I came from the city of Destruction. I am a widow woman, and my husband is dead, his name was Christian, the pilgrim. How! said the Porter, was he your husband? Yes, said she, and these are his children and this, pointing to Mercy, is one of my town's-women. Then the Porter rang his bell, as at such times he is wont, and there come to the door one of the damsels, whose name was Humble-Mind; and to her the Porter said, Go tell it within, that Christiana, the wife of Christian, and her children, are come hither on pilgrimage. She went in, therefore, and told it. But oh, what noise for gladness was there within when the damsel did but drop that out of her mouth!

So they came with haste to the Porter, for Christana stood still at the door. Then some of the most grave said unto her, Come in, Christiana, come in, thou wife of that good man; come in, thou blessed woman, come in, with all that are with thee. So she went in, and they followed her that were her children and companions. Now when they were gone in, they were had into a large room, where they were bidden to sit down: so they sat down, and the chief of the house were called to see and welcome the guests. Then they came in, and understanding who they were, did salute each other with a kiss, and said, Welcome, ye vessels of the grace of God; welcome to us, your friends.

Now, because it was somewhat late, and because the pilgrims were weary with their journey, and also made faint with the sight of the fight, and of the terrible lions, they desired, as soon as might be, to prepare to go to rest. Nay, said those of the family, refresh yourselves first with a morsel of meat; for they had prepared for them a lamb, with the accustomed sauce belonging thereto, for the Porter had heard before of their coming, and had told it to them within. So when they had supped, and ended their prayer with a psalm, they desired they might go to rest.

But let us, said Christiana, if we may be so bold as to choose, be in that chamber that was my husband's when he was here; so they had them up thither, and they all lay in a room. When they were at rest, Christiana and Mercy entered into discourse about things that were convenient.

Christiana: Little did I think once, when my husband went on pilgrimage, that I should ever have followed him.

Mercy: And you as little thought of lying in his bed, and in his chamber to rest, as you do now.

Christiana: And much less did I ever think of seeing his face with comfort, and of worshiping the Lord the King with him; and yet now I believe I shall.

Mercy: Hark, don't you hear a noise?

Christiana: Yes, it is, as I believe, a noise of music, for joy that we are here.

Mercy: Wonderful! Music in the house, music in the heart, and music also in heaven, for joy that we are here! Thus they talked a while, and then betook themselves to sleep.

So in the morning when they were awake, Christiana said to Mercy, What was the matter that you did laugh in your sleep to-night? I suppose you were in a dream.

Mercy: So I was, and a sweet dream it was; but are you sure I laughed?

Christiana: Yes, you laughed heartily; but prithee, Mercy, tell me thy dream.

Mercy: I was a dreaming that I sat all alone in a solitary place, and was bemoaning of the hardness of my heart. Now I had not sat there long but methought many were gathered about me to see me, and to hear what it was that I said. So they hearkened, and I went on bemoaning the hardness of my heart. At this, some of them laughed at me, some called me fool, and some began to thrust me about. With that, methought I looked up and saw one coming with wings towards me. So he came directly to me, and said, Mercy, what aileth thee? Now when he had heard me make my complaint, he said, Peace be to thee; he also wiped my eyes with his handkerchief, and clad me in silver and gold. He put a chain about my neck, and ear-rings in mine ears, and a beautiful crown upon my head. Then he took me by the hand, and said, Mercy, come after me. So he went up, and I followed till we came at a golden gate. Then he knocked; and when they within had opened, the man went in, and I followed him up to a throne, upon which one sat; and he said to me, Welcome, daughter. The place looked bright and twinkling, like the stars, or rather like the sun, and I thought that I saw your husband there; so I awoke from my dream. But did I laugh?

Christiana: Laugh! aye, and well you might to see yourself so well. For you must give me leave to tell you that it was a good dream; and that, as you have begun to find the first part true, so you shall find the second at last. "God speaks once, yea, twice, yet man perceiveth it not; in a dream, in a vision of the night, when deep sleep falleth upon men, in slumberings upon the bed." We need not, when abed, to lie awake to talk with God; he can visit us while we sleep, and cause us then to hear his voice. Our heart oftentimes wakes when we sleep, and God can speak to that, either by words, by proverbs, by signs and similitudes, as well as if one was awake.

Mercy: Well, I am glad of my dream; for I hope ere long to see it fulfilled, to the making me laugh again.

Christiana: I think it is now high time to rise, and to know what we must do.

Mercy: Pray, if they invite us to stay a while, let us willingly accept of the proffer. I am the more willing to stay a while here, to grow better acquainted with these maids: methinks Prudence, Piety, and Charity, have very comely and sober countenances.

Christiana: We shall see what they will do.

So when they were up and ready, they came down, and they asked one another of their rest, and if it was comfortable or not.

Mercy: Very good, said Mercy: it was one of the best night's lodgings that ever I had in my life.

Then said Prudence and Piety, If you will be persuaded to stay here a while, you shall have what the house will afford.

Charity: Aye, and that with a very good will, said Charity. So they consented, and stayed there about a month or above, and became very profitable one to another. And because Prudence would see how Christiana had brought up her children, she asked leave of her to catechise them. So she gave her free consent. Then she began with her youngest, whose name was James.

Prudence: And she said, Come, James, canst thou tell me who made thee?

James: God the Father, God the Son, and God the Holy Ghost.

Prudence: Good boy. And canst thou tell who saved thee?

James: God the Father, God the Son, and God the Holy Ghost.

Prudence: Good boy still. But how doth God the Father save thee?

James: By his grace.

Prudence: How doth God the Son save thee?

James: By his righteousness, death and blood, and life.

Prudence: And how doth God the Holy Ghost save thee?

James: By his illumination, by his renovation, and by his preservation.

Then said Prudence to Christiana, You are to be commended for thus bringing up your children. I suppose I need not ask the rest these questions, since the youngest of them can answer them so well. I will therefore now apply myself to the next youngest.

Prudence: Then she said, Come, Joseph, (for his name was Joseph,) will you let me catechise you?

Joseph: With all my heart.

Prudence: What is man?

Joseph: A reasonable creature, so made by God, as my brother said.

Prudence: What is supposed by this word, saved?

Joseph: That man, by sin, has brought himself into a state of captivity and misery.

Prudence: What is supposed by his being saved by the Trinity?

Joseph: That sin is so great and mighty a tyrant that none can pull us out of its clutches but God; and that God is so good and loving to man, as to pull him indeed out of this miserable state.

Prudence: What is God's design in saving poor men?

Joseph: The glorifying of his name, of his grace, and justice, etc., and the everlasting happiness of his creature.

Prudence: Who are they that will be saved?

Joseph: They that accept of his salvation.

Prudence: Good boy, Joseph; thy mother hath taught thee well, and thou hast hearkened unto what she has said unto thee.

Then said Prudence to Samuel, who was the eldest but one,

Prudence: Come, Samuel, are you willing that I should catechise you?

Samuel: Yes, forsooth, if you please.

Prudence: What is heaven?

Samuel: A place and state most blessed, because God dwelleth there.

Prudence: What is hell?

Samuel: A place and state most woful, because it is the dwelling-place of sin, the devil, and death.

Prudence: Why wouldst thou go to heaven?

Samuel: That I may see God, and serve him without weariness; that I may see Christ, and love him everlastingly; that I may have that fullness of the Holy Spirit in me which I can by no means here enjoy.

Prudence: A very good boy, and one that has learned well.

Then she addressed herself to the eldest, whose name was Matthew; and she said to him, Come, Matthew, shall I also catechise you?

Matthew: With a very good will.

Prudence: I ask then, if there was ever any thing that had a being antecedent to or before God?

Matthew: No, for God is eternal; nor is there any thing, excepting himself, that had a being until the beginning of the first day. For in six days the Lord made heaven and earth, the sea, and all that in them is.

Prudence: What do you think of the Bible?

Matthew: It is the holy word of God.

Prudence: Is there nothing written therein but what you understand?

Matthew: Yes, a great deal.

Prudence: What do you do when you meet with places therein that you do not understand?

Matthew: I think God is wiser than I. I pray also that he will please to let me know all therein that he knows will be for my good.

Prudence: How believe you as touching the resurrection of the dead?

Matthew: I believe they shall rise the same that was buried; the same in nature, though not in corruption. And I believe this upon a double account: first, because God has promised it; secondly, because he is able to perform it.

Then said Prudence to the boys, You must still hearken to your mother; for she can teach you more. You must also diligently give ear to what good talk you shall hear from others: for your sakes do they speak good things. Observe also, and that with carefulness, what the heavens and the earth do teach you; but especially be much in the meditation of that book which was the cause of your father's becoming a pilgrim. I, for my part, my children, will teach you what I can while you are here, and shall be glad if you will ask me questions that tend to godly edifying.

Now by that these pilgrim's had been at this place a week, Mercy had a visitor that pretended some good-will unto her, and his name was Mr. Brisk; a man of some breeding, and that pretended to religion, but a man that stuck very close to the world. So he came once or twice, or more, to Mercy, and offered love unto her. Now Mercy was of a fair countenance, and therefore the more alluring.

Her mind also was to be always busying of herself in doing; for when she had nothing to do for herself, she would be making hose and garments for others, and would bestow them upon those that had need. And Mr. Brisk not knowing where or how she disposed of what she made, seemed to be greatly taken, for that he found her never idle. I will warrant her a good housewife, quoth he to himself.

Mercy then revealed the business to the maidens that were of the house, and inquired of them concerning him, for they did know him better than she. So they told her that he was a very busy young man, and one who pretended to religion, but was, as they feared, a stranger to the power of that which is good.

Nay then, said Mercy, I will look no more on him; for I purpose never to have a clog to my soul.

Prudence then replied, that there needed no matter of great discouragement to be given to him; her continuing so as she had begun to do for the poor, would quickly cool his courage.

So the next time he comes he finds her at her old work, making things for the poor. Then said he, What, always at it? Yes, said she, either for myself or for others. And what canst thou earn a day? said he. I do these things, said she, that I may be rich in good works, laying up in store for myself a good foundation against the time to come, that I may lay hold on eternal life. Why, prithee, what doest thou with them? said he. Clothe the naked, said she. With that his countenance fell. So he forbore to come at her again. And when he was asked the reason why, he said, that Mercy was a pretty lass, but troubled with ill conditions.

When he had left her, Prudence said, Did I not tell thee that Mr. Brisk would soon forsake thee? yea, he will rise up an ill report of thee; for, notwithstanding his pretence to religion, and his seeming love to Mercy, yet Mercy and he are of tempers so different that I believe they will never come together.

Mercy: I might have had husbands before now, though I spoke not of it to any; but they were such as did not like my conditions, though never did any of them find fault with my person. So they and I could not agree.

Prudence: Mercy in our days is but little set by any further than as to its name: the practice which is set forth by thy conditions, there are but few that can abide.

Mercy: Well, said Mercy, if nobody will have me, I will die unmarried, or my conditions shall be to me as a husband: for I cannot change my nature; and to have one who lies cross to me in this, that I purpose never to admit of as long as I live. I had a sister named Bountiful, that was married to one of these churls, but he and she could never agree; but because my sister was resolved to do as she had begun, that is, to show kindness to the poor, therefore her husband first cried her down at the cross, and then turned her out of his doors.

Prudence: And yet he was a professor, I warrant you?

Mercy: Yes, such a one as he was, and of such as he the world is now full: but I am for none of them all.

Now Matthew, the eldest son of Christiana, fell sick, and his sickness was sore upon him, for he was much pained in his bowels, so that he was with it at times pulled, as it were, both ends together. There dwelt also not far from thence one Mr. Skill, an ancient and well-approved physician. So Christiana desired it, and entered the room, and had a little observed the boy, he concluded that he was sick of the gripes. Then he said to his mother, What diet has Matthew of late fed upon? Diet! said Christiana, nothing but what is wholesome. The physician answered, This boy has been tampering with something that lies in his stomach undigested, and that will not away without means. And I tell you he must be purged, or else he will die.

Samuel: Then said Samuel, Mother, what was that which my brother did gather up and eat as soon as we were come from the gate that is at the head of this way? You know that there was an orchard on the left hand, on the other side of the wall, and some of the trees hung over the wall, and my brother did pluck and eat.

Christiana: True, my child, said Christiana, he did take thereof, and did eat: naughty boy as he was, I chid him, and yet he would eat thereof.

Mr. Skill: I knew he had eaten something that was not wholesome food; and that food, to wit, that fruit, is even the most hurtful of all. It is the fruit of Beelzebub's orchard. I do marvel that none did warn you of it; many have died thereof.

Christiana: Then Christiana began to cry; and she said, Oh, naughty boy! and Oh, careless mother! what shall I do for my son?

Mr. Skill: Come, do not be too much dejected; the boy may do well again, but he must purge and vomit.

Christiana: Pray, sir, try the utmost of your skill with him, whatever it costs.

Mr. Skill: Nay, I hope I shall be reasonable. So he made him a purge, but it was too weak; it was said it was made of the blood of a goat, the ashes of a heifer, and some of the juice of hyssop. When Mr. Skill had seen that that purge was too weak, he made one to the purpose. It was made *ex carne et sanguine Christi*, [of the flesh and blood of Christ]. (you know physicians give strange medicines to their patients:) and it was made into pills, with a promise or two, and a proportionable quantity of salt. Now, he was to take them three at a time, fasting, in half a quarter of a pint of the tears of repentance.

When this potion was prepared, and brought to the boy, he was loth to take it, though torn with the gripes as if he should be pulled in pieces. Come, come, said the physician, you must take it. It goes against my stomach, said the boy. I must have you take it, said his mother. I shall vomit it up again, said the boy. Pray, sir, said Christiana to Mr. Skill, how does it taste? It has no ill taste, said the doctor;

and with that she touched one of the pills with the tip of her tongue. Oh, Matthew, said she, this potion is sweeter than honey. If thou lovest thy mother, if thou lovest thy brothers, if thou lovest Mercy, if thou lovest thy life, take it. So, with much ado, after a short prayer for the blessing of God upon it, he took it, and it wrought kindly with him. It caused him to purge; it caused him to sleep, and to rest quietly; it put him into a fine heat and breathing sweat, and did quite rid him of his gripes. So in a little time he got up, and walked about with a staff, and would go from room to room, and talk with Prudence, Piety, and Charity, of his distemper, and how he was healed.

So when the boy was healed, Christiana asked Mr. Skill, saying, Sir, what will content you for your pains and care to and of my child? And he said, You must pay the master of the College of Physicians, according to rules made in that case and provided.

Christiana: But, sir, said she, what is this pill good for else?

Mr. Skill: It is a universal pill; it is good against all the diseases that pilgrims are incident to; and when it is well prepared, it will keep good, time out of mind.

Christiana: Pray, sir, make me up twelve boxes of them; for if I can get these, I will never take other physic.

Mr. Skill: These pills are good to prevent diseases, as well as to cure when one is sick. Yea, I dare say it, and stand to it, that if a man will but use this physic as he should, it will make him live for ever. But, good Christiana, thou must give these pills no other way but as I have prescribed; for if you do, they will do no good. So he gave unto Christiana physic for herself, and her boys, and for Mercy; and bid Matthew take heed how he ate any more green plums; and kissed them, and went his way.

It was told you before, that Prudence bid the boys, that if at any time they would, they should ask her some questions that might be profitable and she would say something to them.

Matthew: Then Matthew, who had been sick, asked her, why for the most part physic should be bitter to our palates.

Prudence: To show how unwelcome the word of God and the effects thereof are to a carnal heart.

Matthew: Why does physic, if it does good, purge, and cause to vomit?

Prudence: To show that the word, when it works effectually, cleanseth the heart and mind. For look, what the one doth to the body, the other doth to the soul.

Matthew: What should we learn by seeing the flame of our fire go upwards, and by seeing the beams and sweet influences of the sun strike downwards?

Prudence: By the going up of the fire, we are taught to ascend to heaven by fervent and hot desires. And by the sun sending his heat, beams, and sweet influences downwards, we are taught the Saviour of the world, though high, reaches down with his grace and love to us below.

Matthew: Whence have the clouds their water?

Prudence: Out of the sea.

Matthew: What may we learn from that?

Prudence: That ministers should fetch their doctrine from God.

Matthew: Why do they empty themselves upon the earth?

Prudence: To show that ministers should give out what they know of God to the world.

Matthew: Why is the rainbow caused by the sun?

Prudence: To show that the covenant of God's grace is confirmed to us in Christ.

Matthew: Why do the springs come from the sea to us through the earth?

Prudence: To show that the grace of God comes to us through the body of Christ.

Matthew: Why do some of the springs rise out of the tops of high hills?

Prudence: To show that the Spirit of grace shall spring up in some that are great and mighty, as well as in many that are poor and low.

Matthew: Why doth the fire fasten upon the candle-wick?

Prudence: To show that unless grace doth kindle upon the heart, there will be no true light of life in us.

Matthew: Why are the wick, and tallow and all, spent to maintain the light of the candle?

Prudence: To show that body and soul, and all, should be at the service of, and spend themselves to maintain in good condition that grace of God that is in us.

Matthew: Why doth the pelican pierce her own breast with her bill?

Prudence: To nourish her young ones with her blood, and thereby to show that Christ the blessed so loved his young, (his people,) as to save them from death by his blood.

Matthew: What may one learn by hearing the cock to crow?

Prudence: Learn to remember Peter's sin, and Peter's repentance. The cock's crowing shows also, that day is coming on: let, then, the crowing of the cock put thee in mind of that last and terrible day of judgment.

Now about this time their month was out; wherefore they signified to those of the house, that it was convenient for them to up and be going. Then said Joseph to his mother, It is proper that you forget not to send to the house of Mr. Interpreter, to pray him to grant that Mr. Great-Heart should be sent unto us, that he may be our conductor for the rest of the way. Good boy, said she, I had almost forgot. So she drew up a petition, and prayed Mr. Watchful the porter to send it by some fit man to her good friend Mr. Interpreter; who, when it was come, and he had seen the contents of the petition, said to the messenger, Go, tell them that I will send him.

When the family where Christiana was, saw that they had a purpose to go forward, they called the whole house together, to give thanks to their King for sending of them such profitable guests as these. Which done, they said unto Christiana, And shall we not show thee something, as our custom is to do to pilgrims, on which thou mayest meditate when thou art upon the way? So they took Christiana, her children, and Mercy, into the closet, and showed them one of the apples that Eve ate of, and that she also did give to her husband, and that for the eating of which they were both turned out of paradise, and asked her what she thought that was. Then Christiana said, It is food or poison, I know not which. So they opened the matter to her, and she held up her hands and wondered.

Then they had her to a place, and showed her Jacob's ladder. Now at that time there were some angels ascending upon it. So Christiana looked and looked to see the angels go up: so did the rest of the company. Then they were going into another place, to show them something else; but James said to his mother, Pray, bid them stay here a little longer, for this is a curious sight. So they turned again, and stood feeding their eyes with this so pleasant a prospect.

After this, they had them into a place where did hang up a golden anchor. So they bid Christiana take it down; for said they, You shall have it with you, for it is of absolute necessity that you should, that you may lay hold of that within the veil, and stand stedfast in case you should meet with turbulent weather, so they were glad thereof.

Then they took them, and had them to the mount upon which Abraham our father offered up Isaac his son, and showed them the altar, the wood, the fire, and the knife, for they remain to be seen to this very day. When they had seen it, they held up their hands, and blessed themselves, and said, Oh, what a man for love to his Master, and for denial to himself, was Abraham!

After they had showed them all these things, Prudence took them into a dining room, where stood a pair of excellent virginals [a musical instrument]; so she played upon them, and turned what she had showed them into this excellent song, saying,

"Eve's apple we have showed you;

  Of that be you aware:
You have seen Jacob's ladder too,
  Upon which angels are.
An anchor you received have;
  But let not these suffice,
Until with Abra'm you have gave
  Your best, a sacrifice."

Now, about this time, one knocked at the door; so the Porter opened, and behold, Mr. Great-Heart was there. But when he was come in, what joy was there! for it came now afresh again into their minds, how but a while ago he had slain old Grim Bloody-man the giant, and had delivered them from the lions.

Then said Mr. Great-Heart to Christiana and to Mercy, My Lord has sent each of you a bottle of wine, and also some parched corn, together with a couple of pomegranates; he has also sent the boys some figs and raisins; to refresh you in your way.

Then they addressed themselves to their journey, and Prudence and Piety went along with them. When they came to the gate, Christiana asked the Porter if any of late went by. He said, No; only one, some time since, who also told me, that of late there had been a great robbery committed on the King's highway as you go. But, said he, the thieves are taken, and will shortly be tried for their lives. Then Christiana and Mercy were afraid; but Matthew said, Mother, fear nothing, as long as Mr. Great-Heart is to go with us, and to be our conductor.

Then said Christiana to the Porter, Sir, I am much obliged to you for all the kindnesses that you have showed to me since I came hither; and also for that you have been so loving and kind to my children. I know not how to gratify your kindness; wherefore, pray, as a token of my respect to you, accept of this small mite. So she put a gold angel [a coin valued at ten shillings sterling] in his hand; and he made her a low obeisance, and said, "Let thy garments be always white; and let thy head want no ointment." Let Mercy live and not die, and let not her works be few. And to the boys he said, Do you fly youthful lusts, and follow after godliness with them that are grave and wise, so shall you put gladness into your mother's heart, and obtain praise of all that are sober-minded. So they thanked the Porter, and departed.

Lesson 85

- Read Book 2, Stage 5 of *The Pilgrim's Progress.*

Book 2, Stage 5

Now I saw in my dream, that they went forward until they were come to the brow of the Hill; where Piety, bethinking herself, cried out, Alas, I have forgot what I intended to bestow upon Christiana and her companions: I will go back and fetch it. So she ran and fetched it. While she was gone, Christiana thought she heard, in a grove a little way off on the right hand, a most curious melodious note, with words much like these:

"Through all my life thy favor is
  So frankly showed to me,
That in thy House for evermore
  My dwelling-place shall be."

And listening still, she thought she heard another answer it, saying,

"For why? The Lord our God is good;
  His mercy is forever sure;
His truth at all times firmly stood,
  And shall from age to age endure."

So Christiana asked Prudence who it was that made those curious notes. They are, answered she, our country birds: they sing these notes but seldom, except it be at the spring, when the flowers appear, and the sun shines warm, and then you may hear them all day long. I often, said she, go out to hear them; we also oft-times keep them tame in our house. They are very fine company for us when we are melancholy: also they make the woods, and groves, and solitary places, places desirable to be in.

By this time Piety was come again. So she said to Christiana, Look here, I have brought thee a scheme of all those things that thou hast seen at our house, upon which thou mayest look when thou findest thyself forgetful, and call those things again to remembrance for thy edification and comfort.

Now they began to go down the hill into the Valley of Humiliation. It was a steep hill, and the way was slippery; but they were very careful; so they got down pretty well. When they were down in the valley, Piety said to Christiana, This is the place where Christian your husband met with the foul fiend Apollyon, and where they had that dreadful fight that they had: I know you cannot but have heard thereof. But be of good courage; as long as you have here Mr. Great-Heart to be your guide and conductor, we hope you will fare the better. So when these two had committed the pilgrims unto the conduct of their guide, he went forward, and they went after.

Mr. Great-Heart: Then said Mr. Great-Heart, We need not be so afraid of this valley, for here is nothing to hurt us, unless we procure it to ourselves. It is true, Christian did here meet with Apollyon, with whom he had also a sore combat: but that fray was the fruit of those slips that he got in his going down the hill: for they that get slips there, must look for combats here. And hence it is, that this valley has got so hard a name. For the common people, when they hear that some frightful thing has befallen such an one in such a place, are of opinion that that place is haunted with some foul fiend, or evil spirit; when, alas! it is for the fruit of their doing, that such things do befal them there. This Valley of Humiliation is of itself as fruitful a place as any the crow flies over; and I am persuaded, if we could hit upon it, we might find somewhere hereabouts something that might give us an account why Christian was so hardly beset in this place.

Then said James to his mother, Lo, yonder stands a pillar, and it looks as if something was written thereon; let us go and see what it is. So they went and found there written, "Let Christian's slips, before he came hither, and the battles that he met with in this place, be a warning to those that come after." Lo, said their guide, did not I tell you that there was something hereabouts that would give intimation of the reason why Christian was so hard beset in this place? Then turning to Christiana, he said, No disparagement to Christian more than to any others whose hap and lot it was. For it is easier going up than down this hill, and that can be said but of few hills in all these parts of the world. But we will leave the good man; he is at rest: he also had a brave victory over his enemy. Let Him grant, that dwelleth above, that we fare no worse, when we come be tried, than he.

But we will come again to this Valley of Humiliation. It is the best and most fruitful piece of ground in all those parts. It is fat ground, and as you see, consisteth much in meadows; and if a man was to come here in the summer-time, as we do now, if he knew not any thing before thereof, and if he also delighted himself in the sight of his eyes, he might see that which would be delightful to him. Behold how green this valley is; also how beautified with lillies. I have known many laboring men that have got good estates in this Valley of Humiliation; for God resisteth the proud, but giveth grace to the humble. Indeed it is a very fruitful soil, and doth bring forth by handfuls. Some also have wished that the next way to their Father's house were here, that they might be troubled no more with either hills or mountains to go over; but the way is the way, and there is an end.

Now, as they were going along, and talking, they espied a boy feeding his father's sheep. The boy was in very mean clothes, but of a very fresh and well-favored countenance; and as he sat by himself, he sung. Hark, said Mr. Great-Heart, to what the shepherd's boy saith. So they hearkened and he said,

"He that is down, needs fear no fall;
  He that is low, no pride:
He that is humble, ever shall
  Have God to be his guide.

I am content with what I have,
  Little be it or much;
And, Lord, contentment still I crave,
  Because thou savest such.

Fulness to such, a burden is,
  That go on pilgrimage;
Here little, and hereafter bliss,
  Is best from Age to Age."

Then said the guide, Do you hear him? I will dare to say, that this boy lives a merrier life, and wears more of that herb called heart's-ease in his bosom, than he that is clad in silk and velvet. But we will proceed in our discourse.

In this valley our Lord formerly had his country-house: he loved much to be here. He loved also to walk these meadows, for he found the air was pleasant. Besides, here a man shall be free from the noise, and from the hurryings of this life: all states are full of noise and confusion; only the Valley of Humiliation is that empty and solitary place. Here a man shall not be so let and hindered in his contemplation as in other places he is apt to be. This is a valley that nobody walks in but those that love a pilgrim's life. And though Christian had the hard hap to meet here with Apollyon, and to enter with him in a brisk encounter, yet I must tell you, that in former times men have met with angels here, have found pearls here, and have in this place found the words of life.

Did I say our Lord had here in former days his country-house, and that he loved here to walk? I will add-in this place, and to the people that love and trace these grounds, he has left a yearly revenue, to be faithfully paid them at certain seasons, for their maintenance by the way, and for their further encouragement to go on in their pilgrimage.

Samuel: Now, as they went on, Samuel said to Mr. Great-Heart, Sir, I perceive that in this valley my father and Apollyon had their battle; but whereabout was the fight? for I perceive this valley is large.

Mr. Great-Heart: Your father had the battle with Apollyon at a place yonder before us, in a narrow passage, just beyond Forgetful Green. And indeed that place is the most dangerous place in all these parts. For if at any time pilgrims meet with any brunt, it is when they forget what favours they have received, and how unworthy they are of them. This is the place also where others have been hard put to it. But more of the place when we are come to it; for I persuade myself that to this day there remains either some sign of the battle, or some monument to testify that such a battle there was fought.

Mercy: Then said Mercy, I think I am as well in this valley as I have been anywhere else in all our journey: the place, methinks, suits with my spirit. I love to be in such places, where there is no rattling with coaches, nor rumbling with wheels.

Methinks, here one may, without much molestation, be thinking what he is, whence he came, what he has done, and to what the King has called him. Here one may think, and break at heart, and melt in one's spirit, until one's eyes become as the fish-pools in Heshbon. They that go rightly through this valley of Baca, make it a well; the rain that God sends down from heaven upon them that are here, also filleth the pools. This valley is that from whence also the King will give to his their vineyards; and they that go through it shall sing, as Christian did, for all he met with Apollyon.

Mr. Great-Heart: 'Tis true, said their guide; I have gone through this valley many a time, and never was better than when here. I have also been a conduct to several pilgrims, and they have confessed the same. "To this man will I look," saith the King, "even to him that is poor, and of a contrite spirit, and trembleth at my word."

Now they were come to the place where the aforementioned battle was fought: Then said the guide to Christiana, her children, and Mercy, This is the place; on this ground Christian stood, and up there came Apollyon against him; and look. And, look, did I not tell you? here is some of your husband's blood upon these stones to this day: Behold, also, how here and there are yet to be seen upon the place, some of the shivers of Apollyon's broken darts. See, also, how they did beat the ground with their feet as they fought, to make good their places against each other; how also with their by-blows they did split the very stones in pieces. Verily, Christian did here play the man, and showed himself as stout as Hercules could, had he been there, even he himself. When Apollyon was beat, he made his retreat to the next valley, that is called, the Valley of the Shadow of Death, unto which we shall come anon. Lo, yonder also stands a monument, on which is engraven this battle, and Christian's victory, to his fame, throughout all ages: So because it stood just on the way-side before them, they stepped to it, and read the writing, which word for word was this:

"Hard by here was a battle fought,
  Most strange, and yet most true;
Christian and Apollyon fought
  Each other to subdue.

The man so bravely play'd the man,
  He made the fiend to fly;

Of which a monument I stand,
  The same to testify."

When they had passed by this place, they came upon the borders of the Shadow of Death. This Valley was longer than the other; a place also most strangely haunted with evil things, as many are able to testify: but these women and children went the better through it, because they had daylight, and because Mr. Great-Heart was their conductor.

When they were entering upon this valley, they thought they heard a groaning, as of dying men; a very great groaning. They thought also that they did hear words of lamentation, spoken as of some in extreme torment. These things made the boys to quake; the women also looked pale and wan; but their guide bid them be of good comfort.

So they went on a little further, and they thought that they felt the ground begin to shake under them, as if some hollow place was there: they heard also a kind of hissing, as of serpents, but nothing as yet appeared. Then said the boys, Are we not yet at the end of this doleful place? But the guide also bid them be of good courage, and look well to their feet; lest haply, said he, you be taken in some snare.

Now James began to be sick; but I think the cause thereof was fear: so his mother gave him some of that glass of spirits that had been given her at the Interpreter's house, and three of the pills that Mr. Skill had prepared, and the boy began to revive. Thus they went on till they came to about the middle of the valley; and then Christiana said, Methinks I see something yonder upon the road before us, a thing of a shape such as I have not seen. Then said Joseph, Mother, what is it? An ugly thing, child; an ugly thing, said she. But, mother, what is it like? said he. 'Tis like I cannot tell what, said she; and now it is but a little way off. Then said she, It is nigh.

Well, said Mr. Great-Heart, let them that are most afraid keep close to me. So the fiend came on, and the conductor met it; but when it was come to him, it vanished to all their sights. Then remembered they what had been said some time ago: "Resist the devil, and he will flee from you."

They went therefore on, as being a little refreshed. But they had not gone far, before Mercy, looking behind her, saw, as she thought, something most like a lion, and it came at a great padding pace after: and it had a hollow voice of roaring; and at every roar it gave, it made the valley echo, and all their hearts to ache, save the heart of him that was their guide. So it came up and Mr. Great-Heart went behind, and put the pilgrims all before him. The lion also came on apace, and Mr. Great-Heart addressed himself to give him battle. But when he saw that it was determined that resistance should be made, he also drew back, and came no further.

Then they went on again, and their conductor went before them, till they came to a place where was cast up a pit the whole breadth of the way; and before they could be prepared to go over that, a great mist and a darkness fell upon them, so that they could not see. Then said the pilgrims, Alas! what now shall we do? But their guide made answer, Fear not; stand still, and see what an end will be put to this also; so they stayed there, because their path was marred. They then also thought that they did hear more apparently the noise and rushing of the enemies; the fire also and the smoke of the pit were much easier to be discerned. Then said Christiana to Mercy, Now I see what my poor husband went through. I have heard much of this place, but I never was here before now. Poor man! he went here all alone in the night; he had night almost quite through the way: also these fiends were busy about him, as if they would have torn him in pieces. Many have spoken of it; but none can tell what the Valley of the Shadow of Death should mean until they come in themselves. The heart knoweth its own bitterness; and a stranger intermeddleth not with its joy. To be here is a fearful thing.

Mr. Great-Heart: This is like doing business in great waters, or like going down into the deep. This is like being in the heart of the sea, and like going down to the bottoms of the mountains. Now it seems as if the earth, with its bars, were about us for ever. But let them that walk in darkness, and have no light, trust in the name of the Lord, and stay upon their God. For my part, as I have told you already, I have gone often through this valley, and have been much harder put to it than now I am: and yet you see I am alive. I would not boast, for that I am not mine own saviour; but I trust we shall have a good deliverance. Come, let us pray for light to Him that can lighten our darkness, and that can rebuke not only these, but all the Satans in hell.

So they cried and prayed, and God sent light and deliverance, for there was now no let in their way; no, not there where but now they were stopped with a pit. Yet they were not got through the valley. So they went on still, and met with great stinks and loathsome smells, to the great annoyance of them. Then said Mercy to Christiana, It is not so pleasant being here as at the gate, or at the Interpreter's, or at the house where we lay last.

O but, said one of the boys, it is not so bad to go through here, as it is to abide here, always; and for aught I know, one reason why we must go this way to the house prepared for us is, that our home might be the sweeter to us.

Well said, Samuel, quoth the guide; thou hast now spoke like a man. Why, if ever I get out here again, said the boy, I think I shall prize light and good way better than I ever did in all my life. Then said the guide, We shall be out by and by.

So on they went, and Joseph said, Cannot we see to the end of this valley as yet? Then said the guide, Look to your feet, for we shall presently be among the snares: so they looked to their feet, and went on; but they were troubled much with the snares. Now, when they were come among the snares, they espied a man cast into the ditch on the left hand, with his flesh all rent and torn. Then said the guide, That is one Heedless, that was going this way: he has lain there a great while. There was one Take-Heed with him when he was taken and slain, but he escaped their hands. You cannot imagine how many are killed hereabouts, and yet men are so foolishly venturous as to set out lightly on pilgrimage, and to come without a guide. Poor Christian! it was a wonder that he here escaped; but he was beloved of his God: also he had a good heart of his own, or else he could never have done it.

Now they drew towards the end of this way; and just there where Christian had seen the cave when he went by, out thence came forth Maul, a giant. This Maul did use to spoil young pilgrims with sophistry; and he called Great-Heart by his name, and said unto him, How many times have you been forbidden to do these things? Then said Mr. Great-Heart, What things? What things! quoth the giant; you know what things: but I will put an end to your trade.

But, pray, said Mr. Great-Heart, before we fall to it, let us understand wherefore we must fight. Now the women and children stood trembling, and knew not what to do. Quoth the giant, You rob the country, and rob it with the worst of thefts. These are but generals, said Mr. Great-Heart; come to particulars, man.

Then said the giant, Thou practisest the craft of a kidnapper; thou gatherest up women and children, and carriest them into a strange country, to the weakening of my master's kingdom. But now Great-Heart replied, I am a servant of the God of heaven; my business is to persuade sinners to repentance. I am commanded to do my endeavors to turn men, women, and children, from darkness to light, and from the power of Satan unto God; and if this be indeed the ground of thy quarrel, let us fall to it as soon as thou wilt.

Then the giant came up, and Mr. Great-Heart went to meet him; and as he went he drew his sword, but the giant had a club. So without more ado they fell to it, and at the first blow the giant struck Mr. Great-Heart down upon one of his knees. With that the women and children cried out. So Mr. Great-Heart recovering himself, laid about him in full lusty manner, and gave the giant a wound in his arm. Thus he fought for the space of an hour, to that height of heat that the breath came out of the giant's nostrils as the heat doth out of a boiling cauldron.

Then they sat down to rest them; but Mr. Great-Heart betook himself to prayer. Also the women and children did nothing but sigh and cry all the time that the battle did last.

When they had rested them, and taken breath, they both fell to it again; and Mr. Great-Heart, with a blow, fetched the giant down to the ground. Nay, hold, let me recover, quoth he: so Mr. Great-Heart fairly let him get up. So to it they went again, and the giant missed but little of all to breaking Mr. Great-Heart's scull with his club.

Mr. Great-Heart seeing that, runs to him in the full heat of his spirit, and pierceth him under the fifth rib. With that the giant began to faint, and could hold up his club no longer. Then Mr. Great-Heart seconded his blow, and smit the head of the giant from his shoulders. Then the women and children rejoiced, and Mr. Great-Heart also praised God for the deliverance he had wrought.

When this was done, they amongst them erected a pillar, and fastened the giant's head thereon, and wrote under in letters that passengers might read,

"He that did wear this head was one
  That pilgrims did misuse;

He stopped their way, he spared none,
  But did them all abuse;
Until that I Great-Heart arose,
  The pilgrims guide to be;
Until that I did him oppose
  That was their enemy."

Lesson 86

- Read Book 2, Stage 6 of *The Pilgrim's Progress*.

Book 2, Stage 6

Now I saw that they went on to the ascent that was a little way off, cast up to be a prospect for pilgrims. That was the place from whence Christian had the first sight of Faithful his brother. Wherefore, here they sat down and rested. They also here did eat and drink, and make merry, for that they had gotten deliverance from this so dangerous an enemy. As they sat thus and did eat, Christiana asked the guide, if he had caught no hurt in the battle? Then said Mr. Great-Heart, No, save a little on my flesh; yet that also shall be so far from being to my detriment, that it is at present a proof of my love to my master and you, and shall be a means, by grace, to increase my reward at last.

Christiana: But were you not afraid, good sir, when you saw him come with his club?

Mr. Great-Heart: It is my duty, said he, to mistrust my own ability, that I may have reliance on Him who is stronger than all.

Christiana: But what did you think when he fetched you down to the ground at the first blow?

Mr. Great-Heart: Why, I thought, quoth he, that so my Master himself was served, and yet he it was that conquered at last.

Matthew: When you all have thought what you please, I think God has been wonderfully good unto us, both in bringing us out of this valley, and in delivering us out of the hand of this enemy. For my part, I see no reason why we should distrust our God any more, since he has now, and in such a place as this, given us such testimony of his love. Then they got up, and went forward.

Now a little before them stood an oak; and under it, when they came to it, they found an old pilgrim fast asleep. They knew that he was a pilgrim by his clothes, and his staff, and his girdle.

So the guide, Mr. Great-Heart, awaked him; and the old gentleman, as he lifted up his eyes, cried out, What's the matter? Who are you; and what is your business here?

Mr. Great-Heart: Come, man, be not so hot; here are none but friends. Yet the old man gets up, and stands upon his guard, and will know of them what they are. Then said the guide, My name is Great-Heart: I am the guide of these pilgrims that are going to the Celestial country.

Mr. Honest: Then said Mr. Honest, I cry you mercy: I feared that you had been of the company of those that some time ago did rob Little-Faith of his money; but, now I look better about me, I perceive you are honester people.

Mr. Great-Heart: Why, what would or could you have done to have helped yourself, if indeed we had been of that company?

Mr. Honest: Done! Why, I would have fought as long as breath had been in me: and had I so done, I am sure you could never have given me the worst on't; for a Christian can never be overcome, unless he shall yield of himself.

Mr. Great-Heart: Well said, father Honest, quoth the guide; for by this I know thou art a cock of the right kind, for thou hast said the truth.

Mr. Honest: And by this also I know that thou knowest what true pilgrimage is; for all others do think that we are the soonest overcome of any.

Mr. Great-Heart: Well, now we are so happily met, pray let me crave your name, and the name of the place you came from.

Mr. Honest: My name I cannot tell you, but I came from the town of Stupidity: it lieth about four degrees beyond the city of Destruction.

Mr. Great-Heart: Oh, Are you that countryman? Then I deem I have half a guess of you: your name is Old Honesty, is it not?

Mr. Honest: So the old gentleman blushed, and said, Not honesty in the abstract, but Honest is my name; and I wish that my nature may agree to what I am called. But, sir, said the old gentleman, how could you guess that I am such a man, since I came from such a place?

Mr. Great-Heart: I had heard of you before, by my Master; for he knows all things that are done on the earth. But I have often wondered that any should come from your place; for your town is worse than is the city of Destruction itself.

Mr. Honest: Yes, we lie more off from the sun, and so are more cold and senseless. But were a man in a mountain of ice, yet if the Sun of righteousness will arise upon him, his frozen heart shall feel a thaw; and thus it has been with me.

Mr. Great-Heart: I believe it, father Honest, I believe it; for I know the thing is true.

Then the old gentleman saluted all the pilgrims with a holy kiss of charity, and asked them their names, and how they had fared since they set out on their pilgrimage.

Christiana: Then said Christiana, My name I suppose you have heard of; good Christian was my husband, and these four are his children. But can you think how the old gentleman was taken, when she told him who she was? He skipped, he smiled, he blessed them with a thousand good wishes, saying,

Mr. Honest: I have heard much of your husband, and of his travels and wars which he underwent in his days. Be it spoken to your comfort, the name of your husband rings all over these parts of the world: his faith, his courage, his enduring, and his sincerity under all, had made his name famous. Then he turned him to the boys, and asked them of their names, which they told him. Then said he unto them, Matthew, be thou like Matthew the publican, not in vice, but in virtue. Samuel, said he, be thou like Samuel the prophet, a man of faith and prayer. Joseph, said he, be thou like Joseph in Potiphar's house, chaste, and one that flees from temptation. And James, be thou like James the just, and like James the brother of our Lord. Then they told him of Mercy, and how she had left her town and her kindred to come along with Christiana and with her sons. At that the old honest man said, Mercy is thy name: by mercy shalt thou be sustained and carried through all those difficulties that shall assault thee in thy way, till thou shalt come thither where thou shalt look the Fountain of mercy in the face with comfort. All this while the guide, Mr. Great-Heart, was very well pleased, and smiled upon his companions.

Now, as they walked along together, the guide asked the old gentleman if he did not know one Mr. Fearing, that came on pilgrimage out of his parts.

Mr. Honest: Yes, very well, said he. He was a man that had the root of the matter in him; but he was one of the most troublesome pilgrims that ever I met with in all my days.

Mr. Great-Heart: I perceive you knew him, for you have given a very right character of him.

Mr. Honest: Knew him! I was a great companion of his; I was with him most an end; when he first began to think upon what would come upon us hereafter, I was with him.

Mr. Great-Heart: I was his guide from my Master's house to the gates of the Celestial City.

Mr. Honest: Then you knew him to be a troublesome one.

Mr. Great-Heart: I did so; but I could very well bear it; for men of my calling are oftentimes intrusted with the conduct of such as he was.

Mr. Honest: Well then, pray let us hear a little of him, and how he managed himself under your conduct.

Mr. Great-Heart: Why, he was always afraid that he should come short of whither he had a desire to go. Every thing frightened him that he heard any body speak of, if it had but the least appearance of opposition in it. I heard that he lay roaring at the Slough of Despond for above a month together; nor durst he, for all he saw several go over before him, venture, though they many of them offered to lend him their hands. He would not go back again, neither. The Celestial City-he said he should die if he came not to it; and yet he was dejected at every difficulty, and stumbled at every straw that any body cast in his way. Well, after he had lain at the Slough of Despond a great while, as I have told you, one sunshiny morning, I do not know how, he ventured, and so got over; but when he was over, he would scarce believe it. He had, I think, a Slough of Despond in his mind, a slough that he carried every where with him, or else he could never have been as he was. So he came up to the gate, you know what I mean, that stands at the head of this way, and there also he stood a good while before he would venture to knock. When the gate was opened, he would give back, and give place to others, and say that he was not worthy. For, all he got before some to the gate, yet many of them went in before him. There the poor man would stand shaking and shrinking; I dare say it would have pitied one's heart to have seen him. Nor would he go back again. At last he took the hammer that hanged on the gate, in his hand, and gave a small rap or two; then one opened to him, but he shrunk back as before. He that opened stepped out after him, and said, Thou trembling one, what wantest thou? With that he fell down to the ground. He that spoke to him wondered to see him so faint, so he said to him, Peace be to thee; up, for I have set open the door to thee; come in, for thou art blessed. With that he got up, and went in trembling; and when he was in, he was ashamed to show his face. Well, after he had been entertained there a while, as you know how the manner is, he was bid go on his way, and also told the way he should take. So he went on till he came out to our house; but as he behaved himself at the gate, so he did at my Master the Interpreter's door. He lay there about in the cold a good while, before he would adventure to call; yet he would not go back: and the nights were long and cold then. Nay, he had a note of necessity in his bosom to my master to receive him, and grant him the comfort of his house, and also to allow him a stout and valiant conductor, because he was himself so chicken-hearted a man; and yet for all that he was afraid to call at the door. So he lay up and down thereabouts, till, poor man, he was almost starved; yea, so great was his dejection, that though he saw several others for knocking get in, yet he was afraid to venture. At last, I think I looked out of the window, and perceiving a man to be up and down about the door, I went out to him, and asked what he was: but, poor man, the water stood in his eyes; so I perceived what he wanted. I went therefore in, and told it in the house, and we showed the thing to our Lord: so he sent me out again, to entreat him to come in; but I dare say, I had hard work to do it. At last he came in; and I will say that for my Lord, he carried it wonderful lovingly to him. There were but a few good bits at the table, but some of it was laid upon his trencher. Then he presented the note; and my Lord looked thereon, and said his desire should be granted. So when he had been there a good while, he seemed to get some heart, and to be a little more comfortable. For my Master, you must know, is one of very tender bowels, especially to them that are afraid; wherefore he carried it so towards him as might tend most to his encouragement. Well, when he had had a sight of the things of the place, and was ready to take his journey to go to the city, my Lord, as he did to Christian before, gave him a bottle of spirits, and some comfortable things to eat. Thus we set forward, and I went before him; but the man was but of few words, only he would sigh aloud.

When we were come to where the three fellows were hanged, he said that he doubted that that would be his end also. Only he seemed glad when he saw the cross and the sepulchre. There I confess he desired to stay a little to look; and he seemed for a while after to be a little cheery. When he came to the Hill Difficulty, he made no stick at that, nor did he much fear the lions: for you must know, that his troubles were not about such things as these; his fear was about his acceptance at last.

I got him in at the house Beautiful, I think, before he was willing. Also, when he was in, I brought him acquainted with the damsels of the place; but he was ashamed to make himself much in company. He desired much to be alone; yet he always loved good talk, and often would get behind the screen to hear it. He also loved much to see ancient things, and to be pondering them in his mind. He told me afterward, that he loved to be in those two houses from which he came last, to wit, at the gate, and that of the Interpreter, but that he durst not be so bold as to ask.

When we went also from the house Beautiful, down the hill, into the Valley of Humiliation, he went down as well as ever I saw a man in my life; for he cared not how mean he was, so he might be happy at last. Yea, I think there was a kind of sympathy betwixt that Valley and him; for I never saw him better in all his pilgrimage than he was in that Valley.

Here he would lie down, embrace the ground, and kiss the very flowers that grew in this valley. He would now be up every morning by break of day, tracing and walking to and fro in the valley.

But when he was come to the entrance of the Valley of the Shadow of Death, I thought I should have lost my man: not for that he had any inclination to go back; that he always abhorred; but he was ready to die for fear. Oh, the hobgoblins will have me! the hobgoblins will have me! cried he; and I could not beat him out of it. He made such a noise, and such an outcry here, that had they but heard him, it was enough to encourage them to come and fall upon us.

But this I took very great notice of, that this valley was as quiet when we went through it, as ever I knew it before or since. I suppose those enemies here had now a special check from our Lord, and a command not to meddle until Mr. Fearing had passed over it.

It would be too tedious to tell you of all; we will therefore only mention a passage or two more. When he was come to Vanity Fair, I thought he would have fought with all the men in the fair. I feared there we should have been both knocked on the head, so hot was he against their fooleries. Upon the Enchanted Ground he was very wakeful. But when he was come at the river where was no bridge, there again he was in a heavy case. Now, now, he said, he should be drowned forever, and so never see that face with comfort that he had come so many miles to behold.

And here also I took notice of what was very remarkable: the water of that river was lower at this time than ever I saw it in all my life; so he went over at last, not much above wetshod. When he was going up to the gate, I began to take leave of him, and to wish him a good reception above. So he said, I shall, I shall. Then parted we asunder, and I saw him no more.

Mr. Honest: Then it seems he was well at last?

Mr. Great-Heart: Yes, yes, I never had doubt about him. He was a man of a choice spirit, only he was always kept very low, and that made his life so burdensome to himself, and so troublesome to others. He was, above many, tender of sin: he was so afraid of doing injuries to others, that he often would deny himself of that which was lawful, because he would not offend.

Mr. Honest: But what should be the reason that such a good man should be all his days so much in the dark?

Mr. Great-Heart: There are two sorts of reasons for it. One is, the wise God will have it so: some must pipe, and some must weep. Now Mr. Fearing was one that played upon the bass. He and his fellows sound the sackbut, whose notes are more doleful than the notes of other music are: though indeed, some say, the bass is the ground of music. And for my part, I care not at all for that profession which begins not in heaviness of mind. The first string that the musician usually touches is the bass, when he intends to put all in tune. God also plays upon this string first, when he sets the soul in tune for himself. Only there was the imperfection of Mr. Fearing; he could play upon no other music but this till towards his latter end.

[I make bold to talk thus metaphorically for the ripening of the wits of young readers, and because, in the book of Revelation, the saved are compared to a company of musicians, that play upon their trumpets and harps, and sing their songs before the throne.]

Mr. Honest: He was a very zealous man, as one may see by the relation you have given of him. Difficulties, lions, or Vanity Fair, he feared not at all; it was only sin, death, and hell, that were to him a terror, because he had some doubts about his interest in that celestial country.

Mr. Great-Heart: You say right; those were the things that were his troublers; and they, as you have well observed, arose from the weakness of his mind thereabout, not from weakness of spirit as to the practical part of a pilgrim's life. I dare believe that, as the proverb is, he could have bit a firebrand, had it stood in his way; but the things with which he was oppressed, no man ever yet could shake off with ease.

Christiana: Then said Christiana, This relation of Mr. Fearing has done me good; I thought nobody had been like me. But I see there was some semblance betwixt this good man and me: only we differed in two things. His troubles were so great that they broke out; but mine I kept within. His also lay so hard upon him, they made him that he could not knock at the houses provided for entertainment; but my trouble was always such as made me knock the louder.

Mercy: If I might also speak my heart, I must say that something of him has also dwelt in me. For I have ever been more afraid of the lake, and the loss of a place in paradise, than I have been of the loss other things. O, thought I, may I have the happiness to have a habitation there! 'Tis enough, though I part with all the world to win it.

Matthew: Then said Matthew, Fear was one thing that made me think that I was far from having that within me which accompanies salvation. But if it was so with such a good man as he, why may it not also go well with me?

James: No fears no grace, said James. Though there is not always grace where there is the fear of hell, yet, to be sure, there is no grace where there is no fear of God.

Mr. Great-Heart: Well said, James; thou hast hit the mark. For the fear of God is the beginning of wisdom; and to be sure, they that want the beginning have neither middle nor end. But we will here conclude our discourse of Mr. Fearing, after we have sent after him this farewell.

"Well, Master Fearing, thou didst fear
  Thy God, and wast afraid
Of doing any thing, while here,
  That would have thee betrayed.
And didst thou fear the lake and pit?
  Would others do so too!
For, as for them that want thy wit,
  They do themselves undo."

Now I saw that they still went on in their talk. For after Mr. Great-Heart had made an end with Mr. Fearing, Mr. Honest began to tell them of another, but his name was Mr. Self-will. He pretended himself to be a pilgrim, said Mr. Honest; but I persuade myself he never came in at the gate that stands at the head of the way.

Mr. Great-Heart: Had you ever any talk with him about it?

Mr. Honest: Yes, more than once or twice; but he would always be like himself, self-willed. He neither cared for man, nor argument, nor yet example; what his mind prompted him to, that he would do, and nothing else could he be got to do.

Mr. Great-Heart: Pray, what principles did he hold? for I suppose you can tell.

Mr. Honest: He held that a man might follow the vices as well as the virtues of pilgrims; and that if he did both, he should be certainly saved.

Mr. Great-Heart: How? If he had said, it is possible for the best to be guilty of the vices, as well as to partake of the virtues of pilgrims, he could not much have been blamed; for indeed we are exempted from no vice absolutely, but on condition that we watch and strive. But this, I perceive, is not the thing; but if I understand you right, your meaning is, that he was of opinion that it was allowable so to be.

Mr. Honest: Aye, aye, so I mean, and so he believed and practised.

Mr. Great-Heart: But what grounds had he for his so saying?

Mr. Honest: Why, he said he had the Scripture for his warrant.

Mr. Great-Heart: Prithee, Mr. Honest, present us with a few particulars.

Mr. Honest: So I will. He said, to have to do with other men's wives had been practised by David, God's beloved; and therefore he could do it. He said, to have more women than one was a thing that Solomon practised, and therefore he could do it. He said, that Sarah and the godly midwives of Egypt lied, and so did save Rahab, and therefore he could do it. He said, that the disciples went at the bidding of their Master, and took away the owner's ass, and therefore he could do so too. He said, that Jacob got the inheritance of his father in a way of guile and dissimulation, and therefore he could do so too.

Mr. Great-Heart: High base indeed! And are you sure he was of this opinion?

Mr. Honest: I heard him plead for it, bring Scripture for it, bring arguments for it, etc.

Mr. Great-Heart: An opinion that is not fit to be with any allowance in the world!

Mr. Honest: You must understand me rightly: he did not say that any man might do this; but that they who had the virtues of those that did such things, might also do the same.

Mr. Great-Heart: But what more false than such a conclusion? For this is as much as to say, that because good men heretofore have sinned of infirmity, therefore he had allowance to do it of a presumptuous mind; or that if, because a child, by the blast of the wind, or for that it stumbled at a stone, fell down and defiled itself in the mire, therefore he might wilfully lie down and wallow like a boar therein. Who could have thought that any one could so far have been blinded by the power of lust? But what is written must be true: they "stumble at the word, being disobedient; whereunto also they were appointed." His supposing that such may have the godly men's virtues, who addict themselves to their vices, is also a delusion as strong as the other. To eat up the sin of God's people, as a dog licks up filth, is no sign that one is possessed with their virtues. Nor can I believe that one who is of this opinion, can at present have faith or love in him. But I know you have made strong objections against him; prithee what can he say for himself?

Mr. Honest: Why, he says, to do this by way of opinion, seems abundantly more honest than to do it, and yet hold contrary to it in opinion.

Mr. Great-Heart: A very wicked answer. For though to let loose the bridle to lusts, while our opinions are against such things, is bad; yet, to sin, and plead a toleration so to do, is worse: the one stumbles beholders accidentally, the other leads them into the snare.

Mr. Honest: There are many of this man's mind, that have not this man's mouth; and that makes going on pilgrimage of so little esteem as it is.

Mr. Great-Heart: You have said the truth, and it is to be lamented: but he that feareth the King of paradise, shall come out of them all.

Christiana: There are strange opinions in the world. I know one that said, it was time enough to repent when we come to die.

Mr. Great-Heart: Such are not overwise; that man would have been loth, might he have had a week to run twenty miles in his life, to defer his journey to the last hour of that week.

Mr. Honest: You say right; and yet the generality of them who count themselves pilgrims, do indeed do thus. I am, as you see, an old man, and have been a traveller in this road many a day; and I have taken notice of many things.

I have seen some that have set out as if they would drive all the world before them, who yet have, in a few days, died as they in the wilderness, and so never got sight of the promised land. I have seen some that have promised nothing at first setting out to be pilgrims, and who one would have thought could not have lived a day, that have yet proved very good pilgrims. I have seen some who have run hastily forward, that again have, after a little time, run just as fast back again. I have seen some who have spoken very well of a pilgrim's life at first, that after a while have spoken as much against it. I have heard some, when they first set out for paradise, say positively, there is such a place, who, when they have been almost there, have come back again, and said there is none. I have heard some vaunt what they would do in case they should be opposed, that have, even at a false alarm, fled faith, the pilgrim's way, and all.

Now, as they were thus on their way, there came one running to meet them, and said, Gentlemen, and you of the weaker sort, if you love life, shift for yourselves, for the robbers are before you.

Mr. Great-Heart: Then said Mr. Great-Heart, They be the three that set upon Little-Faith heretofore. Well, said he, we are ready for them: so they went on their way. Now they looked at every turning when they should have met with the villains; but whether they heard of Mr. Great-Heart, or whether they had some other game, they came not up to the pilgrims.

Christiana then wished for an inn to refresh herself and her children, because they were weary. Then said Mr. Honest, There is one a little before us, where a very honorable disciple, one Gaius, dwells. So they all concluded to turn in thither; and the rather, because the old gentleman gave him so good a report. When they came to the door they went in, not knocking, for folks use not to knock at the door of an inn. Then they called for the master of the house, and he came to them. So they asked if they might lie there that night.

Gaius: Yes, gentlemen, if you be true men; for my house is for none but pilgrims. Then were Christiana, Mercy, and the boys the more glad, for that the innkeeper was a lover of pilgrims. So they called for rooms, and he showed them one for Christiana and her children and Mercy, and another for Mr. Great-Heart and the old gentleman.

Mr. Great-Heart: Then said Mr. Great-Heart, good Gaius, what hast thou for supper? for these pilgrims have come far to-day, and are weary.

Gaius: It is late, said Gaius, so we cannot conveniently go out to seek food; but such as we have you shall be welcome to, if that will content.

Mr. Great-Heart: We will be content with what thou hast in the house; for as much as I have proved thee, thou art never destitute of that which is convenient.

Then he went down and spake to the cook, whose name was, Taste-that-which-is-good, to get ready supper for so many pilgrims. This done, he comes up again, saying, Come, my good friends, you are welcome to me, and I am glad that I have a house to entertain you in; and while supper is making ready, if you please, let us entertain one another with some good discourse: so they all said, Content.

Gaius: Then said Gaius, Whose wife is this aged matron? and whose daughter is this young damsel?

Mr. Great-Heart: This woman is the wife of one Christian, a pilgrim of former times; and these are his four children. The maid is one of her acquaintance, one that she hath persuaded to come with her on pilgrimage. The boys take all after their father, and covet to tread in his steps; yea, if they do but see any place where the old pilgrim hath lain, or any print of his foot, it ministereth joy to their hearts, and they covet to lie or tread in the same.

Gaius: Then said Gaius, Is this Christian's wife, and are these Christian's children? I knew your husband's father, yea, also his father's father. Many have been good of this stock; their ancestors dwelt first at Antioch. Christian's progenitors (I suppose you have heard your husband talk of them) were very worthy men. They have, above any that I know, showed themselves men of great virtue and courage for the Lord of the pilgrims, his ways, and them that loved him. I have heard of many of your husband's relations that have stood all trials for the sake of the truth. Stephen, that was one of the first of the family from whence your husband sprang, was knocked on the head with stones. James, another of this generation, was slain with the edge of the sword. To say nothing of Paul and Peter, men anciently of the family from whence your husband came, there was Ignatius, who was cast to the lions; Romanus, whose flesh was cut by pieces from his bones; and Polycarp, that played the man in the fire. There was he that was hanged up in a basket in the sun for the wasps to eat; and he whom they put into a sack, and cast him into the sea to be drowned. It would be impossible utterly to count up all of that family who have suffered injuries and death for the love of a pilgrim's life. Nor can I but be glad to see that thy husband has left behind him four such boys as these. I hope they will bear up their father's name, and tread in their father's steps, and come to their father's end.

Mr. Great-Heart: Indeed, sir, they are likely lads: they seem to choose heartily their father's ways.

Gaius: That is it that I said. Wherefore Christian's family is like still to spread abroad upon the face of the ground, and yet to be numerous upon the face of the earth; let Christiana look out some damsels for her sons, to whom they may be betrothed, etc., that the name of their father, and the house of his progenitors, may never be forgotten in the world.

Mr. Honest: 'Tis pity his family should fall and be extinct.

Gaius: Fall it cannot, but be diminished it may; but let Christiana take my advice, and that is the way to uphold it. And, Christiana, said this innkeeper, I am glad to see thee and thy friend Mercy together here, a lovely couple. And if I may advise, take Mercy into a nearer relation to thee: if she will, let her be given to Matthew thy eldest son. It is the way to preserve a posterity in the earth. So this match was concluded, and in process of time they were married: but more of that hereafter.

Gaius also proceeded, and said, I will now speak on the behalf of women, to take away their reproach. For as death and the curse came into the world by a woman, so also did life and health: God sent forth his Son, made of a woman. Yea, to show how much they that came after did abhor the act of the mother, this sex in the Old Testament coveted children, if happily this or that woman might be the mother of the Saviour of the world. I will say again, that when the Saviour was come, women rejoiced in him, before either man or angel. I read not that ever any man did give unto Christ so much as one groat; but the women followed him, and ministered to him of their substance. 'Twas a woman that washed his feet with tears, and a woman that anointed his body at the burial. They were women who wept when he was going to the cross, and women that followed him from the cross, and sat over against his sepulchre when he was buried. They were women that were first with him at his resurrection-morn, and women that brought tidings first to his disciples that he was risen from the dead. Women therefore are highly favored, and show by these things that they are sharers with us in the grace of life.

Now the cook sent up to signify that supper was almost ready, and sent one to lay the cloth, and the trenchers, and to set the salt and bread in order.

Then said Matthew, The sight of this cloth, and of this forerunner of the supper, begetteth in me a greater appetite for my food than I had before.

Gaius: So let all ministering doctrines to thee in this life beget in thee a greater desire to sit at the supper of the great King in his kingdom; for all preaching, books, and ordinances here, are but as the laying of the trenchers, and the setting of salt upon the board, when compared with the feast which our Lord will make for us when we come to his house.

So supper came up. And first a heave-shoulder and a wave-breast were set on the table before them; to show that they must begin their meal with prayer and praise to God. The heave-shoulder David lifted up his heart to God with; and with the wave-breast, where his heart lay, he used to lean upon his harp when he played. These two dishes were very fresh and good, and they all ate heartily thereof.

The next they brought up was a bottle of wine, as red as blood. So Gaius said to them, Drink freely; this is the true juice of the vine, that makes glad the heart of God and man. So they drank and were merry.

The next was a dish of milk well crumbed; Gaius said, Let the boys have that, that they may grow thereby.

Then they brought up in course a dish of butter and honey. Then said Gaius, Eat freely of this, for this is good to cheer up and strengthen your judgments and understandings. This was our Lord's dish when he was a child: "Butter and honey shall he eat, that he may know to refuse the evil, and choose the good."

Then they brought them up a dish of apples, and they were very good-tasted fruit. Then said Matthew, May we eat apples, since it was such by and with which the serpent beguiled our first mother?

Then said Gaius,

"Apples were they with which we were beguil'd,
Yet sin, not apples, hath our souls defil'd:
Apples forbid, if ate, corrupt the blood;
To eat such, when commanded, does us good:
Drink of his flagons then, thou church, his dove,
And eat his apples, who art sick of love."

Then said Matthew, I made the scruple, because I a while since was sick with the eating of fruit.

Gaius: Forbidden fruit will make you sick; but not what our Lord has tolerated.

While they were thus talking, they were presented with another dish, and it was a dish of nuts. Then said some at the table, Nuts spoil tender teeth, especially the teeth of children: which when Gaius heard, he said,

"Hard texts are nuts, (I will not call them cheaters,)
Whose shells do keep the kernel from the eaters:
Open the shells, and you shall have the meat;
They here are brought for you to crack and eat."

Then were they very merry, and sat at the table a long time, talking of many things. Then said the old gentleman, My good landlord, while we are cracking your nuts, if you please, do you open this riddle:

"A man there was, though some did count him mad,
The more he cast away, the more he had."

Then they all gave good heed, wondering what good Gaius would say; so he sat still a while, and then thus replied:

"He who bestows his goods upon the poor,
Shall have as much again, and ten times more."

Then said Joseph, I dare say, sir, I did not think you could have found it out.

Oh, said Gaius, I have been trained up in this way a great while: nothing teaches like experience. I have learned of my Lord to be kind, and have found by experience that I have gained thereby. There is that scattereth, and yet increaseth; and there is that withholdeth more than is meet, but it tendeth to poverty: There is that maketh himself rich, yet hath nothing; there is that maketh himself poor, yet hath great riches.

Then Samuel whispered to Christiana, his mother, and said, Mother, this is a very good man's house: let us stay here a good while, and let my brother Matthew be married here to Mercy, before we go any further. The which Gaius the host overhearing, said, With a very good will, my child.

So they stayed there more than a month, and Mercy was given to Matthew to wife.

While they stayed here, Mercy, as her custom was, would be making coats and garments to give to the poor, by which she brought a very good report upon the pilgrims.

But to return again to our story: After supper the lads desired a bed, for they were weary with travelling: Then Gaius called to show them their chamber; but said Mercy, I will have them to bed. So she had them to bed, and they slept well: but the rest sat up all night; for Gaius and they were such suitable company, that they could not tell how to part. After much talk of their Lord, themselves, and their journey, old Mr. Honest, he that put forth the riddle to Gaius, began to nod. Then said Great-Heart, What, sir, you begin to be drowsy; come, rub up, now here is a riddle for you. Then said Mr. Honest, Let us hear it. Then replied Mr. Great-heart,

"He that would kill, must first be overcome:
Who live abroad would, first must die at home."

Ha, said Mr. Honest, it is a hard one; hard to expound, and harder to practise. But come, landlord, said he, I will, if you please, leave my part to you: do you expound it, and I will hear what you say.

No, said Gaius, it was put to you, and it is expected you should answer it. Then said the old gentleman,

"He first by grace must conquered be,
  That sin would mortify;
Who that he lives would convince me,
  Unto himself must die."

It is right, said Gaius; good doctrine and experience teach this. For, first, until grace displays itself, and overcomes the soul with its glory, it is altogether without heart to oppose sin. Besides, if sin is Satan's cords, by which the soul lies bound, how should it make resistance before it is loosed from that infirmity? Secondly, Nor will any one that knows either reason or grace, believe that such a man can be a living monument of grace that is a slave to his own corruptions. And now it comes into my mind, I will tell you a story worth the hearing. There were two men that went on pilgrimage; the one began when he was young, the other when he was old. The young man had strong corruptions to grapple with; the old man's were weak with the decays of nature. The young man trod his steps as even as did the old one, and was every way as light as he. Who now, or which of them, had their graces shining clearest, since both seemed to be alike?

Mr. Honest: The young man's, doubtless. For that which makes head against the greatest opposition, gives best demonstration that it is strongest; especially when it also holdeth pace with that which meets not with half so much, as to be sure old age does not. Besides, I have observed that old men have blessed themselves with this mistake; namely, taking the decays of nature for a gracious conquest over corruptions, and so have been apt to beguile themselves. Indeed, old men that are gracious are best able to give advice to them that are young, because they have seen most of the emptiness of things: but yet, for an old and a young man to set out both together, the young one has the advantage of the fairest discovery of a work of grace within him, though the old man's corruptions are naturally the weakest. Thus they sat talking till break of day.

Now, when the family were up, Christiana bid her son James that he should read a chapter; so he read 53d of Isaiah. When he had done, Mr. Honest asked why it was said that the Saviour was to come "out of a dry ground;" and also, that "he had no form nor comeliness in him."

Mr. Great-Heart: Then said Mr. Great-Heart, To the first I answer, because the church of the Jews, of which Christ came, had then lost almost all the sap and spirit of religion. To the second I say, the words are spoken in the person of unbelievers, who, because they want the eye that can see into our Prince's heart, therefore they judge of him by the meanness of his outside; just like those who, not knowing that precious stones are covered over with a homely crust, when they have found one, because they know not what they have found, cast it away again, as men do a common stone.

Well, said Gaius, now you are here, and since, as I know, Mr. Great-Heart is good at his weapons, if you please, after we have refreshed ourselves, we will walk into the fields, to see if we can do any good. About a mile from hence there is one Slay-good, a giant, that doth much annoy the King's highway in these parts; and I know whereabout his haunt is. He is master of a number of thieves: 't would be well if we could clear these parts of him. So they consented and went: Mr. Great-Heart with his sword, helmet, and shield; and the rest with spears and staves.

When they came to the place where he was, they found him with one Feeble-mind in his hand, whom his servants had brought unto him, having taken him in the way. Now the giant was rifling him, with a purpose after that to pick his bones; for he was of the nature of flesheaters.

Well, so soon as he saw Mr. Great-Heart and his friends at the mouth of his cave, with their weapons, he demanded what they wanted.

Mr. Great-Heart: We want thee; for we are come to revenge the quarrels of the many that thou hast slain of the pilgrims, when thou hast dragged them out of the King's highway: wherefore come out of thy cave. So he armed himself and came out, and to battle they went, and fought for above an hour, and then stood still to take wind.

Slay-Good: Then said the giant, Why are you here on my ground?

Mr. Great-Heart: To revenge the blood of pilgrims, as I told thee before. So they went to it again, and the giant made Mr. Great-Heart give back; but he came up again, and in the greatness of his mind he let fly with such stoutness at the giant's head and sides, that he made him let his weapon fall out of his hand. So he smote him, and slew him, and cut off his head, and brought it away to the inn. He also took Feeble-mind the pilgrim, and brought him with him to his lodgings. When they were come home, they showed his head to the family, and set it up, as they had done others before, for a terror to those that should attempt to do as he hereafter.

Then they asked Mr. Feeble-Mind how he fell into his hands.

Mr. Feeble-Mind: Then said the poor man, I am a sickly man, as you see: and because death did usually once a day knock at my door, I thought I should never be well at home; so I betook myself to a pilgrim's life, and have traveled hither from the town of Uncertain, where I and my father were born. I am a man of no strength at all of body, nor yet of mind, but would, if I could, though I can but crawl, spend my life in the pilgrim's way. When I came at the gate that is at the head of the way, the Lord of that place did entertain me freely; neither objected he against my weakly looks, nor against my feeble mind; but gave me such things as were necessary for my journey, and bid me hope to the end. When I came to the house of the Interpreter, I received much kindness there: and because the hill of Difficulty was judged too hard for me, I was carried up that by one of his servants. Indeed, I have found much relief from pilgrims, though none were willing to go so softly as I am forced to do: yet still as they came on, they bid me be of good cheer, and said, that it was the will of their Lord that comfort should be given to the feeble-minded, and so went on their own pace. When I was come to Assault-lane, then this giant met with me, and bid me prepare for an encounter. But, alas, feeble one that I was, I had more need of a cordial; so he came up and took me. I conceited he would not kill me. Also when he had got me into his den, since I went not with him willingly, I believed I should come out alive again; for I have heard, that not any pilgrim that is taken captive by violent hands, if he keeps heart whole towards his Master, is, by the laws of providence, to die by the hand of the enemy. Robbed I looked to be, and robbed to be sure I am; but I have, as you see, escaped with life, for the which I thank my King as the author, and you as the means. Other brunts I also look for; but this I have resolved on, to wit, to run when I can, to go when I cannot run, and to creep when I cannot go. As to the main, I thank him that loved me, I am fixed; my way is before me, my mind is beyond the river that has no bridge, though I am, as you see, but of a feeble mind.

Mr. Honest: Then said old Mr. Honest, Have not you, sometime ago, been acquainted with one Mr. Fearing, a pilgrim?

Mr. Feeble-Mind: Acquainted with him! Yes, he came from the town of Stupidity, which lieth four degrees to the northward of the city of Destruction, and as many off of where I was born: yet we were well acquainted, for indeed he was my uncle, my father's brother. He and I have been much of a temper: he was a little shorter than I, but yet we were much of a complexion.

Mr. Honest: I perceive you knew him, and I am apt to believe also that you were related one to another; for you have his whitely look, a cast like his with your eye, and your speech is much alike.

Mr. Feeble-Mind: Most have said so that have known us both: and, besides, what I have read in him I have for the most part found in myself.

Gaius: Come, sir, said good Gaius, be of good cheer; you are welcome to me, and to my house. What thou hast a mind to, call for freely; and what thou wouldst have my servants do for thee, they will do it with a ready mind.

Then said Mr. Feeble-mind, This is an unexpected favor, and as the sun shining out of a very dark cloud. Did giant Slay-good intend me this favor when he stopped me, and resolved to let me go no further? Did he intend, that after he had rifled my pockets I should go to Gaius mine host? Yet so it is.

Now, just as Mr. Feeble-mind and Gaius were thus in talk, there came one running, and called at the door, and said, that about a mile and a half off there was one Mr. Not-right, a pilgrim, struck dead upon the place where he was, with a thunderbolt.

Mr. Feeble-Mind: Alas! said Mr. Feeble-mind, is he slain? He overtook me some days before I came so far as hither, and would be my company-keeper. He was also with me when Slay-good the giant took me, but he was nimble of his heels, and escaped; but it seems he escaped to die, and I was taken to live.

"What one would think doth seek to slay outright,
Ofttimes delivers from the saddest plight.
That very Providence whose face is death,
Doth ofttimes to the lowly life bequeath.
I taken was, he did escape and flee;
Hands cross'd gave death to him and life to me."

Now, about this time Matthew and Mercy were married; also Gaius gave his daughter Phebe to James, Matthew's brother, to wife; after which time they yet stayed about ten days at Gaius' house, spending their time and the seasons like as pilgrims use to do.

When they were to depart, Gaius made them a feast, and they did eat and drink, and were merry. Now the hour was come that they must be gone; wherefore Mr. Great-heart called for a reckoning. But Gaius told him, that at his house it was not the custom for pilgrims to pay for their entertainment. He boarded them by the year, but looked for his pay from the good Samaritan, who had promised him, at his return, whatsoever charge he was at with them, faithfully to repay him. Then said Mr. Great-heart to him,

Mr. Great-Heart: Beloved, thou doest faithfully whatsoever thou doest to the brethren, and to strangers, who have borne witness of thy charity before the church, whom if thou yet bring forward on their journey, after a godly sort, thou shalt do well. Then Gaius took his leave of them all, and his children, and particularly of Mr. Feeble-mind. He also gave him something to drink by the way.

Now Mr. Feeble-mind, when they were going out of the door, made as if he intended to linger. The which, when Mr. Great-Heart espied, he said, Come, Mr.

Feeble-mind, pray do you go along with us: I will be your conductor, and you shall fare as the rest.

Mr. Feeble-Mind: Alas! I want a suitable companion. You are all lusty and strong, but I, as you see, am weak; I choose, therefore, rather to come behind, lest, by reason of my many infirmities, I should be both a burden to myself and to you. I am, as I said, a man of a weak and feeble mind, and shall be offended and made weak at that which others can bear. I shall like no laughing; I shall like no gay attire; I shall like no unprofitable questions. Nay, I am so weak a man as to be offended with that which others have a liberty to do. I do not yet know all the truth: I am a very ignorant Christian man. Sometimes, if I hear some rejoice in the Lord, it troubles me because I cannot do so too. It is with me as it is with a weak man among the strong, or as with a sick man among the healthy, or as a lamp despised; so that I know not what to do. "He that is ready to slip with his feet is as a lamp despised in the thought of him that is at ease."

Mr. Great-Heart: But, brother, said Mr. Great-Heart, I have it in commission to comfort the feeble-minded, and to support the weak. You must needs go along with us; we will wait for you; we will lend you our help; we will deny ourselves of some things, both opinionative and practical, for your sake: we will not enter into doubtful disputations before you; we will be made all things to you, rather than you shall be left behind.

Now, all this while they were at Gaius' door; and behold, as they were thus in the heat of their discourse, Mr. Ready-to-halt came by, with his crutches in his hand, and he also was going on pilgrimage.

Mr. Feeble-Mind: Then said Mr. Feeble-mind to him, Man, how camest thou hither? I was but now complaining that I had not a suitable companion, but thou art according to my wish. Welcome, welcome, good Mr. Ready-to-halt; I hope thou and I may be some help.

Mr. Ready-To-Halt: I shall be glad of thy company, said the other; and, good Mr. Feeble-mind, rather than we will part, since we are thus happily met, I will lend thee one of my crutches.

Mr. Feeble-Mind: Nay, said he, though I thank thee for thy good-will, I am not inclined to halt before I am lame. Howbeit, I think when occasion is, it may help me against a dog.

Mr. Ready-To-Halt: If either myself or my crutches can do thee a pleasure, we are both at thy command, good Mr. Feeble-mind.

Thus, therefore, they went on. Mr. Great-Heart and Mr. Honest went before, Christiana and her children went next, and Mr. Feeble-mind came behind, and Mr. Ready-to-halt with his crutches. Then said Mr. Honest,

Mr. Honest: Pray, sir, now we are upon the road, tell us some profitable things of some that have gone on pilgrimage before us.

Mr. Great-Heart: With a good will. I suppose you have heard how Christian of old did meet with Apollyon in the Valley of Humiliation, and also what hard work he had to go through the Valley of the Shadow of Death. Also I think you cannot but have heard how Faithful was put to it by Madam Wanton, with Adam the First, with one Discontent, and Shame; four as deceitful villains as a man can meet with upon the road.

Mr. Honest: Yes, I have heard of all this; but indeed good Faithful was hardest put to it with Shame: he was an unwearied one.

Mr. Great-Heart: Aye; for, as the pilgrim well said, he of all men had the wrong name.

Mr. Honest: But pray, sir, where was it that Christian and Faithful met Talkative? That same was also a notable one.

Mr. Great-Heart: He was a confident fool; yet many follow his ways.

Mr. Honest: He had like to have beguiled Faithful.

Mr. Great-Heart: Aye, but Christian put him into a way quickly to find him out.

Thus they went on till they came to the place where Evangelist met with Christian and Faithful, and prophesied to them what should befall them at Vanity Fair. Then said their guide, Hereabouts did Christian and Faithful meet with Evangelist, who prophesied to them of what troubles they should meet with at Vanity Fair.

Mr. Honest: Say you so? I dare say it was a hard chapter that then he did read unto them.

Mr. Great-Heart: It was so, but he gave them encouragement withal. But what do we talk of them? They were a couple of lion-like men; they had set their faces like a flint. Do not you remember how undaunted they were when they stood before the judge?

Mr. Honest: Well: Faithful bravely suffered.

Mr. Great-Heart: So he did, and as brave things came on't; for Hopeful, and some others, as the story relates it, were converted by his death.

Mr. Honest: Well, but pray go on; for you are well acquainted with things.

Mr. Great-Heart: Above all that Christian met with after he had passed through Vanity Fair, one By-ends was the arch one.

Mr. Honest: By-ends! what was he?

Mr. Great-Heart: A very arch fellow, a downright hypocrite; one that would be religious, whichever way the world went; but so cunning, that he would be sure never to lose or suffer for it. He had his mode of religion for every fresh occasion, and his wife was as good at it as he. He would turn from opinion to opinion; yea, and plead for so doing, too. But, so far as I could learn, he came to an ill end with his by-ends; nor did I ever hear that any of his children were ever of any esteem with any that truly feared God.

Now by this time they were come within sight of the town of Vanity, where Vanity Fair is kept. So, when they saw that they were so near the town, they consulted with one another how they should pass through the town; and some said one thing, and some another. At last Mr. Great-Heart said, I have, as you may understand, often been a conductor of pilgrims through this town. Now, I am acquainted with one Mr. Mnason, a Cyprusian by nation, an old disciple, at whose house we may lodge. If you think good, we will turn in there.

Content, said old Honest; Content, said Christiana; Content, said Mr. Feeble-mind; and so they said all. Now you must think it was eventide by that they got to the outside of the town; but Mr. Great-Heart knew the way to the old man's house. So thither they came; and he called at the door, and the old man within knew his tongue as soon as ever he heard it; so he opened the door, and they all came in. Then said Mnason, their host, How far have ye come to-day? So they said, from the house of Gaius our friend. I promise you, said he, you have gone a good stitch. You may well be weary; sit down. So they sat down.

Mr. Great-Heart: Then said their guide, Come, what cheer, good sirs? I dare say you are welcome to my friend.

Mr. Mnason: I also, said Mr. Mnason, do bid you welcome; and whatever you want, do but say, and we will do what we can to get it for you.

Mr. Honest: Our great want, a while since, was harbor and good company, and now I hope we have both.

Mr. Mnason: For harbor, you see what it is; but for good company, that will appear in the trial.

Mr. Great-Heart: Well, said Mr. Great-Heart, will you have the pilgrims up into their lodging?

Mr. Mnason: I will, said Mr. Mnason So he had them to their respective places; and also showed them a very fair dining-room, where they might be, and sup together until the time should come to go to rest.

Now, when they were seated in their places, and were a little cheery after their journey, Mr. Honest asked his landlord if there was any store of good people in the town.

Mr. Mnason: We have a few: for indeed they are but a few when compared with them on the other side.

Mr. Honest: But how shall we do to see some of them? for the sight of good men to them that are going on pilgrimage, is like the appearing of the moon and stars to them that are sailing upon the seas.

Mr. Mnason: Then Mr. Mnason stamped with his foot, and his daughter Grace came up. So he said unto her, Grace, go you, tell my friends, Mr. Contrite, Mr. Holy-man, Mr. Love-saints, Mr. Dare-not-lie, and Mr. Penitent, that I have a friend or two at my house who have a mind this evening to see them. So Grace went to call them, and they came; and after salutation made, they sat down together at the table.

Then said Mr. Mnason their landlord, My neighbors, I have, as you see, a company of strangers come to my house; they are pilgrims: they come from afar, and are going to Mount Zion. But who, quoth he, do you think this is? pointing his finger to Christiana. It is Christiana, the wife of Christian, the famous pilgrim, who, with Faithful his brother, was so shamefully handled in our town. At that they stood amazed, saying, We little thought to see Christiana when Grace came to call us; wherefore this is a very comfortable surprise. They then asked her of her welfare, and if these young men were her husband's sons. And when she had told them they were, they said, The King whom you love and serve make you as your father, and bring you where he is in peace.

Mr. Honest: Then Mr. Honest (when they were all sat down) asked Mr. Contrite and the rest, in what posture their town was at present.

Mr. Contrite: You may be sure we are full of hurry in fair-time. 'T is hard keeping our hearts and spirits in good order when we are in a cumbered condition. He that lives in such a place as this is, and has to do with such as we have, has need of an item to caution him to take heed every moment of the day.

Mr. Honest: But how are your neighbors now for quietness?

Mr. Contrite: They are much more moderate now than formerly. You know how Christian and Faithful were used at our town; but of late, I say, they have been far more moderate. I think the blood of Faithful lieth as a load upon them till now; for since they burned him, they have been ashamed to burn any more. In those days we were afraid to walk the street; but now we can show our heads. Then the name of a professor was odious; now, especially in some parts of our town, (for you know our town is large,) religion is counted honorable. Then said Mr. Contrite to them, Pray how fareth it with you in your pilgrimage? how stands the country affected towards you?

Mr. Honest: It happens to us as it happeneth to wayfaring men: sometimes our way is clean, sometimes foul; sometimes up hill, sometimes down hill; we are seldom at a certainty. The wind is not always on our backs, nor is every one a friend that we meet with in the way. We have met with some notable rubs already, and what are yet behind we know not; but for the most part, we find it true that has been talked of old, A good man must suffer trouble.

Mr. Contrite: You talk of rubs; what rubs have you met withal?

Mr. Honest: Nay, ask Mr. Great-Heart, our guide; for he can give the best account of that.

Mr. Great-Heart: We have been beset three or four times already. First, Christiana and her children were beset by two ruffians, who they feared would take away their lives. We were beset by Giant Bloody-man, Giant Maul, and Giant Slay-good. Indeed, we did rather beset the last than were beset by him. And thus it was: after we had been some time at the house of Gaius mine host, and of the whole church, we were minded upon a time to take our weapons with us, and go see if we could light upon any of those that are enemies to pilgrims; for we heard that there was a notable one thereabouts. Now Gaius knew his haunt better than I, because he dwelt thereabout. So we looked, and looked, till at last we discerned the mouth of his cave: then we were glad, and plucked up our spirits. So we approached up to his den; and lo, when we came there, he had dragged, by mere force, into his net, this poor man, Mr. Feeble-mind, and was about to bring him to his end. But when he saw us, supposing, as we thought, he had another prey, he left the poor man in his hole, and came out. So we fell to it full sore, and he lustily laid about him; but, in conclusion, he was brought down to the ground, and his head cut off, and set up by the way-side for a terror to such as should after practise such ungodliness. That I tell you the truth, here is the man himself to affirm it, who was as a lamb taken out of the mouth of the lion.

Mr. Feeble-Mind: Then said Mr. Feeble-mind, I found this true, to my cost and comfort: to my cost, when he threatened to pick my bones every moment; and to my comfort, when I saw Mr. Great-Heart and his friends, with their weapons, approach so near for my deliverance.

Mr. Holy-Man: Then said Mr. Holy-man, There are two things that they have need to possess who go on pilgrimage; courage, and an unspotted life. If they have not courage, they can never hold on their way; and if their lives be loose, they will make the very name of a pilgrim stink.

Mr. Love-Saints: Then said Mr. Love-saints, I hope this caution is not needful among you: but truly there are many that go upon the road, who rather declare themselves strangers to pilgrimage, than strangers and pilgrims on the earth.

Mr. Dare-Not-Lie: Then said Mr. Dare-not-lie, 'Tis true. They have neither the pilgrim's weed, nor the pilgrim's courage; they go not uprightly, but all awry with their feet; one shoe goeth inward, another outward; and their hosen are out behind: here a rag, and there a rent, to the disparagement of their Lord.

Mr. Penitent: These things, said Mr. Penitent, they ought to be troubled for; nor are the pilgrims like to have that grace put upon them and their Pilgrim's Progress as they desire, until the way is cleared of such spots and blemishes. Thus they sat talking and spending the time until supper was set upon the table, unto which they went, and refreshed their weary bodies: so they went to rest.

Now they staid in the fair a great while, at the house of Mr. Mnason, who in process of time gave his daughter Grace unto Samuel, Christian's son, to wife, and his daughter Martha to Joseph.

The time, as I said, that they staid here, was long, for it was not now as in former times. Wherefore the pilgrims grew acquainted with many of the good people of the town, and did them what service they could. Mercy, as she was wont, labored much for the poor: wherefore their bellies and backs blessed her, and she was there an ornament to her profession. And, to say the truth for Grace, Phebe, and Martha, they were all of a very good nature, and did much good in their places. They were also all of them very fruitful; so that Christian's name, as was said before, was like to live in the world.

While they lay here, there came a monster out of the woods, and slew many of the people of the town. It would also carry away their children, and teach them to suck its whelps. Now, no man in the town durst so much as face this monster; but all fled when they heard the noise of his coming.

The monster was like unto no one beast on the earth. Its body was like a dragon, and it had seven heads and ten horns. It made great havoc of children, and yet it was governed by a woman. This monster propounded conditions to men; and such men as loved their lives more than their souls, accepted of those conditions. So they came under.

Now Mr. Great-Heart, together with those who came to visit the pilgrims at Mr. Mnason's house, entered into a covenant to go and engage this beast, if perhaps they might deliver the people of this town from the paws and mouth of this so devouring a serpent.

Then did Mr. Great-Heart, Mr. Contrite, Mr. Holy-man, Mr. Dare-not-lie, and Mr. Penitent, with their weapons, go forth to meet him. Now the monster at first was very rampant, and looked upon these enemies with great disdain; but they so belabored him, being sturdy men at arms, that they made him make a retreat: so they came home to Mr. Mnason's house again.

The monster, you must know, had his certain seasons to come out in, and to make his attempts upon the children of the people of the town. At these seasons did these valiant worthies watch him, and did still continually assault him; insomuch that in process of time he became not only wounded, but lame. Also he has not made that havoc of the townsmen's children as formerly he had done; and it is verily believed by some that this beast will die of his wounds.

This, therefore, made Mr. Great-Heart and his fellows of great fame in this town; so that many of the people that wanted their taste of things, yet had a reverent esteem and respect for them. Upon this account, therefore, it was, that these pilgrims got not much hurt here. True, there were some of the baser sort, that could see no more than a mole, nor understand any more than a beast; these had no reverence for these men, and took no notice of their valor and adventures.

Lesson 87

- Read Book 2, Stage 7 of *The Pilgrim's Progress.*

Book 2, Stage 7

Well, the time grew on that the pilgrims must go on their way; wherefore they prepared for their journey. They sent for their friends; they conferred with them; they had some time set apart therein to commit each other to the protection of their Prince. There were again that brought them of such things as they had, that were fit for the weak and the strong, for the women and the men, and so laded them with such things as were necessary. Then they set forward on their way; and their friends accompanying them so far as was convenient, they again committed each other to the protection of their King, and parted.

They therefore that were of the pilgrims' company went on, and Mr. Great-Heart went before them. Now, the women and children being weakly, they were forced to go as they could bear; by which means Mr. Ready-to-halt and Mr. Feeble-mind, had more to sympathize with their condition.

When they were gone from the townsmen, and when their friends had bid them farewell, they quickly came to the place where Faithful was put to death. Therefore they made a stand, and thanked him that had enabled him to bear his cross so well; and the rather, because they now found that they had a benefit by such a manly suffering as his was.

They went on therefore after this a good way further, talking of Christian and Faithful, and how Hopeful joined himself to Christian after that Faithful was dead.

Now they were come up with the hill Lucre, where the silver mine was which took Demas off from his pilgrimage, and into which, as some think, By-ends fell and perished; wherefore they considered that. But when they were come to the old monument that stood over against the hill Lucre, to wit, to the pillar of salt, that stood also within view of Sodom and its stinking lake, they marvelled, as did Christian before, that men of such knowledge and ripeness of wit as they were, should be so blinded as to turn aside here. Only they considered again, that nature is not affected with the harms that others have met with, especially if that thing upon which they look has an attracting virtue upon the foolish eye.

I saw now, that they went on till they came to the river that was on this side of the Delectable Mountains; to the river where the fine trees grow on both sides, and whose leaves, if taken inwardly, are good against surfeits; where the meadows are green all the year long, and where they might lie down safely.

By this river-side, in the meadows, there were cotes and folds for sheep, a house built for the nourishing and bringing up of those lambs, the babes of those women that go on pilgrimage. Also there was here one that was intrusted with them, who could have compassion; and that could gather these lambs with his arm, and carry them in his bosom, and gently lead those that were with young. Now, to the care of this man Christiana admonished her four daughters to commit their little ones, that by these waters they might be housed, harbored, succored, and nourished, and that none of them might be lacking in time to come. This man, if any of them go astray, or be lost, will bring them again; he will also bind up that which was broken, and will strengthen them that are sick. Here they will never want meat, drink, and clothing; here they will be kept from thieves and robbers; for this man will die before one of those committed to his trust shall be lost. Besides, here they shall be sure to have good nurture and admonition, and shall be taught to walk in right paths, and that you know is a favor of no small account. Also here, as you see, are delicate waters, pleasant meadows, dainty flowers, variety of trees, and such as bear wholesome fruit: fruit, not like that which Matthew ate of, that fell over the wall out of Beelzebub's garden; but fruit that procureth health where there is none, and that continueth and increaseth it where it is. So they were content to commit their little ones to him; and that which was also an encouragement to them so to do, was, for that all this was to be at the charge of the King, and so was as an hospital to young children and orphans.

Now they went on. And when they were come to By-path Meadow, to the stile over which Christian went with his fellow Hopeful, when they were taken by Giant

Despair and put into Doubting Castle, they sat down, and consulted what was best to be done: to wit, now they were so strong, and had got such a man as Mr. Great-Heart for their conductor, whether they had not best to make an attempt upon the giant, demolish his castle, and if there were any pilgrims in it, to set them at liberty before they went any further. So one said one thing, and another said the contrary. One questioned if it was lawful to go upon unconsecrated ground; another said they might, provided their end was good; but Mr. Great-Heart said, Though that assertion offered last cannot be universally true, yet I have a commandment to resist sin, to overcome evil, to fight the good fight of faith: and I pray, with whom should I fight this good fight, if not with Giant Despair? I will therefore attempt the taking away of his life, and the demolishing of Doubting Castle. Then said he, Who will go with me? Then said old Honest, I will. And so will we too, said Christiana's four sons, Matthew, Samuel, Joseph, and James; for they were young men and strong. So they left the women in the road, and with them Mr. Feeble-mind, and Mr. Ready-to-halt with his crutches, to be their guard until they came back; for in that place the Giant Despair dwelt so near, they keeping in the road, a little child might lead them.

So Mr. Great-Heart, old Honest, and the four young men, went to go up to Doubting Castle, to look for Giant Despair. When they came at the castle gate, they knocked for entrance with an unusual noise. At that the old Giant comes to the gate, and Diffidence his wife follows. Then said he, Who and what is he that is so hardy, as after this manner to molest the Giant Despair? Mr. Great-Heart replied, It is I, Great-Heart, one of the King of the Celestial country's conductors of pilgrims to their place; and I demand of thee that thou open thy gates for my entrance: prepare thyself also to fight, for I am come to take away thy head; and to demolish Doubting Castle.

Now Giant Despair, because he was a giant, thought no man could overcome him: and again thought he, Since heretofore I have made a conquest of angels, shall Great-Heart make me afraid? So he harnessed himself, and went out. He had a cap of steel upon his head, a breast-plate of fire girded to him, and he came out in iron shoes, with a great club in his hand. Then these six men made up to him, and beset him behind and before: also, when Diffidence the giantess came up to help him, old Mr. Honest cut her down at one blow. Then they fought for their lives, and Giant Despair was brought down to the ground, but was very loth die. He struggled hard, and had, as they say, as many lives as a cat; but Great-Heart was his death, for he left him not till he had severed his head from his shoulders.

Then they fell to demolishing Doubting Castle, and that you know might with ease be done, since Giant Despair was dead. They were seven days in destroying of that; and in it of pilgrims they found one Mr. Despondency, almost starved to death, and one Much-afraid, his daughter: these two they saved alive. But it would have made you wonder to have seen the dead bodies that lay here and there in the castle yard, and how full of dead men's bones the dungeon was.

When Mr. Great-Heart and his companions had performed this exploit, they took Mr. Despondency, and his daughter Much-afraid, into their protection; for they were honest people, though they were prisoners in Doubting Castle to that tyrant Giant Despair. They, therefore, I say, took with them the head of the giant, (for his body they had buried under a heap of stones,) and down to the road and to their companions they came, and showed them what they had done. Now, when Feeble-mind and Ready-to-halt saw that it was the head of Giant Despair indeed, they were very jocund and merry. Now Christiana, if need was, could play upon the viol, and her daughter Mercy upon the lute: so, since they were so merry disposed, she played them a lesson, and Ready-to-halt would dance. So he took Despondency's daughter, Much-afraid, by the hand, and to dancing they went in the road. True, he could not dance without one crutch in his hand, but I promise you he footed it well: also the girl was to be commended, for she answered the music handsomely.

As for Mr. Despondency, the music was not so much to him; he was for feeding rather than dancing, for that he was almost starved. So Christiana gave him some of her bottle of spirits for present relief, and then prepared him something to eat; and in a little time the old gentleman came to himself, and began to be finely revived.

Now I saw in my dream, when all these things were finished, Mr. Great-Heart took the head of Giant Despair, and set it upon a pole by the highway-side, right over against the pillar that Christian erected for a caution to pilgrims that came after, to take heed of entering into his grounds.

Then he writ under it upon a marble stone these verses following:
"This is the head of him whose name only

In former times did pilgrims terrify.
His castle's down, and Diffidence his wife
Brave Mr. Great-Heart has bereft of life.
Despondency, his daughter Much-afraid,
Great-Heart for them also the man has play'd.
Who hereof doubts, if he'll but cast his eye
Up hither, may his scruples satisfy.
This head also, when doubting cripples dance,
Doth show from fears they have deliverance."

When these men had thus bravely showed themselves against Doubting Castle, and had slain Giant Despair, they went forward, and went on till they came to the Delectable Mountains, where Christian and Hopeful refreshed themselves with the varieties of the place. They also acquainted themselves with the shepherds there, who welcomed them, as they had done Christian before, unto the Delectable Mountains.

Now the shepherds seeing so great a train follow Mr. Great-Heart, (for with him they were well acquainted,) they said unto him, Good sir, you have got a goodly company here; pray where did you find all these?

Then Mr. Great-Heart replied,

"First, here is Christiana and her train,
Her sons, and her sons' wives, who, like the wain,
Keep by the pole, and do by compass steer
From sin to grace, else they had not been here.
Next here's old Honest come on pilgrimage,
Ready-to-halt too, who I dare engage
True-hearted is, and so is Feeble-mind,
Who willing was not to be left behind.
Despondency, good man, is coming after,
And so also is Much-afraid, his daughter.
May we have entertainment here, or must
We further go? Let's knew whereon to trust."

Then said the shepherds, This is a comfortable company. You are welcome to us; for we have for the feeble, as well as for the strong. Our Prince has an eye to what is done to the least of these; therefore Infirmity must not be a block to our entertainment. So they had them to the palace door, and then said unto them, Come in, Mr. Feeble-Mind; come in Mr. Ready-to-halt; Come in, Mr. Despondency, and Mrs. Much-afraid his daughter. These, Mr. Great-Heart, said the shepherds to the guide, we call in by name, for that they are most subject to draw back; but as for you, and the rest that are strong, we leave you to your wonted liberty. Then said Mr. Great-Heart, This day I see that grace doth shine in your faces, and that you are my Lord's shepherds indeed; for that you have not pushed these diseased neither with side nor shoulder, but have rather strewed their way into the palace with flowers, as you should.

So the feeble and weak went in, and Mr. Great-Heart and the rest did follow. When they were also set down, the shepherds said to those of the weaker sort, What is it that you would have? for, said they, all things must be managed here to the supporting of the weak, as well as to the warning of the unruly. So they made them a feast of things easy of digestion, and that were pleasant to the palate and nourishing; the which when they had received, they went to their rest, each one respectively unto his proper place.

When morning was come, because the mountains were high and the day clear, and because it was the custom of the shepherds to show the pilgrims before their departure some rarities, therefore, after they were ready, and had refreshed themselves, the shepherds took them out into the fields, and showed them first what they had shown to Christian before.

Then they had them to some new places. The first was Mount Marvel, where they looked, and beheld a man at a distance that tumbled the hills about with words. Then they asked the shepherds what that should mean. So they told them, that that man was the son of one Mr. Great-grace, of whom you read in the first part of the records of the Pilgrim's Progress; and he is set there to teach pilgrims how to believe down, or to tumble out of their ways, what difficulties they should meet with, by faith. Then said Mr. Great-Heart, I know him; he is a man above many.

Then they had them to another place, called Mount Innocence. And there they saw a man clothed all in white; and two men, Prejudice and Ill-will, continually casting dirt upon him. Now behold, the dirt, whatsoever they cast at him, would in a little time fall off again, and his garment would look as clear as if no dirt had been cast thereat. Then said the pilgrims, What means this? The shepherds answered, This man is named Godlyman, and this garment is to show the innocency of his life. Now, those that throw dirt at him are such as hate his well-doing; but, as you see the dirt will not stick upon his clothes, so it shall be with him that liveth innocently in the world. Whoever they be that would make such men dirty, they labor all in vain; for God, by that a little time is spent, will cause that their innocence shall break forth as the light, and their righteousness as the noonday.

Then they took them, and had them to Mount Charity, where they showed them a man that had a bundle of cloth lying before him, out of which he cut coats and garments for the poor that stood about him; yet his bundle or roll of cloth was never the less. Then said they, What should this be? This is, said the shepherds, to show you, that he who has a heart to give of his labor to the poor, shall never want wherewithal. He that watereth shall be watered himself. And the cake that the widow gave to the prophet did not cause that she had the less in her barrel.

They had them also to the place where they saw one Fool and one Want-wit washing an Ethiopian, with intention to make him white; but the more they washed him, the blacker he was. Then they asked the shepherds what that should mean. So they told them, saying, Thus it is with the vile person; all means used to get such a one a good name, shall in conclusion tend but to make him more abominable. Thus it was with the pharisees; and so it shall be with all hypocrites.

Then said Mercy, the wife of Matthew, to Christiana her mother, Mother, I would, if it might be, see the hole in the hill, or that commonly called the By-way to hell. So her mother brake her mind to the shepherds. Then they went to the door; it was on the side of an hill; and they opened it, and bid Mercy hearken a while. So she hearkened, and heard one saying, Cursed be my father for holding of my feet back from the way of peace and life. Another said, Oh that I had been torn in pieces before I had, to save my life, lost my soul! And another said, If I were to live again, how would I deny myself, rather than to come to this place! Then there was as if the very earth groaned and quaked under the feet of this young woman for fear; so she looked white, and came trembling away, saying, Blessed be he and she that is delivered from this place!

Now, when the shepherds had shown them all these things, then they had them back to the palace, and entertained them with what the house would afford. But Mercy, being a young and married woman, longed for something that she saw there, but was ashamed to ask. Her mother-in-law then asked her what she ailed, for she looked as one not well. Then said Mercy, There is a looking-glass hangs up in the dining-room, off which I cannot take my mind; if, therefore, I have it not, I think I shall miscarry. Then said her mother, I will mention thy wants to the shepherds, and they will not deny thee. But she said, I am ashamed that these men should know that I longed. Nay, my daughter, said she, it is no shame, but a virtue, to long for such a thing as that. So Mercy said, Then mother, if you please, ask the shepherds if they are willing to sell it.

Now the glass was one of a thousand. It would present a man, one way, with his own features exactly; and turn it but another way, and it would show one the very face and similitude of the Prince of pilgrims himself. Yes, I have talked with them that can tell, and they have said that they have seen the very crown of thorns upon his head by looking in that glass; they have therein also seen the holes in his hands, his feet, and his side. Yea, such an excellency is there in this glass, that it will show him to one where they have a mind to see him, whether living or dead; whether in earth, or in heaven; whether in a state of humiliation, or in his exaltation; whether coming to suffer, or coming to reign.

Christiana therefore went to the shepherds apart, (now the names of the shepherds were Knowledge, Experience, Watchful, and Sincere,) and said unto them, There is one of my daughters, a breeding woman, that I think doth long for something that she hath seen in this house; and she thinks that she shall miscarry if she should by you be denied.

Experience: Call her, call her, she shall assuredly have what we can help her to. So they called her, and said to her, Mercy, what is that thing thou wouldst have? Then she blushed, and said, The great glass that hangs up in the dining-room. So Sincere ran and fetched it, and with a joyful consent it was given her. Then she bowed her head, and gave thanks, and said, By this I know that I have obtained favor in your eyes.

They also gave to the other young women such things as they desired, and to their husbands great commendations, for that they had joined with Mr. Great-Heart in the slaying of Giant Despair, and the demolishing of Doubting Castle.

About Christiana's neck the shepherds put a bracelet, and so did they about the necks of her four daughters; also they put ear-rings in their ears, and jewels on their foreheads.

When they were minded to go hence, they let them go in peace, but gave not to them those certain cautions which before were given to Christian and his companion. The reason was, for that these had Great-Heart to be their guide, who was one that was well acquainted with things, and so could give them their cautions more seasonably, to wit, even when the danger was nigh the approaching. What cautions Christian and his companion had received of the shepherds, they had also lost by that the time was come that they had need to put them in practice. Wherefore, here was the advantage that this company had over the other.

From thence they went on singing, and they said,

"Behold how fitly are the stages set
  For their relief that pilgrims are become,
And how they us receive without one let,
  That make the other life our mark and home!

What novelties they have to us they give,
  That we, though pilgrims, joyful lives may live;
They do upon us, too, such things bestow,
  That show we pilgrims are, where'er we go."

Lesson 88

- Read Book 2, Stage 8 of *The Pilgrim's Progress*.

Book 2, Stage 8

When they were gone from the shepherds, they quickly came to the place where Christian met with one Turn-away that dwelt in the town of Apostasy. Wherefore of him Mr. Great-Heart their guide now put them in mind, saying, This is the place where Christian met with one Turn-away, who carried with him the character of his rebellion at his back. And this I have to say concerning this man; he would hearken to no counsel, but once a falling, persuasion could not stop him. When he came to the place where the cross and sepulchre were, he did meet with one that did bid him look there; but he gnashed with his teeth, and stamped, and said he was resolved to go back to his own town. Before he came to the gate, he met with Evangelist, who offered to lay hands on him, to turn him into the way again; but this Turn-away resisted him, and having done much despite unto him, he got away over the wall, and so escaped his hand.

Then they went on; and just at the place where Little-Faith formerly was robbed, there stood a man with his sword drawn, and his face all over with blood. Then said Mr. Great-Heart, Who art thou? The man made answer, saying, I am one whose name is Valiant-for-truth. I am a pilgrim, and am going to the Celestial City. Now, as I was in my way, there were three men that did beset me, and propounded unto me these three things: 1. Whether I would become one of them. 2. Or go back from whence I came. 3. Or die upon the place. To the first I answered, I had been a true man for a long season, and therefore it could not be expected that I should now cast in my lot with thieves. Then they demanded what I would say to the second. So I told them that the place from whence I came, had I not found incommodity there, I had not forsaken it at all; but finding it altogether unsuitable to me, and very unprofitable for me, I forsook it for this way. Then they asked me what I said to the third. And I told them my life cost far more dear than that I should lightly give it away. Besides, you have nothing to do thus to put things to my choice; wherefore at your peril be it if you meddle. Then these three, to wit, Wild-head, Inconsiderate, and Pragmatic, drew upon me, and I also drew upon them. So we fell to it, one against three, for the space of above three hours. They have left upon me, as you see, some of the marks of their valor, and have also carried away with them some of mine. They are but just now gone; I suppose they might, as the saying is, hear your horse dash, and so they betook themselves to flight.

Mr. Great-Heart: But here was great odds, three against one.

Valiant-For-Truth: 'Tis true; but little and more are nothing to him that has the truth on his side: "Though an host should encamp against me," said one, "my heart shall not fear: though war should rise against me, in this will I be confident," etc. Besides, said he, I have read in some records, that one man has fought an army: and how many did Samson slay with the jawbone of an ass!

Mr. Great-House: Then said the guide, Why did you not cry out, that some might have come in for your succor?

Valiant-For-Truth: So I did to my King, who I knew could hear me, and afford invisible help, and that was sufficient for me.

Mr. Great-Heart: Then said Great-Heart to Mr. Valiant-for-truth, Thou hast worthily behaved thyself; let me see thy sword. So he showed it him.

When he had taken it in his hand, and looked thereon awhile, he said, Ha, it is a right Jerusalem blade.

Valiant-For-Truth: It is so. Let a man have one of these blades, with a hand to wield it, and skill to use it, and he may venture upon an angel with it. He need not fear its holding, if he can but tell how to lay on. Its edge will never blunt. It will cut flesh and bones, and soul, and spirit, and all.

Mr. Great-Heart: But you fought a great while; I wonder you was not weary.

Valiant-For-Truth: I fought till my sword did cleave to my hand; and then they were joined together as if a sword grew out of my arm; and when the blood ran through my fingers, then I fought with most courage.

Mr. Great-Heart: Thou hast done well; thou hast resisted unto blood, striving against sin. Thou shalt abide by us, come in and go out with us; for we are thy companions. Then they took him and washed his wounds, and gave him of what they had, to refresh him: and so they went together.

Now, as they went on, because Mr. Great-Heart was delighted in him, (for he loved one greatly that he found to be a man of his hands,) and because there were in company those that were feeble and weak, therefore he questioned with him about many things; as first, what countryman he was.

Valiant-For-Truth: I am of Dark-land; for there was I born, and there my father and mother are still.

Mr. Great-Heart: Dark-land! said the guide; doth not that lie on the same coast with the City of Destruction?

Valiant-For-Truth: Yes, it doth. Now that which caused me to come on pilgrimage was this. We had one Mr. Tell-true come into our parts, and he told it about what Christian had done, that went from the City of Destruction; namely, how he had forsaken his wife and children, and had betaken himself to a pilgrim's life. It was also confidently reported, how he had killed a serpent that did come out to resist him in his journey; and how he got through to whither he intended. It was also told what welcome he had at all his Lord's lodgings, especially when he came to the gates of the Celestial City; for there, said the man, he was received with sound of trumpet by a company of shining ones. He told also how all the bells in the city did ring for joy at his reception, and what golden garments he was clothed with; with many other things that now I shall forbear to relate. In a word, that man so told the story of Christian and his travels that my heart fell into a burning haste to be gone after him; nor could father or mother stay me. So I got from them, and am come thus far on my way.

Mr. Great-Heart: You came in at the gate, did you not?

Valiant-For-Truth: Yes, yes; for the same man also told us, that all would be nothing if we did not begin to enter this way at the gate.

Mr. Great-Heart: Look you, said the guide to Christiana, the pilgrimage of your husband, and what he has gotten thereby, is spread abroad far and near.

Valiant-For-Truth: Why, is this Christian's wife?

Mr. Great-Heart: Yes, that it is; and these also are his four sons.

Valiant-For-Truth: What, and going on pilgrimage too?

Mr. Great-Heart: Yes, verily, they are following after.

Valiant-For-Truth: It glads me at the heart. Good man, how joyful will he be when he shall see them that would not go with him, yet to enter after him in at the gates into the Celestial City.

Mr. Great-Heart: Without doubt it will be a comfort to him; for, next to the joy of seeing himself there, it will be a joy to meet there his wife and children.

Valiant-For-Truth: But now you are upon that, pray let me hear your opinion about it. Some make a question whether we shall know one another when we are there.

Mr. Great-Heart: Do you think they shall know themselves then, or that they shall rejoice to see themselves in that bliss? And if they think they shall know and do this, why not know others, and rejoice in their welfare also? Again, since relations are our second self, though that state will be dissolved there, yet why may it not be rationally concluded that we shall be more glad to see them there than to see they are wanting?

Valiant-For-Truth: Well, I perceive whereabouts you are as to this. Have you any more things to ask me about my beginning to come on pilgrimage?

Mr. Great-Heart: Yes; were your father and mother willing that you should become a pilgrim?

Valiant-For-Truth: O no; they used all means imaginable to persuade me to stay at home.

Mr. Great-Heart: Why, what could they say against it?

Valiant-For-Truth: They said it was an idle life; and if I myself were not inclined to sloth and laziness, I would never countenance a pilgrim's condition.

Mr. Great-Heart: And what did they say else?

Valiant-For-Truth: Why, they told me that it was a dangerous way; yea, the most dangerous way in the world, said they, is that which the pilgrims go.

Mr. Great-Heart: Did they show you wherein this way is so dangerous?

Valiant-For-Truth: Yes; and that in many particulars.

Mr. Great-Heart: Name some of them.

Valiant-For-Truth: They told me of the Slough of Despond, where Christian was well-nigh smothered. They told me, that there were archers standing ready in Beelzebub-castle to shoot them who should knock at the Wicket-gate for entrance. They told me also of the wood and dark mountains; of the hill Difficulty; of the lions; and also of the three giants, Bloody-man, Maul, and Slay-good. They said, moreover, that there was a foul fiend haunted the Valley of Humiliation; and that Christian was by him almost bereft of life. Besides, said they, you must go over the Valley of the Shadow of Death, where the hobgoblins are, where the light is darkness, where the way is full of snares, pits, traps, and gins. They told me also of Giant Despair, of Doubting Castle, and of the ruin that the pilgrims met with here. Further they said I must go over the Enchanted Ground, which was dangerous; And that after all this I should find a river, over which there was no bridge; and that that river did lie betwixt me and the Celestial country.

Mr. Great-Heart: And was this all?

Valiant-For-Truth: No. They also told me that this way was full of deceivers, and of persons that lay in wait there to turn good men out of the path.

Mr. Great-Heart: But how did they make that out?

Valiant-For-Truth: They told me that Mr. Worldly Wiseman did lie there in wait to deceive. They said also, that there were Formality and Hypocrisy continually on the road. They said also, that By-ends, Talkative, or Demas, would go near to gather me up; that the Flatterer would catch me in his net; or that, with green-headed Ignorance, I would presume to go on to the gate, from whence he was sent back to the hole that was in the side of the hill, and made to go the by-way to hell.

Mr. Great-Heart: I promise you this was enough to discourage you; but did they make an end here?

Valiant-For-Truth: No, stay. They told me also of many that had tried that way of old, and that had gone a great way therein, to see if they could find something of the glory there that so many had so much talked of from time to time, and how they came back again, and befooled themselves for setting a foot out of doors in that path, to the satisfaction of all the country. And they named several that did so, as Obstinate and Pliable, Mistrust and Timorous, Turn-away and old Atheist, with several more; who, they said, had some of them gone far to see what they could find, but not one of them had found so much advantage by going as amounted to the weight of a feather.

Mr. Great-Heart: Said they any thing more to discourage you?

Valiant-For-Truth: Yes. They told me of one Mr. Fearing, who was a pilgrim, and how he found his way so solitary that he never had a comfortable hour therein; also, that Mr. Despondency had like to have been starved therein: yea, and also (which I had almost forgot) that Christian himself, about whom there has been such a noise, after all his adventures for a celestial crown, was certainly drowned in the Black River, and never went a foot further; however it was smothered up.

Mr. Great-Heart: And did none of these things discourage you?

Valiant-For-Truth: No; they seemed but as so many nothings to me.

Mr. Great-Heart: How came that about?

Valiant-For-Truth: Why, I still believed what Mr. Tell-true had said; and that carried me beyond them all.

Mr. Great-Heart: Then this was your victory, even your faith.

Valiant-For-Truth: It was so. I believed, and therefore came out, got into the way, fought all that set themselves against me, and, by believing, am come to this place.

"Who would true valor see,

  Let him come hither;
One here will constant be,
  Come wind, come weather
There's no discouragement
Shall make him once relent
His first avow'd intent
To be a pilgrim.

Whoso beset him round
  With dismal stories,
Do but themselves confound;
  His strength the more is.
No lion can him fright,
He'll with a giant fight,
But he will have a right
To be a pilgrim.

Hobgoblin nor foul fiend
  Can daunt his spirit;
He knows he at the end
  Shall life inherit.
Then fancies fly away,
He'll not fear what men say;
He'll labor night and day
To be a pilgrim.

By this time they were got to the Enchanted Ground, where the air naturally tended to make one drowsy. And that place was all grown over with briars and thorns, excepting here and there, where was an enchanted arbor, upon which if a man sits, or in which if a man sleeps, it is a question, some say, whether ever he shall rise or wake again in this world. Over this forest, therefore, they went, both one and another, and Mr. Great-Heart went before, for that he was the guide; and Mr. Valiant-for-truth came behind, being rear-guard, for fear lest peradventure some fiend, or dragon, or giant, or thief, should fall upon their rear, and so do mischief. They went on here, each man with his sword drawn in his hand; for they knew it was a dangerous place. Also they cheered up one another as well as they could.

Feeble-mind, Mr. Great-Heart commanded should come up after him; and Mr. Despondency was under the eye of Mr. Valiant.

Now they had not gone far, but a great mist and darkness fell upon them all; so that they could scarce, for a great while, the one see the other. Wherefore they were forced, for some time, to feel one for another by words; for they walked not by sight. But any one must think, that here was but sorry going for the best of them all; but how much worse for the women and children, who both of feet and heart were but tender! Yet so it was, that through the encouraging words of him that led in the front, and of him that brought them up behind, they made a pretty good shift to wag along.

The way also here was very wearisome, through dirt and slabbiness. Nor was there, on all this ground, so much as one inn or victualling-house wherein to refresh the feebler sort. Here, therefore, was grunting, and puffing, and sighing, while one tumbleth over a bush, another sticks fast in the dirt, and the children, some of them, lost their shoes in the mire; while one cries out, I am down; and another, Ho, where are you? and a third, The bushes have got such fast hold on me, I think I cannot get away from them.

Then they came at an arbor, warm, and promising much refreshing to the pilgrims; for it was finely wrought above-head, beautified with greens, furnished with benches and settles. It also had in it a soft couch, whereon the weary might lean. This, you must think, all things considered, was tempting; for the pilgrims already began to be foiled with the badness of the way: but there was not one of them that made so much as a motion to stop there. Yea, for aught I could perceive, they continually gave so good heed to the advice of their guide, and he did so faithfully tell them of dangers, and of the nature of the dangers when they were at them, that usually, when they were nearest to them, they did most pluck up their spirits, and hearten one another to deny the flesh. This arbor was called The Slothful's Friend, and was made on purpose to allure, if it might be, some of the pilgrims there to take up their rest when weary.

I saw them in my dream, that they went on in this their solitary ground, till they came to a place at which a man is apt to lose his way. Now, though when it was light their guide could well enough tell how to miss those ways that led wrong, yet in the dark he was put to a stand. But he had in his pocket a map of all ways leading to or from the Celestial City; wherefore he struck a light (for he never goes without his tinder-box also), and takes a view of his book or map, which bids him to be careful in that place to turn to the right hand. And had he not been careful here to look in his map, they had all, in probability, been smothered in the mud; for just a little before them, and that at the end of the cleanest way too, was a pit, none knows how deep, full of nothing but mud, there made on purpose to destroy the pilgrims in.

Then thought I with myself, Who that goeth on pilgrimage but would have one of these maps about him, that he may look, when he is at a stand, which is the way he must take?

Then they went on in this Enchanted Ground till they came to where there was another arbor, and it was built by the highway-side. And in that arbor there lay two men, whose names were Heedless and Too-bold. These two went thus far on pilgrimage; but here, being wearied with their journey, they sat down to rest themselves, and so fell fast asleep. When the pilgrims saw them, they stood still, and shook their heads; for they knew that the sleepers were in a pitiful case. Then they consulted what to do, whether to go on and leave them in their sleep, or to step to them and try to awake them; so they concluded to go to them and awake them, that is, if they could; but with this caution, namely, to take heed that they themselves did not sit down nor embrace the offered benefit of that arbor.

So they went in, and spake to the men, and called each by his name, for the guide, it seems, did know them; but there was no voice nor answer. Then the guide did shake them, and do what he could to disturb them. Then said one of them, I will pay you when I take my money. At which the guide shook his head. I will fight so long as I can hold my sword in my hand, said the other. At that, one of the children laughed.

Then said Christiana, What is the meaning of this? The guide said, They talk in their sleep. If you strike them, beat them, or whatever else you do to them, they will answer you after this fashion; or, as one of them said in old time, when the waves of the sea did beat upon him, and he slept as one upon the mast of a ship, When I awake, I will seek it yet again. You know, when men talk in their sleep, they say any thing; but their words are not governed either by faith or reason. There is an incoherency in their words now, as there was before betwixt their going on pilgrimage and sitting down here. This, then, is the mischief of it: when heedless ones go on pilgrimage, 'tis twenty to one but they are served thus. For this Enchanted Ground is one of the last refuges that the enemy to pilgrims has; wherefore it is, as you see, placed almost at the end of the way, and so it standeth against us with the more advantage. For when, thinks the enemy, will these fools be so desirous to sit down as when they are weary? and when so like to be weary as when almost at their journey's end? Therefore it is, I say, that the Enchanted Ground is placed so nigh to the land Beulah, and so near the end of their race. Wherefore let pilgrims look to themselves, lest it happen to them as it has done to these that, as you see, are fallen asleep, and none can awake them.

Then the pilgrims desired with trembling to go forward; only they prayed their guide to strike a light, that they might go the rest of their way by the help of the light of a lantern. So he struck a light, and they went by the help of that through the rest of this way, though the darkness was very great. But the children began to be sorely weary, and they cried out unto him that loveth pilgrims, to make their way more comfortable. So by that they had gone a little further, a wind arose that drove away the fog, so the air became more clear. Yet they were not off (by much) of the Enchanted Ground; only now they could see one another better, and the way wherein they should walk.

Now when they were almost at the end of this ground, they perceived that a little before them was a solemn noise, as of one that was much concerned. So they went on and looked before them: and behold they saw, as they thought, a man upon his knees, with hands and eyes lifted up, and speaking, as they thought, earnestly to one that was above. They drew nigh, but could not tell what he said; so they went softly till he had done. When he had done, he got up, and began to run towards the Celestial City. Then Mr. Great-Heart called after him, saying, Soho, friend, let us have your company, if you go, as I suppose you do, to the Celestial City. So the man stopped, and they came up to him. But as soon as Mr. Honest saw him, he said, I know this man. Then said Mr. Valiant-for-truth, Prithee, who is it? It is one, said he, that comes from whereabout I dwelt. His name is Standfast; he is certainly a right good pilgrim.

So they came up to one another; and presently Standfast said to old Honest, Ho, father Honest, are you there? Aye, said he, that I am, as sure as you are there. Right glad am I, said Mr. Standfast, that I have found you on this road. And as glad am I, said the other, that I espied you on your knees. Then Mr. Standfast blushed, and said, But why, did you see me? Yes, that I did, quoth the other, and with my heart was glad at the sight. Why, what did you think? said Standfast. Think! said old Honest; what could I think? I thought we had an honest man upon the road, and therefore should have his company by and by. If you thought not amiss, said Standfast, how happy am I! But if I be not as I should, 't is I alone must bear it. That is true, said the other; but your fear doth further confirm me that things are right betwixt the Prince of pilgrims and your soul. For he saith, "Blessed is the man that feareth always."

Valiant-For-Truth: Well but, brother, I pray thee tell us what was it that was the cause of thy being upon thy knees even now: was it for that some special mercy laid obligations upon thee, or how?

Standfast: Why, we are, as you see, upon the Enchanted Ground; and as I was coming along, I was musing with myself of what a dangerous nature the road in this place was, and how many that had come even thus far on pilgrimage, had here been stopped and been destroyed. I thought also of the manner of the death with which this place destroyeth men. Those that die here, die of no violent distemper: the death which such die is not grievous to them. For he that goeth away in a sleep, begins that journey with desire and pleasure. Yea, such acquiesce in the will of that disease.

Mr. Honest: Then Mr. Honest interrupting him, said, Did you see the two men asleep in the arbor?

Standfast: Aye, aye, I saw Heedless and Too-bold there; and for ought I know, there they will lie till they rot. But let me go on with my tale. As I was thus musing, as I said, there was one in very pleasant attire, but old, who presented herself to me, and offered me three things, to wit, her body, her purse, and her bed. Now the truth is, I was both weary and sleepy. I am also as poor as an owlet, and that perhaps the witch knew. Well, I repulsed her once and again, but she put by my repulses, and smiled. Then I began to be angry; but she mattered that nothing at all. Then she made offers again, and said, if I would be ruled by her, she would make me great and happy; for, said she, I am the mistress of the world, and men are made happy by me. Then I asked her name, and she told me it was Madam Bubble. This set me further from her; but she still followed me with enticements. Then I betook me, as you saw, to my knees, and with hands lifted up, and cries, I prayed to Him that had said he would help. So, just as you came up, the gentlewoman went her way. Then I continued to give thanks for this my great deliverance; for I verily believe she intended no good, but rather sought to make stop of me in my journey.

Mr. Honest: Without doubt her designs were bad. But stay, now you talk of her, methinks I either have seen her, or have read some story of her.

Standfast: Perhaps you have done both.

Mr. Honest: Madam Bubble! Is she not a tall, comely dame, something of a swarthy complexion?

Standfast: Right, you hit it: she is just such a one.

Mr. Honest: Doth she not speak very smoothly, and give you a smile at the end of a sentence?

Standfast: You fall right upon it again, for these are her very actions.

Mr. Honest: Doth she not wear a great purse by her side, and is not her hand often in it, fingering her money, as if that was her heart's delight.

Standfast: 'Tis just so; had she stood by all this while, you could not more amply have set her forth before me, nor have better described her features.

Mr. Honest: Then he that drew her picture was a good limner, and he that wrote of her said true.

Mr. Great-Heart: This woman is a witch, and it is by virtue of her sorceries that this ground is enchanted. Whoever doth lay his head down in her lap, had as good lay it down on that block over which the axe doth hang; and whoever lay their eyes upon her beauty are counted the enemies of God. This is she that maintaineth in their splendor all those that are the enemies of pilgrims. Yea, this is she that has bought off many a man from a pilgrim's life. She is a great gossiper; she is always, both she and her daughters, at one pilgrim's heels or another, now commending, and then preferring the excellences of this life. She is a bold and impudent slut: she will talk with any man. She always laugheth poor pilgrims to scorn, but highly commends the rich. If there be one cunning to get money in a place, she will speak well of him from house to house. She loveth banqueting and feasting mainly well; she is always at one full table or another. She has given it out in some places that she is a goddess, and therefore some do worship her. She has her time, and open places of cheating; and she will say and avow it, that none can show a good comparable to hers. She promiseth to dwell with children's children, if they will but love her and make much of her. She will cast out of her purse gold like dust in some places and to some persons. She loves to be sought after, spoken well of, and to lie in the bosoms of men. She is never weary of commending her commodities, and she loves them most that think best of her. She will promise to some crowns and kingdoms, if they will but take her advice; yet many has she brought to the halter, and ten thousand times more to hell.

Standfast: Oh, said Standfast, what a mercy is it that I did resist her; for whither might she have drawn me!

Mr. Great-Heart: Whither? nay, none but God knows whither. But in general, to be sure, she would have drawn thee into many foolish and hurtful lusts, which drown men in destruction and perdition. 'T was she that set Absalom against his father, and Jeroboam against his master. 'T was she that persuaded Judas to sell his Lord; and that prevailed with Demas to forsake the godly pilgrim's life. None can tell of the mischief that she doth. She makes variance betwixt rulers and subjects, betwixt parents and children, betwixt neighbor and neighbor, betwixt a man and his wife, betwixt a man and himself, betwixt the flesh and the spirit. Wherefore, good Mr. Standfast, be as your name is, and when you have done all, stand.

At this discourse there was among the pilgrims a mixture of joy and trembling; but at length they broke out and sang,

"What danger is the Pilgrim in!
  How many are his foes!
How many ways there are to sin
  No living mortal knows.

Some in the ditch are spoiled, yea, can
  Lie tumbling in the mire:

Some, though they shun the frying-pan
Do leap into the fire."

After this, I beheld until they were come into the land of Beulah, where the sun shineth night and day. Here, because they were weary, they betook themselves a while to rest. And because this country was common for pilgrims, and because the orchards and vineyards that were here belonged to the King of the Celestial country, therefore they were licensed to make bold with any of his things. But a little while soon refreshed them here; for the bells did so ring, and the trumpets continually sound so melodiously, that they could not sleep, and yet they received as much refreshing as if they had slept their sleep ever so soundly. Here also all the noise of them that walked the streets was, More pilgrims are come to town! And another would answer, saying, And so many went over the water, and were let in at the golden gates to-day! They would cry again, There is now a legion of shining ones just come to town, by which we know that there are more pilgrims upon the road; for here they come to wait for them, and to comfort them after all their sorrow. Then the pilgrims got up, and walked to and fro. But how were their ears now filled with heavenly noises, and their eyes delighted with celestial visions! In this land they heard nothing, saw nothing, felt nothing, smelt nothing, tasted nothing that was offensive to their stomach or mind; only when they tasted of the water of the river over which they were to go, they thought that it tasted a little bitterish to the palate; but it proved sweeter when it was down.

In this place there was a record kept of the names of them that had been pilgrims of old, and a history of all the famous acts that they had done. It was here also much discoursed, how the river to some had had its flowings, and what ebbings it has had while others have gone over. It has been in a manner dry for some, while it has overflowed its banks for others.

In this place the children of the town would go into the King's gardens, and gather nosegays for the pilgrims, and bring them to them with much affection. Here also grew camphire, with spikenard and saffron, calamus and cinnamon, with all the trees of frankincense, myrrh, and aloes, with all chief spices. With these the pilgrims' chambers were perfumed while they stayed here; and with these were their bodies anointed, to prepare them to go over the river, when the time appointed was come.

Now, while they lay here, and waited for the good hour, there was a noise in the town that there was a post come from the Celestial City, with matter of great importance to one Christiana, the wife of Christian the pilgrim. So inquiry was made for her, and the house was found out where she was. So the post presented her with a letter. The contents were, Hail, good woman; I bring thee tidings that the Master calleth for thee, and expecteth that thou shouldst stand in his presence in clothes of immortality within these ten days.

When he had read this letter to her, he gave her therewith a sure token that he was a true messenger, and was come to bid her make haste to be gone. The token was, an arrow with a point sharpened with love, let easily into her heart, which by degrees wrought so effectually with her, that at the time appointed she must be gone.

When Christiana saw that her time was come, and that she was the first of this company that was to go over, she called for Mr. Great-Heart her guide, and told him how matters were. So he told her he was heartily glad of the news, and could have been glad had the post come for him. Then she bid him that he should give advice how all things should be prepared for her journey. So he told her, saying, Thus and thus it must be, and we that survive will accompany you to the river-side.

Then she called for her children, and gave them her blessing, and told them that she had read with comfort the mark that was set in their foreheads, and was glad to see them with her there, and that they had kept their garments so white. Lastly, she bequeathed to the poor that little she had, and commanded her sons and daughters to be ready against the messenger should come for them.

When she had spoken these words to her guide, and to her children, she called for Mr. Valiant-for-truth, and said unto him, Sir, you have in all places showed yourself true-hearted; be faithful unto death, and my King will give you a crown of life. I would also entreat you to have an eye to my children; and if at any time you see them faint, speak comfortably to them. For my daughters, my sons' wives, they have been faithful, and a fulfilling of the promise upon them will be their end. But she gave Mr. Standfast a ring.

Then she called for old Mr. Honest, and said of him, "Behold an Israelite indeed, in whom is no guile!" Then said he, I wish you a fair day when you set out for

Mount Sion, and shall be glad to see that you go over the river dry-shod. But she answered, Come wet, come dry, I long to be gone; for however the weather is in my journey, I shall have time enough when I come there to sit down and rest me and dry me.

Then came in that good man Mr. Ready-to-halt, to see her. So she said to him, Thy travel hitherto has been with difficulty; but that will make thy rest the sweeter. Watch, and be ready; for at an hour when you think not, the messenger may come.

After him came Mr. Despondency and his daughter Much-afraid, to whom she said, You ought, with thankfulness, forever to remember your deliverance from the hands of Giant Despair, and out of Doubting Castle. The effect of that mercy is, that you are brought with safety hither. Be ye watchful, and cast away fear; be sober, and hope to the end.

Then she said to Mr. Feeble-mind, Thou wast delivered from the mouth of Giant Slay-good, that thou mightest live in the light of the living, and see thy King with comfort. Only I advise thee to repent of thine aptness to fear and doubt of his goodness, before he sends for thee; lest thou shouldst, when he comes, be forced to stand before him for that fault with blushing.

Now the day drew on that Christiana must be gone. So the road was full of people to see her take her journey. But behold, all the banks beyond the river were full of horses and chariots, which were come down from above to accompany her to the city gate. So she came forth, and entered the river, with a beckon of farewell to those that followed her. The last words that she was heard to say were, I come, Lord, to be with thee and bless thee! So her children and friends returned to their place, for those that waited for Christiana had carried her out of their sight. So she went and called, and entered in at the gate with all the ceremonies of joy that her husband Christian had entered with before her. At her departure, the children wept. But Mr. Great-Heart and Mr. Valiant played upon the welltuned cymbal and harp for joy. So all departed to their respective places.

In process of time there came a post to the town again, and his business was with Mr. Ready-to-halt. So he inquired him out, and said, I am come from Him whom thou hast loved and followed, though upon crutches; and my message is to tell thee, that he expects thee at his table to sup with him in his kingdom, the next day after

Easter; wherefore prepare thyself for this journey. Then he also gave him a token that he was a true messenger, saying, "I have broken thy golden bowl, and loosed thy silver cord."

After this, Mr. Ready-to-halt called for his fellow-pilgrims, and told them, saying, I am sent for, and God shall surely visit you also. So he desired Mr. Valiant to make his will. And because he had nothing to bequeath to them that should survive him but his crutches, and his good wishes, therefore thus he said, These crutches I bequeath to my son that shall tread in my steps, with a hundred warm wishes that he may prove better than I have been.

Then he thanked Mr. Great-Heart for his conduct and kindness, and so addressed himself to his journey. When he came to the brink of the river, he said, Now I shall have no more need of these crutches, since yonder are chariots and horses for me to ride on. The last words he was heard to say were, Welcome life! So he went his way.

After this, Mr. Feeble-mind had tidings brought him that the post sounded his horn at his chamber door. Then he came in, and told him, saying, I am come to tell thee that thy Master hath need of thee, and that in a very little time thou must behold his face in brightness. And take this as a token of the truth of my message: "Those that look out at the windows shall be darkened." Then Mr. Feeble-mind called for his friends, and told them what errand had been brought unto him, and what token he had received of the truth of the message. Then he said, since I have nothing to bequeath to any, to what purpose should I make a will? As for my feeble mind, that I will leave behind me, for that I shall have no need of it in the place whither I go, nor is it worth bestowing upon the poorest pilgrims: wherefore, when I am gone, I desire that you, Mr. Valiant, would bury it in a dunghill. This done, and the day being come on which he was to depart, he entered the river as the rest. His last words were, Hold out, faith and patience! So he went over to the other side.

When days had many of them passed away, Mr. Despondency was sent for; for a post was come, and brought this message to him: Trembling man! these are to summon thee to be ready with the King by the next Lord's day, to shout for joy for thy deliverance from all thy doubtings. And, said the messenger, that my message is true, take this for a proof: so he gave him a grasshopper to be a burden unto him.

Now Mr. Despondency's daughter, whose name was Much-afraid, said, when she heard what was done, that she would go with her father. Then Mr. Despondency said to his friends, Myself and my daughter, you know what we have been, and how troublesomely we have behaved ourselves in every company. My will and my daughter's is, that our desponds and slavish fears be by no man ever received, from the day of our departure, forever; for I know that after my death they will offer themselves to others. For, to be plain with you, they are ghosts which we entertained when we first began to be pilgrims, and could never shake them off after; and they will walk about, and seek entertainment of the pilgrims: but for our sakes, shut the doors upon them. When the time was come for them to depart, they went up to the brink of the river. The last words of Mr. Despondency were, Farewell, night; welcome, day! His daughter went through the river singing, but none could understand what she said.

Then it came to pass a while after, that there was a post in the town that inquired for Mr. Honest. So he came to the house where he was, and delivered to his hand these lines: Thou art commanded to be ready against this day seven-night, to present thyself before thy Lord at his Father's house. And for a token that my message is true, "All the daughters of music shall be brought low." Then Mr. Honest called for his friends, and said unto them, I die, but shall make no will. As for my honesty, it shall go with me; let him that comes after be told of this. When the day that he was to be gone was come, he addressed himself to go over the river. Now the river at that time over-flowed its banks in some places; but Mr. Honest, in his lifetime, had spoken to one Good-conscience to meet him there, the which he also did, and lent him his hand, and so helped him over. The last words of Mr. Honest were, Grace reigns! So he left the world.

After this it was noised abroad that Mr. Valiant-for-truth was taken with a summons by the same post as the other, and had this for a token that the summons was true, "That his pitcher was broken at the fountain." When he understood it, he called for his friends, and told them of it. Then said he, I am going to my Father's; and though with great difficulty I have got hither, yet now I do not repent me of all the trouble I have been at to arrive where I am. My sword I give to him that shall succeed me in my pilgrimage, and my courage and skill to him that can get it. My marks and scars I carry with me, to be a witness for me that I have fought His battles who will now be my rewarder. When the day that he must go hence was come, many accompanied him to the river-side, into which as he went, he said, "Death, where is thy sting?" And as he went down deeper, he said, "Grave, where is thy victory?" So he passed over, and all the trumpets sounded for him on the other side.

Then there came forth a summons for Mr. Standfast. This Mr. Standfast was he whom the rest of the pilgrims found upon his knees in the Enchanted Ground. And the post brought it him open in his hands: the contents thereof were, that he must prepare for a change of life, for his Master was not willing that he should be so far from him any longer. At this Mr. Standfast was put into a muse. Nay, said the messenger, you need not doubt of the truth of my message; for here is a token of the truth thereof, "Thy wheel is broken at the cistern." Then he called to him Mr. Great-Heart, who was their guide, and said unto him, Sir, although it was not my hap to be much in your good company during the days of my pilgrimage, yet, since the time I knew you, you have been profitable to me. When I came from home, I left behind me a wife and five small children; let me entreat you, at your return, (for I know that you go and return to your Master's house, in hopes that you may yet be a conductor to more of the holy pilgrims,) that you send to my family, and let them be acquainted with all that hath and shall happen unto me. Tell them moreover of my happy arrival at this place, and of the present and late blessed condition I am in. Tell them also of Christian and Christiana his wife, and how she and her children came after her husband. Tell them also of what a happy end she made, and whither she is gone. I have little or nothing to send to my family, unless it be prayers and tears for them; of which it will suffice that you acquaint them, if peradventure they may prevail. When Mr. Standfast had thus set things in order, and the time being come for him to haste him away, he also went down to the river. Now there was a great calm at that time in the river; wherefore Mr. Standfast, when he was about half-way in, stood a while, and talked with his companions that had waited upon him thither. And he said, This river has been a terror to many; yea, the thoughts of it also have often frightened me; but now methinks I stand easy; my foot is fixed upon that on which the feet of the priests that bare the ark of the covenant stood while Israel went over Jordan. The waters indeed are to the palate bitter, and to the stomach cold; yet the thoughts of what I am going to, and of the convoy that waits for me on the other side, do lie as a glowing coal at my heart. I see myself now at the end of my journey; my toilsome days are ended. I am going to see that head which was crowned with thorns, and that face which was spit upon for me. I have formerly lived by hearsay and faith; but now I go where I shall live by sight, and shall be with him in whose company I delight myself. I have loved to hear my Lord spoken of; and wherever I have seen the print of his shoe in the earth, there I have coveted to set my foot too. His name has been to me as a civet-box; yea, sweeter than all perfumes. His voice to me has been most sweet, and his countenance I have more desired than they that have most desired the light of the sun. His words I did use to gather for my food, and for antidotes against my faintings. He hath held me, and hath kept me from mine iniquities; yea, my steps hath he strengthened in his way.

Now, while he was thus in discourse, his countenance changed; his strong man bowed under him: and after he had said, Take me, for I come unto thee, he ceased to be seen of them.

But glorious it was to see how the open region was filled with horses and chariots, with trumpeters and pipers, with singers and players upon stringed instruments, to welcome the pilgrims as they went up, and followed one another in at the beautiful gate of the city.

As for Christiana's children, the four boys that Christiana brought, with their wives and children, I did not stay where I was till they were gone over. Also, since I came away, I heard one say that they were yet alive, and so would be for the increase of the church, in that place where they were, for a time.

Should it be my lot to go that way again, I may give those that desire it an account of what I here am silent about: meantime I bid my reader

FAREWELL.
THE END.

Lesson 90 (no reading for Lesson 89)

- We're going to start a new book. We learned early this year that the poet Poe influenced the beginnings of science fiction as a genre (type of writing). We're going to read a novel by a famous science fiction author, Jules Verne. The mood of the book is mysterious and dark, just like Poe's writing. Like in *Treasure Island* (7th level), you'll find a commander who can be both kind and evil. (Just because a man is capable of *some* good doesn't make him "good." Only Christ's life in someone can make someone good. These characters reveal their true nature when greed comes into play.)

- Read this summary of the book.

Twenty Thousand Leagues Under the Sea is a science fiction novel written by Jules Verne. It is written in the first person, and was first published in 1870. The book takes place in the year 1866. There's a mysterious creature in the ocean that has been sinking ships. So the government of the United States sends out the *Abraham Lincoln* to capture the creature.

The ship is attacked by the creature and Aronnax the scientist, Conseil his servant, and Ned Land a skilled harpooner, go overboard. They land on top of the creature, which turns out to be a submarine known as the *Nautilus*. They are placed in a cell and told they can roam the submarine as long as they return to the cell whenever asked. The commander of the submarine, Captain Nemo, treats them well.

The book explores the many thrilling adventures the men experience while on the *Nautilus*. They visit the lost city of Atlantis. They fish for pearls. They almost run out of oxygen when the submarine gets stuck in ice in the south pole. They fight off a giant squid that cannot be killed with bullets.

There are also many upsetting moments like the time they are given sleeping pills and awake to find a crew member horribly injured. When he later dies and they bury him in an underground cemetery, they find many other crewmen have been laid to rest there as well.

Eventually, Captain Nemo attacks a warship and sinks it. The three men decide they must escape the *Nautilus*. The find that they are headed toward a giant whirlpool that no ship is known to have ever survived. But somehow they come out of it safely. They awake in the hut of a fisherman. Aronnax awaits his return to France where he can write all about his journeys 20,000 leagues under the sea.

- Read this overview of the setting, characters, and plot conflict.

Setting

20,000 Leagues Under the Sea begins in 1866 and is largely set on the submarine the *Nautilus*, commanded by Captain Nemo. It traverses all of the oceans of the world throughout the book.

Major Characters

Dr. Pierre Aronnax: He is the 40-year-old French narrator of the book. He was a doctor and became a scientist. He lives in Paris with his servant, Conseil.

Conseil: He is Aronnax's compliant 30-year-old servant.

Ned Land: 40-year-old Canadian master harpooner.

Captain Nemo: He is the commander and designer of the *Nautilus*. He's a former engineer whose nationality is unknown.

Minor Characters

Captain Anderson: He is the captain of the ship that sank (the *Scotia*), prompting the United States to send the *Abraham Lincoln* in search of the "creature" that is bringing down ships.

Captain Farragut: He is the captain of the *Abraham Lincoln.*

Sir Samuel Cunard: He owns many "unsinkable" ships. The world is outraged when his ship, the *Scotia* is attacked.

Protagonist

The protagonist, or main character, of *Twenty Thousand Leagues Under the Sea* is Dr. Arronax. He is the narrator and main character of the book. He is a scientist, but throughout the course of the book sees how science can be used for evil, and ends up choosing his companions over science.

Antagonist
The antagonist, or character that provides the obstacle for the protagonist, of *Twenty Thousand Leagues Under the Sea* is Captain Nemo. He imprisons Arronax and his companions.

Climax
The climax, or major turning point that determines the outcome, of *Twenty Thousand Leagues Under the Sea* is in Chapter 22 when the three men decide to escape the *Nautilus*.

Resolution
The resolution, or the outcome of the climax, of *Twenty Thousand Leagues Under the Sea* is that the men survive an "un-survivable" whirlpool and plan to return home. Captain Nemo remains a mystery and no one knows if he survives or where he ends up.

- Read this vocabulary list. The book uses many scientific words that can make it hard to understand. Hopefully this list will help.

Vocabulary

Acre: a unit of measurement approximately the size of a football field (more precisely, 43,560 square feet).

Annelids: worms

Babiroussa: an East Indian pig

Byssus: filament by which mussels and other mollusks attach themselves to rocks

Cetacean: a classification of marine mammals such as dolphins and whales.

Dugong: a plant-eating animal with flippers found in the Indian Ocean, Red Sea, and Pacific Ocean

Echeneis: a type of fish that can suction itself to things

Echinoderm: a classification of invertebrate that has parts coming symmetrically from center (like a starfish)

Fathom: a measure of depth around 6 feet

Fucus: brown algae

Hydrophytes: a plant that can grow in water

Hyracotherium: an extinct horse

Ichthyologist: a scientist who studies fish

Kraken: a mythological sea monster

League: a unit of distance equivalent to 2.5-3.5 miles

Leviathan: a biblical sea monster

Narwhal: a whale found in the arctic with an ivory horn on its head.

Nereocysti: giant seaweed

Oreodon: an extinct, deer-like mammal

Pintadine: a shellfish capable of producing pearls

Polyp: can be solitary, such as a sea anemone, or can be colonial, such as coral

Poop: on a ship, an enclosed structure at the stem

Port: the left side of a ship

Starboard: the right side of a ship

Terra firma: solid ground

Zoophytes: invertebrates such as a sea anemone or sponge

Other Units of Measure

Cable length: In Verne's context, 600 feet

Centigrade: 0° - freezing water; 37° - human body temperature; 100° - boiling water

Gram: roughly 1/28 of an ounce

Milligram: Roughly 1/28,000 of an ounce

Kilogram (kilo): Roughly 2.2 pounds

Hectare: Roughly 2.5 acres

Knot: 1.15 miles per hour

Liter: Roughly 1 quart

Meter: Roughly 1 yard, 3 inches

Millimeter: Roughly 1/25 of an inch

Centimeter: Roughly 2/5 of an inch

Decimeter: Roughly 4 inches

Kilometer: Roughly 6/10 of a mile

Myriameter: Roughly 6.2 miles

Metric ton: Roughly 2,200 pounds

Congratulations! You're halfway through Literature and Composition I! Your reading lessons will continue in the Literature & Composition I Reader: Lessons 91-180.

Made in United States
Orlando, FL
02 April 2024

45356631R00300